Contents

SHORTER ARTICLES

English Manuscript Studies
1100–1700

English Manuscript Studies
1100–1700

VOLUME 5

Edited by
Peter Beal & Jeremy Griffiths

THE BRITISH LIBRARY

The British Library is grateful to The British Academy and
the 27 Foundation for their support for this publication.

First published 1995 by
The British Library
Great Russell Street
London WC1B 3DG

British Library Cataloguing in Publication Data

A cataloguing record for this publication is
available from The British Library.

ISBN 0-7123-0310-3

Typeset in Linotron 300 Baskerville by
Bexhill Phototypesetters
Printed in England by
Redwood Books, Trowbridge

Annotation in Some Manuscripts of *Troilus and Criseyde*

JULIA BOFFEY

Recent studies of *Troilus and Criseyde* have drawn attention to a flexibility of structure which allows for oscillation between narrative and lyrical modes.[1] Modern editors of the text have made this characteristic visible by inserting headings to indicate the start of the most clearly discernible groups of lyrical stanzas. Three of Troilus's songs (I, 400–420; III, 1744–71; V, 638–44) usually receive such emphasis, as does his plaintive letter to the departed Criseyde (V, 1317–1421), and the letter which forms her own last word in the course of the narrative (V, 1590–1631). Antigone's love-song (II, 827–75) is also sometimes highlighted.[2] Further set-pieces of various kinds have been elsewhere identified: Troilus's philosophical disquisition in Book IV (958–1078), his lament after Criseyde's departure (V, 218–45), and his address to her empty house (V, 540–53) are the most frequently-cited examples.[3] Editorial practice and critical understanding have of course responded in their different ways to precedents set in the early manuscripts of *Troilus and Criseyde*, where some lyrical or otherwise isolable passages are drawn to the reader's attention by means of headings or marginal glosses. The discussion which follows takes the early annotation of the poem as a starting point for some speculations about the manner in which scribal headings and marginal notes may have informed or may reflect early perceptions of the work's structure and appeal.

Little scholarly attention has been paid to the general question of the presentation and apparatus of *Troilus and Criseyde* in its surviving manuscripts. Study of the text has tended either to follow the efforts of Root in establishing different versions of the poem and illustrating Chaucer's successive revisions to it, or more recently to propose a situation which involves no clear-cut earlier or later redactions but rather a fluid grouping of manuscripts which reflect different scribal traditions.[4] Matters such as layout and annotation have been discussed selectively according to the extent to which they support editorial commentary, or in more specific terms in connection with facsimile reproductions of individual manuscripts.[5] Annotation of the kind which signals the lyrical passages in the poem clearly needs to be studied in the context of the overall features of its *ordinatio*, which offers some pointers towards the establishment of which annotations might be authorial, which scribal, and which the additions of later readers.[6] The most significant and consistent feature of the formal layout of the text in its sixteen more or less complete surviving manuscripts is its division into five books by means of varying combinations of scribal incipits, explicits, and decorated or ornamented borders and capitals.[7] The proems to Books II to IV are also signalled, although with more variation.[8] Extracts from Joseph of Exeter's *De excidio Trojano*, and from the *Thebaid* of Statius are occasionally supplied at points in the text to which they relate. Structural markers which draw attention to lyrics or to passages which are in some other sense self-contained are almost all provided in the form of marginal glosses, although a small number appear in the column of text. The unique description of the final two stanzas of the poem as it appears in London, British Library MS Harley 1239 as 'Lenuoye Du Chaucer', like the words 'Cantus Troyli versus Criseide' copied into Oxford, Bodleian Library MS Selden supra 56 at the start of Troilus's letter at Book V, line 1317, for example, are strictly headings rather than marginal glosses. Usually the structural markers are less imposingly presented than the indications of book division, although there are exceptions, such as one of the three 'Canticus Troili' glosses in Cambridge, Corpus Christi College MS 61 (on fol. 91r), which has been formally displayed by the scribe in an enclosing box.

The full range of marginal glosses in the sixteen surviving manuscripts can be sub-divided into different categories of indicator.[9] Some point out the source of particular passages. A note in Bodleian MS Rawlinson poet. 163 recalls 'Baicius de consolacione philosophie' at the point when Pandarus, trying to wake Troilus from an amorous trance, asks him 'artow lik an asse to the harpe . . .?' (I, 731), in words with which Philosophy upbraids Boethius (*Boece*, I, prosa iv, 1–3). Marginal glosses in Bodleian MSS Digby 181 and Selden supra 56 identify 'Cato' as the source of the proverb 'firste vertu is to kepe tonge' which Pandarus cites to Troilus after his first encounter with Criseyde (III, 294). No less than six manuscripts[10] gloss the reference to 'the cok, comune astrologer', which crows after the lovers' first night together (III, 1415), most adding variations on 'vulgarus astrologus' and one (BL MS Harley 2392) specifying the source of the reference in Alanus's *De Planctu Naturae*. Other Latin glosses serve explanatory purposes, providing information about figures or practices of the pagan past which might have seemed obscure to the poem's audience, and they occasionally come in bursts, as for instance with the proems to Books II, III, and IV, or with Criseyde's oath of faithfulness in Book IV (1534–54). Sometimes too these explanatory glosses clarify lexical problems or ambiguities caused by potentially confusing orthography. Troilus's 'vessell that men clepeth an urne' (V, 311) causes some difficulty, prompting the note 'id est vrna. vrne' in BL MS Harley 2392, while his plea to his soul, 'lurkinge in this wo' (IV, 305–6) that it 'unneste,/Fle forth out of myn herte . . .', is accompanied in three manuscripts (Durham University Library MS Cosin V. II. 13, BL MS Harley 2280, and Bodleian MS Selden B.24) with the illuminating alternative 'go out of thi neste'.

These explanatory and source glosses are numerous, and in many cases common to manuscripts from different textual groupings, as if they quickly became part of the various scribal traditions in which the poem was transmitted. Much more randomly placed across the whole range of witnesses are the briefer indicators which appear to mark passages which must have seemed especially pleasing or valuable to some individual taste, and whose commonest formulation is the terse 'nota'. The significance of some of these is now to a large extent irrecoverable. We have no way of knowing why some particular lines or sections should have been especially appealing. The thrust of the enigmatic pointers in St John's MS L.1 which read 'nota k' is virtually impossible to comprehend.[11]

A large number of these notes signal proverbs or aphorisms, perhaps because these were either familiar and readily recognized, or pithy enough to be memorized for some future need. They occur with particular frequency in Bodleian MS Selden B.24 and BL MS Harley 2392, which both highlight, for example, Pandarus's early counsel to Troilus, 'Unknowe, unkist, and lost that is unsought' (I, 809), and his advice to Criseyde, 'Thenk ek how elde wasteth every houre/In ech of yow a partie of beautee' (II, 393–4). In this latter instance, the significant association of most of the proverbial lore in the poem with Pandarus's machinations is made explicit in the gloss of Bodleian MS Selden B.24: 'nota bene de proverbis pandar'. Significantly, there are noticeable coincidences of location between some of these indicators and certain proverbial stanzas or groups of stanzas which are known to have circulated as independent extracts: Pandarus's short homilies on the whetstone (I, 631–37), on weedy ground (I, 946–52), and on unguarded tongues (III, 302–8), all in some way singled out in one or more manuscripts, fall into this category.[12]

Rather differently from glosses designed for mnemonic purposes, or to locate sources, annotation of the designedly lyrical passages in the poem tends to occur in the body of marginalia which supplies some form of structural analysis, signalling changes and new departures in the action, or discrete rhetorical units in the dialogue. Such commentary ranges from the brief speech indicators especially prominent in Bodleian MS Selden B.24 and BL MS Harley 4912 – 'Pandarus', 'Criseid', 'Troilus', 'Auctour'[13] – to the lengthy summaries favoured in Bodleian MS Rawlinson poet. 163: 'How troilus on the nyght that Cress*eyd* shuld han comen on the morn myght han no reste & how on the morn he sent after Pandar & how they two alday & al that nyght bood on the wallis & yet cam nat Cress*eyd*' (V, 1100). Such glosses are provided in both English and in Latin. Bodleian MS Rawlinson poet. 163 is annotated almost entirely in English; Bodleian MS Selden B.24, with the next most extensive annotation, in English and Latin; and BL MS Harley 2392, the next most fully glossed, almost exclusively in Latin (sometimes to nice effect: 'Quod Pandarus, "Thow wrecched mouses herte/Artow agast so that she wol the bite?"', III, 736–37, is signalled by 'no*ta* q*uo* p. dicebat T. h*abe*re cor muris').

The nature and full range of marginal annotations to the poem can best be illustrated by detailed consideration of Bodleian MSS Rawlinson poet. 163 and Selden B.24, both later fifteenth-century copies. In Bodleian MS Selden B.24, *Troilus and Criseyde* is the first and most substantial item in a large paper anthology of poems by Chaucer and his followers, keeping company with works such as Lydgate's *Complaint of the Black Knight,* Hoccleve's *Letter of Cupid,* and the unique surviving text of *The Kingis Quair.*[14] The major part of the anthology (fols 1–209v, line 14) was copied by one scribe, whose hand has also been identified in the Haye Manuscript in the Scott collection at Abbotsford, an anthology of translations of French texts made in Scotland for Oliver Sinclair.[15] Bodleian MS Selden B.24 includes notes on members of the same Sinclair family, notably an inscription naming Henry Lord Sinclair on fol. 230v, whose arms are depicted at the end of *Troilus and Criseyde* (fol. 118v). The production of the manuscript can be set fairly precisely some time between 1488, a date suggested by a note on fol. 120r which refers to King James IV, who came to the throne in that year, and 1513, the year of Henry Sinclair's death at Flodden. Some care has been taken in the presentation of the text of *Troilus* to remind readers of its division into books. Rubrics usually signal the book divisions and the proems, and decorated borders and capitals draw attention to the beginnings of Books I, III, IV, and V. Unusually, the stanza which follows the end of Troilus's letter at Book V, line 1421 (with its extra-metrical sign manual, 'le vostre T') begins with a decorated capital and border of the same kind.

The copious marginal notes in this manuscript appear to me to be the work of the main scribe. Tight rebinding has meant that many of them disappear into the gutter and are now illegible, and Root indeed suggested that they were supplied by the main scribe and a later annotator,[16] but the differences would seem rather to be connected with the apparently arbitrary hierarchy of scripts and layout used for the glosses, some of which are engrossed or enclosed in boxes. Few sources are noted, beyond the occasional Latin equivalent of a stated or implied English proverb, such as 'Acriores in pri*n*cipio franguntur in fine' which is set next to 'Ful sharp bygynnyng breketh ofte at ende' (II, 791). There are several injunctions to 'nota bene', some placed with proverbial or sententious matter, like the statement 'he that departed is in everi place/Is nowher hol, as writen clerkes wyse' (I, 960), but others of more enigmatic import (as, for instance, at I, 378). Numerous speech indicators are supplied, some of which single out 'auctour' at moments of significant intrusion by the narrator (for example, at II, 22 and 29). Occasionally, the glosses emphasize features of literary and linguistic interest, as does the note 'heir chaucer prayis his buk salbe lail vritin & veill vnderstandin in sentence and metir', next to the comments on the 'gret diversite/In Englissh and in writyng of oure tonge' (V, 1793–4).

By far the greatest number of marginal notes here concern the rhetorical texture of the poem, apportioning appropriate terms to particular sequences, such as 'Troylus skorni*ng* all v*err*y lovar*is*' (I, 187); 'her troylus repentit ye skorni*ng* of luvaris' (I, 316); 'consolacio [miserorum] est haber[e consort]em in pe[na]' (I, 708); 'De pandar bon*o* *con*silio' (I, 954); 'pa*n*dar de troylus comendacio' (II, 163); 'confessio troily' (II, 528); 'diu*er*se argume*ntis* in creseid avis ys syd' (II, 750); 'here maketh troyl*us* his compleynt vpon fortune' (IV, 260). Notes of 'cantus' and 'litera' designate songs and letters which are both directly quoted[17] and more indirectly summarized or reported, such as the letter which Troilus writes on Pandarus's advice (II, 1065) which is termed 'prima littera Troilus missa ad Criseid'. The density of annotation varies noticeably throughout the text. Book I and most of Book II, until the point at which Criseyde replies to Troilus's letter, are heavily glossed. From here to almost the end of Book V there are few notes apart from some terse speech indicators, until a final flurry of glosses appears next to the concluding stanzas. The tight rebinding of the manuscript renders impossible any attempt to check whether the variations in the amount of annotation correspond with different gatherings, but they may well reflect features of the exemplar or

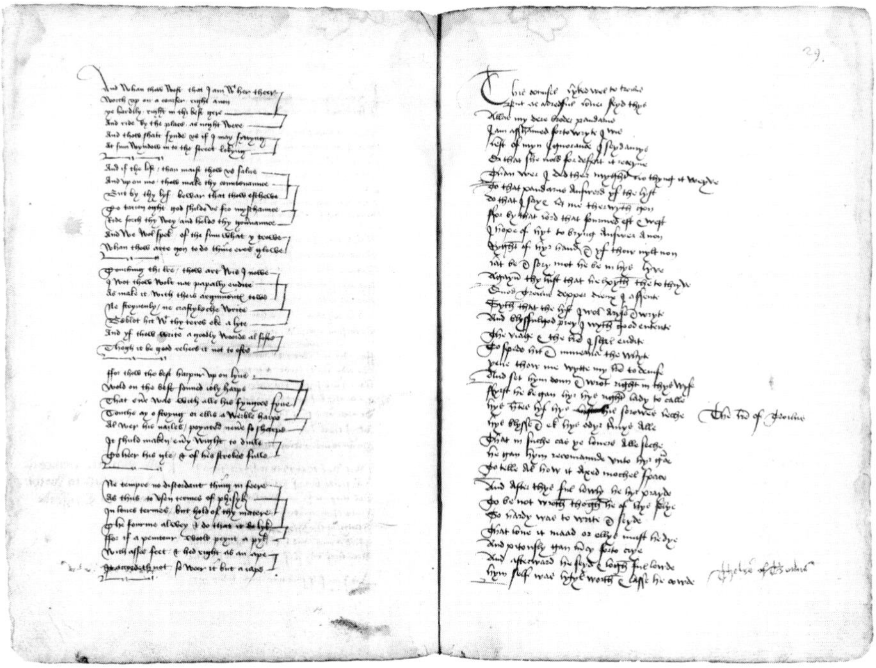

PLATE 1 *Oxford, Bodleian Library,* MS *Rawlinson poet. 163, fols 28v–29r.* Troilus and Criseyde, *II, 1010–1078. Hand C on fol. 28v, and Hand A on fol. 29r. Next to II, 1066: 'The* lettre *of Troilus' (also copied below by a different hand). Reproduced with the permission of the Bodleian Library.*

exemplars which the scribe used; as Windeatt notes, this text of the poem has been 'edited' between two textual traditions, and it is interesting that Book II, line 1210 – approximately the part of the poem where the annotation in Bodleian MS Selden B.24 begins to decrease – marks a point of the change in affiliation in at least two other manuscripts.[18] The occasional and apparently random extra prominence given to marginal notes by means of engrossing the comments or boxing them in may also be connected with the precedent of exemplars.

Bodleian MS Rawlinson poet. 163, datable on palaeographical grounds to the second half of the fifteenth century, and containing only the Chaucerian lyric *To Rosemounde* in addition to its text of *Troilus and Criseyde*, is the work of a number of collaborating scribes.[19] The provision of its numerous glosses to *Troilus* varies significantly throughout the course of the manuscript, and provokes questions about individual scribal practice. The text was copied by four scribes,

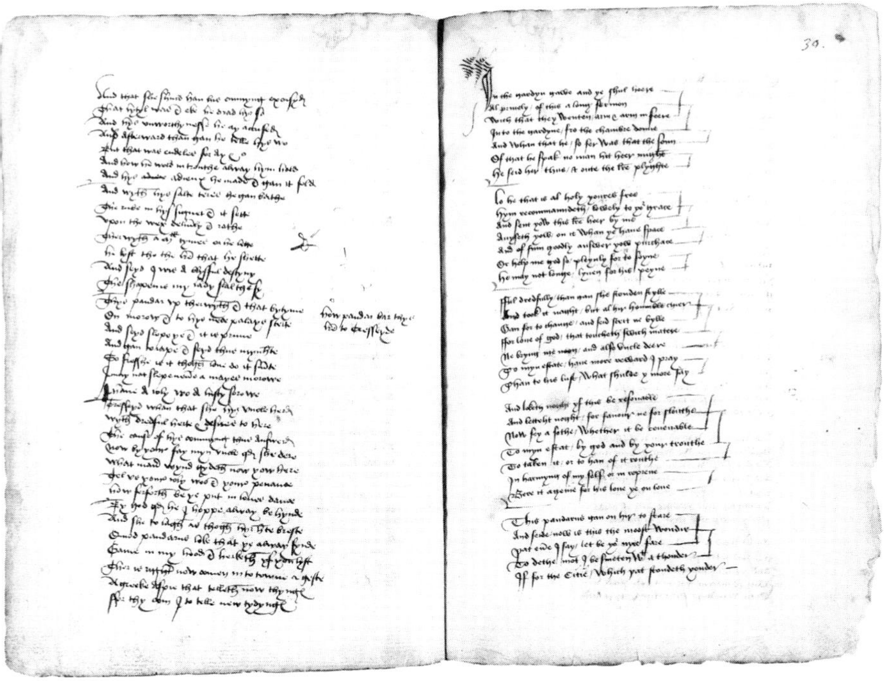

PLATE 2 *Oxford, Bodleian Library,* MS *Rawlinson poet. 163, fols 29v–30r.* Troilus and Criseyde, *II, 1079–1146. Hand A on fol. 29v, and Hand C on fol. 30r. Next to II, 1093–94: 'how pandar bar thys/*lettre *to Cresseyde'. Reproduced with the permission of the Bodleian Library.*

one of whom probably organized the division of labour and in fact carried out most of the work. This scribe, A, copied the first gathering (fols 1–9; I, 1–700), and worked on the final leaves of the second gathering (fols 16–19; II, 118–433), which had been begun by another scribe, B (fols 10–16; I, 701–II, 117). The division of work at this point became more complicated. Scribe C copied nine leaves of the third gathering (fols 20–28; II, 434–1043), was interrupted for a single leaf by A (fol. 29; II, 1044–1113), and then completed the third gathering (fols 30–31) and copied the whole of the fourth (fols 32–42; II, 1114–III, 305). B reappeared for most of the fifth gathering (fols 43–51; III, 306–912), although the final part of this (fols 51v–52) and the first part of the next gathering (fols 53–59r; III, 913–1372) was the work of a new contributor, scribe D. Scribe A returned at the end of the sixth gathering (fols 59r–60), and went on to complete the remainder of the copying.

The manuscript seems to have been designed from the outset as a more modest volume than Bodleian MS Selden B.24. Some decoration was intended for a few large capitals (at the start of Books I and V, and at II, 50, and IV, 24, the resumption of the narrative after the proems), but it was never completed. Only the stint of scribe C, and part of that of scribe B, have been rubricated. The scribes in general wrote mixed hands, with a preponderance of secretary forms (particularly in the hand of scribe A), but some chose to write more formal scripts for particular purposes: C and occasionally B supplied their glosses in larger scripts modelled on *textura*, and D wrote his few annotations in a script distinct from that used for the main body of the text. Scribe A's colophon at the end of the poem, written in a more formal hand than his usual secretary, is enclosed by the words 'tregentyll . . . chaucer' in cursive script. This may have been intended as a compliment to the author of the poem, or a record of the scribe's own name.[20] The words are written again in a more clumsy *textura* at the end of the stanzas *To Rosemounde*, copied by scribe A and supplied on a singleton which follows the last gathering of the main item in the manuscript.

The text of *Troilus* is presented here with the usual care to mark book divisions. Unusually, the proems to Books II, III and IV are absent. No gaps have been left, and the incipits of these books are simply placed at what are in fact Book II, line 50, Book III, line 50, and Book IV, line 29. The Latin extract from Statius's *Thebaid*, which is included in all other manuscripts except BL MS Harley 2392 as an adjunct to Cassandra's interpretation of Troilus's dream (after V, 1498), is also missing.[21] The marginal annotation, as often elsewhere, includes information about sources ('Re*qui*re in metamorphosies' after the reference to Niobe at I, 699–700, for example), a few speech indicators which make particular reference to 'Auctor' (as at II, 666: 'Now myghte som envious jangle thus . . .'), and several 'nota' directives. Its overwhelming tendency, however, is towards a kind of discourse analysis, undertaken by means of often lengthy descriptive sentences: 'How Crysseide mused what was best to do touchyng the loue of Troylus' (II, 694); 'How Pandar counceiled troilus to write a lettyr to Crisseide' (II, 1002); 'How Cresseide and troylus leyn anothyr nyght togyder in Pandarus hows and gannen eft dispyse day whan it app*ro*ched (III, 1667); 'How troilus shewed resons to Panda[r] why he myght not rauysshe Cresseyd' (IV, 547); 'How Cresseyd seyd she wold be trewe vnto Diomede' (V, 1065), and so on. These notes are both so numerous and so copious, compared with those of any other extant manuscript, that they prompt suspicion of a practical function: are they a refined kind of running-title, to help a reader find his or her place in the text? That many occur half-way down the outside margins of the rectos and versos, as if in an appointed position, might support this notion, but there is no marked consistency, and the fact that some pages carry two or more lengthy notes suggests in the end an informed intellectual response to the poem rather than a summarizing pragmatic one.

The incidence of annotation varies considerably between the stints of the different scribes, as to some extent does its nature. Scribe A, who on the evidence of his work on gatherings produced both independently and in conjunction with others seems to have been the director of operations, is the chief purveyor of the discourse analysis which characterizes the manuscript, and, particularly in his later stints, supplies indicators of 'Auctor' and glosses of 'nota'. Scribe B, who similarly provides marginal notes of these three kinds, also introduces a number of source glosses, attributing proverbs to Solomon, and directing readers to the works of Ovid and Boethius. These annotations are noticeably concentrated in the first and absent from the second of his two stints, a discrepancy which is not easily explained by the nature of the text at the two different points of the poem.[22] Scribe C, whose range of glosses reflects that of A, nonetheless gives his marginalia a distinctive appearance by flourishing and touching them in red. Scribe D, apart from one summarizing gloss, completely abandons the precedents set by his colleagues, and adds only two rather obscure comments. Next to Criseyde's playful reproaches to Troilus, 'Wol ye the childissh jalous contrefete?/Now were it worthi that ye were ybete' (III, 1168–9), he inserts the aside 'ye *with* a ffether', and he adds at the later point of the comparison between the two lovers and the sparrowhawk and lark (III, 1191), the faintly sinister remark: 'How bace phisik come in honde betwene Cresseyde & Troylys'. Although it is conceivable that the precedent of exemplars may have been a factor in the differing kinds of annotation here, the practices of the four scribes are distinct enough to suggest individual decisions about what to emphasize and how to do so. There are too faint indications that scribal practice could become infectious (or that an editor or overseer modified instructions as work proceeded): the 'nota' and 'auctor' glosses introduced in C's stint (fols 20–28) are not evident in the work of the other scribes until then, but seem to be picked up in B's second contribution (fols 43–51), and in A's lengthy final one. The summarizing glosses which become fuller in B's second contribution increase significantly in length over A's copy of the last two and a half books.

The amount of structural pointing of this sort supplied with different texts of the poem varies widely. Bodleian MS Rawlinson poet. 163 contains just over one hundred such indicators (excluding marginal notes about sources, and the apparatus of book-structure); Bodleian MS Selden B.24 between about sixty and seventy – the total is hard to compute because some notes disappear into the tight binding; BL MSS Harley 3943 and 1239 have only one or two. But a significant small corpus of notes appears with some consistency in most of the manuscripts. Troilus's first song (I, 400–420) is signalled in eleven of the sixteen witnesses.[23] His letter in Book V (1317–1421) is identified by ten manuscripts.[24] Ten manuscripts single out Criseyde's epistolary attempt to explain her failure to return (V, 1590–1631).[25] Seven manuscripts note Troilus's Boethian song in praise of love at the end of Book III (1744–71),[26] and seven also highlight Antigone's love-song (II, 827–75).[27]

It is notable firstly that this small corpus of annotation survives in manuscripts of all textual traditions, and secondly that its appearance is not conditional upon the affiliations of a particular copy: New York, Pierpont Morgan Library MS M 817, whose text closely agrees with those affiliated to Corpus MS 61, is virtually bare of this kind of commentary.[28] It is present in manuscripts of provably early and later date,[29] and it focuses very clearly on the sequence of songs and letters whose sentiments effectively encapsulate the flavour of successive points in the larger narrative, as if reflecting some sense of their importance in the unfolding structure. Further marginal notes, occurring less consistently over a range of manuscripts but still with sufficient frequency to represent something more than individual scribal whim, draw attention to the contribution which other kinds of non-narrative material make to the poem. Troilus's complaint against fortune in Book IV (260–336) is signalled in Bodleian Library MS Selden B.24 – '[H]ere maketh troyl*us* his compleynt vpon fortune' – and by a longer note in Bodleian MS Rawlinson poet. 163. Criseyde's private lament that she is to be exchanged for Antenor (IV, 742–98) is also given some formal status, noted in three manuscripts (BL MS Harley 2392, Huntington MS HM 114, and Bodleian MS Selden supra 56) as her 'lamentacio'. Troilus's melodramatic disposition of his effects, as he is gripped by mortal sorrow early in the action of Book V (295–322), is in three manuscripts (Bodleian MSS Rawlinson poet. 163, Selden B.24, and Selden supra 56) termed his 'testament', and his address to Criseyde's empty house (V, 540–53) is indicated in two (Bodleian MS Selden B.24 and BL MS Harley 2392). A marked interest in the epistolary dimension of the poem is emphasized by the highlighting in five manuscripts (BL MSS Harley 2392 and 4912; Bodleian MSS Rawlinson poet. 163, Selden B.24, and Selden supra 56) of the summary of the first letter which Troilus writes to Criseyde (II, 1065–85); the noting in three manuscripts (BL MS Harley 4912

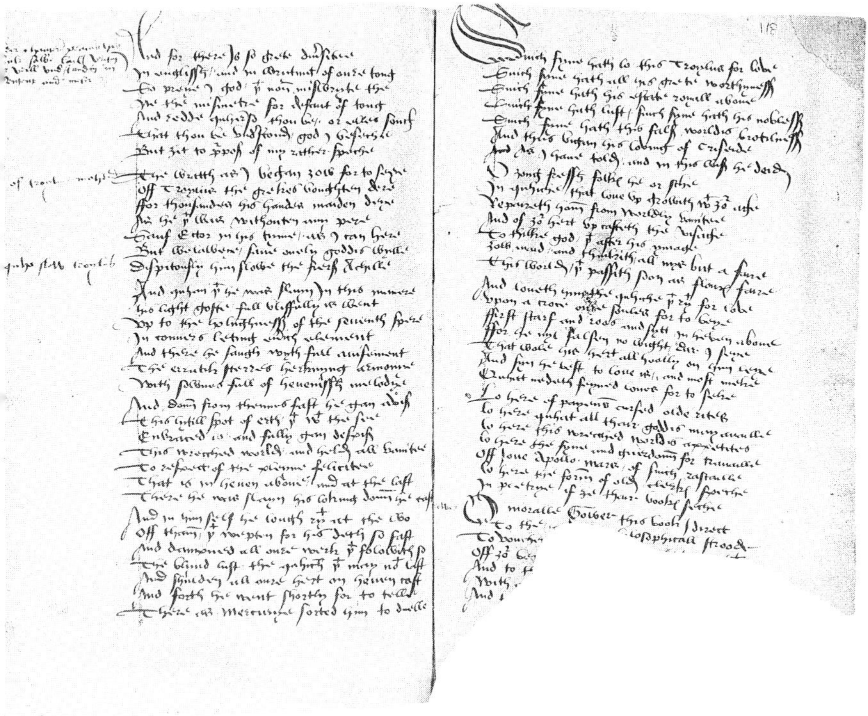

PLATE 3 *Oxford, Bodleian Library,* MS *Arch. Selden B. 24, fols 117v–118r.* Troilus and Criseyde, *V, 1793–1682. Main scribe of the manuscript. Next to V, 1793–94: 'heir chaucer prayis his buk/salbe laill vritin/& veill vnderstandin in/sentens and meter'. Next to V, 1800: 'of troylus manheid'. Next to V, 1806: 'quho slew troylus'. Reproduced with the permission of the Bodleian Library.*

and Bodleian MSS Rawlinson poet. 163 and Selden B.24) of her reply to this (II, 1219–25); and by the signalling in three manuscripts (Bodleian MSS Rawlinson poet. 163, Selden B.24, and Selden supra 56) of Pandarus's abbreviation of Oenone's *Heroides* epistles (I, 659–72), cited to Troilus as evidence that even the wisest physician cannot always heal himself.

To ascertain the point in the poem's genesis or circulation at which these remarks originated, and to locate any evidence about the nature of their possible transmission from manuscript to manuscript would clearly be revealing. Do they constitute variations on some authorized or even authorial early apparatus, or are they rather the individual responses of the particular scribes and editors who were involved in the poem's transmission? Here, the complicated textual history of the work, and moreover the relative unchartedness of the whole practice of the glossing and annotation of vernacular texts, rather impede understanding. Moreover, no manuscripts of *Troilus and Criseyde* seems to stand as close to Chaucer's presumed original as do the Hengwrt and Ellesmere copies of *The Canterbury Tales*.[30] Analysis of the apparatus in this body of manuscripts does however supply some illuminating comparison to the case of *Troilus*.[31] It has been argued from the evidence of the Hengwrt and Ellesmere manuscripts that some glosses, particularly those quoting sources, may derive from Chaucer's originals, whether representing 'authorial memoranda', or prompts to the reader's interpretation, or devices to lend a special authority to the text. The lines from Statius which preface The Knight's Tale and some of the glosses from Pope Innocent III which accompany The Man of Law's Tale, have been cited as likely examples.[32] On the other hand, the extensiveness of the Hengwrt and Ellesmere marginalia, the variety of its functions, and the evidence that a programme which began in one manuscript was maintained and expanded in the other, where more room was made for it at the planning stage, argue for the intervention of an editor, if not the scribe himself, in its compilation.[33] In the end, the contention that 'the Chaucer glosses . . . have no one single function and possibly no single author' seems the only reasonable one.[34]

Such a situation might well also obtain for the *Troilus* manuscripts, with a small number of glosses, such as the Statius argument attached to Cassandra's words (V, after 1498), and possibly the quotations from Joseph of Exeter which in two manuscripts (St John's MS L.1 and Cambridge, University Library Gg. 4. 27) accompany the descriptions of Diomede, Criseyde, and Troilus (V, 800–840), deriving from the author's original, and with more extensive annotation, such as explanatory lexical glosses, which are surely more likely to be supplied by scribes or editors than by authors,[35] overlaid on top of this by a process of gradual accretion. How might the rubrics indicating letters and lyrics, and the larger body of comments which supply a more detailed structural analysis of the text, fit into this developing process? At first sight they may seem more a part of the poem's reception than its composition. If comments like these are designed to provide a response to the text, or more practically to indicate a way round it, and a key to its contents at any particular point, then, like lexical glosses, they are probably the work of copyists or readers. But the sheer consistency with which rubrics or headings draw attention to Troilus's major songs and to the letters in Book V is provoking. And the evidence that at least one of these sections – Troilus's

Boethian song in Book III, which is absent in one manuscript (BL MS Harley 3943) and a later addition in another (Huntington MS HM 114) – might originally have existed in Chaucer's original as an inserted leaf, gives pause for thought.[36] When we bear in mind that Troilus's first song, like this one, is also woven into the Boccaccian narrative from a further source (in this case, from Petrarch),[37] it comes to seem not impossible that various of the songs, and the letters as well, once existed as physically discrete fragments with headings which clarified their relationship to the text into which they were to be fitted. Such headings might then almost accidentally have become a traditional part of the poem's apparatus. Later readers and copyists, perhaps taking them primarily as comments on the rhetorical rather than the physical structure of the text, may well have been inspired to search for and to highlight what seemed like similar passages. The accretion of extensive marginalia in later manuscripts, in contrast to the spare annotation in the earliest ones such as Corpus MS 61, Pierpont Morgan MS M. 817, and Cambridge, University Library MS Gg. 4. 27, would seem to support the hypothesis of such a process.

While no conclusive generalizations can be made about the derivation of the extensive annotation of *Troilus* in later manuscripts such as Bodleian MSS Rawlinson poet. 163 and Selden B. 24, such witnesses clearly demonstrate the availability in the later fifteenth century of what had effectively become a certain critical perspective on the poem, concerned with its structure and its subtle welding together of distinct rhetorical set-pieces, in which lyrics and letters play an important role. Such contemporary commentary nicely anticipates twentieth-century readings which address the poem's compounding of these speech-acts in the context of an investigation of the forms and effectiveness of different modes of discourse.[38] It could be further argued that a tradition of such commentary on *Troilus* had some significance for the history of English poetry in the fifteenth century. Bodleian MS Selden B. 24 incorporates with it a large number of poems which include interpolated lyrics: in the main scribe's hand, *The Complaint of Mars, The Parliament of Fowls, The Legend of Good Women,* and Lydgate's *Complaint of the Black Knight;* in the hand of his collaborator, *The Quare of Jelusy,* and the anonymous poems now called *the Lay of Sorrow* and *The Lufaris Complaynt.* Shared between them is the unique surviving copy of *The Kingis Quair.* None of these texts as copied here has the extensive apparatus of *Troilus,* but the birds' song in *The Kingis Quair* (232–38) has been singled out as 'cantus', as if to acknowledge some structural similarity between it and its Chaucerian models.

Copies of *Troilus* with annotation of a kind to inspire the extensive commentary of this manuscript may furthermore have been accessible to two identifiable Chaucerian disciples. It has been suggested that the contents of Bodleian MS Selden B. 24 derive from a collection of Chauceriana compiled, some time in the 1420s, for James I of Scotland, the probable author of *The Kingis Quair*, during his imprisonment in England.[39] Its connection with Henry Lord Sinclair, whose maternal grandmother was James's sister, and its inclusion of the unique surviving copy of *The Kingis Quair*, would seem to support this argument. It may therefore be that the *Troilus* annotation in Bodleian MS Selden B. 24 derives from apparatus in James's own copy – apparatus which might have informed or reflected his own perception of the poem's construction, and hence played some part in his own creative practice.[40] Looking further forward, we might speculate that Henryson also had some acquaintance with *Troilus* as annotated in this way. Without necessarily countenancing the suggestion that the anonymous lord to whom Henryson attributes the commandment to write his *Fables* is to be identified as Sinclair, the owner of Bodleian MS Selden B. 24, we might just about legitimately hypothesize that whatever text of *Troilus* Henryson knew would have been related to that of this manuscript, which is known to have been in Scotland at an appropriate time (1488–1513).[41] Henryson's own effective use of lyrical set-pieces, notably in the *Testament of Cresseid* and *Orpheus and Erudice*, might then be seen in the context of a reading of Chaucer's poems guided by attempts to emphasize these same elements of their own construction. While the early incorporation into manuscripts of the notes highlighting the *Troilus* lyrics might be due to nothing more than scribal serendipity, it is tempting to see the gradual formalizing and extension of their role as influential in the processes of the poem's early reception.[42]

NOTES

1 *See*, for example, W. A. Davenport, *Chaucer: Complaint and Narrative* (Cambridge, 1988), pp.129–77; Eugene Vance, *Mervelous Signals: Poetics and Sign Theory in the Middle Ages* (Lincoln, Nebraska, 1987), pp.256–310; J. I. Wimsatt, 'The French Lyric Element in *Troilus and Criseyde*', *Year's Work in English Studies*, 15 (1985), 18–32.

2 All are signalled in B. A. Windeatt, ed., *Geoffrey Chaucer: Troilus and Criseyde. A New Edition of 'The Book of Troilus'* (London and New York, 1984); other modern editions highlight different selections. The edition of the poem from which quotations in this article have been taken is that of Larry D. Benson, ed., *The Riverside Chaucer* (Boston, 1987).

3 *See*, for example, R. H. Robbins, 'The Lyrics', in *A Companion to Chaucer Studies*, ed. Beryl Rowland, second edition (New York and London, 1979), pp.380–402, and

Robert O. Payne, *The Key of Remembrance: A Study of Chaucer's Poetics* (New Haven and London, 1963), pp.173–84.

4 R. K. Root, *The Textual Tradition of Chaucer's Troilus*, Chaucer Society, 1st series, 99 (1916), and ed., *The Book of Troilus and Criseyde* (Princeton, 1926); B. A. Windeatt, 'The Text of the *Troilus*', in *Essays on Troilus and Criseyde*, ed. M. B. Salu (Cambridge, 1979), pp.1–22, and ed., *Troilus and Criseyde;* Derek Brewer, 'Observations on the Text of *Troilus*', in *Medieval Studies for J. A. W. Bennett, Aetatis Suae LXX*, ed. P. L. Heyworth (Oxford, 1981), pp.121–38, and 'Root's Account of the Text of *Troilus*,' *Poetica*, 12 (1981), 36–44; Charles A. Owen, Jr., '*Troilus and Criseyde:* The Question of Chaucer's Revisions', *Studies in the Age of Chaucer*, 9 (1987), 155–72.

5 B. A. Windeatt, 'The Scribes as Chaucer's Early Critics', *Studies in the Age of Chaucer*, 1 (1979), 119–41, considers some of the annotation in the context of the scribes' role in the process of reception; *see* also Margaret Jennings, C. S. J., 'To *Pryke* or to *Prye:* Scribal Delights in the *Troilus*, Book III', in *Chaucer in the Eighties*, ed. Julian N. Wasserman and Robert J. Blanch (Syracuse, 1986), pp.121–33. C. David Benson and Barry A. Windeatt, 'The Manuscript Glosses to Chaucer's *Troilus and Criseyde*', *Chaucer Review*, 25 (1990–91), 33–53, list but make no attempt to analyse the manuscript glosses (my own readings of the annotations differ in some cases from theirs). Examples of the *ordinatio* of the poem are to be found, with discussion, in the following facsimiles: M. B. Parkes and Elizabeth Salter, *Troilus and Criseyde: Geoffrey Chaucer. A Facsimile of Corpus Christi College, Cambridge, MS 61* (Cambridge, 1978); M. B. Parkes and Richard Beadle, *Geoffrey Chaucer: The Poetical Works. A Facsimile of Cambridge, University Library, MS Gg. 4. 27*, 3 vols (Cambridge, 1979–81); Richard Beadle and Jeremy Griffiths, *St John's College, Cambridge, MS L. 1: A Facsimile* (Norman, Oklahoma, 1983); Jeanne Krochalis, *The Pierpont Morgan Library Manuscript M. 817* (Norman, Oklahoma, 1986).

6 *See*, for example, Parkes and Salter, *Corpus MS 61*, pp.4–5; Parkes and Beadle, *Cambridge University Library MS Gg. 4. 27*, iii, pp.40–44; Beadle and Griffiths, *St John's MS L. 1*, pp.xxi–xxiii.

7 For descriptions of the manuscripts *see* Windeatt, ed., *Troilus and Criseyde*, pp.68–76, and R. K. Root, *The Manuscripts of Chaucer's Troilus*, Chaucer Society, 1st Series, 98 (1914), with illustrations. Root and Windeatt supply information on extracts from the poem copied into manuscripts, and on early printed editions. The annotation of these is not considered in the present discussion.

8 Variations are included in the textual notes of Windeatt, ed., *Troilus and Criseyde*.

9 For fuller information about some of these categories, *see* Windeatt, 'The Scribes as Chaucer's Early Critics', and ed., *Troilus and Criseyde*, p.54, note 28.

10 BL MSS Harley 2280 and 2392; St John's MS L. 1; San Marino, Huntington Library MS HM 114; Bodleian Library MSS Selden B. 24 and Selden supra 56.

11 *See* Beadle and Griffiths, *St John's MS L. 1*, p.xxiii. Jeremy Griffiths has suggested to me in correspondence that 'nota k' may be associated with the name 'kayle' that is written in a fifteenth-century hand on the rear flyleaf of the manuscript.

12 *See* Windeatt, ed., *Troilus and Criseyde*, pp.75–76.

13 Changes of speaker are indicated in the later parts of the text in Cambridge University Library MS Gg. 4.27 by means of pen-flourished initials; *see* Parkes and Beadle, *Cambridge University Library MS Gg. 4. 27*, p.41.

14 For descriptions of the contents and make-up of Bodleian MS Selden B. 24 *see* E. P. Hammond, *Chaucer: A Bibliographical Manual* (New York, 1908), pp.341–43; Root, *The MSS of Chaucer's Troilus*, pp.43–45; J. Norton-Smith, ed., *The Kingis Quair* (Oxford, 1961), pp.xxxi–xxxv; M. B. Parkes, *English Cursive Bookhands, 1250–1500*, second edition (London, 1979), p.13. The hand of the main scribe is illustrated in

the studies by Root and Parkes. For analysis of the paper stocks, *see* R. J. Lyall, 'Books and Book Owners in Fifteenth Century Scotland', in *Book Production and Publishing in Britain, 1375–1475*, ed. Jeremy Griffiths and Derek Pearsall (Cambridge, 1989), pp.239–56 (especially pp.250–52).

15 The identity of the hands was first noted by N. R. Ker, *Medieval Manuscripts in British Libraries, II* (Oxford, 1977), p.1, who questions the hypothesis that the scribe was James Graye (*see* Norton-Smith, ed., *The Kingis Quair*). A second hand which supplies a short stint (fols 209v–228v, completing *The Kingis Quair* and adding Hoccleve's *Letter of Cupid* and two anonymous lovers' complaints) has been compared with that of 'V de F' who signs his name in Cambridge, University Library MS Kk. 1. 5; *see* Norton-Smith, ed., *The Kingis Quair*, and, for illustrations, Margaret Muriel Gray, ed., *Lancelot of the Laik*, Scottish Text Society, New Series 2 (1912), frontispiece, and plates facing pp.1 and 96. For information on members of the Sinclair family, *see DNB*.

16 'There are many marginal notes in Latin and in English, which are particularly frequent in Books I and V. They are in at least two hands, one of which seems to be that of the original scribe'; *The MSS of Chaucer's Troilus*, p.45.

17 I, 400: Cantus Troili; II, 827: Cantus Antigonee; III, 1744: [Tr]oilus song [. . .] luf vide*licet*; V, 638: Cantus Troili; V, 1317: Troili [. . .] sho hade [. . .].

18 Windeatt, ed., *Troilus and Criseyde*, pp.66, 74.

19 For a description, *see* Root, *The MSS of Chaucer's Troilus*, pp.37–42.

20 For a summary of opinions, *see* Aage Brusendorff, *The Chaucer Tradition* (Oxford, 1925), pp.439–40.

21 There is an additional unique stanza after II, 1750. *See* Benson, ed., *Riverside Chaucer*, p.1168.

22 *See* Benson and Windeatt, 'MS Glosses', pp.43–44.

23 Corpus MS 61; Durham University Library MS Cosin V. II. 13; Cambridge University Library MS Gg. 4. 27; BL MSS Harley 2280 and 4912; St John's MS L. 1; Huntington MS HM 114; Bodleian MSS Digby 181, Rawlinson poet. 163, Selden B. 24, and Selden supra 56.

24 Corpus MS 61; Durham, University Library MS Cosin V. II. 13; BL MSS Harley 2280, 1239, and 2392; Cambridge, St John's MS L. 1; Huntington MS HM 114; Bodleian MSS Rawlinson poet. 163, Selden B. 24, and Selden supra 56. The beginning of the letter is marked in BL MS Harley 3943 by a large initial.

25 Corpus MS 61; Durham, University Library MS Cosin V. II. 13; BL MSS Harley 2280, 1239, and 2392; St John's MS L. 1; Huntington MS HM 114; Bodleian MSS Rawlinson poet. 163, Selden B. 24, and Selden supra 56. The letter is introduced in Cambridge, University Library MS Gg. 4. 27 and BL MS Harley 3943 by a large initial.

26 Corpus MS 61; BL MSS Harley 2392 and 4912; St John's MS L. 1; Bodleian MSS Rawlinson poet. 163, Selden B. 24, and Selden supra 56.

27 Durham University Library MS Cosin V. II. 13; BL MSS Harley 2392 and 4912; Huntington MS HM 114; Bodleian MSS Rawlinson poet. 163, Selden B. 24, and Selden supra 56. In this instance Benson, ed., *The Riverside Chaucer*, sticks strictly to the copy-text, Corpus MS 61, which contains no gloss. Windeatt, ed., *Troilus and Criseyde*, although also following Corpus MS 61, is sufficiently swayed by the evidence of the other witnesses to include 'Cantus Antigone', the gloss favoured by most of the manuscripts which include one.

28 *See* Windeatt, ed., *Troilus and Criseyde*, pp.36–55, for discussion of textual affiliations.

29 Corpus MS 61 and St John's MS L. 1 are dated on palaeographical grounds respectively to the first and second quarters of the fifteenth century by Parkes and

Salter, *Corpus* MS *61* and Beadle and Griffiths, *St John's* MS *L. 1*. Bodleian MS Selden supra 56 is dated '1441' in a scribal colophon.

30 John M. Manly and Edith Rickert, *The Text of The Canterbury Tales*, 8 vols (Chicago, 1940), and A. I. Doyle and M. B. Parkes, 'The Production of Copies of *The Canterbury Tales* and the *Confessio Amantis* in the Early Fifteenth Century', in *Medieval Scribes, Manuscripts, and Libraries: Essays Presented to N. R. Ker*, ed. M. B. Parkes and Andrew G. Watson (London, 1978), pp.163–210.

31 *See* Manly and Rickert, *The Text of The Canterbury Tales*, iii, 483–527; Graham D. Caie, 'The Significance of the Early Chaucer Manuscript Glosses (With Special Reference to *The Wife of Bath's Prologue*)', *Chaucer Review*, 10 (1975–6), 350–60, 'The Significance of the Glosses in the Earliest Manuscripts of *The Canterbury Tales*', in *Papers from the First Nordic Conference for English Studies*, ed. Stig Johansson and Bjorn Tysdahl (Oslo, 1981), pp.25–34, 'The Significance of Marginal Glosses in the Earliest Manuscripts of *The Canterbury Tales*', in *Chaucer and Scriptural Tradition*, ed. David Lyle Jeffrey (Ottawa, 1984), pp.75–88; Charles A. Owen, Jr., 'The Alternative Reading of *The Canterbury Tales:* Chaucer's Text and the Early Manuscripts', *Proceedings of the Modern Language Association of America*, 97 (1982), 237–50; Susan Schibanoff, 'The New Reader and Female Textuality in Two Early Commentaries on Chaucer', *Studies in the Age of Chaucer*, 10 (1988), 71–108; Doyle and Parkes, 'The Production of Copies of *The Canterbury Tales*', and introduction to *The Canterbury Tales, Geoffrey Chaucer. A Facsimile and Transcription of the Hengwrt Manuscript, with Variants from the Ellemsmere Manuscript*, ed. Paul G. Ruggiers (Norman, Oklahoma, 1979), pp.xxiii–xxiv; N. F. Blake, 'Literary and Other Languages in Middle English', in *Genres, Themes, and Images in English Literature from the 14th to the 15th Century: The J. A. W. Bennett Memorial Lectures, Perugia, 1986*, ed. Piero Boitani and Anna Torti (Tübingen, 1988), pp.166–85 (*see* pp.176–85).

32 Daniel S. Silvia, Jr., 'Glosses to *The Canterbury Tales* from St Jerome's *Epistola Adversus Jovinianum*', *Studies in Philology*, 62 (1965), 28–39. For more recent bibliography, *see* Thomas J. Farrell, 'The Style of the *Clerk's Tale* and the Functions of its Glosses', *Studies in Philology*, 86 (1989), 286–309.

33 Owen, 'The Alternative Reading of *The Canterbury Tales*'.

34 Caie, 'The Significance of Marginal Glosses', p.77.

35 Such glosses are particularly frequent in MS Harley 2392.

36 Windeatt, ed., *Troilus and Criseyde*, pp.38–9.

37 Benson, ed., *Riverside Chaucer*, p.1028, note.

38 *See* above, note 1.

39 Norton-Smith, ed., *The Kingis Quair*, pp.xxxi–xxxv.

40 *See* John Macqueen, 'Poetry – James I to Henryson', in *The History of Scottish Literature. Volume 1, Origins to 1660*, ed. R. D. S. Jack (Aberdeen, 1988), pp.55–72 (especially pp.55–59).

41 A. Lawson, ed., *The Kingis Quair and the Quare of Jelusy*, (London, 1910), pp.xlvii–xlviii. The suggestion has not been pursued by other Henryson scholars, since the reference ('be requeist and precept of ane lord,/Of quhome the name it neidis not record', *Fables*, 34–5) is extremely vague. *See* Denton Fox, ed., *The Poems of Robert Henryson* (Oxford, 1981), p.4.

42 I should like to thank Rosamund Allen, A. S. G. Edwards, and Jeremy Griffiths for their comments on earlier drafts of this article.

Two Fifteenth-Century Manuscripts of the Statutes of the Order of the Garter

LISA JEFFERSON

Early manuscripts of the Statutes of the Order of the Garter are rare, and there are none known to survive that predate the fifteenth century, although the Order was founded by Edward III in or around the year 1348. The earliest surviving statutes decree that all newly elected companions of the Order of the Garter should be issued with a copy of the statutes of the order, and evidence makes it clear that in the fifteenth century these were always in French.[1] The surviving evidence also makes it clear that such documents were always in the form of parchment rolls, until the beginning of the sixteenth century, when bound quarto books first appear.[2] Of the rolls that survive,[3] no two are exactly alike, the decoration in particular being individual to each one; there is however a basic similarity of layout common to all but the Nancy manuscript, which is not a roll but a folded document in charter-type format.

The issuing of copies to newly-elected companions of the Order of the Garter is therefore decreed by the Statutes themselves, which also require that all such copies should be sealed with the Common Seal of the Order. The Statutes also decree '*que l'original soit ensellé avecques ledit seel, et demoinge en la tresoroir dudit college a tousjours*'. No original manuscript survives,[4] and the sparse survival of any copies at all will probably in part be because the early Statutes also decree that after the death of each companion his executors must return his set of the Statutes to the Dean of St George's Chapel in Windsor. We know that this was not always done, but that it was considered sufficiently important for enforcement of the rule to be further strengthened at times by additional chapter ordinances.[5] The survival of the Modena manuscript described here can be attributed to the fact that it was sent abroad to a foreign companion; the Nancy manuscript is more problematical.

The two manuscripts described in this article both date from the reign of Edward IV and form an interesting contrast. Both have seals attached to them which are of an earlier date than any other seals of the Order hitherto recorded. The Nancy manuscript is of particular interest, and is written, signed and dated by the scribe Ricardus Franciscus (or Franceys, the form he himself uses here and which we should perhaps now adopt).

THE NANCY MANUSCRIPT

The Nancy manuscript (housed in the Archives Départementales de Meurthe et Moselle, with the shelfmark MS H 80) is an illuminated parchment document, of two membranes, each measuring 348mm in width and c.1000mm in length (900mm down to the fold, the rest needing to be estimated). It is sealed '*patenter*', with the seal appended on a parchment tag '*sur double queue*'; this tag (or label), measuring 43mm wide and 200mm in length, is threaded through a transverse slit cut across the middle of the lower part of the two layers of parchment whose bottom sections, below the writing, are folded together twice and are held together by the tag with its seal. The document is loosely folded. There are some patches caused by damp, and some slight damage to the edges and corners, but it is generally well-preserved and the whole is legible; the second membrane is noticeably clearer than the first, and this first membrane has been rubbed in places, particularly on the lower portion, in a way consistent with normal wear to the document if it was being regularly consulted. The prickings at both sides are clearly visible, and the central sections of each membrane are carefully ruled. A space of either one or two blank lines has been left between each if the articles of the Statutes (or chapters as they have sometimes been referred to).[6] Incipit: *A lonneur de dieu et de la glorieuse Vierge sainte Marie et de mon*seigneur *Saint George Le Roy Edward le tiers de ce nom . . .*; Explicit: '. . . *se besoing en est*'.

The text is written in a bastard secretary script, and the hand is clearly recognizable as that of Ricardus Franciscus, and displays his usual elegant use of ornate ascenders, descenders and cadels. The text is accurate. At the foot of the first membrane, inside what is now the fold formed for the conjoining of the two membranes by the parchment label holding the seal, is the signature in black ink: 'R. ffranceys. s R' (*see* PLATE 1); on the last ruled line of the second membrane, below the end of the text, is the signature in red ink: 'R. ffranceys. s R 1467' (*see* PLATE 2). The numerals of the date are those of the fifteenth century. The 'S R' are on each side of a paraph; could

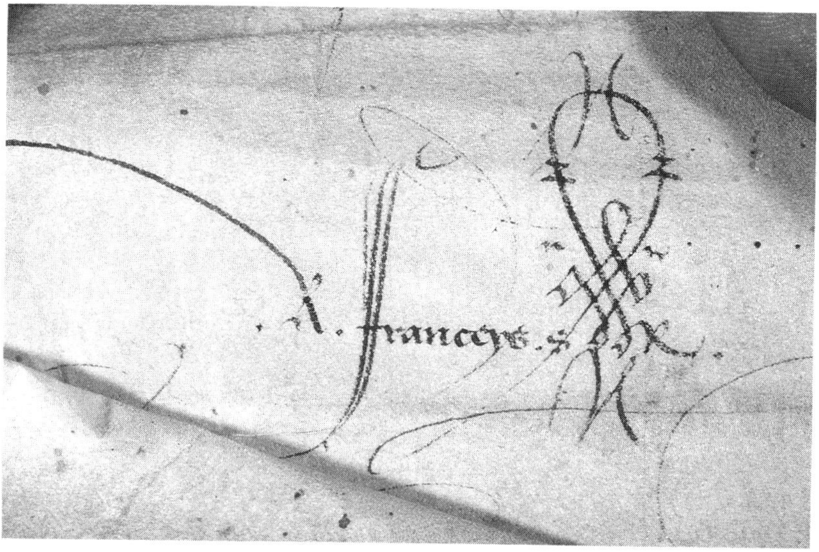

PLATE 1 *Nancy, Archives Départementales de Meurthe et Moselle,* MS *H 80, membrane 1 (detail). The signature of Richard Franceys at the bottom of the first membrane. Reproduced by permission.*

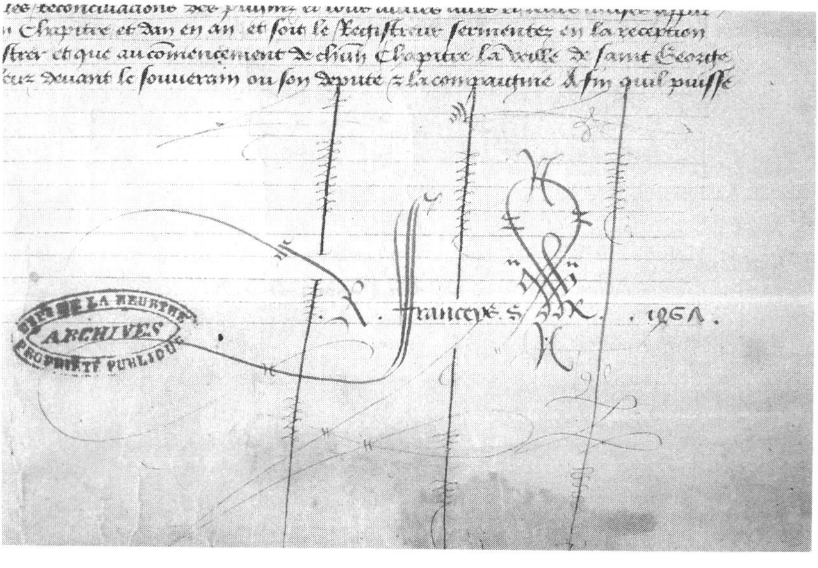

PLATE 2 *Nancy, Archives Départementales de Meurthe et Moselle,* MS *H 80, membrane 2 (detail). The signature of Richard Franceys at the end of the document, with the date 1467. Reproduced by permission.*

it be that these are the reversed first and last letters of the scribe's name? or possibly initials standing for, say, 'Scriba Regis'? or could they perhaps indicate some other epithet?

The top left-hand section of the first membrane is illuminated: the initial 'A' is made to hold two shields, one in each compartment of the letter, the upper one painted with the arms of St George and encircled with the garter bearing the motto of the Order: 'hony soyt qui mal y pense'; the lower one is left blank, but is also encircled with the garter, and it is possible that the arms of a recipient of the manuscript were intended to be painted in here, but also possible that it was intentionally left blank (see further below). Stemming from this initial above and to the left is an ornate floral design, illuminated predominately in gold and blue, and using also red, pink, green and white; the cross of St George in the upper coat of arms is done in a much brighter red than that used in the decoration. A feathered tail of decoration descends some way into the left-hand margin. This illuminated section measures 270mm in length and 100mm in width at the top. Not visible at normal reading distance, but clearly visible at close range, are three areas of the first membrane which have been drafted for further illumination: light pen-sketching of ornate designs have been traced out to the right of the initial 'A', at the top right-hand side, and also towards the base of the membrane, just above where the fold now is and below the end of the text on the first membrane; all being of the same style as that of the illuminated ornamentation at the top left-hand side. This unilluminated sketching (and perhaps the blank shield within the initial 'A') indicate that further decoration of the manuscript was intended but for some reason left unfinished. There is no illumination on the second membrane, nor any sign of any having been intended.

Further ornamentation to the manuscript is provided by elaborate pen-flourishing: both the first and the second membranes have ornate ascenders leading out from the top line of the text into various shapes, including a heart shape in each case; the first lines of each article of the statutes (which are each preceded by a blank space left after the preceding article) also contain ornate ascenders, less exaggerated than those of the first lines; the bottom line of the first membrane has ornate descenders. In addition, throughout the text on both membranes, the initial letter of each article (which is usually an 'I' for 'Item') has been given highly elaborate extensions into the left hand margin, sometimes in red and sometimes in black ink (not in strict alternation). To the left of this appears the number of each article, written at the same time as the rest of the manuscript, and possibly by the scribe himself.

The scribe, Richard Franceys, is known to us from a number of other manuscripts; I list here all those that have so far been attributed to him, although some of these attributions are disputed or uncertain:

1 San Marino, California, Huntington Library, MS HM 932: The Statutes of the Archdeaconry of London;[7] this is the only other manuscript to be signed and dated by the scribe; the language of this text is Latin, and on fol. 13v is found the signature and date: *'Ricardus Franciscus Scripsit Anno Domini 1447'* (*see* PLATE 3).

2 Oxford, Bodleian Library, MS Laud Misc. 570: Christine de Pisan, *L'Epître d'Othéa*; and *Livre des quatre vertus*, in French; this manuscript is dated 1440 and on f. 23v the initials 'R.F.' appear in a decorative motif.

3 Grant of arms to the Tallow Chandlers' Company of the City of London (MS in the possession of the company);[8] dated 24 September 1456; signed and sealed by John Smert, Garter King of Arms; the language is French.[9]

4 Oxford, Bodleian Library, MS Ashmole 789, fols 1–5: writing exercises in Latin, including fols 3v and 4r a decorated alphabetical list of Latin first names and fol. 4v upper- and lower-case alphabets, abbreviations and ligatures.

5 London, British Library, MS Harley 2915: a Book of Hours, in Latin and French.

6 Oxford, University College, MS 85: English translations of Alain Chartier, *Quadrilogue;* of the *Secretum secretorum*;[10] etc.

7 London, British Library, MS Harley 4775: Jacobus de Voragine, *The Golden Legend,* in English.

8 New York, Pierpont Morgan Library, MS M 126: Gower, *Confessio Amantis,* in English.

9 Philadelphia, Rosenbach Foundation, MS 439/16: Lydgate, *The Fall of Princes,* in English.[11]

10 Oxford, Bodleian Library, MS Ashmole 764: an heraldic miscellany, mostly in French.

11 Cambridge, St John's College, MS H 5 (olim 208): Stephen Scrope's English translation of the *Epistle of Othea.*[12]

12 Parts of Coks Cartulary: London, Hospital of St Bartholomew, Smithfield, Cartulary in two volumes.[13]

Scholars have usually stated that Richard Franceys was of French origin,[14] and I believe that the Nancy manuscript provides good evidence for this. First, we have his signature with the French form of his name; but this is not conclusive, since his only other known signature (appended to a Latin text) is in a Latin form; the abbrevia-

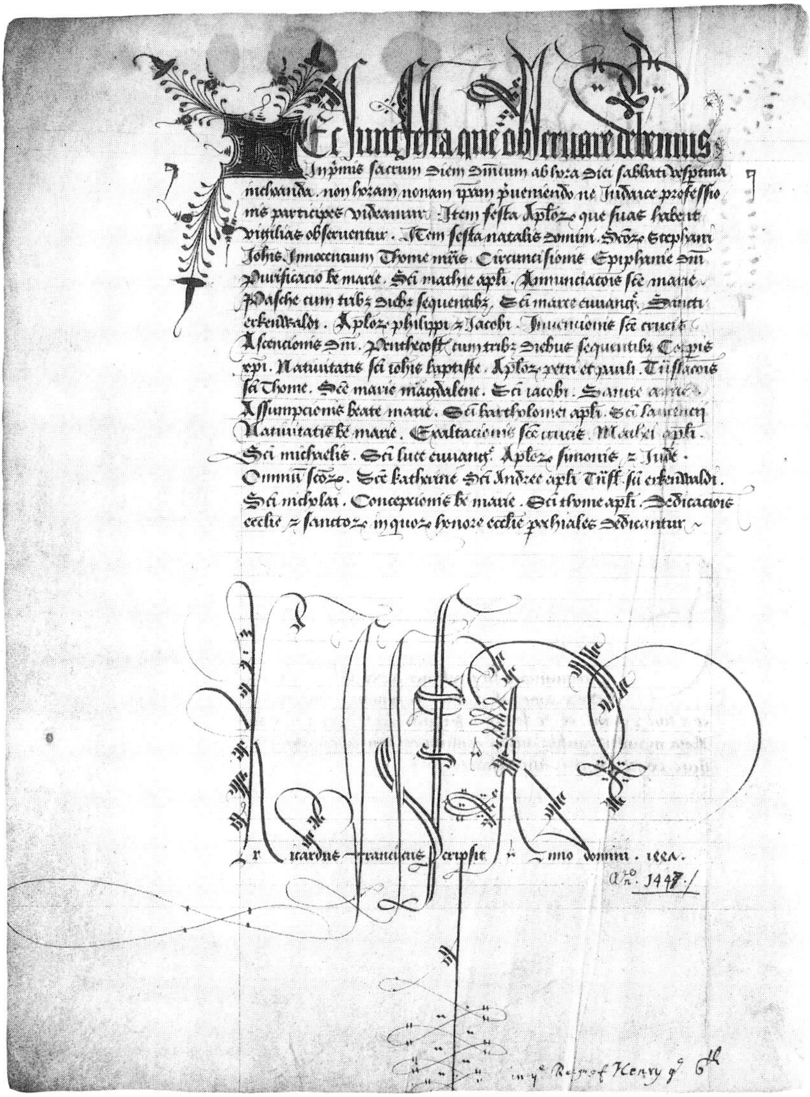

PLATE 3 *Statutes of the Archdeaconry of London, San Marino, California, Huntington Library,* MS *HM 932, fol. 13v (detail). The signature of Richard Franceys, with the date 1447. Reproduced by permission of the Huntington Library.*

tion of Richard to a simple capital 'R' must also be considered, as also whether we should understand 'ffranceys' and 'Franciscus' as being the name 'Francis' or the epithet 'French'. Much better proof lies in the language of the text of the Nancy document. This is too complicated a matter to be gone into here in detail and will have to await treatment in a lengthier article; but, briefly, comparison with other texts of these statutes reveals minor emendations, alterations and small additions to the text which either correct grammatical errors, or rephrase a sentence more logically, or add a synonymic doublet word or phrase. A fairly high degree of scribal variation is common to all fifteenth-century texts of these statutes, and Richard Franceys' variations are such as must have been introduced by someone fully fluent in continental French, not just in Anglo-Norman; there is of course no proof that it was Franceys himself who was responsible for the variations, but my knowledge of the other texts of these statutes makes me feel fairly certain that his exemplar will have contained abbreviated words which he has here expanded to a fully accurate French form, something that cannot be said for the copies of all other scribes.

The remaining question about this manuscript: for whom was it intended? cannot be answered with certainty. There are no marks of ownership upon it, and its present location poses more problems than it solves. It is listed in the Nancy catalogues as having come into the archives there from the Benedictine house of Dieulouard, at the time when all monastic libraries were requisitioned by the State in France.[15] Dieulouard was a house of English Benedictines, founded in 1606, and which flourished (to no small extent on its sale of English beer!)[16] until the Revolution, when the monks were dispersed, the church and library were pillaged, and the building was set on fire; the monks fled to Ampleforth.[17] There is no record to be found of this copy of the Statutes of the Order of the Garter either in the documents from Dieulouard remaining in Nancy or in the (very few) that the monks managed to take back with them to England.[18] As to who might have taken the document to Dieulouard, a large number of possibilities present themselves between 1606 and the French Revolution, any of which might explain its presence there, but none of which I have yet been able to find giving positive confirmation. At some stage, certainly, the document was sent or taken abroad, and arrived in the Archives de Meurthe-et-Moselle in Nancy at the time of the French Revolution; most probably it did come from Dieulouard, and had been taken there at some point, perhaps to someone there with antiquarian interests; but a remaining possibility to consider, given the lack of any confirmation of its previous presence there, is that those cataloguing the newly-acquired archives of Nancy misattributed the provenance of the document: a certain amount of confusion happened when all the holdings of the religious houses were rounded up, and it would be natural for the cataloguers, if in doubt, to assume that such a document had come from a local English community.[19]

More may be learned about its earlier provenance from the manuscript itself: there are scribbled marks at several places across the top of the second membrane, very near the upper edge, written upside-down to the text: 'Dec D Decano Decano': when folded, this edge would be immediately available, and it would seem therefore that the document had been sent 'to the dean', or else been thus labelled as belonging to him or emanating from his hands.[20] The Dean of St George's, Windsor, is almost certainly the individual in question, and is the person to whom, by statute, all copies of the statutes of the Order issued to companions should have been returned by the executors after the death of each companion. Did this then happen in this case, and was the manuscript preserved at Windsor until some unknown date when, for some unknown reason, and by some unknown person, it was taken to Dieulouard?

But for which companion of the Order could this copy have been issued? The date of 1467 provides us with only one real possibility:[21] Duke Charles (the Bold) of Burgundy. He was not elected to the Order until the following year, but negotiations about this (as about his marriage to the King's sister) were taking place in 1467; it is by no means improbable that a highly ornate document could have been commissioned in readiness. He would certainly have been sent some copy, and letters concerning his oath to abide by the statutes of the Order survive; no manuscript has been found to date that can be attributed as his,[22] and the possibility of this Nancy manuscript being his must therefore be considered.[23]

But is it perhaps more possible, given the charter-type format of this document, that it was drawn up not as a copy for one of the companions, but as a replacement for whatever original document may have survived at St George's Chapel in Windsor, and that it was sent to the Dean (in 1467 this was John Faulkes, alias Vaux), as the man responsible for seeing that it be safely housed in the treasury there? Almost everything about this document would be consistent with this explanation, but room for doubt is still present, since one might have expected such a document to be the master-copy from which other copies were made: but the Modena manuscript (described below), whose text is basically the same as that of this Nancy manuscript (although with a large number of scribal mistakes, small omissions etc.) was provably not copied from it,[24] nor was any other copy known to me. But so few survive that this is not safe evidence, and the present physical state of the manuscript is certainly consistent with frequent use and consultation.

If, for whatever reason, it had been decided in 1467 that a new official document should be drawn up to replace the original at Windsor, then the choice of the scribe Richard Franceys would have been an obvious one. We know that he had already done work for John Smert, Garter King of Arms, and had produced for him the grant of arms to the Tallow Chandlers Company, and also the collection of heraldic treatises now contained in MS Ashmole 764 (and very possibly also other manuscripts still awaiting identification). Smert therefore knew Franceys, and, as Garter King of Arms could either have commissioned such a document himself or have been ordered to do so by King Edward IV. Once written, illuminated, and sealed, it would need to be sent to the Dean of Windsor – and hence the scribbled words 'Decano' on the second membrane. How long it could have remained at Windsor we do not know; its version of the statutes was already anachronistic, since amendments and additions to the ordinances had been made, and others followed; in 1522 Henry VIII produced a definitive new version that authoritatively superseded all earlier ones. Perhaps one day evidence will be found for the route this manuscript may have travelled between Windsor and Nancy.

THE MODENA MANUSCRIPT

In complete contrast to the Nancy manuscript is the copy of the Statutes that is now held in the Archivio di Stato of Modena, Archivio per Materie, ordini equestri, b.7, MS no. 4657/92. It is, by comparison, plain, having almost no illumination and very little decoration. The writing is clear and elegant, but the text is by no means accurate and, unlike the Nancy manuscript, reveals a fair degree of scribal carelessness.

It is a parchment roll, 2420mm × 300mm, consisting of three membranes of unequal length [970 + 950 + 500mm], joined lengthwise in sequence; the seal is attached to the third membrane by a label cut out of parchment, 140mm long and 40mm wide.[25] The manuscript has been very well preserved, and is in excellent condition, showing none of the signs of wear that we see on the Nancy manuscript. The ruling has been carefully done and there are 198 lines of writing in all, written in a clear bastard secretary hand. A gap of one line has been left between each of the articles, except near the end, on the last membrane, where a few articles follow directly on the next line below the previous article, the scribe clearly having realised that he needed to economise on space if he was to get the whole text into the remaining space. There is much later pencil numeration of all articles in the left-hand margin, but only one contemporary number here, which is used to indicate the correct order of articles at a point where the scribe has omitted one in error and added it next, thus inverting the order of 2 articles.

Ornate ascenders and descenders are used throughout the text, notably on the first line, but these lack the elegance of Franceys' hand, and are far less numerous. Less elegant and assured also are the initials of each new article, which are however similar in having light pen-flourishes extended into the left-hand margin. The only other decoration is a large initial 'A' at the beginning, surrounded by an ornate floral design executed in blue, pink, white and brown; and a shield bearing the arms of St George, executed in silver and red, drawn above the first line of text, roughly in the middle.[26] Incipit: *A Lonneur de dieu et de la glorieuse Vierge Sainte Mar ooo de monseigneur Saint George A le Roy dangleterre nostre Seigneur Edward le tiers . . .*; Explicit: . . . *se besoing en soit.*

This manuscript is datable to 1480, when it was sent to Ercole I, Duke of Ferrara.[27] Its present location, among the archives of the Este family held now in Modena, sufficiently supports this attribution, and two old shelf marks on the dorse of the third membrane make it certain: the first, 'N. 7' can be identified as dating from the sixteenth century, when the archives of the Este family were catalogued in Ferrara; the other, 'N. 443', dates from the seventeenth century when the Este family's holdings in Modena were catalogued.[28]

THE SEALS

Let us turn now to the seals attached to each of these manuscripts. They are both earlier than any other of the Order known to survive.[29] Both are round pendent seals, and are impressions into red wax; both are affixed to the documents with parchment tags, but the threading method is different in each case (see descriptions above); a small signet seal has been used for the counterseal on the back of each.

The diameter of the Nancy seal is 50mm (*see* PLATE 4). It is now rather chipped around the edges, and lacks a small outer section on the dexter side, but is otherwise well-preserved. The Modena seal is very slightly larger in overall diameter (60mm) (*see* PLATE 5). The

PLATE 4 *(left) Nancy, Archives Départementales de Meurthe et Moselle,* MS *H 80 (actual diameter 50mm). The obverse of the earliest surviving seal of the Order of the Garter, 1467. Reproduced by permission.*

PLATE 5 *(right) Modena, Archivio di Stato di Modena, Archivio per Materie, ordini equestri, b.7,* MS *no. 4657/92 (actual diameter 60mm). The obverse of the 1480 seal of the Order of the Garter. Reproduced by permission.*

central part of the obverse is very rubbed, but is still quite discernible, and there has been slight damage to the lower sinister corner; all is otherwise well-preserved.

The obverse of the two seals is identical: in the centre is a large shield bearing the arms of St George dexter impaling the Royal Arms sinister; the shield is surmounted by a crown with five fleur-de-lis points, the base having a ribbon design of alternating crosses and double superimposed points (x:x:x:); it is encircled with the garter, bearing the motto of the Order, '*hony soyt qui mal y pense*' in black letter type lettering, reading (as is usual) from the lower corner of the dexter side, above the buckle of the garter, upwards and then down to the lower sinister side, with three words on each side; each word is separated from the next by a small vertically-elongated quatrefoil. On the Nancy seal the first words of the motto are now missing, whereas on the Modena seal the last word has mostly disappeared, but the other words are still visible. The initials 'E' and 'R', also in black letter, are placed centrally, one on each side of the shield, in

PLATE 6 *(left) Nancy, Archives Départementales de Meurthe et Moselle,* MS *H 80 (actual diameter 15mm), The 1467 counterseal of the Order of the Garter. Reproduced by permission.*

PLATE 7 *(right) Modena, Archivio di Stato di Modena, Archivio per Materie, ordini equestri, b.7,* MS *no. 4657/92 (actual diameter 15mm). The 1480 counterseal of the Order of the Garter, with added initials 'E' – 'R'. Reproduced by permission.*

the field between the motto and the coat of arms. The field is diapered with a pattern of intertwining rose leaves and flowers.

On the back of both seals is a small counterseal; these are very small, having a diameter of only 15mm; both are well-preserved and their detail is clearly visible. On these the Royal arms and those of St George are in reversed positions, the Royal Arms dexter and the Arms of St George sinister. The encircling with the garter and the surmounting with a crown are as on the obverse, but the crown here just four fleur-de-lis points. The whole field is occupied, leaving no more than a very narrow gap between the garter ribbon and the shield. The same signet has been used for both, but it has been modified, for on the Modena seal alone we see the initials 'E' and 'R' (*see* PLATES 6 and 7); these have been superimposed on the garter ribbon, each placed centrally one on each side of the shield; this placing was necessitated by the small size of this seal, on which almost no field is left between the shield and the encircling garter.

These initials must be those of Edward IV, and there is no possibility of the seals having been those of Edward III, still in use by his successor as Sovereign of the Order of the Garter, although later monarchs did employ the seals of their predecessors (and the current Garter seal is the Hanoverian one of 1716). The Royal Arms are those in use between c.1401 and 1603: quarterly, 1 and 4 France Modern, 2 and 3 England. Edward III's shield used France Ancient, the difference between this and France Modern being that in the former the fleurs-de-lis appear 'semy', whereas in the latter just three fleurs-de-lis appear.[30]

In addition, the first use of a counterseal on the back of the Common Seal of the Order can be dated, although no earlier examples of it remain than these two. In 1421, Henry V and his Companions of the Order formally agreed in chapter to a set of amendments to the existing statutes; article 27 of these latter had decreed that

> le commun seel soit fait, lequel demourra en la garde de celui que le souverain vouldra assigner

and article 32

> que toutes les licences des chevaliers de l'ordre qui yront hors pour acquerir honneur, et tous certificas ou mandemens a faire touchans ledit ordre, doresenavant par le souverain soient faits soubz le commun seel, lequel remaindra en la garde d'un des compaignons dudit ordre, a la voulenté dudit souverain.[31] Et ce celui qui l'aura en garde se parte pour cause raisonnable hors de la presence dudit souverain, que adoncques il laissera ledit seel en garde d'un autre compaignon dudit ordre, estant present avecques le souverain, par son assignement; ainsi que le seel ne soit nulle fois hors de la presence dudit souverain tant qu'il sera dedens le royaume. Et pareillement en son absence sera son deputé avecques ledit seel.

The amendment was made at the end of this article and reads:

> Et pour tant que le souverain propose de soy absenter et de aler hors du royaume a cause raisonnable, il est ordonné par assent de la compaignie qu'il aura ung signet convenable a l'ordre du gartier, pour mettre au dox du seel commun de l'ordre, qui sera avecques lui ou qu'il soit, en tous les actes et fais de l'ordre en son absence susdicte, encontre les actes par le deputté faiz en Angleterre.

It would seem from this that Henry V had intended this signet seal to be used only as a seal of absence when the Sovereign was abroad; his deputy, who remained in England, would be responsible for affixing the common seal of the Order to any document requiring it.

Edward IV and his companions of the Order modified the ruling of the statutes concerning the safe-keeping of the Garter seal when, on 20 April 16.E.IV (1475), a Chancellor was formally appointed to the Order:

> Item: it is accordyd by the Souerain and the companions at the Chapiter holden the xx day of Aprill the xvi yeer of the reigne of King Edward the iiii[th] the Souereigne, that notwithstanding the Chapiter or article in the Statutes of the ordre of the gartyr that beginneth in Frenche:

> *Item que toutes licens*, wherby it apperyth that the seall of the gartyr owght to be in the keping of one of the ordre being present with the souereigne: yet for certayn considerations moving the souvereyn and the seyd companions that were present this day, it is aggred that the right reverent father in god Richard Bishop of Sarum shall have during the Kings pleasure the keping of the seid seall and be called Chanceler of the seid ordre of the gartyr[32]

The rulings on the use of the seals had also been modified on 10 October of the previous year when Edward issued Letters Patent: these letters state that chancellors '*ne pourront seeler nulles lettres se non par la forme et la maniere come il est ordonné par les estatuz dudit ordre ou par le commandement especial de nous et de nos successeurs souverains dudit* ordre' (my underlining).[33] This modification to the rules on use of the seal, specifically giving the Sovereign of the Order the right to issue special commands concerning this, postdates the use of the signet on the Nancy manuscript. Nothing is surprising in this to those familiar with the history of the Order of the Garter, for it is frequent to find disparities between the statutes and actual practices, and to find also that amendments to the statutes are introduced after some change in practice. The statutes in force in 1467 officially required only the common seal of the Order to be affixed to copies issued to companions, and to the original kept at Windsor; but countersealing is common practice, and nothing more natural than that Edward should have wished to affix his signet seal to the Nancy copy of the statutes of the Order of the Garter, which was clearly drawn up to be an elegant, formal and authoritative document; by the time the Modena document was issued in 1480, the use of the signet seal as well as the common seal was covered (had anyone bothered to query it!) by the Letters Patent quoted above.

The modification to the signet (the addition of the initials 'E R') between its use on the Nancy seal in 1467 and that on the Modena seal in 1480 is of interest. Edward IV's reign was interrupted in 1470–71, when Henry VI returned to the throne for a short period and Edward took refuge in Holland. The two seals of the Order of the Garter were clearly safely preserved during this time, although it is impossible to say where, or in whose keeping they may have been, although one may presume that Edward himself held the signet seal. No difference is apparent in the obverse of the impressions here (both show the initials 'E R'), leading one to think that Henry made no use of the common seal of the Order during this second reign of his;[34] the addition of initials to the signet seal used for the counterseal could perhaps have been done after Edward's return from France, and have been occasioned by a wish to authenticate ownership of this seal.

NOTES

I am in the course of preparing a full study of the surviving manuscripts of the Statutes of the Order of the Garter (from the inception of the Order up to the reign of Henry VIII). My research work has been supported by funding arranged by Mr Hubert Chesshyre, L.V.O., Chester Herald, and Mr Peter Begent and my very grateful thanks go to them. I thank in addition here those in Nancy and Modena who have been so helpful: the Director, M. Hubert Collin, and the staff of the Archives de Meurthe-et-Moselle in Nancy; and the Director, Prof. Dott. Angelo Spaggiari, and Dott. Giuseppe Treni and the other staff of the Archivio di Stato in Modena. My thanks go also to Dr M. B. Parkes for his expert guidance and generously-given advice and help; and to Jeremy Griffiths who read and commented upon an earlier draft of this article.

1 Latin versions survive, and, right at the end of the fifteenth century, an English version, but these were done for other purposes, not for issue to companions of the Order.

2 There are earlier copies in such a format, but these are not copies as issued to companions of the Order, but copies done for heralds and contained in their manuals of useful reference texts.

3 There are three others from the fifteenth century: one dates from the reign of Henry VI (London, British Library, MS Harley Roll Y 27: second quarter of the fifteenth century); and two from the reign of Henry VII (Copenhagen, Rigsarkivet, MS Egeskabene England, no 12 (1493); Edinburgh, National Library of Scotland, MS Ch A 43 (c.1500). Sources survive which mention and in some cases transcribe other parchment rolls, but without giving full physical details; there are also a few other surviving later rolls, but these are for various reasons different and not comparable. Diethard Schneider's 1988 doctoral thesis, *Der englische Hosenbandorden: Beiträge zur Entstehung und Entwicklung des 'The Most Noble Order of the Garter' (1348–1702), mit einem Ausblick bis 1983*, 4 vols, (Bonn, 1988), lists all these manuscripts, and provides an (inadequate) edition of the text; I am indebted to this work for the listing of manuscripts (which is however incomplete); Schneider was working from microfilms, did not describe the manuscripts, gives no information about the seals, and did not recognise Richard Franceys as the scribe of the Nancy manuscript.

4 *See* my article: 'MS Arundel 48 and the Earliest Statutes of the Order of the Garter', *English Historical Review*, 109 (1994), 356–385.

5 *See* for instance N. H. Nicolas, *History of the Orders of Knighthood of the British Empire* (London, 1842), 4 vols, I, 97.

6 *See* quotation below on pp.30–31.

7 C. W. Dutschke, *Guide to Medieval and Renaissance MSS in the Huntington Library* (San Marino, 1989), 2 vols, 277–8; and *see* K. L. Scott, 'A mid-fifteenth-century illuminating shop and its customers', *Journal of the Warburg & Courtauld Institute*, 31, (1968), 170–96, note 3.

8 This identification was made by J. Alexander, 'William Abell 'lymnour' and 15th Century English Illumination', in *Kunsthistorische Forschungen: Otto Pächt zu seinem 70. Geburtstag*, ed. A. Rosenauer and G. Weber, (Salzburg, 1972), 166–72, p.170, note 37; *see also* p.167 note 19.

9 Reproductions of this are to be found in J. Bromley and H. Child, *The Armorial Bearings of the Guilds of London* (London, 1960), Plate 50 (and *see* pp.236–39); F. J. Grant, *Illustrated Catalogue of the Heraldic Exhibition, Edinburgh, MDCCCXCI* (Edinburgh, 1891), Plate 5 (no.34); R. J. Mitchell and M. D. R. Leys, *A History of the English People* (London, 1950), plate facing p.224. *See also* M. F. Monier-Williams,

Records of the Worshipful Company of the Tallow-Chandlers, London (London, 1897), Vol. I, pp.22–36.

10 ed. M. A. Manzalaoui, *EETS*, Vol.276, (1977); *see* pp.xxxix–xl for comments on the scribe.

11 *See Sixty Bokes Olde and Newe: Manuscripts and Early Printed Books from Libraries in and near Philadelphia illustrating Chaucer's Sources, his Works and their Influence*, ed. D. Anderson, (Knoxville, 1986), no.55, pp.105–110.

12 *See* A. I. Doyle, 'A note on St John's College, Cambridge, MS H 5', Appendix B in *The Epistle of Othea*, ed. C. F. Bühler, *EETS*, (London, 1970), pp.125–7.

13 Also suggested by Alexander, 'William Abell "lymnour"', note 37.

14 R. Hamer, 'Spellings of the fifteenth-century scribe Ricardus Franciscus', in *Five Hundred Years of Words and Sounds: A Festschrift for Eric Dobson*, ed. E. G. Stanley and D. Gray, (Cambridge, 1983), pp.63–73 pp.69: 'He seems to have been French, or at least strongly influenced by French scribal models'); C. Meale, 'Patrons, Buyers and Owners: Book Production and Social Status', in *Book Production and Publishing in Britain, 1375–1475*, ed. Jeremy Griffiths and Derek Pearsall, (Cambridge, 1989), pp.201–38 (p.202 states he was not English); *see also* C. Paul Christianson, *A Dictionary of London Stationers and Book Artisans*, 1300–1500 (New York, 1990); Christianson, 'Evidence for the study of London's late medieval manuscript-book trade', in *Book Production and Publishing in Britain, 1375–1475*, ed. Griffiths and Pearsall, pp.87–108.

15 Hubert Collin, *Guide des Archives de Meurthe-et-Moselle. Première Partie* (Nancy, 1984); H. Lepage, *Inventaire Sommaire des Archives Départementales antérieurs à 1790: Meurthe et Moselle, Archives Ecclésiastiques, Série H*, Tome IV (Nancy, 1881).

16 L'abbé G. Clanché, *La Bière des bénédictins anglais de Dieulouard et leur abbaye actuelle d'Ampleforth* (Nancy, 1933).

17 J. I. Cummins, 'The foundation of St Lawrence at Dieulouard', *The Ampleforth Journal*, 4, (1899), 14–29; L'abbé Melnotte, *Notice historique sur Scarpone et Dieulouard* (Nancy, 1895); P. Marton, *Les Bénédictins anglais de Dieulouard et la fuite du Révérend Père Marsh, dernier prieur du couvent de Saint Laurent* (Nancy, *1884);* Dom Aug. Calmet, *Notice de la Lorraine* (Nancy, 1756), cols 327–331: 'Dieulouard'.

18 Nancy, Archives, MS H 83: *Catalogus Librorum Bibliothecae Monasterii Sancti Laurentij de Deicustodia*; I am most grateful to Fr. Anselm Cramer, O.S.B., the Monastery Librarian of Ampleforth, for his confirmation that there is no known record of our manuscript's having been at Dieulouard.

19 *See* J. Favier, 'Coup d'oeil sur les bibliothèques des couvents du district de Nancy pendant la Révolution', *Mémoires de la Société d'Archéologie Lorraine*, 3e série, 11, (1883), 139–94.

20 There is also a largely indecipherable notation on the dorse here: possibly 'L ? J.'

21 The only other two names one could consider are those of Anthony Wydville, Lord Scales, elected c.1465: he should have had a copy issued to him earlier than 1467, but could perhaps have wanted some rather grander-looking document, perhaps in connection with the Smithfield tournament of that year? or else Inigo d'Avalos, Count of Monte Odorisio, elected c.1466: he would seem to have been of too little importance to the Order to have rated this exceptional document. There were no further elections after that of Duke Charles until 1471.

22 I am indebted to Dr A. I. Doyle of University College, Durham and Dr C. F. R. de Hamel of Sotheby's for their information about copies at auction.

23 Duke Charles of Burgundy died in battle at Nancy, but I suspect this to be a coincidence and not pertinent to the provenance of the manuscript and its present housing in the Archives in Nancy.

24 I shall deal with this in detail in a separate article.

25 This label was obviously cut from a scrap sheet, and some of what was written on this is clearly legible on the inside sections of the ends of the tags; it is written in English, and perhaps in the same hand as that of the scribe of the manuscript (which is in French). The central part of each line cannot be read as it is within the seal; the legible words are:

Di ([or Du]	most noble and habaundaunt grace
tend	of xij yeris and an half and
more by	ney hath hathe taken frome your said
besecher	the Valor of ij^{c} li. vnto there

26 There is also an erasure of some words above the first line, but from what can still be made out this must have been a later annotation.

27 We have proof of its being sent in the effusive letter written by Ercole I to Edward IV, thanking him for the honour accorded him: "... *Verum quod in me fuit ipsa Insignia cum statutis suis, gratanter et hilarissima fronte, ac reverenter accepi et quantum in ipsis statutis continetur me observare policitus sum et polliceor, ac me ut semper fui, sic deinceps futurum Maiestati Vestri obsequentissimum et deditissimum filium et servitorem plane profiteor.*' Cited here from the edition of C. Foucard, *Lo Statuto della Compagnia della Giarretiera istituita da Edoardo III, Re d'Inghilterra, MCCCL (Con riproduzione dell'esemplare consegnato ad Ercole, Duca di Ferrara, nell'anno 1480)* (Modena, 1878).

28 I am most grateful to the director of the Archivio di Stato in Modena, Prof. Angelo Spaggiari, for providing me with information about these shelfmarks. The Este family were forced to transfer their capital from Ferrara to Modena in 1598; they took almost everything with them, including a vast collection of archive papers; the Este archives now form the basis of Modena's State Archive, which was brought into being between 1860 and 1863; most of the contents of the Archivio per materie came from the Ducal Chancellery; *see Guida Generale degli Archivi di Stato Italiani* (Rome, 1983), II, 993ff. On the earlier catalogues *see* Angelo Spaggiari, 'Rapporti politico-amministrativi fra corte e periferia negli archivi dello 'stato' estense', *La corte e la spazio: Ferrara estense*, ed. G. Papagno and A. Quondam, (Bulzoni: Rome, 1982), pp.93–106. Three inventories of the Este family archive remain, dated 1488, 1517 and 1545, that were all made before the move to Modena; unfortunately only the last of these could be found when I visited Modena (MS entitled: *Inventario de li Instrumenti. Inuestiture. et altre cose de la Tore*) where unfortunately this manuscript of the Garter Statutes cannot be traced, but whose numbering style is identical to that of the N.7 on our manuscript.

29 It had been thought that the earliest surviving seal of the Order of the Garter was that dating from the reign of Henry VII to be found in the Rigsarkivet in Copenhagen, attached to the copy of the Statutes of the Order sent to John, King of Denmark, Norway and Sweden, who was elected to the Order in 1493 (MS Egeskabene England, no.12).

30 *See* T. Woodcock and J. M. Robinson, *The Oxford Guide to Heraldry* (Oxford, 1990), p.188.

31 The only keeper of the Seal mentioned in the early French Register of the Order is Sir John Robsart appointed in 1422; *see* Oxford, Bodleian Library, MS Ashmole 1128, fol. 49v. (This is Ashmole's transcript of this Register, the original of which is now lost.)

32 MS Ashmole 1128, fol. 86r.

33 *See* J. Hussey, 'Letters Patent of Edward the Fourth, creating the Chancellorship of the Order of the Garter, and appointing Richard Beauchamp, Bishop of

Salisbury, as first Chancellor, A.D. 1476', *The Wiltshire Archaeological and Natural History Magazine*, 17, (1878), 93–94.

34 The relevant case to compare is that of the Great Seal of England: during the period of his exile in Holland, Edward IV's Great Seal came into the possession of Henry VI, who had it altered for his own use, substituting his name 'Henricus' for 'Edwardus' in the legend. When he returned to the throne, Edward IV had a new Royal Seal made. *See* A. B. and A. Wyon, *The Great Seals of England* (London, 1887), pp.60–61.

Manuscripts in The Schøyen Collection Copied or Owned in the British Isles before 1700

JEREMY GRIFFITHS

The list that follows comprises summary descriptions of the manuscripts in The Schøyen Collection, copied or owned in the British Isles before 1700, covering acquisitions up to MS 257, purchased in June 1989. Future volumes of *English Manuscript Studies* will list the manuscripts of British origin in The Schøyen Collection from MS 257 – at the time of writing there are over 570 of these, including documents.

The list is derived from the preliminary catalogue of The Schøyen Collection being compiled by Mr Schøyen, with the assistance of his librarian, Elizabeth Sørenssen, and is published by kind permission.

The collection is kept in Oslo and in London. The correct form of reference is: Oslo & London, The Schøyen Collection, MS —.

In the list that follows, the contents of manuscripts are noted summarily. Numbers of leaves are not noted, unless the item is a single leaf or similar fragment of a complete manuscript. The form of dates follows N. R. Ker, *Medieval Manuscripts in British Libraries: I London* (Oxford, 1969), p.vii. Only significant illumination is noted. Details of bindings are not noticed, unless the binding is original or otherwise significant. The provenance of individual items includes references to auction sale or booksellers' catalogues, where possible, as convenient sources of further detailed description. Immediate book trade provenance is generally omitted, unless it comprises a published catalogue description.

MS 10 Bible, with Jerome prologues
in Latin, Italy, s.xiii 2, decoration apparently completed in England, s.xvi English or Scottish, blind-stamped calf binding.
John Maude, c.1600; Sir James Colquhoun of Luss, Bt., s.xviii; E. H. M. Cox of Longforgan, Dundee; Sotheby's, 17 November 1943, lot 451; Foster W. Bond, London; Sotheby's, 2 December 1986 lot 36

MS 11 Bible, with Jerome prefaces
in Latin, England, s.xiii 2, modern red morocco binding, with medieval edge painting
Given in 1492 by John Sterr to Thomas Brent, Dean of the Secular College of St. Michael, South Malling, Sussex (not in Ker, *MLGB*); Hans Sallander, Uppsala, Sweden, 1946; Sven Ericsson, Stockholm, until 1986; Sotheby's, 2 December 1986, lot 37

MS 15 Bible, with Jerome prologues
in Latin, England, Canterbury?, s.xiii 3/4, historiated initials and Genesis initial
Christ Church, Canterbury, s.xiii, with ownership inscription of William Lighfield, monk of Christ Church, Canterbury; Magister Thomas Trussel, s.xv; William Cockes, 'clerici', s.xvi; Henry Munster; Sotheby's, 12 December 1967, lot 19; Sanders, Oxford; Christie's, 9 December 1981, lot 231

MS 33 Chronicle and other texts
Chronicle of the Kings of England from Lear to Arthur; 'In welth is no sekernes', macaronic verse; Geoffrey of Monmouth, *Historia Regum Britanniae*, Books 7.3–12.8 (*Prophetia Merlini*); King Edwin's Wars, in Latin pentameter verse; Chronicle of the Kings of England from Alfred to Henry V; Chronological list of the Kings of England, Popes and Roman Emperors from Arthur to Edward the Elder, partly a continuation of Bede's *Historia Ecclesiastica* from 1225; Metrical Chronicle of the Kings of England from William the Conqueror to Edward III; Mnemonic of the order of the kings of England from William the Conqueror to Edward III; Diagrammatic table of the descent of the French crown to Edward III; Bernard of Graves, Account of the death of Edward III and the campaigns of Edward the Black Prince; Copy of the letters by which King John resigned the throne to Pope Innocent III, dated Dover, 15 May 1213; Form of allegiance to King Charles IV of France by King Edward II as Duke of Guyenne; Account of the descent of Edward III, from a document submitted to Parliament by the Duke of York; History of Bordeaux, based on a text copied by Vitalis de St Sever in the chronicles of the church at Vienne, transcribed from a copy by Raymundus Guillaume de Puy; Pseudo-Bede, *Imago Mundi*; Old Testament History from Noah to David; John of Garland, *Alium Compotum Metricum*; Mnemonic calendar verses; Alexander de Villa Dei, *Carmen* de *Algorismo*; Johannes de Sacrobosco, *Tractatus de Sphera*; History of Britain from Caesar to Guthlac, possibly excerpted from Bede's *Historia Ecclesiastica*; Bede, *Historia Ecclesiastica*, 1–3; Political prophecy and satire from the reigns of Edward I–III, apparently based upon Geoffrey of Monmouth,

Prophetia Merlini; 'De Adventu Britonum in Istam Insulam'; Description of the rule of Gascony by the English from 1220–1259; Copy of letter of King Edward III to Pope Clement VI concerning papal privileges, dated Westminster, 10 September 1343 in Latin, Middle English, French and Gascon, England, c.1325–1430, copied by Bernard of Graves and 15 further scribes, 13 portraits of the English kings, including the Black Prince, a classroom scene, the White Ship and various royal coats-of-arms by the illuminator of the Belknap Hours and Oxford, Bodleian Library, MS Bodley 581 and other artists
Bernard of Graves, London, c.1375–1400; possibly King James VI of Scotland, s.xvi; John Napier of Merchistoun, Scotland, s.xvii; ?David, Earl of Huntingdon, Scotland, s.xvii; Colonel Robert Graham of Grahamstown, South Africa, s.xix; Christie's, 25 June 1986, lot 208

MS 76 Bede, *De Tabernaculo*
in Latin, England(?), s.xi/xii, large initial **L**
Quaritch, Catalogue 1088 (1988), item 4

MS 79 Gregory, *Moralia in Job*, 21:24–30
in Latin, 1 leaf, England, s.xi/xii
2 further leaves are pastedowns in Magdalen College H.14,10, now MS Lat. 267, fols 60–61
Quaritch, Catalogue 1088 (1988), item 17

MS 94 Peter Lombard, *Commentary on the Epistle to the Romans*, Chapters 1, 3, 5, 7, 8, 13, 14, 15
in Latin, 23 leaves, England, s.xii 2
Sir Thomas Phillipps; Katharine, John, Thomas & Alan Fenwick; Robinson Bros.; H. P. Kraus; Bernard Rosenthal; Quaritch, Catalogue 1088 (1988), item 23

MS 95 Gregory, *Moralia in Job*, Chapters 10 and 11; Gregory, *Homilies on Ezekiel*
in Latin, England, s.xii ex, 12 leaves
another leaf is in Tokyo, Takamiya Collection
Sir Thomas Phillipps; Katharine, John, Thomas & Alan Fenwick; Robinson Bros.; H. P. Kraus; Bernard Rosenthal; Quaritch, Catalogue 1088 (1988), item 24 (8 leaves); Quaritch, Catalogue 1147 (1991), item 93 (4 leaves)

MS 101 Bible, Ecclesiastes 2:17–3:14
in Latin, 1 leaf, England, c.1350–1365, champe initial with sprays from a four-volume Bible, of which volume 1 is London, British Library, Royal MS I.E.IV, with further leaves: Quaritch, Catalogue 1056 (1985), item 21; Oxford, Bodleian Library, MS

Bibl.lat.b.4; New Zealand, Dunedin Public Library; New York, Pierpont Morgan Library, MS M. 471
Richard Legh, Cheshire, 1613; Richard Maria Domville, Cheshire; Sir Peter Leicester, Cheshire, 1614–1678

MS 106 Bible, 1 Maccabees 1:1–39, and capitula
in Latin, 1 leaf, England, s.xii med, uncompleted initial **E**
Sotheby's, 11 December 1979, lot 10; Bernard Rosenthal; Quaritch, Catalogue 1088 (1988), item 61

MS 107 Bible, Matthew 2:11–18 and Commentary
in Latin, 1 leaf, England, s.xii/xiii, initial **Q**
Sotheby's 12 November 1987, lot 12; Bernard Rosenthal; Quaritch, Catalogue 1088 (1988), item 65

MS 127 Bede, *Homily* 1.16 from a Homiliary
in Latin, 1 leaf, England, s.xii/xiii
medieval library shelfmark 'I, 16 15'; Quaritch, Catalogue 1088 (1988), item 8

MS 194 Ranulph Higden, *Polychronicon*, translated by John Trevisa in Middle English, London, c.1420, copied by the same scribe as Oxford, Bodleian Library, MS Bodley 693 and MS Laud Misc.609, borders, initials and 2 views of Noah's Ark, in a style associated with Hermann Sheere
Roger Morgan and William, Hertfordshire; William Smith and John Roper, Taunton, Somerset, s.xv ex; Gabriel Barwyke, 1523–1561; Alice Draycott; Lord Middleton, Wollaton Hall; Sotheby's, 16 July 1928, lot 557; E. P. Goldschmidt, London; Boies Penrose, Pennsylvania; Sotheby's, 20 May 1947, lot 288; Foster W. Bond, London; Sotheby's, 8 December 1981, lot 80; Sotheby's, 6 December 1988, lot 45

MS 197 Aldhelm, *De Laude Virginitatis*, Chapters 47, 49, 50 in Latin and Anglo-Saxon, 2 leaves, England, Worcester or Canterbury?, s.viii/ix with s.x Anglo-Saxon glosses
Other leaves from the same manuscript: New Haven, Yale University Library, MS Beinecke 401 (28 leaves); Cambridge, University Library, Additional MS 3330 (2 leaves); London, British Library, Additional MS 50483 (1 leaf); Oxford, Bodleian Library, MS Lat.th.d.24 & MS.Don.f.458 (4 leaves); Philadelphia, Free Library, Lewis Collection, MS ET. 121 (1 leaf)
Owned in the s.xix by an unnamed bookseller in Brighton; James Tregaskis, London, until 1921; Wilfred Merton, Slindon, MS 41; Bernard Breslauer, Catalogue 90 (1958), item 3; H. P. Kraus, Catalogue 88 (1958), item 5 and Catalogue 95 (1961), item 3; Dr. Peter and Irene Ludwig, Aachen and Cologne, MS XI,5; The J.

Paul Getty Museum, Malibu, California; Sotheby's, 6 December 1988, lot 33

MS 209/5 Liber Extra 10:5.33 and Commentary
in Latin, 2 leaves, England, s.xiv med, pen-flourished initials

MS 209/9 Breviary, Use of York?
in Latin, 3 leaves, England, York?, s.xiv/xv, pen-flourished initials
Other leaves from the same manuscript: Marvin Colker, University of Virginia (2 leaves); Bernard Rosenthal (4 leaves)
Sir Thomas Phillipps; Katharine, John, Thomas & Alan Fenwick; Robinson Bros.; H. P. Kraus

MS 209/10 Life of the Virgin and the Conception of Christ
in Latin, 1 leaf, England, s.xv med
Sir Thomas Phillipps; Katharine, John, Thomas & Alan Fenwick; Robinson Bros.; H. P. Kraus

MS 209/11 Unidentified legal text
in Latin, 1 leaf, England, s.xv med
Sotheby's, 11 December 1979, lot 12

MS 209/12 Psalms 87:4–90 and antiphon
in Latin, 1 leaf, England, s.xv med, pen-flourished initials
Sir Thomas Phillipps; Katharine, John, Thomas & Alan Fenwick; Robinson Bros.; H. P. Kraus

MS 209/13 Jacobus de Voragine, *Legendea Aurea*, Chapters 12–13; Ranulph Cestrensis, *Polychronicon*, Book 3, Chapters 18–20
in Latin, 2 leaves, England, s.xv med
Sir Thomas Phillipps; Katharine, John, Thomas & Alan Fenwick; Robinson Bros.; H. P. Kraus

MS 209/17 Noted Breviary
in Latin, 1 leaf, England, s.xii 2
Sotheby's, 11 December 1979, lot 10

MS 209/25 Missal, with Commemoration of St Laurence
in Latin, 1 leaf, England, s.xiii 2/4, with s.xv ex marginal annotation in Middle English

MS 209/26 Psalms 20:12–21:6, with Peter Lombard, *Commentary*
in Latin, 1 leaf, England, s.xiii med, pen-flourished initials
Sotheby's, 11 December 1979, lot 12

MS 209/27 Gregory, *Moralia in Job*, 26:6
in Latin, 1 leaf, England, s.xiii med
Sotheby's, 11 December 1979, lot 12

MS 209/28 Psalms 48:17–49:5; 51:10–53:1, with Peter Lombard, *Commentary*
in Latin, 2 leaves, s.xiii med, initial **O**, pen-flourished initials
Sir Thomas Phillipps; Katharine, John, Thomas & Alan Fenwick; Robinson Bros.; H. P. Kraus

MS 209/29 Bible, Ecclesiastes 1:1, with Jerome Prologue
in Latin, 1 leaf, England, s.xiii 2
Erik von Scherling, Leiden; Sotheby's, 11 December 1979, lot 12

MS 209/30 Aristotle, *De Anima*, Book 3:8–10
in Latin, 1 leaf, England, s.xiii ex, with later annotations
Sotheby's, 11 December 1979, lot 12

MS 209/31 Peter Lombard, *Sententiae* 4:19.1.3–4.4 with title for 4:20.1.1
in Latin, 2 leaves, England, s.xiii/xiv, flourished initials
Sotheby's, 11 December 1979, lot 12

MS 209/48 Philosophical disputations on the vices and virtues, 'Utrum quilibet virtuosus in operibus sibi propriis dilectatur'
in Latin, 2 leaves, England, s.xiv med
Sotheby's, 11 December 1979, lot 12

MS 209/49 Astrological treatises, apparently composed of extracts from Raymund Lull
in Latin, 2 leaves, England, s.xiv 2
Sotheby's, 11 December 1979, lot 12

MS 209/50 Homily on the Apocalypse
in Latin, 1 partial leaf, England, s.xiv ex
Sotheby's, 11 December 1979, lot 12

MS 209/51 Flores Bernardi
in Latin, 1 leaf, England, s.xix/xv

MS 213 Breviary: Temporal, services for the 3rd week of Advent
in Latin, 2 leaves, England, s.xii med, decorated initials including initial **L** and initial **I** with foliate ornament
Sotheby's, 11 December 1979, lot 9

MS 214 Bible: Ezekiel 34:1–36:10
in Latin, 2 leaves, England, s.xii 2
Sotheby's, 11 December 1979, lot 10

MS 237 Bible: John 21:16 and Commentary
in Latin, 1 leaf, England, s.xii 2
Philip Bliss, Oxford, s.xix; Sotheby's, 21 August 1858, lots

100&119; Sir Thomas Phillipps, MS 18133; Katharine, John, Thomas & Alan Fenwick; Sotheby's, 24 April 1911, lot 390; E. H. Dring, London (1911–1928); E. M. Dring, London (1928–1984); Quaritch, Catalogue 1036 (1984), item 79

MS 242 Hrabanus Maurus, *Homiliae in Evangelia et Epistolas*
in Latin, 7 leaves, England, s.xiii 2
formerly pastedowns with s.xviii fragmentary bookplates and All Souls shelfmarks, 'MM–9–9, 'MM–9–10'
All Souls College, Oxford (s.xviii); Sir Thomas Phillipps; Katharine, John, Thomas & Alan Fenwick; Robinson Bros.; H. P. Kraus; Bernard Rosenthal; Quaritch, Catalogue 1088, (1988), item 46

MS 250 Genealogical Chronicle Roll of the Kings of England to Henry IV
in Anglo-Norman, 9 membranes, England, East Anglia?, 1321–27, with additions between 1399 and 1413, 161 pen drawings of the English kings in roundels, 3 large opening circular miniatures of the Saxon heptarchy, the Roman roads of Britain and the Wheel of Fortune by two artists, one from the Queen Mary's Psalter group and the other in the style of the Queen Mary Apocalypse (London, British Library, Royal MS 19.B.XV)
Apparently the immediate exemplar of Oxford, Bodleian Library, MS French d.1(R); Cambridge, University Library, MSS Dd.3.58 and Oo.7.32
Maud de Chaworth, wife of Henry, Earl of Lancaster (s.xiv in); Blanche, wife of John of Gaunt, mother of Henry IV (s.xv); Chaworth family (until 1988); Robert Holden Ltd., London; Sam Fogg, Catalogue 12 (1989), item 10

MS 257 Godfrey Babion and Hildebert of Lavardin, *Sermones Catholicorum*
in Latin, England, East Anglia, s.xii 2/4, 76 large initials, English s.xiv/xv binding on wooden boards
Augustinian Abbey of St. Osyth, near Colchester, Essex (from s.xii); Tollemache family, Helmingham Hall, Suffolk (s.xv); Sotheby's, 14 June 1965, lot 1; Major J. R. Abbey, MS JA. 7341; Sotheby's, 19 June 1989, lot 3008

Sir John Harington: Six Letters, a Postscript, and a Case in Chancery

HUGH CRAIG

I

The life of the writer and courtier Sir John Harington (1560–1612) has always seemed relatively well documented.[1] Harington was confessional by nature, and recorded much about his own activities and about his circle in the annotations to his translation of Ariosto (1591), in his extraordinary prose miscellany *The Metamorphosis of Ajax* (1596), and in various other writings on state and church affairs, as well as in his letters, a collection of which was published in 1930. In recent years, nevertheless, a great deal more has come to light. The principal source has been the letters and documents preserved in the papers of the Charterhouse. Thomas Sutton, the founder of Charterhouse, was the greatest money-lender of his day, corresponded with multitudinous clients and suitors, and preserved hundreds of letters and documents which passed into the care of his foundation and thus survived to the present.[2] Harington's connection with Sutton was already known through letters in McClure's collection – Harington urged Sutton to buy a number of family properties, promoted a scheme to make the King's son Charles, Duke of York, Sutton's heir, and helped Sutton to get his Act establishing the Charterhouse foundation through Parliament – but N. R. Shipley has been able to elucidate through the Charterhouse papers and other records the complex negotiations over the sale to Sutton of a manor, Castle Camps, which involved Harington intimately, clarifying much about Harington's affairs at the time along the way[3]; and Robert C. Evans has found and printed eight new letters from Harington in the collection.[4]

The present article offers a supplement to Shipley's account, based on documents in Chancery proceedings cited briefly elsewhere[5] but not previously quoted in connection with Harington, and prints the text of six unpublished letters and a postscript of Harington's. McClure printed sixty-two Harington letters in his edition of 1930. Another letter by Harington to Cecil had been printed in 1903 in the *State Papers*, as was pointed out by R. H. Miller in 1979.[6] In 1988, as noted above, Evans added substantially to the tally, with eight hitherto unnoticed letters from Harington to Thomas Sutton and Sir William Smith, discovered by Evans in the Charterhouse papers.[7] A number of other letters have been cited in print. McClure summarised the contents of three letters to Gilbert Talbot, seventh Earl of Shrewsbury, which he was not able to print in full.[8] A review of McClure's book referred to a draft letter in the British Library overlooked by McClure.[9] A letter from Harington to Lady Arbella Stuart, not in McClure, was listed by F. W. Steer in 1968 as in the Arundel Castle archives.[10] These five letters are printed in the present article, along with a new letter from the Charterhouse papers and a postscript overlooked by McClure from a letter in Gonville and Caius College, Cambridge. (For convenience, the items are given numbers corresponding to those in McClure.)

II

At one stage in the long and forbiddingly complicated disputes between Harington's uncle Thomas Markham, Markham's son Sir Griffin, and Harington himself (on one side) and Sir John Skinner (on the other) – disputes given the fullest account to date in Shipley – Harington brought a case in Chancery against Skinner. Two sets of documents from the case, not noticed by Shipley, are preserved in the Public Record Office. They consist of Harington's original bill of complaint of November 1604, suing for a conveyance of the manor of Castle Camps to him from Sir John Skinner and Thomas Arundel in satisfaction of a debt of £4,000, with answers from Arundel and Skinner and a replication by Harington, and a second bill from Harington, dating from 1606, with an answer from Skinner and a further replication by Harington.[11] This bill of complaint is probably the one Harington refers to in a letter from earlier in 1604. Harington asks Shrewsbury there 'to favor us in our bill agaynst Sir John Skinner, whose frawd, wastfullnes, and willfullness, hathe been the fyrst concussyon, and is lyke to be the fynall rewin of the markhams credyt.'[12]

Shipley notes that '[t]he relationship between the Skinner and the Markham families dated back to at least Dec[ember] 1593,' when Sir

Griffin Markham entered into a recognizance with Alderman Skinner.[13] According to Skinner's demurrer and answer of 1606, the connection between the families had in fact begun some years earlier, in 1588–9 or thereabouts, when Harington's uncle Thomas Markham came to Alderman Thomas Skinner, Sir John Skinner's father, in the Fleet Prison, where he lay as the result of being censured and fined by the Star Chamber.[14] Markham offered to use his influence at court and with Sir Christopher Hatton in particular[15] to have the case re-heard, the fine discharged, and Skinner released. This was to be in return for Skinner agreeing to a match between his son and heir John Skinner and Markham's daughter Jane. If Markham failed he was to pay a marriage portion of £2,000. The couple was to receive from Alderman Skinner the manors of Castle Camps (in Cambridgeshire, near the Essex border), Lavenham or Lannam (Suffolk), and Fowlmere or Fulmer (also in Cambridgeshire). Skinner had bought the manors some years before from Edward de Vere, seventeenth Earl of Oxford.[16] The marriage took place, but, Skinner says, Markham neither succeeded in having Thomas Skinner released nor paid the promised dowry. Jane Skinner remained at her father's house,[17] where John Skinner was entertained over a period of years, though 'not to the value of two thowsand pounds.' Skinner says that his father, finding the marriage 'to bringe nether benefytt not proffytt to his reputacon nor purse did therevppon conceave deepe displeasure against the said Markham,' and conveyed away from Sir John more than half of the lands he had promised him.[18] Certainly the manor of Lavenham seems to have passed to Sir Thomas Skinner, Sir John's younger brother.[19] According to Harington's Chancery deposition of 1606, Skinner, after encumbering the Castle Camps estate with entails, persuaded Markham to accept a book of his father's debts as part settlement of his own debts to him, urging that Markham would be better able to collect the debts, especially those owed by Court figures, than Skinner himself.[20]

In the middle of 1601 Thomas Markham and his son Sir Griffin, who by that time claimed an interest in Castle Camps, together arranged a mortgage of the manor to Thomas Arundel (later Baron Arundel of Wardour, and a schoolfellow and family friend of Harington's[21]). Shipley comments that the role of Arundel in the dispute over Castle Camps is the most obscure of all the phases of the affair.[22] The details added by the Chancery documents serve to clear up some of the mystery. Arundel's own account is that the Markhams begged him to buy Castle Camps or take a mortgage on it. Believing that it had been conveyed to the Markhams, and with Skinner's knowledge, he promised to take a mortgage on the manor for £5,000 or thereabouts, provided that it was cleared of various encumbrances and that Kirby Bellers, the Markham manor in Leicestershire, was conveyed to him as collateral assurance. It was agreed in June 1601 that he would receive rent from Castle Camps. He advanced various moneys to the other side, being in the end, as he calculates, £1,100 or £1,200 out of pocket over the affair. Since neither of his conditions were met, he goes on, he resolved not to proceed any further in the business and told the Markhams as much. Evidently he retained certain papers connected with Castle Camps, papers he says in 1604 he will not give up until Skinner in particular has paid him what he is owed. He received none of the promised rent.[23] Other versions of this part of the story suggest that Arundel had advanced further along the path to ownership of Castle Camps. On 22 January 1601/2, Thomas Markham wrote to Robert Taylor, Teller of the Exchequer, asking for Taylor's help in providing £5,500 in cash which was apparently to serve as a sham tender to redeem Castle Camps from Arundel. He assured Taylor that the mortgage held by Arundel was 'mearly in trust and no monye at all thearvppon'.[24] On the same day, according to Skinner, the Markhams attempted to redeem Camps from Arundel with a tender of 'Counters, stones and other trashe.' Skinner made a counter-tender of five shillings. In September 1602, a servant of Arundel's actually took possession of the manor.[25] At some later date Harington by his own account paid Arundel £900 to redeem the manor from him, clearly in the belief that this might lead to its sale and thus the repayment of debts to Harington himself.[26] At the time of his first bill in the case, late 1604, he apparently believed that Arundel and Skinner were in conspiracy against him, and jointly owned Castle Camps. It seems also that Arundel acted as an arbitrator in the dispute between Skinner and the Markhams in late 1602,[27] without any lasting success.

Reading the Chancery documents with Harington in mind, it is his credulity that emerges as the first issue. Essentially, he seems to have trusted Skinner, or to have believed at least that Skinner's ownership of Castle Camps would mean that Skinner's creditors could not fail to be paid. In the summer of 1602, already embroiled in the dispute through his bond to provide Skinner with the funds to buy his office at Berwick,[28] Harington 'interposed' himself between Skinner and Sir Griffin Markham, and 'p[re]vayled' on Skinner to make an offer to give the whole of Castle Camps to the other side in exchange for £6,000 more from the Markhams, an offer Sir Griffin refused, 'to the great discontent' of Harington as well as Skinner.[29] Evidently Harington felt at the time that Skinner's offer was reasonable, and that Skinner could be trusted to carry it through. He says himself that his loans to the Markhams were made after being persuaded by Skinner's assurances that his own debts to the Markhams would be covered by the sale or mortgage of Camps. There is a revealing note of indignation at good-naturedness betrayed in his picture of himself convinced after 'conference' with Skinner of the worth of his promises, and relying so implicitly on 'the honest p[er]formance thereof' that he provided the Markhams with large sums of money without the extra security he might otherwise have had from them.[30] Skinner, incidentally, expresses satisfaction at Harington's come-uppance after his outspokenness in the past: Harington, he says, had 'heertofore ymputed it vnto other men as greate ffollye to become bounde as suretyes for such greate som[m]es of money.'[31] This echo of Harington's tendency to bombast recalls Cecil's tart reflection (under provocation) on Harington's 'rayling' on the Queen's memory at his dinners.[32] In May 1603, when Harington was in prison for his Markham debts, he apparently lent Skinner £25 more, Skinner persuading him that it would be used to help in arrangements to discharge his debts.[33] In July the King was persuaded to write to Skinner on Harington's behalf; this resulted in Skinner's being interviewed by Egerton, the Lord Chancellor, and Lord Kinloss, and in more promises to mortgage Castle Camps to discharge Harington's debts, but not in any action.[34] It took all Thomas Sutton's shrewdness and patience to complete an advantageous transaction with Skinner;[35] Harington, for all his powerful allies, was out of his depth. On the whole, the evidence of the Chancery case bears out Harington's own summary judgement of his disastrous involvement in the dispute: he had 'playd the foole to[o] frendly.'[36]

III

Letter 6 in McClure's collection concerns a grant of arms to the Harington family, to be agreed between Sir William Dethick, Garter King-of-Arms, and William Camden, Clarenceux King-of-Arms.[37] In a postscript to the original letter, not printed in McClure, Harington refers somewhat disparagingly to a William Stubbs, and calls him 'my brother.' Harington had a half-sister Hester, offspring of the marriage between Harington's father, John Harington, and his first wife Ethelreda Malte. The latter was reputedly a natural daughter of Henry VIII, though brought up as the daughter of his tailor, John Malte.[38] The postscript indicates that Hester had married Stubbs, who was for many years in the service of the Duchy of Lancaster, and M.P. for Yarmouth (Isle of Wight) in 1584. He was working for

Walsingham in 1587, and was one of those employed to find Walsingham's will in 1590.[39] The relationship with Harington is confirmed by the fact that Stubbs stood surety for a loan by Harington and Sir Griffin Markham in 1603, and took a bond for £1,400 from Harington in early 1604, as two Recognisances for Debt show.[40] In the second of these Stubbs is described as of Watchfield, Berkshire; this was one of the manors which came originally to John Malte from the Crown, and so to Hester, who passed it to Harington's father.[41] Stubbs is also mentioned in a letter of Harington's to Sutton.[42]

POSTSCRIPT TO McCLURE LETTER 6

From an autograph letter to Sir William Dethick, 24 June 1597 (Cambridge, Gonville & Caius College MS 606/513*, pasted to the verso of fol. 62). Published by permission of the Master and Fellows of Gonville & Caius College, Cambridge.

> Heer ys a seale of a gentlemans that w^th^in thease xx^ty^ yeers was no gentleman and yet yow see how prety a show yt makes yt ys my brother Mr Willim Stubbs that served m^r^ Secretary walsingham.

The first of the new letters to the Earl of Shrewsbury was probably written in the summer of 1603, during Harington's first period of imprisonment for debt.[43] Harington asks Shrewsbury to press his suit for the forfeiture of the property of Sir Griffin Markham and his brothers, who had taken part in the Bye Plot against King James.[44]

32a

Autograph letter to the Earl of Shrewsbury, undated (London, Lambeth Palace Library, Talbot Papers MS 3203, fol. 84).[45]

> My very good Lord.
>
> It ys not sufficient to geve yor lo^p^ a complementall thanks for so compleat a favor as I receaved from yor lo^p^. Yf I bee honest or gratefull I ame bownd to performe more then I promist, yf god make mee able, and doe send mee lyfe and helth in this contagiows tyme.
>
> I thowght good furder to advertyse yor lo^p^ that I have moved his Matie. for the benefyt soch as yt ys of Sr Griphin Markham and his brothers forfeyture; soche as yt ys I say, for yt ys moch entangled; but yf I may have yor lo^ps^ favor heer to advawnce the equytye of my suyte specially to my Lo Thresorer of Scotland s^r^ george Hume; and after yor furderawnce in the cowntry I dowbt not but I shall bothe do my selfe good and yor Lo^p^ servyce in yt. My Lo of Mar, and my Lo. of

Kinlosse have promist mee to furder yt all they may. And Sr Thomas Lake yf yor lo^{p} wowld anymat him yn yt I know wold do moche, and ys in place to geve very quyck dispatch to yt. this ys all I will troble yor Lo^{p} wth and rest

Humbly at yor servyce
Iohn Haryngton./[46]

At the beginning of the next year, Harington was again in prison, and was negotiating with the Earl over the sale of his land at Lenton, in Nottinghamshire, as the pair of new letters to Shrewsbury printed below, and a letter printed in McClure from later in the same month, show.[47] These lands, over 600 acres in extent, and formerly belonging to Lenton Priory, had been granted to Harington's parents by Queen Elizabeth.[48] As he says in Letter 35c, they lay close to the estate of his friend Sir Francis Willoughby.[49] On June 23 1604, Harington was granted the King's reversion to the Lenton property, in fee farm, as he anticipates here. It was sold immediately to Sir Michael Hickes.[50]

In the letter below, Harington refers to Shrewsbury's help in securing pardons for Charles and Thomas Markham, twin sons of Thomas Markham of Ollerton, who had confessed that their brother Sir Griffin swore them to an oath binding them to support of the Bye Plot.[51] He also alludes to the quarrel between Shrewsbury and Thomas and Mary Markham, the parents of the Markham brothers. Thomas Markham senior was once among Shrewsbury's closest confidants: in 1592 he headed a list of 'notorious Papists and dangerous recusants in the household, or in great account with, Lord Shrewsbury,' with Mary Markham, 'chief companion to the young Countess when she is in Nottinghamshire, and whom she calls sister'[52]. By 1595 the Countess regarded Markham, with Shrewsbury's neighbour and bitter enemy Sir Thomas Stanhope, as one of the factions which might poison the Earl.[53] Francis Markham says that the loss of Shrewsbury's friendship 'was one of the first steps to Markham's ruin.'[54]

35b

Autograph letter to the Earl of Shrewsbury, 11 March 1603/4 (London, Lambeth Palace Library, Talbot Papers MS 3203, fol. 204).

My speciall good Lord.

Yowr Lo^{p} hath donne mee many favors since this my dismall distresse but my case ys not yet capable of releefe by any favor. Since yor Lo^{p}

vowtsafed last to speak with mee, I have receaved some comfort from his Matie. fyrst that I have now powr to sell my land in notingamsheer in fee farme (which yf I had been wyse I showld have sowght at the fyrst) secondly that I understand his Matie hath gevn speciall charge that I shall have satisfaccion of my det and charges from Sr Griphin Markham, before hee have his pardon, which I ame sory to thinke how hard yt will bee for hym to doe. except hee had better means to compell Sr Iohn Skinner to make satisfaccion of his dett.

In which, sith yor Lo^{p} hath so nobly procured favor for poor Charls and Thomas Markham (who wear only seduced by theyr brother) and that in so doing, yor Lo^{p} hath been content to forget all theyr fathers and mothers former unkyndnesses; Let mee entreat yor Lo^{p} now for all owr sakes, at my earnest request, (that have honord yor Lo^{p} and my Lady with an vninterupted cowrse of more then common regard,) to lend vs yor Lo^{ps} good Cowntenawnce in owr Iust complayntes of Sr Iohn Skinner. Who hath indeed been the rewin of theyr estates, and the shaking of myne; and that I may have the favor to have my complaynt hard agaynst him, before all my Lords or at least some one or two that may report theyr Lo^{ps} opinions to the rest./

My Lord Chawncellor vppon a word speaking of yor Lo^{p} or any of my Lords, will grawnt an *habeas corpus* for mee to come to the Cownsell chamber on tewsday, whear I long exceedingly to satisfy, especially My Lord Hary Howard, of some exceptions have been taken to mee. In w^{ch}, hoping of yor Lo^{ps} accustomed honorable furderawnce I humbly take my leave
the xith of March.
1603.

Yowr Lo^{ps} at commawndment
Iohn Haryngton.[55]

35C

Autograph letter to the Earl of Shrewsbury, 12 March 1603/4 (London, Lambeth Palace Library, Talbot Papers MS 3203, fol. 210).

My speciall good Lord

According to yor Lordships desyre, I send heer enclosed a breefe note of the demaynes of lenton, very trewly set downe as Mr Dan[?] who ys my tenawnt thearto at that rate for 13 yeer to come doth pay mee. I have been very credyble enformd thear ys Cole in my grownd, and last yeer a gentleman offerd mee a hunderd pownd a yeer for xxi yeer to let him a lease of yt, but by my imprysonment, sicknes, and other crosses, I ame now dryvn to sell yt before I can searche yt. It Ioyns to Sr Persyvall willowghbyes howse wthin forty yards, whear yor Lo^{p} knows S^{r} ffr. Willowghby made 1000^{li} a yeer of cole. I have often been told and yt ys lyke enowgh to proove trew that the neyghborhood of that howse to this land will one day eyther cawse that the owner of that howse will buy this land deer, or the owner of this land will get that howse [*deletion*[56]] cheap; my selfe have been offerd very proffitable exchawnges for yt, but yt was never in my powr till now to performe a bargen, yf I had made yt.

I have been offerd 16 yeers purchase for yt allredy in the behalfe of one who they say may come from his howse by water to yt my thirst of lyberty makes mee sell in hast which ys not good for a seller, but the gentleman yor lo^{p} named to mee, ys a man both of good vnderstandinge and reasonable good conscyence and thearfore I showld bee most willing to deale with him: so I humbly take leave
this 12th of March.
1603

Yo^{r} Lo^{ps} at commawndment
Iohn Haryngton./[57]

In November 1607 Harington was promoting a scheme to have Thomas Sutton declare Charles, Duke of York (later Charles I) his heir, in exchange for a title. In a letter of that month printed in McClure he expresses confidence that Camps, the centre of the fierce disputes involving the Markhams, the Skinners, Harington and Arundel, and which Sutton had finally bought, will pass to the Duke on Sutton's death.[58] In Letter 50b, below, he asks Lady Arbella Stuart to promote the scheme. The project alarmed Sutton greatly, threatening to upset his cherished plan for creating a great charitable foundation out of his estate. It came to nothing.[59] Lady Arbella (1575–1615) was first cousin to the King, and next in succession to the throne. Rumours connected her to various plots against James. She was married secretly to William Seymour in 1610, and from 1611 to her death was imprisoned in the Tower.[60] She evidently had a close association with Sir John Skinner's wife Jane. Harington reports Lady Skinner attending her while sick with smallpox in December 1609; in the same month she is reported committed to her chamber after what was seen as a dangerous association with Lady Skinner, 'a great Papist.'[61]

50b

Autograph letter to Lady Arbella Stuart, 19 November, probably 1607 (Arundel Castle Manuscripts, Autograph Letters, 1585–1617, No. 169). Published by permission of His Grace The Duke of Norfolk.

Most noble Lady

Geve mee leave thus boldly to put yor honor in mynde of my humble suyt for acquaynting her Royall Matie, wth my endevor and proceeding, in the busynes concerning Duke Charls, allredy in part notyfyed to her highnes, thowgh not in that fashion perhaps as I wold have wyshed.

I know soch affayrs are comonly wayed by the successe, and yf y^{t} fayl yt ys imputed allwayes to the execucion rather then ye direccion But for meaner censures I will not discorage my selfe, among whome I may bee styled a busy offycer withowt an offyce or soche lyke. Only I desyre that my soveraygn King and Queen may conceave, as the truthe ys, that my endeavors heerin have no other prospect nor retrospect, but my Loyall affection and dewty to them and theyr most deer Children whose good I wold purchase not with paper and Inke but with my best blood, as knoweth God to whose holly proteccion I commit yor honor remayning ever

19. Novembr:

At yor honors Comawndment.
Iohn Haryngton./[62]

In 1601, Sir John Skinner entered into a statute making Castle Camps security for a loan of £10,000. The statute named Sebastian Harvey, a well-known London merchant, as the lender. It seems that Harvey in fact knew nothing about the statute at the time: the money came from Thomas Markham, and the security was in trust for him. In July of 1609, when the manor was his, Sutton visited Harvey to ask about the statute. Sir Griffin Markham's wife Anne was Harvey's niece, and she seems to have prompted Harington to put Sutton's mind at rest about it.[63] The 'trew report' Harington wrote in November of the same year, explaining the circumstances behind the statute, has long been in print,[64] but without Harington's covering letter, a copy of which appears with the report in a document in the Charterhouse papers. Neither report nor letter are in Harington's hand, and neither is dated or signed; no doubt they were given to Sutton so he would have copies of the originals which went off to Cecil. The letter is now printed here. Skinner's statute continued to haunt Sutton. A letter from 1610 warns him that Lady Arbella had secured the benefit of the statute, presumably through Lady Skinner, and might attempt to extract some payment from Sutton for it since it could be represented as an encumbrance on Castle Camps.[65]

55a

Letter to Sir Robert Cecil, Lord Salisbury, 23 November 1609

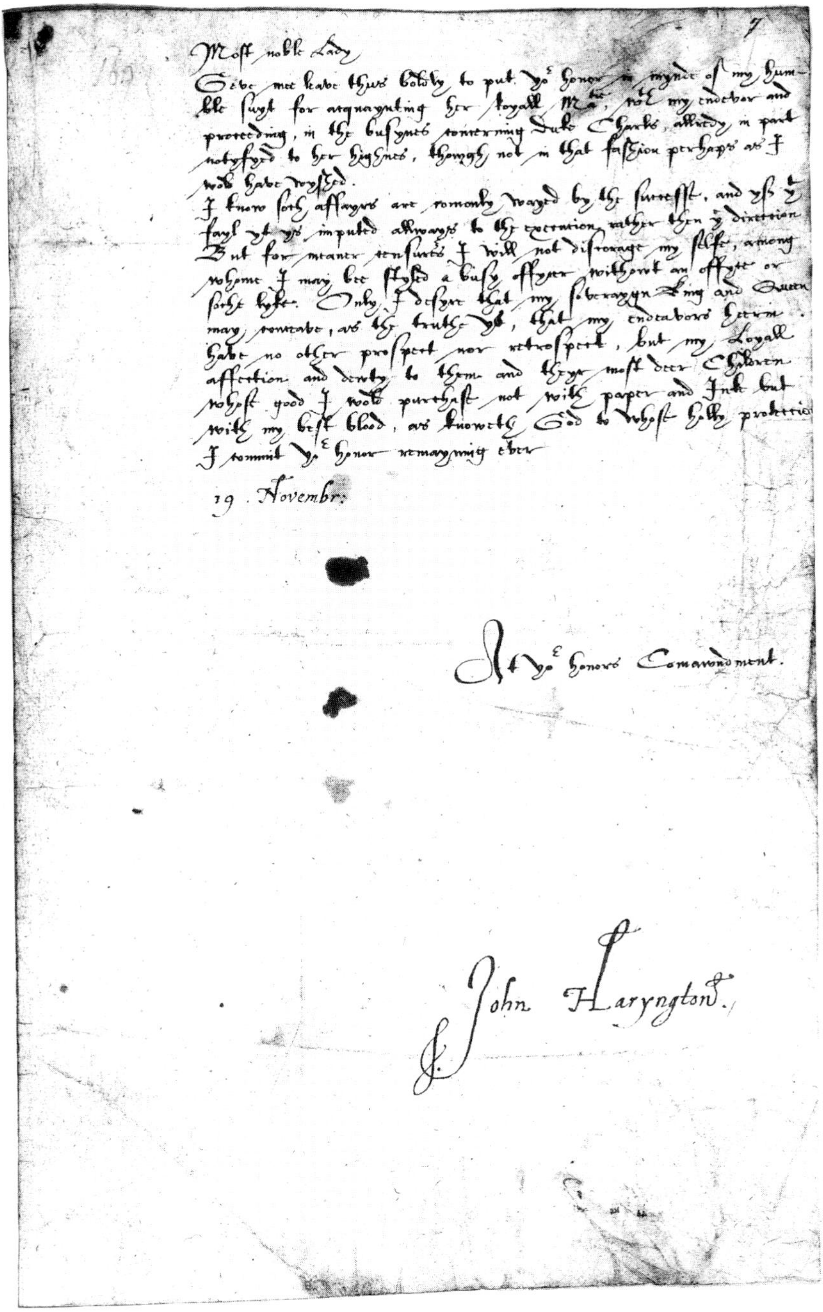

Most noble Lady
Geve mee leave thus boldly to put yor honor in mynde of my humble suyt for acquaynting her Royall Mtie, wth my endevor and proceeding, in the busynes concerning Duke Charls, allredy in part notyfyed to her highnes, though not in that fashion perhaps as I wold have wyshed.
I know such affayrs are comonly wayed by the successe, and yf I fayl yt ys imputed allwayes to the occasion rather then ye direction
But for meaner censures I will not discorage my selfe, among whome I may bee styled a busy offycer without an offyce or such lyke. Only I desyer that my soveraygn King and Queen may conceave, as the truthe ys, that my endeavors herein have no other prospect nor retrospect, but my Loyall affection and duety to them and theyr most deer Children whose good I wold purchase not with paper and Ink but with my best blood, as knoweth God to whose holly protection I commit yor honor remayning ever

19 . Novembr:

At yor honors Comaundment.

John Haryngton.

PLATE 1 *Harington's letter to Arbella Stuart: Arundel Castle Manuscripts, Autograph Letters, 1585–1617, No. 169. (Original size 296 × 109mm). Reproduced by permission of His Grace The Duke of Norfolk.*

(Greater London Record Office, Charterhouse Papers, Acc. 1876/F5/42). Published by permission of The Governors of Sutton's Hospital in the Charterhouse.

> Right hono^{r}able, and my verie good Lord./
> Being lately to visit Mr^{r}. Thomas Sutton, I fownde him somwhat more troubled in minde, then he was accustomed, and the reason was as he told me, y^{t} Sr Iohn Skinner sought to draw him in daunger of a statute of 10000^{li}./
> It movd me much, y^{t} Sr Iohn Skinner, who in law, equitie, and Conscience, ys speciallie bownde to warrant and procure m^{r} Suttons securitie, would offer to make himselfe an Instrument of his vniust trouble, but much more, bycause I had bene a principall perswader to draw m^{r} Sutton into this purchase. Whereof I was resolved, if oportunitie had served me, to haue made a trew report to his Maiestie of my knowledge, in a matter, in wch I haue spent some yeares to my great chardge, and trouble, assuring my selfe y^{t} a prince of y^{t} Iustice, and sanctified affection, vpon due Information would never once give eare to a motion of this nature, trenching[?] so deepe into the state of eu^{r}ie[?] purchase in England. And failing of y^{t} Importunitie, I p[re]sume to write the same to yor Lordship in theis few lynes, wch if yor Lordship out of yor zeale to Iustice will p[re]sent to his sacred Maties. view, I will iustifie to be trew, both in substance and Circumstance.

The last item printed here is Harington's draft letter asking its unnamed recipient (recently made a Privy Councillor) to put in a word for a grant of timber by the crown for the repair of the abbey church of Bath. The church had been left roofless since the dissolution of the abbey itself; Harington also tried to interest Sutton and Lord Compton in this pious work.[66] A rough date for the letter is given by the mention of *Coryats Crudities* (1611), which seems to be a new book at the time of writing. This also suggests that the recipient is William Herbert, third Earl of Pembroke (1580–1630), made a Privy Councillor on 29 September 1611.[67] He was Warden of the Forest of Dean, which also figures in the letter, and had been granted mining rights to the forest earlier in 1611.[68] His father, the second Earl, had been Harington's godfather.[69] Harington also records here an interview with the King. Elsewhere he describes meeting James when the King was newly on the English throne.[70] It is fascinating to hear of an exhange of learned wit between the two on this later occasion: Harington says he showed the King the poem in *Coryats Crudities* asking Harington to shelter Coryate's odorous pages under the shield of Ajax.[71] The King is also reported discussing Harington's water closet invention and its installation in various royal houses, suggesting that it was still regarded as useful at this late date.[72] Just beneath the letter, much crossed out and added to, there are some lines in Harington's hand which indicate what was to be in the note to King James he talks about in the body of the letter. It seems that the King was to be referred to Nicholas Sanders' remark in an anti-Reformation tract that cunning courtiers at Henry VIII's court waited until the king was in a good mood after relieving himself on the lavatory to press suits like the grant of bells and roofing lead from dissolved monasteries.[73] To refute Sanders Harington suggests James should grant timber for the Bath abbey church roof when moved to do so after one of his own evacuations.

60a

Autograph draft letter to a lord, 1611 or 1612 (London, British Library Additional MS 27,632, fol. 46r).

Ryght honorable and my very good lord

I haue d[irecte]d the ymplement I showd yor lo^{P} to his ma^{tie}, and I had so fit a tyme and fownd his ma^{tie} so well disposed as bred ~~good~~ a grave discowrse, in the beginninge ~~and so~~ of the mortalyty of princes (wch discowrs his Matie compared wth the doctrine[?] of ye sermon afore dinner) but so pleasawnt conceyt in the end, when I produced ~~the~~ Mr Coriats booke with the verses that commend yt to ye proteccion *Aiax* sheeld that his matie was exceeding ~~pleasant~~ mery & made mee thinke of a verse in Ariosto of the kynge of Lombardy

That down he lay and fell in soch a lafter

Hee skarce *could see* ~~*nor*~~ or *speak a good whyle after.*

Yesterday at my going away his[?] ma^{tie} laying his graciows hand[?] on my — spake to mee ~~him selfe~~ in myne ear to provyde one more of the XXX fashion and to ~~mend one~~ alter — — at Thibballs and ~~one~~[?] at Hamton Cowrt that annoys him often. W^{ch} I will goe in hand wth presently not dowbting but yow^{r} lo^{P} shall see and say that I shall doe 1000^{li} worth of good to his ma^{tie} pallaces and not coste ~~his~~ ma^{tie} 1000^{li} neyther shall yt bee longe in doinge./

One thing specially I would — yor lo^{P} in, that whearas at yor coming from — yow lost much love of all sorts thear, and consequently — exspectaciones of yor favor, wch after allso yo^{wr} Lo^{P} showd in furdering — peticion for —, yt wold please yow being a Cownselor now to speak wth my lo Threseror or wth Mr Chawncellor of the eschequer as a thing belonging to the K^{s} honor, to grawnt warrant ffor 100^{okes} out of Broccars wood in Wiltshyer yf they may have the 300 owt of the forest of dean. peticion. . My Lo Chamberlane, hath nobly promist 100 frome[?] Markham[?] ~~I~~ And yf yt please yor Lo^{P} in furtherawnce of theys seut — to show his m^{atie} at some pryvat[?] oportunytye — this XXX note of my observacion in reeding story ys — — XXX ~~showd~~ XXX

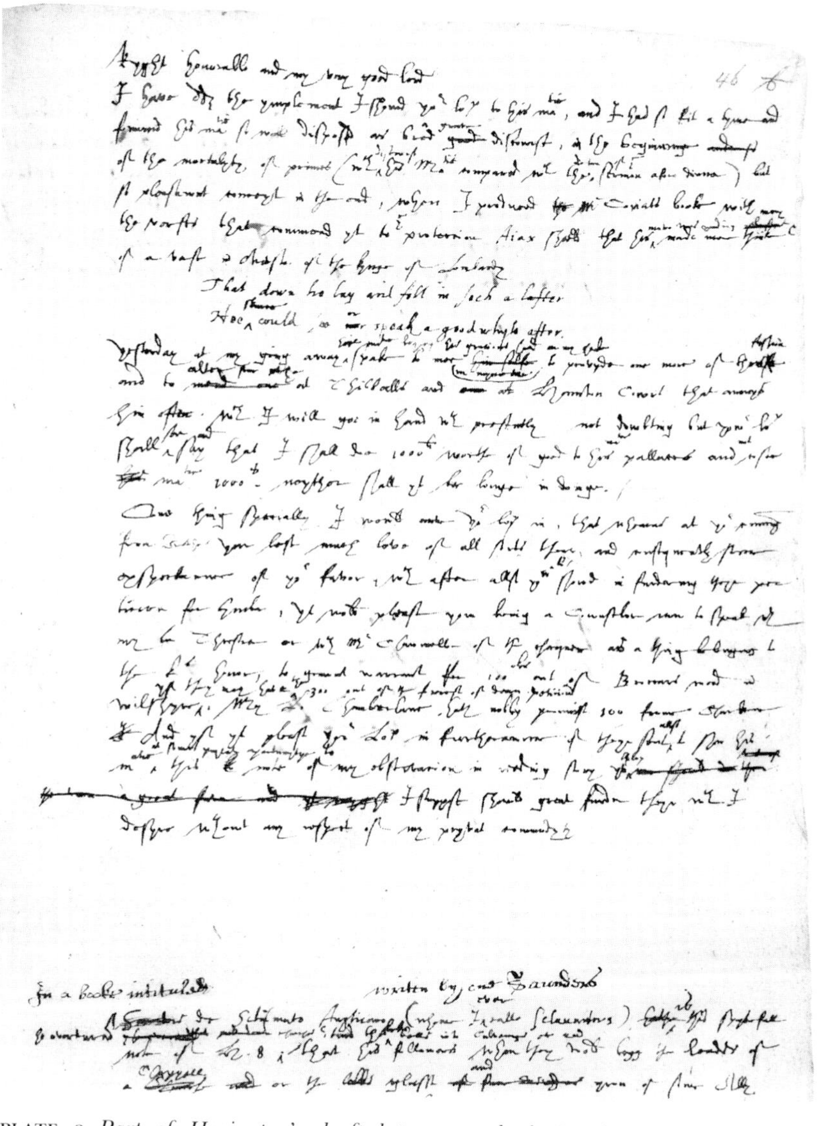

PLATE 2 *Part of Harington's draft letter to a lord: London, British Library, Additional* MS *27632, fol. 46r. (Original size of this portion 222 × 189mm; whole page 308 × 189mm).*

~~yow~~ – ~~the~~ XXX ~~a great favour and yt myght~~ I suppose should great furder theys wch I desyre wthowt any respect of my pryvat commodyty[74]

IV

The materials gathered here give some interesting shading to Harington's own biography. His amusement at the new-found gentility of his brother-in-law suggests a certain complacency about his own claims to patrician status; his foolhardiness in embroiling himself in the disputes between the Markhams and Skinner indicates over-confidence in his own abilities and influence. On the broader canvas of social and economic history, the story of the dispute between the Markham and Skinner families begins (if Sir John Skinner is to be believed) with an offer by a gentleman to a merchant to trade influence at court for a good match for his daughter. Jane Markham was to marry the son of a clothworker turned alderman, enriched by manors like Castle Camps bought by his father not long before from one of the noblest families in the country. There is a parallel in Harington's dealings with Sutton: the knight from Somerset had the idea of using his influence to arrange a peerage for the money-lender in return for a legacy for the King's second son. H. R. Trevor-Roper suggests that the plan was that 'Harington, as the skilful broker, would receive a rake-off from both sides.'[75] Shipley pictures Harington as approaching Sutton in an entirely venal spirit, having 'repeatedly demonstrated his firm commitment to court and market place.'[76] Harington's adversary Skinner, in a similar vein, had suggested that Harington had hoped to win 'some place of dignitye and p[r]eeferrment in Courte' by standing surety for his uncle.[77] Motives in such cases are unfathomable, but I suspect the truth in both instances was more complicated. Harington shows a great affection for his uncle in the boisterous pages of *The Metamorphosis of Ajax*, written in happier times, and the consequences of his pledging himself on his behalf seem to have been uniformly painful. With the scheme to have Sutton leave his money to the Duke of York there is less to go on, but there is no evidence that Harington expected tangible rewards for his efforts. The project has in any case a quality of the bizarre, suggesting a desire on Harington's part to achieve a bold stroke in what he saw as the public interest, rather than mercenary calculation. Robert C. Evans remarks on the 'self-respect' evident in Harington's letters to Sutton: far from the uniformly deferential tone one might expect from 'a would-be manipulator intent on courting a rich old man,' Harington, as Evans rightly says, frequently takes the high moral ground, expressing a sense of 'injured merit,' and frequently 'moralizing' to his correspondent.[78] Harington's half-sister was Henry VIII's daughter; he was himself Elizabeth's godson; evidently he was intimate enough with James to discuss literary novelties and sanitary improvements with him. He may have been disappointed in grandiose projects of one kind and another, but he clearly did not doubt his claims to a status which put him beyond dependence on a Sutton, however rich. This sturdy self-esteem, infuriating as it obviously was to uneasy allies like Cecil, and to adversaries like Skinner, is part of the independence which also gives a particular interest to all his writings, even down to a postscript or to letters seeking buyers for an estate or timber for a ruined church.

NOTES

1 The letters and postscript printed here (with the exception of No. 55b) were originally collected and transcribed by M. H. M. MacKinnon of Guelph, Ontario, Canada. MacKinnon completed a draft essay containing transcriptions of the letters with commentary and summaries of the material from Chancery Proceedings quoted below. The essay was put aside and after a number of years, no longer wishing to proceed with publication, he passed the essay to the present writer with an invitation to take the material forward to publication. New transcriptions have been made for the purpose and a new commentary compiled, drawing on that in the unpublished essay. Responsibility for errors in transcription and annotation in what follows is (naturally) the present writer's. In the transcriptions below, marks of contraction have been expanded and shown between square brackets. Words in an italic hand are printed in italics. Indecipherable words are shown thus: '—'; and if crossed out, thus: 'XXX.'

2 The Charterhouse papers are now in the care of the Greater London Record Office.

3 N. R. Shipley, 'The History of a Manor: Castle Campes, 1580–1629', *Bulletin of the Institute of Historical Research*, 48 (1975), 162–181.

4 Robert C. Evans, 'Sir John Harington and Thomas Sutton: New Letters from Charterhouse', *John Donne Journal*, 7 (1988), 213–37, with errata in 8 (1989), 195. I am grateful to Dr Peter Beal for drawing my attention to this article. It may be useful to offer some corrections, and some additional annotations, for these Charterhouse letters and for the new versions of letters already printed in McClure published in the article. In Evans's 'New Letter 43A' (p.216; GLRO, Acc. 1876/F3/146), line 9, for 'remit' read 'comit'; for the identity of the William Stubbs mentioned in the letter, *see* the 'Postscript to McClure Letter 6' below. In 'New Letter 48A' (pp.218–9; Acc. 1876/F3/149), line 7, for 'story' read 'stay'; and in line 9, for 'honor' read 'howr.' In 'New Letter 48B' (pp.219–20; Acc. 1876/F3/150), line 4, for 'y^{t}' read 'y^{e}' (the lineation of this letter is unreliable in the printed version, and this line is presented there as line 3). 'Haverell parke' is Haverhill End or Park, which adjoined the Great Park of Castle Camps: *see* the map, 'Castle Camps in the Late 16th Century', in *Victoria County History, Cambridge and the Isle of Ely*, VI, 38.

In 'New Letter 48C' (pp.221–2; Acc. 1876/F3/148), line 14, the scored-out words are 'a p[a]'t of'; in line 20, the word Evans reads as 'y^m' appears to be a thorn which has been crossed out before any superior letter was written in and is thus meant to be ignored; in the first line of the second postscript, for 'Saue' read 'have'. In 'New Letter 48D' (pp.223–4; Acc. 1876/F3/317), line 11, for '[him]' read 'Win'. This is a reference to William Wynne, who married Juliana Markham, one of Thomas and Mary Markham's daughters. The Wynnes' claims on Castle Camps are detailed in Shipley, pp.165ff. In line 13 of the same letter, for 'Sr William Stowes' read 'S^r willim Stones': this must be the William Stone, later Sir William, who was a fellow clothworker of Thomas Skinner's (Thomas Girtin, *The Golden Ram: A Narrative History of the Clothworkers' Company, 1528–1958* [London, 1958], pp.73–4), is mentioned as an associate of Skinner's in a Star Chamber case (PRO, STAC5/W6/76: *see* note 14 below), and who was one of the executors of his will (Shipley, p.165). The petition from Skinner mentioned in the letter, claiming that Sutton had refused to pay the bulk of the £10,800 agreed for the sale of his land, leaving Skinner and his family destitute, is in the Charterhouse papers, GLRO, Acc. 1876/F3/108B. In 'Old Letter 49' (pp.224–5; Acc. 1876/F3/152), line 24, for 'remit' read 'comit'. In 'New letter 50B' (p.226; Acc. 1876/F3/151), line 8, for 'elise' read 'ellse'. '[T]he title deed' mentioned in line 1 apparently refers to the second entail by Sir John Skinner on Castle Camps: *see* Shipley, p.169. In 'Old Letter 53' (pp.229–30; Acc. 1876/F3/155), line 30, for 'honest' read 'howse'. Evans discusses 'Old Letter 57' further in his 'Thomas Sutton: Ben Jonson's Volpone?', *Philological Quarterly*, 68 (1989), 295–314 (*see* pp.305–6 in particular).

5 *Victoria County History, Cambridge and the Isle of Ely*, VI, 39n.

6 'Sir John Harington's Irish Journals', *Studies in Bibliography*, 32 (1979), 179–186; the reference to the letter is on p.182. It was printed in *Calendar of State Papers, Ireland, 1600, March-October*, pp.233–4.

7 Shipley, p.176n, refers to the letters but assumes they have already been printed in nineteeth-century volumes on Sutton.

8 *The Letters and Epigrams of Sir John Harington: Together with 'The Prayse of Private Life'* (Philadelphia, 1930), pp.397, 399–400.

9 *The Times Literary Supplement*, 4 September 1930, p.697.

10 *Arundel Castle Archives: Interim Handlists Nos. 1–12* (Chichester, 1968), p.203. *See also* Peter Beal, *Index of English Literary Manuscripts*, I (London, 1980), Part 2, pp.123–4.

11 PRO, Chancery Proceedings, C2/James I/H13/47 and H2/68.

12 McClure, p.112. There is a similar appeal in No. 35b below.

13 Shipley, p.165n.

14 PRO, C2/James I/H2/68. Alderman Skinner was arrested in 1589 by order of Queen in council for failing to contribute to a forced loan: Girtin, p.321. In a Star Chamber suit of Michaelmas, Eliz. 30/31 (late 1588), Thomas Skinner is accused by Thomas Blande of London, gentleman, of assault and battery over a dispute about Blande's claims to the office of under-sheriff, in Skinner's gift as Sheriff (PRO, STAC5/B4/4). He had earlier been accused in the Star Chamber of corrupting a jury in York on behalf of William Stone (PRO, STAC5/W76/6, from Eliz. 28, *i.e.* 1585–6). The results of these two cases are not known.

15 Markham had been standard-bearer to the Queen's band of gentleman pensioners, as Harington himself notes elsewhere: *A New Discourse of a Stale Subject, Called The Metamorphosis of Ajax*, ed. Elizabeth Story Donno (London, 1962), p.252. There is a letter in the Harington papers by Hatton, written by command of the Queen, directing Edward Manners, third Earl of Rutland, to allow Markham the quiet enjoyment of his 'walkes or offices' in Sherwood Forest (BL, Additional MS 46,367, fol. 63; cp. *Calendar of State Papers, Domestic, 1547–80*, p.689).

16 *Victoria County History, Cambridge and the Isle of Ely*, II, 21, VI, 39, VIII, 157, and H. R. Trevor-Roper, *The Gentry 1540–1640*, Economic History Review Supplements, 1 (London, 1954), pp.13–14. The de Veres had held Castle Camps and Lavenham since the Norman Conquest.

17 As 'Joane' she is mentioned in Harington's *The Metamorphosis of Ajax*, ed. Donno, p.254, with a glance at stories that are circulating about her. It is reported in Henry Foley, *Records of the English Province of the Society of Jesus*, III (London, 1878), 782, that Lady Skinner was married against her will for the sake of Sir John's wealth (cited in Shipley, p.164).

18 Skinner, demurrer and answer, PRO, C2/James I/H2/68.

19 W. A. Copinger, *The Manors of Suffolk . . . The Hundreds of Babergh and Blackbourn* (London, 1905), p.122.

20 Harington, replication, PRO, C2/James I/H2/68.

21 There are frequent references to Arundel's father, Sir Matthew, and his mother, Lady Margaret, in Harington's letters and in the *Metamorphosis of Ajax*. Harington mentions Arundel himself in a note to his translation of *Orlando Furioso* (1591), Book 45: ed. McNulty (Oxford, 1972), pp.541–2.

22 Shipley, p.171.

23 Arundel, answer, 1 December 1604, PRO, C2/James I/H13/47.

24 GLRO, Acc. 1876/F3/373. Skinner confirms that Arundel 'did not paie one groate' on the mortgage: demurrer and answer, PRO, C2/James I/H2/68.

25 Skinner, demurrer and answer, 12 September 1606, PRO, C2/James I/H2/68.

26 Harington, bill, 4 August 1606, PRO, C2/James I/H2/68.

27 Skinner, demurrer and answer, PRO, C2/James I/H2/68; letter to Thomas Sutton from George Gascoigne, 18 December 1602, Charterhouse Papers, GLRO, Acc. 1876/F3/137; Harington, bill, PRO, C2/James I/H2/68. In the latter Harington says that Tobie Matthew, Bishop of Durham, attempted to arbitrate in the case in 1605–6, but was unable to resolve it before the deadline for the award in June 1606.

28 Shipley, p.169.

29 Harington, bill, PRO, C2/James I/H2/68.

30 Harington, replication, PRO, C2/James I/H13/47.

31 Skinner, demurrer and answer, PRO, C2/James I/H13/47.

32 McClure, p.398.

33 Harington, bill, PRO, C2/James I/H2/68.

34 Harington, bill, and Skinner, demurrer and answer, PRO, C2/James I/H13/47.

35 James Peller Malcolm remarks that the negotiations over Castle Camps 'caused Mr. Sutton more uneasiness than any other that I know of during his long life': *Londinium Redivivum; or, an Antient History and Modern Description of London*, I (London, 1802), 397n.

36 Harington, *A Short View of the State of Ireland*, ed W. Dunn Macray (Oxford, 1879), pp.23–4.

37 McClure, pp.66–7.

38 Ruth Hughey, *John Harington of Stepney: Tudor Gentleman: His Life and Works* (Columbus, Ohio, 1971), pp.17–18.

39 P. W. Hasler, *The House of Commons 1558–1603*, III (London, 1981), 462.

40 PRO, L.C. 4/195, ff. 213v, 246v.

41 Hughey, pp.18, 62; *Victoria County History, Berkshire*, IV, 536–7.

42 Evans, 'New Letters', p.216. Another Harington letter thanks the unnamed recipient for reconciling 'my sister' with her husband, presumably referring to Hester and William Stubbs: McClure, p.142.

43 Sir Griffin's forfeiture is mentioned also in a letter of June 1603 (McClure, p.104), and the plague in a letter of October that year (McClure, p.105).

44 On Sir Griffin's part in the plot, *see* Trevor-Roper, *The Gentry 1540–1640*, p.38.

45 The Talbot Papers are available on microfilm as *Social and Political Affairs in the Age of the Tudors: The Talbot Papers from the Lambeth Palace Library, London*, 9 reels (Brighton: Harvester Press Microform Publications, 1984).

46 For John Erskine, second or seventh Earl of Mar in the Erskine line (1558–1634), Edward Bruce, Lord Kinloss and Baron Bruce of Kinloss (1549?–1611), and Sir Thomas Lake (1567?–1630), then Latin Secretary to the King, *see DNB*.

47 McClure, p.112.

48 *Calendar of the Patent Rolls, 1560–1563* (London, 1948), pp.510–11; Alan G. R. Smith, *Servant of the Cecils: The Life of Sir Michael Hickes, 1543–1612* (London, 1977), p.175.

49 Harington makes Sir Francis Willoughby, with whom he had many family connections, one of his jurors in *The Metamorphosis of Ajax*: ed. Donno, p.234.

50 *Calendar of State Papers, Domestic, 1603–10*, pp.124, 125; Smith, p.175.

51 Historical Manuscripts Commission, *Salisbury*, XV, 231–4.

52 *Calendar of State Papers, Domestic, 1591–4*, p.174, and cp. Shrewsbury's letter of 1591 in Historical Manuscripts Commission, *Salisbury*, IV, 112–15, defending himself from the charge that he is too much under the sway of Markham.

53 Historical Manuscripts Commission, *Salisbury*, V, 253. Nicholas Williamson, who reported this speech, says he asked one of Markham's former servants to solicit Markham to make his peace with Stanhope (Historical Manuscripts Commission, *Salisbury*, V, 227).

54 Joseph Hunter, *Familiae Minorum Gentium*, ed. John W. Clay, Publications of the Harleian Society, 37–39 (London, 1895), III, 967.

55 The Lord Chancellor was Thomas Egerton, Lord Ellesmere. Henry Howard (1540–1614), younger brother of the Duke of Norfolk, gained a great deal of influence at court under the new king. He was created Earl of Northampton later in the same month.

56 What appears to be a 't' and the top loop of an 'h' have been crossed through.

57 Sir Francis Willoughby was a pioneer in coal mining, iron smelting, and glass making. He had completed the building of the prodigy house Wollaton Hall on the site in 1588; on his death in 1596 the estate passed to his son-in-law, Sir Percival Willoughby. *See* Mary E. Finch, *The Wealth of Five Northamptonshire Families 1540–1640*, Publications of the Northamptonshire Record Society 19 (Oxford, 1956), pp.54–55. Finch gives a figure of £1,000 for the profits from Sir Francis's woods and coal-mines, giving some support to Harington's estimate in the letter (p.55n).

58 McClure, pp.129–30.

59 On Harington's activities after 1608 promoting the Act of Parliament setting up Sutton's foundation, the Charterhouse, *see* Neal R. Shipley, '"Full Hand and Worthy Purposes": The Foundation of Charterhouse 1610–1616', in *A Charterhouse Miscellany*, ed. R. L. Arrowsmith (London, 1982), pp.6–10. Shipley states wrongly there that the only connection between Sutton and Harington was over arrangements for Sutton's will (p.6), and that Harington was an M.P. (p.9).

60 *See* DNB.

61 Evans, 'New Letters', p.231; Historical Manuscripts Commission, *Downshire*, II, 211 (cited in Evans, 'New Letters', p.237, n. 30). An informant in Foley, III, 782–3, testifies to Lady Skinner's devoutness.

62 The date is written in paler ink.

63 Malcolm, I, 400; Shipley, 'Castle Campes', p.170n. There is another reference to the statute in a memorandum from Sir William Smith in the Charterhouse papers, GLRO, Acc. 1876/F3/486.

64 Malcolm, I, 401. It is reprinted in McClure, pp.406–7. The version of the report

Malcolm transcribed has a date and a signature, so would seem to be distinct from the one in Acc. 1876/F3/42. The new version reads 'S[r] Griphin Markham' and 'S[r] Iohn Skinner' for Malcolm's nonsensical 'sir Griffin Martin' and 'sir John Harvie' (McClure silently corrected the former, but miscopies the date of the statute as 1600 rather than 1601).

65 Letter from Robert Dawe, 6 April 1610, GLRO, Acc. 1876/F3/94.

66 *See* Evans, 'New Letters', p.228, and McClure, pp.141–2. Harington's notes just beneath the letter make it clear the timber is for the abbey church. He gives a history of the building in *A Supplie or Addicion to the Catalogue of Bishops to the Yeare 1608*, ed. R. H. Miller (Potomac, Maryland, 1979), pp.106–13.

67 *See DNB.*

68 *Calendar of State Papers, Domestic, 1603–10*, p.395 (grant of 10 January 1608); *George III: Reports of the Commissioners of Land Revenue, 1–7: 1778–1790, House of Commons Sessional Papers of the Eighteenth Century*, ed. Sheila Lambert, LXXVI (Wilmington, Delaware, 1975), 91 (grant of 13 June 1611).

69 Harington, *A Treatise on Playe*, in Henry Harington and Thomas Park, eds., *Nugae Antiquae* (London, 1804), I, 220.

70 McClure, pp.109–11.

71 Thomas Coryate, *Coryats Crudities* (London, 1611), sig. e[v]–e2[r].

72 Echoing his boast in the letter, Harington had declared in his *Metamorphosis of Ajax* that the closet would be worth £1,000 in a house like Theobalds, £10,000 in a palace like Hampton Court: ed. Donno, pp.177–8.

73 Sanders, *De Origine ac Progressu Schismati Anglicani* (Rheims, 1585), fol. 104r. Harington rearranges Sanders' remarks slightly.

74 In the transcription of this letter insertions above and below the line and in the margin have been silently incorporated into the text, in the order which seems to be indicated by the markings and arrangement of the manuscript. Dr Beal was kind enough to check parts of the transcription for me. There is a slightly different translation of the couplet from Ariosto in Harington's *Orlando Furioso*, 28.71.7–8: ed. McNulty, p.320. The Lord Treasurer was Sir Robert Cecil, Earl of Salisbury, the Chancellor of the Exchequer was Sir Julius Caesar, and the Lord Chamberlain was Lord Thomas Howard. 'Broccars wood' is possibly Brokerswood, near Westbury, Wiltshire.

75 H. R. Trevor-Roper, 'Carthusiana – XV: Thomas Sutton', *The Carthusian*, 20 (1948), 2–8; the quoted passage is on p.7.

76 Shipley, 'Castle Campes', pp.171–2. This view of Harington's character and career seems to derive from Trevor-Roper's in 'Thomas Sutton', p.6, which has Harington running himself 'elegantly but inextricably' into debts which finally land him in prison. Trevor-Roper neglects to mention that Harington's imprisonment was not the result of failed intrigues or extravagances at court but for pledging security for his uncle. By his own account Harington had not previously been troubled with debt (Evans, 'New Letters', p.215); and he told Sutton in 1608 that he had money enough for his needs, despite his losses (Evans, 'New Letters', p.229).

77 Skinner, demurrer and answer, PRO, C2/James I/H13/47.

78 Evans, 'New Letters', pp.233–4.

Donne's 1622 Sermon on the Gunpowder Plot: His Original Presentation Manuscript Discovered

JEANNE SHAMI

DESCRIPTION

The discovery in the British Library of a manuscript sermon by John Donne corrected in his own hand (Royal MS 17 B.XX) is a cause for celebration among Donne scholars, particularly for readers of the sermons. Manuscript sources exist for only nineteen sermons, out of a total of one hundred and sixty, and, to date, no 'authorial' manuscript has been identified.[1] Since 1962, with the publication of the ten-volume California edition of Donne's sermons, a generation of students has come to rely on the 'definitive' text supplied by George Potter and Evelyn Simpson. That text was based on the three folio editions of sermons printed in the seventeenth century, and supplemented by information derived from early printed editions and manuscript sources. Potter and Simpson relied on six manuscript collections of sermons, and supplemented their findings with a seventh manuscript discovered by Sir Geoffrey Keynes when they had nearly completed their edition. None of these is in Donne's autograph.[2]

It should not be too surprising, however, that an unidentified manuscript of a Donne sermon should now come to light. Most of the collections in the British Library were catalogued in the eighteenth and nineteenth centuries, when Donne's reputation as the 'monarch of wit' had waned,[3] and when no edition of the sermons was readily available (before Henry Alford's 1839 edition).[4] Today, sermons remain out of fashion as a subject of academic inquiry; clearly, few people read anonymous manuscript sermons. But the British Library's index of miscellaneous sermons and theological tracts, though seldom used, offers rich possibilities for scholars interested in and familiar with texts of early modern sermons.

I discovered the Donne sermon in December 1992, catalogued simply as a sermon on Lamentations 4:20 among miscellaneous sermon manuscripts in the British Library's indices. The fuller entry in the Royal Manuscripts Catalogue reads 'Sermon on Lamentations iv.20, in commemoration of the King's deliverance from the Gunpowder plot. Beg. "Of the Author of this book". The preacher's name does not appear. Paper; ff. 36. Quarto. 8in. × 6in. Circ. 1620–1625. Not in the old catalogues'. The manuscript is a single sermon, rebound in 1984 by the British Library, the leaves mounted on guards, and placed with three other sermons in a miscellaneous collection of early seventeenth-century sermon separates numbered Royal MSS 17 B.XVIII–XXI. The sermon does not have a title-page and is not mentioned in Peter Beal's *Index of English Literary Manuscripts*.

Fortunately, however, the sermon is one about which we know a great deal.[5] The sermon was, in fact, scheduled to be preached by Donne at Paul's Cross, 5 November 1622, on the anniversary of the Gunpowder Treason, but was delivered inside the Cathedral on account of bad weather. Donne chose as his text Lamentations 4:20: 'The breath of our Nostrills, the Anointed of the Lord was taken in their pitts'. In a letter of 1 December 1622, addressed to Sir Thomas Roe, English Ambassador at Constantinople, Donne alludes specifically to this sermon. With the letter, Donne apparently sent a copy of his first published sermon which had been preached earlier in the year at Paul's Cross (15 September 1622), defending James's *Directions to Preachers* (issued on August 4). The letter to Roe reports that the September 15 sermon had been preached to address the concerns of many persons who had been scandalized by the proposals to marry Prince Charles to the Spanish Infanta and who had 'admitted suspicions of a tepidnes in very high places' as a result of the new restrictions on preaching. Donne compares the September 15 sermon with the Gunpowder Anniversary sermon, commenting that on November 5 he 'was left more to [his] owne liberty'. He continues as follows: 'and therfore I would I could also send your Lordship a Copy of that; but that one, which, also by commandement I did write after the preachinge, is as yet in his Majesties hand, and, I know not whether he will in it, as he did in the other, after his readinge thereof, command it to be printed; and, whilst it is in that suspence, I know your Lordship would call it Indiscretion, to send out any copy thereof; neither truly, ame I able to committ that fault; for I have no Copy'.[6]

However, King James did not in fact order the sermon printed, and the sermon manuscript seems to have remained 'in that suspence' until now. MS Royal 17 B.XX has been carefully corrected in Donne's hand, and is apparently that very copy which the King commanded, and which has remained unrecognized, and uncatalogued as Donne's, in the Royal Manuscripts collection.

The implications of such a discovery are profound. The manuscript and its corrections yield important new information about the process by which Donne's sermons were produced and transmitted. In addition, the existence of an authorial manuscript version of this sermon requires us to reconsider the textual status of the only early printed version of the sermon (XLIII in *Fifty Sermons*, 1649; hereafter cited as F50). Finally, the substantive differences between this manuscript, transcribed immediately after delivery, and the version first printed in F50 reveal much about the political considerations impinging on Donne in the pulpit in 1622.

MS Royal 17 B.XX is a fair copy by a scribe evidently working directly from Donne's own original manuscript and under his supervision. That it is not entirely autograph need not contradict Donne's own statements. The reference to the sermon 'which I did write after the preachinge' and which is now in the King's hand need not be taken literally (that is, it is not necessary to conclude that it refers to Donne's autograph manuscript). These comments can be interpreted in their more inclusive sense to mean that Donne composed and wrote out the sermon itself after it was preached. Since it was customary for Donne to preach only from notes,[7] such a 'writing' would have been necessary once the King had commanded the sermon. The word 'write' could also encompass the scribal 'writing out' (perhaps from Donne's own abbreviated manuscript), especially since the manuscript was clearly produced under Donne's supervision. Donne's statement would then refer to the entire process by which the sermon as delivered orally was produced in written form, and would encompass both meanings of 'write', that is, to compose, and to write out. Similarly, the statement to Roe that 'I have no copy' makes sense if it is taken literally to mean that he has his own original manuscript (from which the scribe obviously copied the sermon for the King), but he has no extra copy. The only copy (corrected by him) is in the hands of the King, and Donne stresses the indiscretion of proliferating copies before he is sure what James's intentions are with regard to the sermon.[8]

This is not the only scenario which could explain the presence of Donne's corrected manuscript in the Royal collection. It is conceivable, for example, that Donne's statement in his letter to Roe means that a copy, written in Donne's own hand, was the one that was given to the King. In that case, MS Royal 17 B.XX might be a copy taken by one of the King's scribes, and sent to Donne for proof-reading. This circumstance would also make literally true Donne's statement that he has no copy of the sermon to send to Roe. However, it seems unlikely that Donne would have sent a sermon in his own hand to the King, and more likely that Donne would have employed a professional scribe for the purpose. It also seems unlikely that King James, whose library contains few contemporary English sermons,[9] would have commanded a copy of the sermon, and then asked Donne to proof-read it, if he did not think he wanted to publish it. But the sermon was not published in Donne's lifetime. It is conceivable, and likely, that Donne's language in the letter to Roe is deliberately ambiguous, and reflects Donne's awareness, expressed in the letter, of the indiscretion of circulating a sermon which was being examined, for whatever reasons, by the King.

Although lacking in decorative polish, the manuscript in the Royal collection is fair enough to be a copy fit for the King, even if it is not such an elaborate piece of calligraphy as can sometimes be found in royal presentation copies made for special occasions. Comparison with the other three sermons with which it is bound indicates that it fits within the parameters of acceptable presentation. The first two sermons in the volume preceding Donne's are, in fact, carefully copied on ruled pages with a neat title-page and an address to a patron. Mildrid Cicill's dedication to the Duchess of Summerside precedes her translation of Basil's homily (MS Royal 17 B.XVIII). James Cleland's 1616 sermon on the Gowry Conspiracy is similarly presented. It includes, in addition to a title-page, a preface to the text, and the prayer before the sermon (MS Royal 17 B.XIX). The final sermon in the volume, however, although it begins with a title-page and dedication to James I, is untidily written, with biblical texts inserted between lines of script which slants considerably to the upper right hand corner, and is in a loose, sprawling hand (MS Royal 17 B.XXI). Donne's sermon certainly fits within the volume, and suggests that the precision and correctness of the text were considered (at least by Donne) to be more suitable to the learned King James than the more formal and decorative aspects of a manuscript. It is also important to remember (as the known example of Donne's autograph verse letter demonstrates) that even in a formal gesture seeking the patronage of the Lady Carew and Essex Riche (with whom Donne was not acquainted at the time) Donne thought it preferable to improve the text by crossing out and replacing words in two places rather than leaving an inferior but cleaner-looking manuscript.[10]

The manuscript, written primarily in secretary hand, is the work of one scribe. It is foliated in pencil in the upper right-hand corner (36 quarto leaves) by a later (probably nineteenth-century) hand. At the very top right-hand corner of the first leaf, also in a later hand, is written in ink '17 B XX. p.264.', indicating the reference to this sermon in Casley's 1734 catalogue of manuscripts of the Royal Collection. In darker ink on almost every leaf, Donne himself has corrected copying errors in the manuscript, and filled in blank spaces, sometimes between punctuation marks, left by the scribe. On the first three leaves, proper nouns and also words which are to be emphasized have been underlined, but this practice is discontinued after the second line of the third leaf. Judging by the ink, this underlining is contemporary with the manuscript, although it is unclear when and by whom it was done. It does not seem likely that the scribe would have copied only those marks if the entire manuscript from which he was copying were underlined. It is possible that Donne himself began underlining those words meant to be italicized. The ink with which Donne has crossed out 'Johns' at fol. 1r, line 14, for example, is similar in colour and stroke to that underlining 'Apocalypse'. This manuscript apparently follows the practice of F50 (believed to be based on authorial manuscript revisions no longer extant) in underlining words which receive rhetorical emphasis. For example, *historicall* and *propheticall* on folio 2v have been underlined to emphasize the logical parts into which the sermon will be divided.[11] It is very unlikely that James I himself read and underlined this part of the sermon, since the underlinings are rhetorical rather than thematic.

The manuscript itself is on unruled paper measuring 157mm × 195mm, and the pages are trimmed. Several of the leaves have been recently repaired but the manuscript is in good condition and the text of the sermon is complete. There is some question as to whether the Prayer before the Sermon which precedes it in *Fifty Sermons* was included with this copy of the sermon, but the catalogue entry in the index to the Royal Manuscripts gives the number of leaves as 36, suggesting that for some time (at least since 1734, the date of Casley's *Catalogue*), the sermon has been preserved in this form.

The entire manuscript is written on one stock of paper, which bears watermark Heawood 3499 (a figure of two posts, which Heawood dates '1617' from blank paper in the Phillipps Collection). The collation based on watermarks is as follows: $1–7^4$, $8–9^1$, $10–11^4$, for a total of 38 leaves, the last two of which are blank.

DONNE'S CORRECTIONS

There is no mistaking Donne's neat italic hand in this manuscript. On the basis of the autograph verse letter discovered in 1970, Croft describes his style as one which is 'free from obtrusive mannerisms yet possesses a personal quality that once discerned is unmistakable.'[12] Petti uses a sample of a letter by Donne to confirm that Donne writes with a firm, compact, unobtrusive, and very cursive hand, even if there are often gaps between letters, especially after Greek *e*.[13] The most obvious example in MS Royal 17 B.XX of Donne's hand is on fol. 36r, lines 9–10 (PLATE 1), where he fills the space with 'mercy and benignity, to let him out'. His epsilon *e* (which leans slightly backwards and appears to rise slightly above the general level of other letters), alternate italic *e*, and curled-back *d* are certainly characteristic of his style. At other times Donne writes single words in his neatest but still usually very distinctive script, and even inks over, in his darker ink, one or two words of the scribe to make them clearer (such as the very first word: 'Lamentati').

Many of Donne's characteristic scribal habits noted by Croft, Petti, and Barker can be observed in the corrections to sermon MS Royal 17.B.XX.[14]

(a) A distinguishing feature of Donne's style is that many of his letters appear in two or three forms, especially *y*, *d*, *t*, *f*, and *e*. The manuscript provides examples which conform to the types identified by Croft and Petti. For example, Petti notes that Donne's hand demonstrates at least three varieties of *y*. One of these can clearly be seen on fol. 18, line 5, where Donne crosses out the scribe's 'that' and adds his characteristic 'yo^{w}'. The *y* in this example is the one Petti describes with a tail ending in a little curl to the left (line 2 of Petti's example, 'any'). This is the same as the *y* in fol. 3, lines 2–4 (historically, prohetically); fol. 20, line 15 (yt); fol. 23v, line 4 (by); fol. 35v, line 7 (necessary); fol. 36, line 10 (mercy). Fol. 36, line 10 (*see* PLATE 1) also has the *y* ending in a loop crossing the tail, as in 'thys' in line 17 of Petti's sample.

(b) While Donne uses several *e*'s, the epsilon *e* is perhaps his most characteristic form and is frequently used in this manuscript: fol. 9, line 2 (th*e*se); fol. 10, line 9 (nowh*e*r*e*); fol. 15v, line 19 (disput*e*d); fol. 19, lines 1–2 (th*e*, anoint*e*d, Br*e*ath); fol. 19, line 7 (insinuat*e*; *see* PLATE 2); fol. 21v, line 10 (*e*specially); fol. 21v, line 19 (pref*e*rd); fol. 25, line 19 (tim*e*); fol. 28, line 1 (dir*e*ct*e*d); fol. 32, line 4 (w*e*); fol. 33, line 21 (onc*e*), fol. 34, line 20 (ar*e*); fol. 35v, line 7 (n*e*c*e*ssary); fol. 36, line 9 (m*e*rcy, b*e*nignity), line 10 (l*e*t, *see* PLATE 1).

(c) Similarly, the *f* described by Petti (that is, straight with a small curved head and separate cross stroke) is like the *f* in 'preferd', fol. 21v, line 19. It closely resembles the *f* in 'free' in line 34 of Petti's example.

(d) Petti also notes that Donne characteristically leaves the top of the *o* open. Examples of this practice occur at fol. 10, line 8

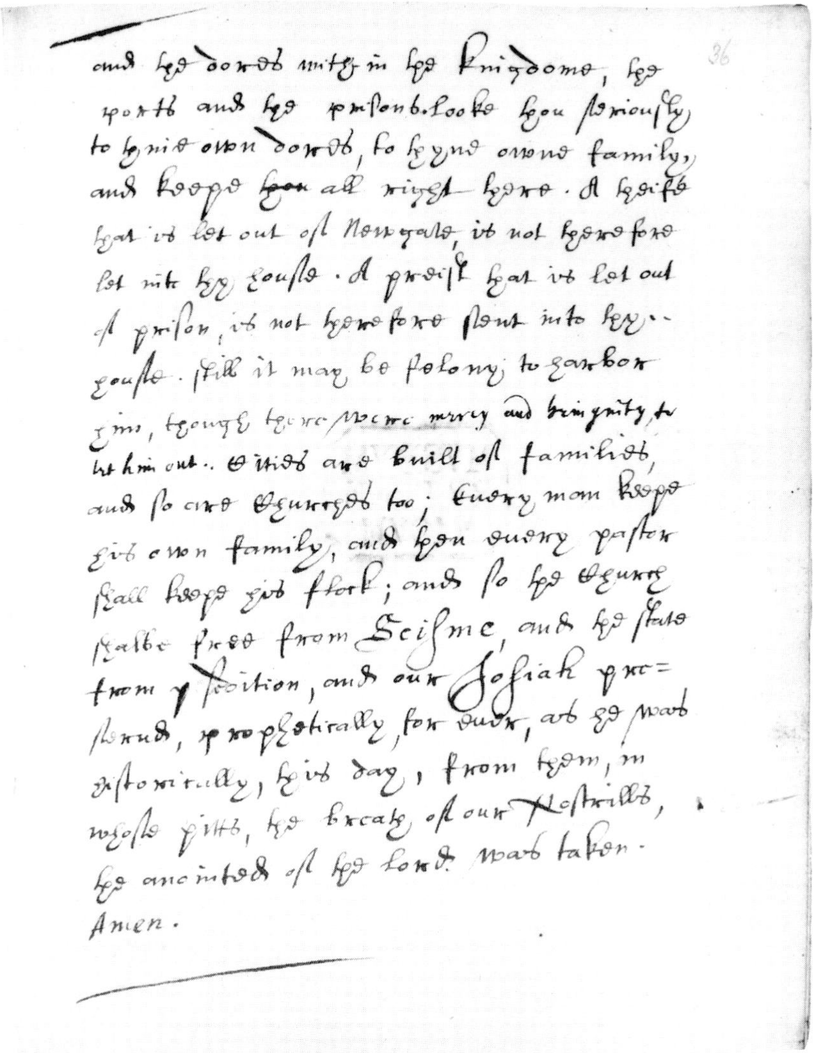
36

and the doores with in the kingdome, the
ports and the prisons. Looke thou seriously
to thine own doores, to thyne owne family,
and keepe ~~thou~~ all right there. A theife
that is let out of Newgate, is not therefore
let into thy house. A preist that is let out
of prison, is not therefore sent into thy
house. still it may be felony to harbor
him, though there were mercy and benignity, to
let him out. Cities are built of families,
and so are Churches too; Every man keepe
his own family, and then every pastor
shall keepe his flock; and so the Church
shalbe free from Scisme, and the state
from sedition, and our Josiah pre=
served, prophetically for ever, as he was
historically, this day, from them, in
whose pitts, the breath of our nostrills,
the anointed of the Lord was taken.
Amen.

PLATE 1 *The last page of the scribal presentation manuscript of Donne's 1622 Sermon on the Gunpowder Plot with seven words in Donne's hand inserted in lines 9–10: London, British Library,* MS *Royal 17 B.XX, fol. 36r. (Original size of page 197 × 157mm).*

(nowhere); fol. 16, line 10 (remou'd); fol. 33, line 21 (once); fol. 34, line 12 (not); fol. 34, line 20 (who, so); fol. 36, line 10 (to, *see* PLATE 1).

(e) Both Petti and Croft note Donne's use of the long shaft on *p* and there are several examples in the manuscript: fol. 15v, line 20 (disputed); fol. 21v, line 10 (especially); fol. 31, line 15 (psalms).

(f) Although experts have not commented specifically on Donne's *s*, it too is characteristic, particularly in the middle of words. Donne's *s*, like many of the letters noted above, also comes in several varieties, but most often resembles the *s* in 'spaine' (Petti, line 9), or 'spanish' (Petti, line 10). This form appears on fol. 1, line 14 (some); fol. 19, line 2 (*s*piritus, no*s*trills, *see* PLATE 2); fol. 21v, line 15 (p*s*alms); and so forth. The looped form of *s* (as in Petti, line 6, *s*car*s*e) appears on fol. 9, line 2 (these). Another form of *s*, best represented by fol. 27, line 14 (vision), and fol. 35v, line 8 (as) is identical to the form of *s* seen in the verse letter holograph reproduced by Croft, line 16 (vertuous).

(g) Donne's *h* also appears to be characteristic in this manuscript. It has a straight, unlooped ascender and a narrow shoulder widening out to a broader base which does not go below the line. It is best represented in fol. 9, line 2 (these); fol. 10, lines 8–9 (nowhere); fol. 24, line 18 (that); fol. 31v, line 12 (Sepher); fol. 35v, line 9 (the); fol. 36, line 10 (him; *see* PLATE 1).

(h) Croft notes that Donne's capitals are often like enlarged miniscules, *see* for instance, M, N. An example of this can be noted on fol. 19, line 2 (Nostrills, Narium; *see* PLATE 2).

(i) Fol. 19, line 2 (PLATE 2) also has a good example of the high-shouldered ligature of 'of' which is a characteristic of Donne's style noted by Croft. It is similar to 'of' in line 24 of the verse letter holograph and to Petti's 'of' in line 29 of his sample.

(j) The word 'directed' on fol. 28, line 1 provides an excellent opportunity to observe similarities between this word and the same word in line 5 of the autograph verse letter. Both have the same long upright ascender on *d*; the *i* in the sermon manuscript is more upright than in the verse letter, but there is the same break after the *i* before the *r* begins; the sermon has the same *r* with high ligature to episilon *e*; the *c* is very similar in both; the *t* in the sermon is not the same as in the verse letter: that is, the cross-bar on the poem's *t* is not a separate stroke. This *t* is more like the *t* on line 2 of Petti's example (nights); the epsilon *e* leading to a curled-back *d* in the sermon is identical to the epsilon *e* leading to straight ascender *d* of the poem, but the curled-back *d* of the sermon is one of the most characteristic of Donne's letter-forms (Petti, line 1 (end), line 2 (safeguarded), line 4 (donne), etc.). On the whole the similarities in handwriting between

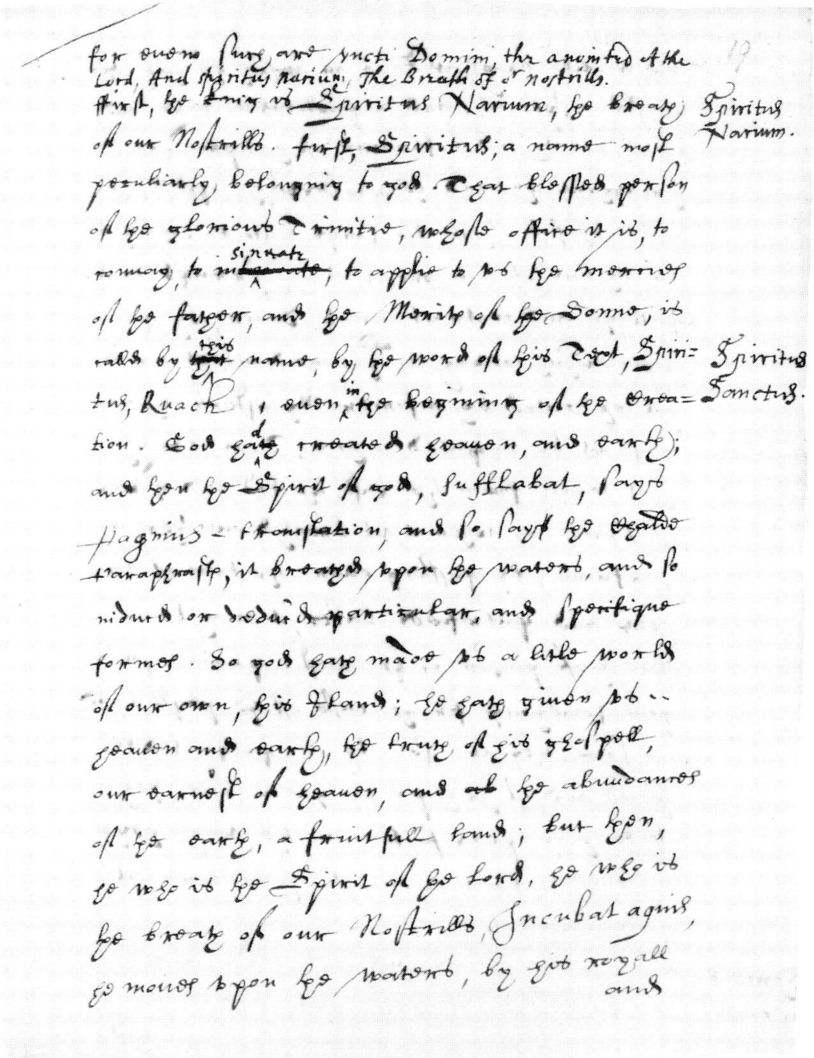
for even they are Uncti Domini, the anointed of the
Lord, And Spiritus Narium, The Breath of o^r nostrills.
First, the King is Spiritus Narium, the breath Spiritus
of our Nostrills. First, Spiritus; a name most Narium.
peculiarly belonging to God. That blessed person
of the glorious Trinitie, whose office it is, to
comfort, to sinnate, to applie to us the mercies
of the father, and the Merits of the Sonne, is
called by this name, by the word of this Text, Spiri- Spiritus
tus, Ruach, even in the beginning of the Crea- Sanctus.
tion. God had created heaven, and earth;
and then the Spirit of God, Sufflabat, sayes
Pagnins translation, and so sayes the Chalde
paraphrase, it breathed upon the waters, and so
induced or deduced particular, and specifique
formes. So God hath made us a little world
of our own, this Island; he hath given us
heaven and earth, the truth of his Gospell,
our earnest of heaven, and all the abundance
of the earth, a fruitfull land; but then,
he who is the Spirit of the Lord, he who is
the breath of our Nostrills, Incubat aquis,
he moves upon the waters, by his royall
and

PLATE 2 *A page of the scribal presentation manuscript of Donne's 1622 Sermon on the Gunpowder Plot with various corrections and insertions in Donne's hand, notably thirteen words inserted in the first two lines: London, British Library,* MS *Royal 17 B.XX, fol. 19r. (Original size of page 197 × 157mm).*

the two words are remarkable, and the variations are ones that have many other precedents in Donne's writing.

Donne's authorial corrections are of great significance to scholars. In the first place, they reveal more than we have hitherto known about his process of preparing a sermon for distribution after his delivery. It appears that Donne produced an original manuscript, in his own hand, either before he delivered the sermon, or more likely afterwards when it was commanded by the King. Donne then had a scribe transcribe the sermon from his own copy; at times the scribe is unable to decipher Donne's words (usually those in Latin or Hebrew, but sometimes in English) and leaves a blank space. The scribe then goes through the sermon again (or perhaps parts of it) and tries to fill in those passages which he omitted on the first run; we see this on folio 8, where he has left insufficient space for a Latin quotation: when he finds he is running out of space, he has to crowd the final two words. It is possible that after filling in the blank spaces the scribe trimmed the pages and then reread the sermon one more time, correcting any errors. This possibility is suggested by the fact that on fol. 33v the marginal reference to 2.reg.23 which has been partially cropped is corrected by putting the 2 above the other words. In general one can note that the scribe speeds up as he goes along, and in the process makes more errors, most of which he goes back to correct. The hand becomes looser as the sermon proceeds, and there are many more scribal errors and corrections in the scribal hand towards the end. In addition, the scribe apparently experiences more difficulty with Donne's handwriting as he goes along. Most of the long blank spaces which were indecipherable to the scribe and later filled in by Donne occur in the last half of the manuscript. It is also probable that Donne's own script became more hurried and difficult to decipher as the sermon progressed. The manuscript appears to have been prepared in haste, although still with concern for accuracy and sense. The haste can be explained by the King's demand to see the sermon, which was preached on November 5 and was in the King's hand by at least December 1 when Donne wrote to Thomas Roe. The entire manuscript also demonstrates that Donne was not as careful about the appearance of the manuscript as he was about the content.

When the scribe had completed his transcription and revisions, Donne then apparently proof-read and corrected the manuscript himself in order to render it presentable to the King. He added letters, changed words, perhaps punctuated, and filled in blank spaces left by the scribe (who usually left more room than Donne needed because Donne's script was more compact, spare). There is no evidence that Donne went over the manuscript more than once, except possibly the evidence of the underlining. In places such as fol. 27, line 14, where the scribe has left too much room, Donne fills the extra space with a flourished tilde. The corrections nevertheless reveal the precision and care with which Donne attended to his task. They reveal that Donne not only corrected obvious scribal errors which obscured sense, but took care to ensure that particular words were also 'accurate'. This included making changes from 'the' to 'that' (fols 12, line 2, 24, line 18) and 'hath' to 'had' (fol. 19, line 11), where either would make sense, for example. In one instance at least (fol. 28, line 1) Donne has corrected the spelling of a word (from 'derected' to 'directed'), a practice which suggests that Donne was more precise in matters of spelling (to the point of marring the appearance of the page for a one-letter correction) than was normal for the period, when spelling was various and inconsistent.[15] In addition, it is possible that Donne actually corrected or added punctuation (the colon at fol. 7v, line 8, the change from a comma to a semi-colon with the addition of a period at fol. 8v, line 22, as he proof-read).

Despite these indications of careful proof-reading and correction, however, Donne missed several errors and even introduced at least one error into the manuscript. On six occasions Donne fails to add words to the top of a leaf which were the catchwords at the bottom of the previous page (at fol. 11r and 11v 'he' is missing before 'can' in both; fol. 13v has 'a' as last word followed by catchword 'gaine' whereas the word at the top of fol. 14 is 'againe'; catchwords 'in his' from fol. 20 are missing at the top of fol. 20v; catchword 'god' from fol. 24 is missing at the top of fol. 24v; catchword 'a' from fol. 30 is missing from the top of fol. 30v). On two occasions (fols 23v, line 18 and 8v, line 11), the word 'there' is mistakenly used for 'their', despite the fact that in the manuscript several scribal corrections indicate that Donne and the scribe distinguished between the two forms. The word 'his' is repeated on fol. 25v, line 4, although normally either the scribe or Donne deletes words carelessly written twice. In addition, Donne does not correct the word 'Hadradrimmon' on fol. 14v, line 5, and allows the clearly mistaken 'them' to remain for 'then' at fol. 2v, line 16.

More remarkable is Donne's failure to correct the phrase 'in *foueis*, in pitts' at fol. 30, line 17. From the paragraph as a whole, and from the marginal annotation at that point, it is clear that the phrase should be in the singular (as it is in F50), that is, 'in *fouea*, in a pit', in order to allow for the contrast with the plural form later in the paragraph. Another curious error is Donne's insertion of the word 'especially' at the end of a phrase on fol. 21v, line 10, thus creating an awkward and redundant sentence: 'and it is theirs especially in our prayers to allmightie god for them especially'. Donne apparently failed to notice the first 'especially'; there seems to be no stylistic reason why Donne would add the second word, and many reasons why he would not have done so if he had noticed the first occurrence.

TEXTUAL IMPLICATIONS

The existence of an authorial manuscript, of course, also has implications for the status of the standard text of this sermon. To this point, the accepted text of the sermon has been based on the first printed version (*Fifty Sermons*, 1649). On the basis of comparison between existing manuscript sources of sermons printed in this volume, Potter and Simpson argue that F50 came from a primary source containing moderate though not radical revisions by Donne himself. They also conclude that if the sole text for the sermon is from F50, an editor must proceed on the probability that the sermons in that volume came from manuscript copy of the same excellence as that from which F80 was printed, but on the certainty that the editing, type-setting, and proof-reading of F50 were considerably less careful than in the preparation of F80 (*LXXX Sermons*, 1640). Consequently, Potter and Simpson have used F50 as their copy-text, but have emended obvious copyists' errors, marginalia, punctuation, and italics.[16]

A collation of MS Royal 17 B.XX with F50 supports Potter and Simpson's view that F50 is derived from an authorial manuscript. On the basis of the differences, few of which are necessary for the sense, it seems safe to say that the changes in F50 represent 'deliberate and intelligent'[17] revisions to the manuscript copy which Donne had of this sermon (though not this very copy, which appears to have remained in the Royal collection of manuscripts since 1622). A consideration of the nature of the changes between Royal MS and F50 does confirm that the version in F50 is a revision, probably by Donne himself. It also raises the question whether an editor is wise invariably to prefer a later, revised version to an earlier one, particularly when that earlier version happens to be corrected in Donne's hand and presumably is in the form in which he wished it to be in November 1622, though perhaps not in 1625 or the latter part of 1630 when it was revised for publication.[18]

From the evidence of this presentation manuscript, the revisions which Donne made to his original manuscript fall into four main categories: significant changes in content, substantive rewordings, stylistic rewordings, and innumerable changes in spelling, punctuation and italics which may or may not be authorial.

F50 obviously offers a revised version of the 1622 manuscript. Four sections in particular were added or significantly revised and indicate more clearly both what Donne intended in his earlier version, and what he cautiously refrained from spelling out at the time of delivery.

(a) The printed version contains 'The Prayer Before the Sermon'. This prayer provides a context within which readers may interpret the content of the sermon and it fulfills the Canon of the Church that required prayer before each sermon.[19] The prayer offers thanks and praise for deliverance from a Catholic plot, and encouragement for continued watchfulness against them. The prayer was suitable both when the sermon was preached (and may have been included in the entire service for the day) and when Donne was revising this sermon. Deliverance from the Gunpowder Plot continued to be celebrated annually in Churches across England. In this prayer, Donne lays the 'only ground of the Treason of this day' upon 'that [Catholic] Religion'.[20]

(b) you said to me says *Samuel*, 1 *Samuel* 12.12. Nay but a king shall raeigne over vs; (MS Royal 17 B.XX, fol. 8v, lines 17–19).

You said to mee (says *Samuel*, by way of Reproofe and Increpation) *You said, Nay but a King shall reigne over us;* Now, that was not their fault; but that which followes, The unseasonablenesse and inconsideration of their clamorous Petition, *You said a King shall reigne over us*, (F50, 170–173).

These lines constitute an important addition. Donne wants to clarify the way in which Samuel was allowed to expostulate with God. Donne distinguishes between Samuel's authorized function of 'Reproofe and Increpation' (the proper behaviour of a prophet, which Donne outlines elsewhere)[21] and the unseasonableness and inconsideration of the clamorous petition of the Jews. Donne contrasts not only the manner of petitioning, but also the words. Samuel's words are simply a reminder to God of what he had promised. The Jews' words indicate that they will not trust in God's means.

(c) That that King that neglects the dutyes of his place, That exercises his prerogative with out iust cause, that vexes his Subiects nay that giues himselfe to intemperate hunting for in that very particular, they instance, that in such cases Kings are as much in theyr mercy, and subiect to censure and correction. we proceed not so in censuring the actions of Kings. we say with Ciril, in *John* 1.12.56. *impium est dicere regi, inique agis.* (MS Royal 17 B.XX, fol. 18v, lines 7–16).

> That that King which neglects the duties of his place (and they must prescribe the duty, and judge the negligence too) That King that exercises his Prerogative, without just cause (and they must prescribe the Prerogative, and judge the cause,) That that King that vexes his Subjects, That that King that gives himself to *intemperate hunting* (for in that very particular they instance) that in such cases, (and they multiply these cases infinitely) Kings are in their mercy, and subject to their censures, and corrections. We proceed not so, in censuring the actions of Kings; we say, with St. *Cyrill, Impium est dicere Regi, Inique agis; It is an impious thing,* (in him, who is onely a private man and hath no other obligations upon him) *to say to the King,* or *of the King, He governs not as a King is bound to do:* (F50, 400–409).

Donne specifies more clearly in his revision that his objection to the King's critics is that they prescribe the King's duties and judge the King's negligence by the standard of their own prescriptions. In the manuscript version Donne is not denying that the King is negligent, or that he exercises his prerogative without just cause. The fault is that the King's critics make themselves the judges of how the prerogative should be exercised, and in what causes. In addition they multiply infinitely the number of cases of the King's bad behaviour, specifically his 'intemperate hunting'. In the revision, Donne explains that it is an impious thing in one who is only a private person and has no other obligations on him (as a preacher does) to criticize the King's government.[22] Nonetheless, Donne does not free those who are authorized counsellors of their responsibility in such matters. For Donne, it is important that people act within the freedom and protection of authorized political and religious functions.

> (d) but princes do not so much as worke therein, and therefore are excusable. (MS Royal 17 B.XX, fol. 21v, lines 5–6).
>
> but Princes doe not so much as worke therein, and so may bee excusable; at least, for any cooperation in the evill of the action, though not for countenancing, and authorising an evill instrument; but that is another case. (F50, 490–92).

This addition in 1649 is the most important revision Donne made. In the manuscript version, Donne appears to be excusing Princes for their part in ill actions. The Prince, he says, does not work so much in these even as God is said to work in evil actions. But in the revision, Donne does not excuse the Prince for countenancing and authorizing an evil instrument. In fact, he explicitly criticizes such blindness, but ends abruptly without discussing further the nature of the King's responsibility to surround himself with wise counsellors. The distinction he makes is an important one, and shifts the focus of responsibility from the agents who execute the Prince's good intentions in a bad way to the Prince himself who authorized these evil instruments. Given the crisis of counsel taking place in the 1620s, and particularly the public sense that evil counsel in the person of Buckingham was responsible for all of the Kingdom's ills, the words added in the revision resonate politically in a way that qualifies substantially Donne's willingness to work within the political fiction of 'the King can do no wrong'.

Some of the most significant rewordings which Donne adopts in the source for F50 also focus more sharply on the politics of the sermon.[23] The theme of the sermon is that even a bad King should be obeyed, although Donne stresses (perhaps too often) that the present situation in England is analogous to that of the good King Josiah rather than the bad King Zedekiah. Accordingly, Donne alters his earlier source to stress the responsibilities of the King's counsellors (74, 775), the specific nature of the King's responsibilities in matters of religion (569–70, 574–5), and the kind of moderate response appropriate even to genuine abuses of that power (88–9, 436–7). Donne also seems to clarify that his primary concern in preaching obedience to the King is political rather than personal. Donne stresses in his revisions the effects on the political stability of the Kingdom of public national obedience, and of the dangers resulting when the King falls in the estimation of other nations (209–10, 579, 776). Two revisions also alter the emphasis in the sermon on the King's religion, a matter which in 1622 was the subject of public concern and which the imposition of the *Directions* had highlighted.[24] The manuscript states unequivocally that the King 'hath not' left his religion while this assertion is omitted from F50, 600. Similarly, Donne revises his manuscript to say not that Princes 'therefore are' excusable when their good intentions are not well executed, but that Princes 'may be' excusable. This is a small verbal difference, but the revisions taken together suggest that Donne is expressing himself more precisely and critically in F50 than in the Royal manuscript.

Apart from these substantive changes, there are innumerable stylistic alterations in F50. These changes and rewordings are of several sorts: those which amplify a meaning in the original; rewordings which clarify; those which translate a Latin phrase; those which improve the syntax; those which alter rhetorical emphasis; those which offer a more precise diction; changes to a less dramatic syntax; and elimination of unnecessary words.

The changes in this sermon from the 1622 Royal manuscript to F50 can be compared with those noted by Potter and Simpson in the other sermon for which we have two distinct versions. In general, Donne revises for clarity, amplification, rhetorical emphasis, and repetition. He clarifies pronoun references, improves the syntax, and occasionally changes the meaning, or makes an 'interpretable' meaning clearer. There are virtually no places where the rewordings in F50 alter the manuscript for the worse: exceptions include the syntax at line 132, wording at line 278 and 740, and a redundancy at line 697 ('from whence') which is not in the manuscript (where Donne has corrected 'when as' to 'whence').

A comparison of the marginalia in both the manuscript and printed versions of the sermon provides an interesting special case that confirms the authorial connections between F50 and Donne. The marginalia in the manuscript differ from those in the printed version. In some cases the manuscript corrects errors that entered into the printed source and confirms editorial emendations made by Potter and Simpson. However, despite the care with which Donne corrected the manuscript, including, it seems, the marginalia, he allows several errors in notation to remain. There are three examples of marginalia which exist in F50, which have been corrected by Potter and Simpson, but which are also found in MS Royal 17 B.XX and are therefore authorial, if incorrect: the manuscript has Job.30.1. as does F50, 584, but Potter and Simpson have corrected this to Job 30.8.9; the manuscript agrees with F50, 604 in having Gen.28.18. rather than the corrected Gen.28.17; both the manuscript and F50, 628 have Iudg.9.8, whereas Potter and Simpson have emended the reference correctly to Iudg.9.14, 15. The presence of these common errors suggests that F50 was copying faithfully from its (authorial) source in printing its text. These common errors also correct, to some extent, Potter and Simpson's claims that the compositor of F50 was 'careless'; perhaps the presumption that Donne always quotes accurately from his Biblical and patristic sources needs to be qualified again by D. C. Allen's observations made some years ago about the varying degree of accuracy in Donne's use of Biblical quotations.[25]

Five other marginalia in Donne's corrected manuscript support Potter and Simpson's emendations of F50: the incorrect citation of Ezek. 2.20 at F50, 47 is correctly cited in the manuscript as [Ezek.] 2.10; the incorrect citation of Ezek. 16.3 at F50 191 is correctly cited as Ezek. 16.13. in the manuscript; F50, 273 has Luke. 14.14. which is correctly cited as Luke. 19.14. in the manuscript; F50, 354 2 Reg.25.ult. is correctly cited as 23 ult. in the manuscript (but without the 2 Reg.); F50, 510 marginal reference reads 1 Cor.7.44. and is emended by Potter and Simpson to 1 Cor.7.40. This is the correct text and is included in the text of the manuscript rather than in the margin. Although the manuscript has more marginal comments than F50 (and for some reason crosses out marginal comments that are accurate and that appear later in F50, such as *Coquaeus*, f. 18 which appears at line 637), no errors not in the manuscript are introduced into F50.

Even where F50 contradicts Donne's corrections in the manuscript, the conclusion is that F50 represents an authorial revision. Most of the changes are neither better nor worse than the early version. For example, F50's replacement of 'both these' (Royal MS fol. 9, line 2) with 'either of these' (176–7) is a more precise statement. The change from fol. 35v, lines 7–8 ('necessary; as much') to 'necessary, so much' at F50, 784–5, while it weakens the parallelism in the sentence, does not alter the sense. Neither does the elimination of 'we' in F50, 703, although it too weakens the parallelism of fol. 32r, line 4. Donne's insertion and positioning of 'and' at fol. 28, line 8 is much preferable to F50's at line 620, but is not strictly necessary for sense. On fol. 21v, line 10, where Donne adds another 'especially' to the end of the line, it seems clear that he didn't see the first one, but corrected the redundancy when he revised. F50, 564 has 'and the fundamentall things' whereas the manuscript (fol. 25, line 15) has 'in' which makes better sense. The difference could be a printing error.

One of the most interesting clues to the text of the sermon is in F50's 'now no where' [202–3] (which seems to combine the 'now here' mistake of Donne's scribe at fol. 10, lines 8–9, with Donne's correction to 'nowhere' in 1622). It is possible that the manuscript from which the text for F50 was taken had the same difficulty as this one (that is, the scribe mistook 'nowhere' for 'now here'). Then Donne, or someone else, corrected the error but did not put the line far enough through 'now', with the consequence that it looked as though he wanted 'now nowhere'. The same wording could also be achieved if the 'nowhere' were interlined above 'where' as a correction for the printer. In any case, this common error between the two versions of the sermon (as with the common marginal errors) suggests that F50 is also derived from an authorial source.

The existence of an early authorial manuscript of the sermon on Lamentations 4:20, therefore, has significant implications for textual editing of this sermon and of Donne's sermons in general. Besides the substantive rhetorical and political considerations outlined above, these two texts raise less substantive questions of italics, punctuation, and capitalization. There are innumerable differences between the Royal manuscript and F50 on these matters, which call in question modern editorial emendations of F50. The punctuation of the manuscript, for example, differs significantly from F50. In themselves, these differences provide the material for a careful study, but it is difficult to know whether the manuscript or the 1649 punctuation is Donne's own. In general F50 is more liberal in its use of commas, but moves towards lighter stops. Potter and Simpson based this conclusion on comparison of other sources with F50, but this new sermon manuscript confirms their general conclusions.[26] It is possible that some of the manuscript corrections include changes in punctuation, suggesting as with the autograph verse letter that Donne's practice with punctuation is to use it for rhetorical pointing rather than for grammatical logic. However, given the status of the two versions of the sermon, the three emendations by Potter and Simpson seem arbitrary in the face of the enormous difference between F50 and the manuscript on these matters.[27]

Similarly, an examination of the manuscript suggests that precise information about italics may be difficult to come by, and that these things were largely controlled by compositors. The use of italics in F50 bears almost no resemblance to that in the manuscript and so Potter and Simpson's four emendations seem somewhat misleading. As with punctuation, there seems to be no good reason for making these few changes when the differences are so numerous.[28]

CONCLUSION

The discovery and identification of an authorial sermon manuscript corrected in Donne's hand, then, is important for many reasons. It documents the text of a sermon written down and transcribed in fair copy soon after its delivery in the pulpit, and indicates a great deal about Donne's processes of composition, proof-reading, correction, and transmission of sermon texts. A common theme in discussion of sermon texts of this period is the frustration caused by not knowing the relation between what was said in the pulpit and what was finally published. While we have always assumed that a sermon for publication would differ from the sermon as delivered, we have not previously had such a precise instrument of comparison. The manuscript indicates that Donne's copy of the sermon made immediately after delivery is more dramatic in syntax and diction than F50. This is indicated not only by the lack of connecting and explanatory words in the manuscript, but by the heavier and more pointed punctuation as well. The stops are more emphatic; the transitions more abrupt.

In addition, a comparison of this early manuscript with the later printed text of the sermon reveals that Donne substantially revised this sermon for publication. The two versions of the sermon raise questions about the textual authority of the modern edition by Potter and Simpson, which is based on F50 and which emends on the basis of assumptions that need to be re-examined. The most useful 'edition' of this sermon would be a parallel-text one which calls attention to the differences between the two versions of the sermon, and their significance in charting the development of Donne's attitudes towards the material and its presentation.

Finally, the two states of the sermon suggest that Donne changed his sermons not only for stylistic or rhetorical reasons but also for political ones; however, both versions of the sermon could be valid for their time and place. This means that the question of determining a text closest to Donne's intentions, either verbally or politically, is probably the wrong question. Many of the revisions indicate that Donne's intentions changed. The circumstances surrounding this sermon, and the nature of Donne's revisions to the manuscript when he prepared it for publication, tell us something of Donne's sense of decorum in the pulpit. A comparison of the two versions reinforces the sense that Donne is concerned with authorized means of criticism, but that in 1622 he was wary of criticizing the King as openly as he did in the revised version. In fact, the crucial passages, politically, reveal both what Donne's views were about the King's responsibility not to countenance bad counsellors, and his own sense that November 1622 was not the right time, given the prevailing conditions of censorship which he himself had defended, for making such a criticism.

It is to be hoped that the significance of this manuscript will become even clearer in the parallel-text edition of the sermon on which I am presently engaged.

APPENDIX: CORRECTIONS IN DONNE'S HAND

Definitely Autograph

Folio Line	Scribe	Donne's Corrections
1.14	*Johns*	**some** ~~*Johns*~~
3.2	historicall	historicall**y**
3.4	propheticall	propheticall**y**
9.2	bide there	~~bide there~~ ^**both these**
10.8	now here	**nowhere** ~~now here~~

10.9	now here	**nowhere** ~~now here~~ ^
13.6	they implicitly	**came** they implicitly ^
16.10	reducd	**mou'd** re~~ducd~~ ^
18.5	affection that	affections ~~that~~ **yow**
18v.13	and	**and** ~~and~~ ^
19.1–2	*vncti Domini* , ,	*vncti Domini* **the anointed of the Lord, And spiritus Narium, The Breath of o^r Nostrills.**
19.7	intreate	**sinuate** in~~treate~~ ^
19.10	euen the	**in** euen the ^
19.11	hath	ha~~th~~**d** ^
19v.8	it, his	**and** it, his ^
20.15	it	**y** ~~i~~t ^
21v.10	for them.	**especially** for them . ^
21v.19	preserud	**ferd** pre~~serud~~
23.12	wars	**was** ~~wars~~ ^
23.24	the	**in** ~~the~~ ^

23v.4	now him	**by** now him ^
24.18	the	**that** ~~the~~ ^
25.19	truth	**time** ~~truth~~ ^
27.14	that sleeping	that **vision** ∼ sleeping
28.1	derected	**directed** ~~derected~~ ^
28.8	out, was	**and** out, was ^
31v.12	when as	**ce** when ~~as~~ ^
31v.14–5	is become	is become **Sepher Te=hillim∼∼.**
31v.15	psalms	**psalms** ~~psalms~~ ^
32.4	therefore know	**we** therefore kn**e**w ^
32.17	cause	cause**s**
33.21	nor	**once** ~~nor~~ ^
34.12	Ambassadors, as	Ambassadors, **is not,** as
34.20	even they may	**who are so** even they may ^
35v.7–8	shall be ; is	shall be **necessary**; **as much,** is
35v.9	be better	**the** be better ^
36.9–10	were , .	were **mercy and benignity**, **to let him out**.

Probably Autograph

Folio 1:	Lame	Lame**ntati**
5v.11	leaue	~~leaue~~ ^**leaue**
7v.8	a King and	a King**:** and
8.18	was	was**t**
15v.19	disparted	dis~~parted~~ ^**puted**
18v.12	the	th~~e~~**at**
25.15	and	~~and~~ **in**
29v.1	*ducendus*	*d*~~*u*~~^**i***cendus*

Possibly Autograph

8v.22	fault,	fault**;**
12.2	the	th**at**
21v.20	Theophyila	Theoph**ylact**
17v.7	speake	speak**s**
17v.9	will	wil**t**
21v.14	Theophyila	Theoph**ylact**

NOTES

I would like to thank the British Library for permission to quote from MS Royal 17 B.XX. In addition, I would like to acknowledge the support of the University of Regina's President's Fund for this research. However, for their patient and learned advice, I am especially indebted to Peter Beal, Hilton Kelliher, Ernie Sullivan, and Cameron Louis.

1 This newly discovered manuscript is the only known manuscript source for the sermon on Lamentations 4:20.

2 For a detailed introduction to the manuscripts and the text of Donne's sermons, *see The Sermons of John Donne* ed. George Potter and Evelyn Simpson, vols I (Berkeley, 1953), pp.33–82, and II (Berkeley, 1955), pp.365–71; hereafter cited as *Sermons*.

3 For a detailed discussion of Donne's reputation during this period *see* Raoul Granqvist, *The Reputation of John Donne: 1779–1873* (Uppsala, 1975) and Roland Botting, 'The Reputation of John Donne During the Nineteenth Century', *Research Studies of the State College of Washington*, 9 (1941), 139–88.

4 John Donne, *The Works of John Donne, D. D.*, ed. Henry Alford, 6 vols (London, 1839).

5 *Sermons*, vol. IV (Berkeley, 1959), pp.34–36.

6 SP 14/134/59.

7 John Sparrow, 'John Donne and Contemporary Preachers: Their Preparation of Sermons for Delivery and for Publication', *Essays and Studies by Members of the English Association*, 16 (1930), 144–178.

8 The importance of discretion for Donne is discussed in Jeanne Shami, 'Donne on Discretion', *Journal of English Literary History*, 47 (1980), 48–66.

9 For a description of the contents of the Royal library *see* David Casley, *A Catalogue of the Manuscripts of the Kings's Library* (London, 1734).

10 Because of these holograph changes, Helen Gardner and Nicolas Barker disagree about whether or not the verse letter is a fair copy. *See* Helen Gardner, *John Donne's holograph of 'A Letter to the Lady Carey and Mrs Essex Riche'* (Oxford, 1972), p.2, and Nicolas Barker, 'Donne's "Letter to the Lady Carey and Mrs. Essex Riche": Text and Facsimile', *The Book Collector*, 22 (1973), 491–2.

11 *Sermons*, vol. I (Berkeley, 1953), pp.77–8.

12 P. J. Croft, *Autograph Poetry in the English Language*, vol. I (New York, 1973), pp.25–6.

13 Anthony G. Petti, *English Literary Hands from Chaucer to Dryden* (Cambridge, Mass., 1977), pp.96–7.

14 Nicolas Barker, '"Goodfriday 1613": by whose hand?', *Times Literary Supplement*, 20 September 1974, pp.996–7.

15 *See* the discussion in Albert C. Baugh and Thomas Cable, *A History of the English Language*, fourth edition (Englewood Cliffs, NJ, 1993), pp.203–09.

16 *Sermons*, vol. I (Berkeley, 1953), pp.78–82.

17 Ibid., p.62.

18 For an excellent discussion of this textual issue, *see* Ted-Larry Pebworth and Ernest W. Sullivan, II, 'Rational Presentation of Multiple Text Traditions', *Papers of the Bibliographical Society of America*, 83 (1989), 43–60.

19 Canon LV of the 1603 *Constitutions and Canons Ecclesiastical* (Wing 4101) required prayer before sermons, lectures, and homilies, and outlined specifically the nature and even the wording of the prayer.

20 *Sermons*, vol. IV (Berkeley, 1959), p.236.

21 *Sermons*, vol. II (Berkeley, 1955), p.303.

22 For a discussion of how Donne balances the King's prerogative with the authority of the preacher *see* Jeanne Shami '"Kings and Desperate Men": John Donne Preaches at Court', *John Donne Journal*, 6 (1987), 9–23.

23 Donne's politics have received much critical attention recently. For the view that Donne's politics are unequivocally absolutist *see* John Carey, *John Donne: Life, Mind and Art* (London, 1981), Debora Shuger, *Habits of Thought in the English Renaissance: Religion, Politics and the Dominant Culture* (Berkeley, 1990). This absolutist view has been challenged recently by David Norbrook, 'The Monarchy of Wit and the Republic of Letters: Donne's Politics', in *Soliciting Interpretation: Literary Theory and Seventeenth-Century English Poetry*, ed. Elizabeth Harvey and Katherine Maus (Chicago, 1990), pp.3–36; Annabel Patterson, 'John Donne, Kingsman?', in *The Mental World of the Jacobean Court*, ed. Linda Levy Peck (Cambridge, 1991), pp.251–72; David Gray and Jeanne Shami, 'Political Advice in Donne's *Devotions*: "No Man is

an Island"', *Modern Language Quarterly*, 50 (1989), 337–56; Jeanne Shami, 'Donne's Sermons and the Absolutist Politics of Quotation', in *Donne's Religious Imagination: Essays in Honour of John T. Shawcross*, ed. Raymond-Jean Frontain and Frances Malpezzi (Conway, AK, 1994).

24 This point is discussed fully in an article by Thomas Cogswell entitled 'England and the Spanish Match', in *Conflict in Early Stuart England*, ed. Richard Cust and Ann Hughes (London, 1989), pp.107–133.

25 *See* D. C. Allen, 'Dean Donne Sets His Text', *Journal of English Literary History*, 10 (1943), pp.208–29. In addition, *see* the comments on Donne's marginal annotations to *Biathanatos* in *Biathanatos* ed. Ernest W. Sullivan, II (Newark, 1984), pp.xxxvii–viii.

26 *Sermons*, vol. I (Berkeley, 1953), pp.75, 81–2.

27 *Sermons*, vol. IV (Berkeley, 1959), pp.410–11.

28 Ibid.

Arthur Young, Jr's 1792 Transcript of Milton's Trinity Manuscript

PETER McCULLOUGH

The Library of Trinity College, Cambridge has housed, since the late seventeenth century, one of the most precious artifacts of England's literary renaissance: the 50-page collection, mostly autograph, of John Milton's shorter works. Trinity MS R.3.4. – the 'Trinity Manuscript' to Milton studies – includes the author's working drafts of many of the English sonnets, 'Lycidas', 'Comus', and the early conceptions of *Paradise Lost* as a drama.[1] Sadly, many leaves of the small volume have suffered significant damage since they were gathered and bound in 1736, and many readings have been lost. Several of Milton's eighteenth-century editors, however, notably Thomas Birch, Thomas Newton, and James Todd, had the advantage of consulting the manuscript before much of the decay occurred, and have preserved many now-lost readings in their annotations. Nonetheless, these editors recorded mostly cancelled readings that appear in the Trinity texts, and none made a complete, systematic transcript. As a result, our picture of the early state of the Trinity Manuscript has been piecemeal at best, and scholars have had to rely on the 1899 facsimile and transcript by W. Aldis Wright as the earliest available view of Milton's manuscript.[2]

This lamentable gap has now been filled by the discovery of a near-verbatim transcript of the entire Trinity Manuscript made by the Trinity undergraduate Arthur Young, Jr in October 1792, now owned by Princeton University Library.[3] The purpose of this essay is not to provide a detailed survey of textual variants between Young's transcript and Wright's. Rather, it is to sketch the biographical circumstances that might suggest why Young undertook such a project, and to assess first the reliability, and finally the significance, of Young's transcript.

The details of Young's biography offer only hints of possible motives for his transcribing Milton's manuscript. Born in 1769, Young was the third child and only son of Arthur Young, Sr of Bradfield Hall, Suffolk, and his wife, Martha Allen of Lynn, Norfolk.[4] Young, Sr (1741–1820), a second son, did not attend university, but after a failed apprenticeship in business, and several false starts in farming, established himself as an author of major importance on the subjects of political and agricultural economy. The elder Young's most recent biographer, in fact, considers him 'unquestionably the most significant figure in the English Agricultural Revolution'.[5] He published several important accounts of tours in Britain, France, and Italy, and edited the monthly journal *Annals of Agriculture* (1784–1809). In 1793 he was appointed Secretary to the Board of Agriculture by Pitt, a post that he held until his death.

The Young household at Bradfield Hall did not lack more direct literary connections. Arthur, Jr attended grammar school at nearby Bury St Edmund's, where he studied under the Rev. Richard Valpy (1754–1836).[6] Valpy, also an amateur poet and dramatist, was noted for his enthusiastic (and at the time unusual) inclusion of English, as well as Classical, literature in his curriculum. Although the evidence is circumstantial, it could be that at the Bury school Valpy first inspired Arthur, Jr's interest in Milton. The elder Young, however, nurtured a lasting friendship with his son's headmaster, and from their correspondence we do know that Arthur Young, Sr himself wrote English verse with some degree of seriousness. Valpy acted as an enthusiastic reader and encouraging critic of Young's poetry, and even urged him in 1782 to 'leave the train of Ceres, & join the choir of the muses'.[7] Later, Valpy wrote to Young that 'there runs a vein of fancy through your poetry which stamps a high character upon it'.[8] As a youth, then, both at school and at his father's house, Arthur, Jr had ample occasion to develop an interest in English verse, and perhaps in Milton.

The Youngs also were related first by friendship and later by marriage to the family of musicologist Dr Charles Burney (1726–1814), which included, of course, Dr Burney's daughter, the novelist and playwright Frances Burney, later Mme d'Arblay (1752–1840). Arthur, Sr's connection with Charles Burney dated from the former's youth spent among the polite society of Lynn, Norfolk, where Burney was organist from 1752 to 1760. The link between the families was strengthened in 1767 when Burney married as his second wife Elizabeth Allen, sister of Young's wife, Martha. The Youngs and Burneys exchanged regular visits and correspondence, and, in a small coincidence of literary history, on the day that Arthur Young, Jr sat down in Cambridge to transcribe Trinity's Milton manuscript –

Friday, 5 October 1792 – his father was entertaining at Bradfield Hall the acclaimed author of *Evelina* and *Cecilia*.[9]

Young the agriculturalist spared no expense in the education of his son, who he seems to have marked-out for a clerical career from an early age. Arthur, Jr left Bury St Edmund's for Eton in 1785 where he studied until 1789 under Assistant Master George Heath.[10] Young, Sr pinned all hopes for his son's advancement on the expected patronage of his elder brother, the Rev. Dr John Young (1727–1786), a rising clergyman who held several livings, enjoyed the personal favour of King George III, and was a Fellow of Eton. During his nephew's second year at Eton, however, the Rev. Dr Young died when thrown from his mount during the last royal hunt of the season.[11] In a letter to his wife from Eton, where he settled his brother's affairs, Arthur, Sr lamented that 'the loss to my poor boy was nothing short of ruin'. While at Eton, Young inquired after his son's academic progress, and Mr Heath's account did little to cheer the father's spirits. 'Sorry I am to say', Young wrote in the same letter, 'that Arthur seems determined to do little for himself. He is now at a crisis, and sinks or swims'.[12]

Arthur, Jr did manage to stay afloat, for he matriculated at Trinity College, Cambridge, in October 1789.[13] Trinity seems to have been selected with the input of Mrs Young and the influence of Dr John Symonds, a Trinity College don and University Professor of Modern History, also one of Arthur, Sr's closest friends among the Suffolk gentry.[14] We get a glimpse of Young, Jr's possible interest or facility in English letters when Symonds wrote to the elder Young that Trinity 'offers so handsome a premium to young men, who declaim well either in English or Latin; & this is surely very advantageous to an Etonian'.[15] On the eve of his son's going up to Cambridge, Arthur, Sr wrote a lengthy letter of advice to his son in which he urged diligence, recommended study 'in ye mathematics' as 'the fashionable study at Cambridge' and hence the surest road to a fellowship and best way to avoid the fate of 'a couple of wretched curacies or a lousy living'. But perhaps the most telling for the purposes of this study is this stern admonition:

> I beg of you consider the importance of yr. time & on no account lose a single day even at Bradfield: and of all things remember (for I confess I fear that most in you) that idle amusive reading is time absolutely lost at yr. age: it gives nothing; but merely kills time that might give every thing.[16]

Perhaps the father would have counted his son's devotion of 5 October 1792 to the project of transcribing Milton's manuscript as 'idle amusive reading' and 'time absolutely lost'. Arthur did fall short of a Trinity fellowship, but nonetheless proceeded scholar in 1792, won first prize for English declamation in the same year, and graduated B.A. in 1793.[17]

One further biographical connection should be mentioned with respect to Young's Milton transcript. In June 1792, only months before Young's transcription, another Suffolk neighbour and friend of the Young family, Capel Lofft (1751–1824), published at Bury St Edmund's the first – and only – volume of a projected multi-volume edition of *Paradise Lost*.[18] Lofft, like most eighteenth-century editors of Milton, reacted against the editorial 'improvements' of Bentley's 1732 edition and declared as his purpose 'to give the PARADISE LOST correctly, and in such manner as MILTON intended'. Significantly, he lamented 'the non-existence of a Manuscript', and so instead took as the next-best available copy-texts the 'two *authentic* Editions, both published in the life time of MILTON'.[19] Lofft was the nephew, heir, and namesake of the great editor and annotator of Shakespeare, Edward Capel (1713–81).[20] Capel's collating energies were near legendary, and he was said to have transcribed the whole of Shakespeare ten times. But Capel's editorial interests extended to Milton as well. At the conclusion of Lofft's preface, he claims that his uncle had actually anticipated his own *Paradise Lost* edition, for,

> There is now, I understand, in *Trinity-College*, CAMBRIDGE, a fair MS. of [Paradise Lost] (which I have formerly seen), carefully transcribed and prepared for the Press, by the Relation whom I have mentioned [*i.e.*, Capel]. If he had lived to publish it . . . I probably should have had no . . . occasion, for this Attempt.[21]

Edward Capel bequeathed most of his outstanding library to Trinity College, Cambridge, and the *Paradise Lost* transcript was part of that bequest.[22] Although this evidence is again circumstantial, it must at least be suggested that Young's decision to transcribe the Trinity Manuscript was in some way encouraged or influenced by an interest in the establishment of authentic Milton texts that had flourished for two generations in Young's Suffolk neighbourhood, indeed among Young's family friends, and that had substantial connections with Arthur's college.

Upon graduating from Cambridge, Arthur Young, Jr took holy orders. His father's fears for his preferment were realized, however, and the new Reverend Arthur Young waited nine years for a living. In the meantime, he published an agrarian survey of Sussex on commission from the Board of Agriculture in 1793, and contributed numerous articles on agriculture to his father's journal. In 1802, the

Rev. Arthur Young received from his patron George Wyndham, third Earl of Egremont, a sizeable Irish living. Young visited his clerical charge only once, and spoke of it with considerable contempt, although he held the living for life.[23] In 1805, he accepted an invitation – first extended to his father who had declined because of age and failing health – to conduct agricultural surveys for the Russian government. In the last twenty years of his life Young made three extended visits to Russia, and in 1810 he purchased an estate in the Crimea where he died in September 1827.[24]

Young's transcription of the Trinity Manuscript consists of seventeen unbound folio sheets of contemporary paper measuring 315 × 415mm.[25] The sheets are gathered and numbered (in the upper margin, recto, near the gutter) somewhat irregularly by Young:[26] first, a bifolium with the title-page [i] on one side, and folio XXIII on the other, then two bifolia numbered I[a^r–b^v] and II[a^r–b^v], followed by a gathering of ten sheets, III–XXII, and finally two more bifolia numbered XXIV[a^r–b^v] and XXV[a^r–b^v]. The transcriber ruled a 2cm left margin in pencil on each page, and used a clear, consistent italic hand. The whole is preserved in a bifolium cover of later paper that bears the inscription (in a different, probably later, hand), 'Copy of Miltons Poems at Cambridge with a Fac Simile of his Hand Writing'. Preserved with Young's transcript is a panelled printed card 22 × 18½cm, titled '*FAC SIMILE of the HAND WRITING of MILTON. From the* MSS. *in TRINITY COLLEGE CAMBRIDGE.*', with 12 lines of verse from six different works found in the Trinity Manuscript reproduced in facsimile, and the footnote '*COMMUNICATED by ARTHUR YOUNG Esq: Jun: 6. Oct: MDCCXCII*'.[27]

With only a few significant exceptions (discussed below) Young copied the contents of the Trinity Manuscript in the order in which they appear in the original, preserved deleted readings, interlinear additions and corrections, and remained faithful to Milton's orthography. When Young erred in transcription, he did so more often by omission than commission, and thereby introduced very few substantive misreadings into the transcript.[28] Young occasionally introduced a comma or possessive apostrophe not found in Milton's holograph, and a few egregious errors of anticipation suggest that he did not carefully proof-read his work. It must be stated clearly that Young's transcription is in fact so accurate as to deserve the Sotheby's sale catalogue description of it as 'an important witness to the original state of Milton's invaluable manuscript', although the assessment of Young's work as a 'verbatim copy' needs some qualification.[29] A collation of Young's transcription with that of Wright reveals that Young, although a generally reliable transcriber, vascillated between purely antiquarian facsimile reproduction and a much more liberal reconstruction of a reading text of the works contained in the Trinity Manuscript.

Perhaps the greatest inconsistency in Young's copying was his varied handling of both single words and larger passages that Milton struck out in the course of revision. For the most part Young reproduced deleted readings, oftentimes even imitating the shape of Milton's crosses and strikes (*see* PLATES 1–4). Nonetheless, if the deleted portion was a single word, and especially if Milton decided to use the deleted word after all, Young does not reproduce the evidence of the poet's indecision. Similarly, Young sometimes does not consider Milton's correction of a misspelt word worth recording (for example, instead of the correction 'that *wond'st* wont'st to love', Young simply gives 'that wont'st to love'[30]). Instances of Young's silent omission of deleted readings do not occur frequently, but some very important glimpses of Milton's process of composition do disappear, as when in 'Comus', Milton's search for the right adjective has the Naiades

potent
culling thire *potent* hearbes, & balefull druggs
(powerfull)
myghty.[31]

Young's sanitized version – 'culling thire potent hearbs, & balefull druggs' – makes the nymphs' job much easier.[32] In Young's defense, most of his omissions of deleted readings (including that just quoted) can be attributed to the near-illegibility of the text found under Milton's more emphatic overstrikes. By far the most significant example is the heavily-struck 22-line passage that stood between lines 754 and 755 of 'Comus'. Young makes no effort to decipher any of the deleted text, nor does he make any editorial note in his transcript of its presence in the original.[33] For the texts of Milton's many deletions in the Trinity Manuscript, Young's 1792 transcript cannot rival the amazing precision of W. Aldis Wright's 1899 work.

In addition to the occasional omission of deleted readings, Young in a few important instances tacitly interpolated or rearranged in his transcript sections that Milton had added or revised in the margins or on separate pages of the original. And on two occasions Young omitted drafts of complete texts that appeared in multiple states in the Trinity original. Young thereby created a more readable text, but abandoned facsimile verisimilitude. The sixth page of the Trinity Manuscript (*Fac.*, p.6) contains the first of two drafts of the so-called 'Letter to an Unknown Friend', in which Milton explains his decision not to take holy orders, and concludes with 'some of my nightward thoughts . . . made up in a Petrarchian stanza', the famous Sonnet 7 ('How soon hath time'). Page seven (*Fac.*, 7) bears a heavily-emended and expanded version of the letter that does not recopy the sonnet but leaves a space to indicate the proper place for its insertion in a final copy. Young, however, silently ignored the first draft, and wrote instead a fair copy of the second draft that (again, silently) incorporated all revisions and inserted Sonnet 7 at the appropriate place (Young, II[a]^{v}–[b]^{r}). Perhaps Young's impatience with the drafts of the 'Letter to an Unknown Friend' and his care to preserve the sonnet suggest that his interest was primarily in Milton's verse – he had titled his transcript 'Poemata Miltoni Manuscripta' – but by any estimate this is the greatest flaw in Young's copy. Young also failed to transcribe the copies of sonnets 11, 12, 13, and 14, found on two pages of a quarto gathering misbound with the Trinity folios (*Fac.*, pp.42, 43). These sonnets are not in Milton's hand, but in that of an anonymous scribe known as 'scribe Y'. Young presumably did not reproduce these scribal copies since holographs of all four (which Young does transcribe) are preserved elsewhere in the Trinity volume.

Every editor who has attempted to present a readable text of Milton's famous outlines for tragedies in the Trinity Manuscript, which include the seminal drafts of *Paradise Lost,* has been forced by basic rules of comprehensibility to rearrange the material as it exists in the original. The outlines are, after all, sketches, and therefore quickly drawn, often heavily revised, and haphazardly expanded in the margins and on facing folios. Young found himself, like the most recent editor of these outlines, 'seeking a degree of precision that Milton himself never anticipated and imposing upon them an artificial coherence alien to Milton's changing and incomplete designs'.[34] Young at least attempted to preserve the look of the Trinity outlines. The two sketches for the five-act 'Paradise Lost' (*Fac.*, p.33; Young, XX^{r}) are executed to high standards of verisimilitude both in layout and orthography, and Young also retains Milton's two-column list format for the Old Testament topics that follow (*Fac.*, p.34; Young XX^{v}–XXI^{r}). If Young's transcript is not as editorially liberal as the reading texts necessary for the purposes of the Columbia *Complete Works* or the Yale *Prose Works,* he does, however, silently move marginal additions into the body of Milton's text. For example, after the entry for the subject 'Hezechias', Milton added the note 'infra' to signal an expansion of the topic as 'Hesechia beseig'd' at the foot of the page. Young moved the addition into its 'proper' place after the original entry, and thereby obscured the evidence of Milton's revision

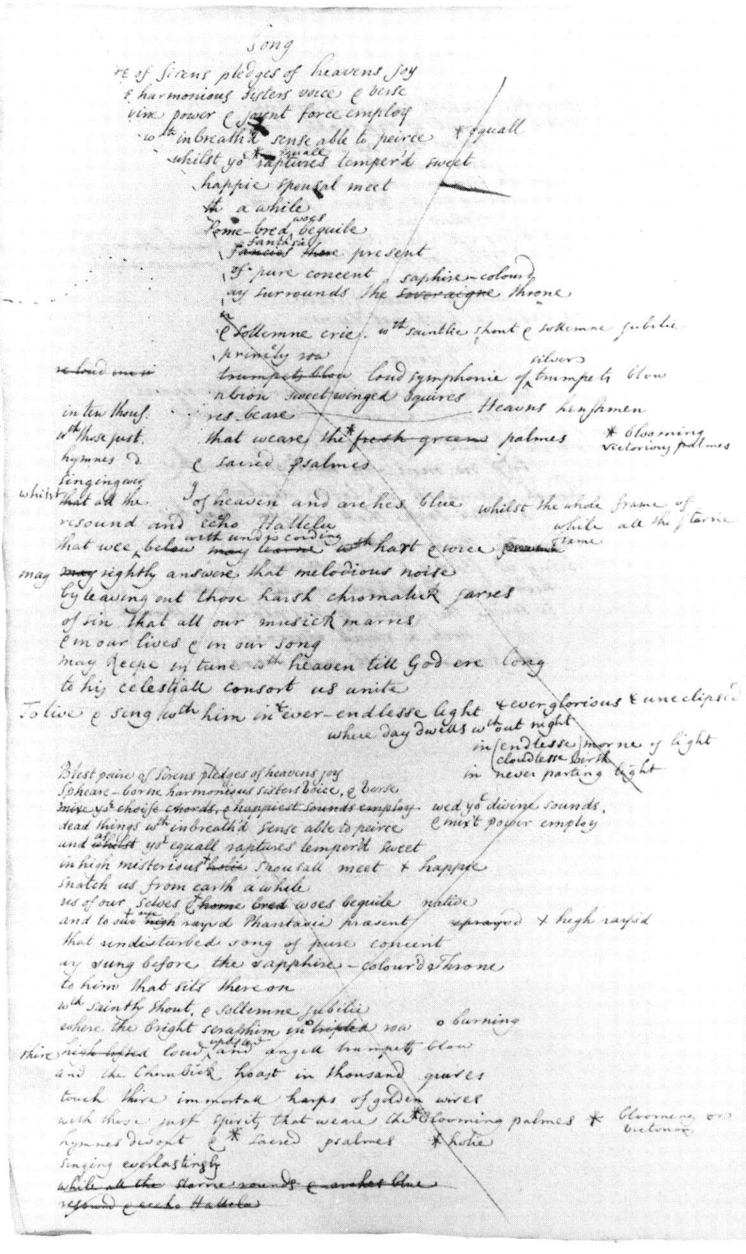
song
re of Sirens pledges of heavens joy
e harmonious sisters voice & verse
vixe power & joint force employ
wth inbreath'd sense able to peirce
whilst yor equall raptures temper'd sweet
happie spousal meet
a while
home-bred woes beguile
fantasie present
of pure concent
ay surrounds the soveraigne sapphire-colour'd throne
& sollemne crie. wth saintlie shout & sollemne jubilie
princely row
trumpets blow loud symphonie of silver trumpets blow
cherubim sweet winged squires Heavens henchmen
in ten thous. ires bease
wth those just. that weare the fresh greene palmes * blooming victorious palmes
hymnes & & sacred psalmes
singing ever
whilst that all the of heaven and arches blue whilst the whole frame of
resound and echo Hallelu while all the starrie frame
that wee below with undiscording may learne wth hart & voice
may rightly answere that melodious noise
by leaving out those harsh chromatick jarres
of sin that all our musick marres
& in our lives & in our song
may keepe in tune wth heaven till God ere long
to his celestiall consort us unite
To live & sing wth him in ever-endlesse light & ever-glorious & unclipsed
where day dwells wthout night
in endlesse morne of light
cloudlesse birth
in never parting light

Blest paire of Sirens pledges of heavens joy
Sphear-borne harmonious sisters voice, & verse
mixe yor choise chords, & happiest sounds employ wed yor divine sounds, & mixt power employ
dead things wth inbreath'd sense able to peirce
and whilst at yor equall raptures temper'd sweet
in high misterious holie spousall meet + happie
Snatch us from earth a while
us of our selves & home bred woes beguile native
and to our high rays'd Phantasie present upraysed + high raysd
that undisturbed song of pure concent
ay sung before the sapphire-colour'd throne
to him that sits thereon
wth saintly shout, & sollemne jubilie
where the bright seraphim in tripled row o burning
thire high lifted loud uplifted and angell trumpets blow
and the Cherubick hoast in thousand quires
touch thire immortall harps of golden wires
with those just spirits that weare the * blooming palmes * blooming or victorious
hymnes devout & * sacred psalmes * holie
singing everlastingly
while all the starrie rounds & arches blue
resound & eccho Hallelu

PLATE 1 *Arthur Young, Jr's transcript of Milton's first and second drafts of 'At a Solemn Musick': Princeton University Library, Coll. No. C0140 (Gen. MSS, Misc.), Box MERS–MIT, fo.1[b^v]. (Original page size 318 × 202mm). Reproduced by permission of Princeton University Library.*

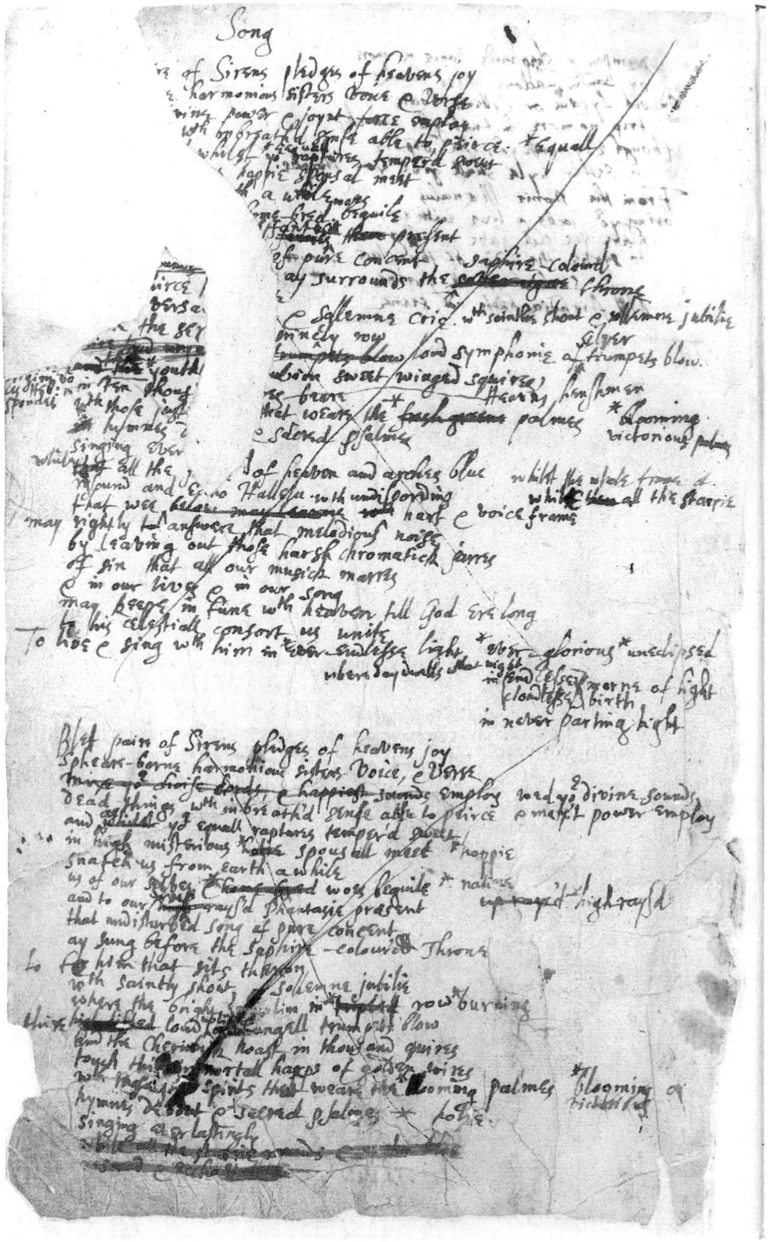

PLATE 2 *Milton's autograph first and second drafts of 'At a Solemn Musick' in the Trinity Manuscript: Cambridge, Trinity College Library, MS R. 3.4., p.4. (Original page size 301 × 187mm).*
Reproduced by permission of Trinity College Library, Cambridge.

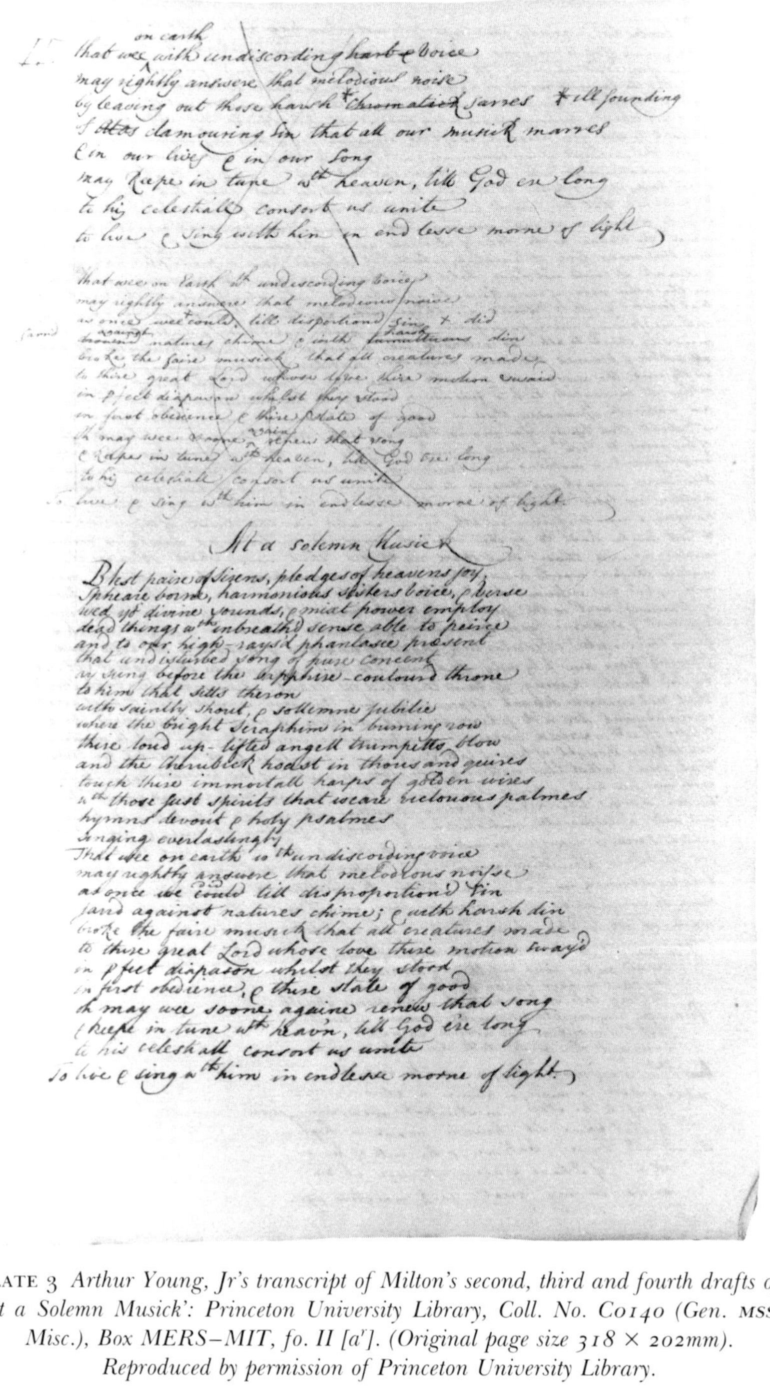
that wee on earth with undiscording harp & voice
may rightly answere that melodious noise
by leaving out those harsh chromaticke jarres & ill sounding
of sin clamouring sin that all our musick marres
& in our lives & in our song
may keepe in tune wth heaven, till God ere long
to his celestiall consort us unite
to live & sing with him in endlesse morne of light

That wee on earth wth undiscording voice
may rightly answere that melodious noise
as once wee could, till disproportion'd sin
jarr'd against natures chime & with harsh din
broke the faire musick that all creatures made
to their great Lord whose love their motion sway'd
in pfect diapason whilst they stood
in first obedience & their state of good
oh may wee soone againe renew that song
& keepe in tune wth heaven, till God ere long
to his celestiall consort us unite
to live & sing wth him in endlesse morne of light

At a solemn Musick

Blest paire of Sirens, pledges of heavens joy,
Sphear borne, harmonious sisters voice, & verse
wed yor divine sounds, & mixt power employ
dead things wth inbreath'd sense able to peirce
and to our high-rays'd phantasie present
that undisturbed song of pure concent
ay sung before the sapphire-colour'd throne
to him that sitts theron
with saintly shout, & sollemne jubilie
where the bright Seraphim in burning row
their loud up-lifted angell trumpetts blow
and the Cherubick hoast in thousand quires
touch their immortall harps of golden wires
wth those just spirits that weare victorious palmes
hymns devout & holy psalmes
singing everlastingly;
That wee on earth wth undiscording voice
may rightly answere that melodious noise
as once we could till disproportion'd sin
jarr'd against natures chime; & with harsh din
broke the faire musick that all creatures made
to their great Lord whose love their motion sway'd
in pfect diapason whilst they stood
in first obedience, & their state of good
oh may wee soone againe renew that song
& keepe in tune wth heaven, till God ere long
to his celestiall consort us unite
To live & sing wth him in endlesse morne of light.

PLATE 3 *Arthur Young, Jr's transcript of Milton's second, third and fourth drafts of 'At a Solemn Musick': Princeton University Library, Coll. No. C0140 (Gen. MSS, Misc.), Box MERS–MIT, fo. II [a^r]. (Original page size 318 × 202mm). Reproduced by permission of Princeton University Library.*

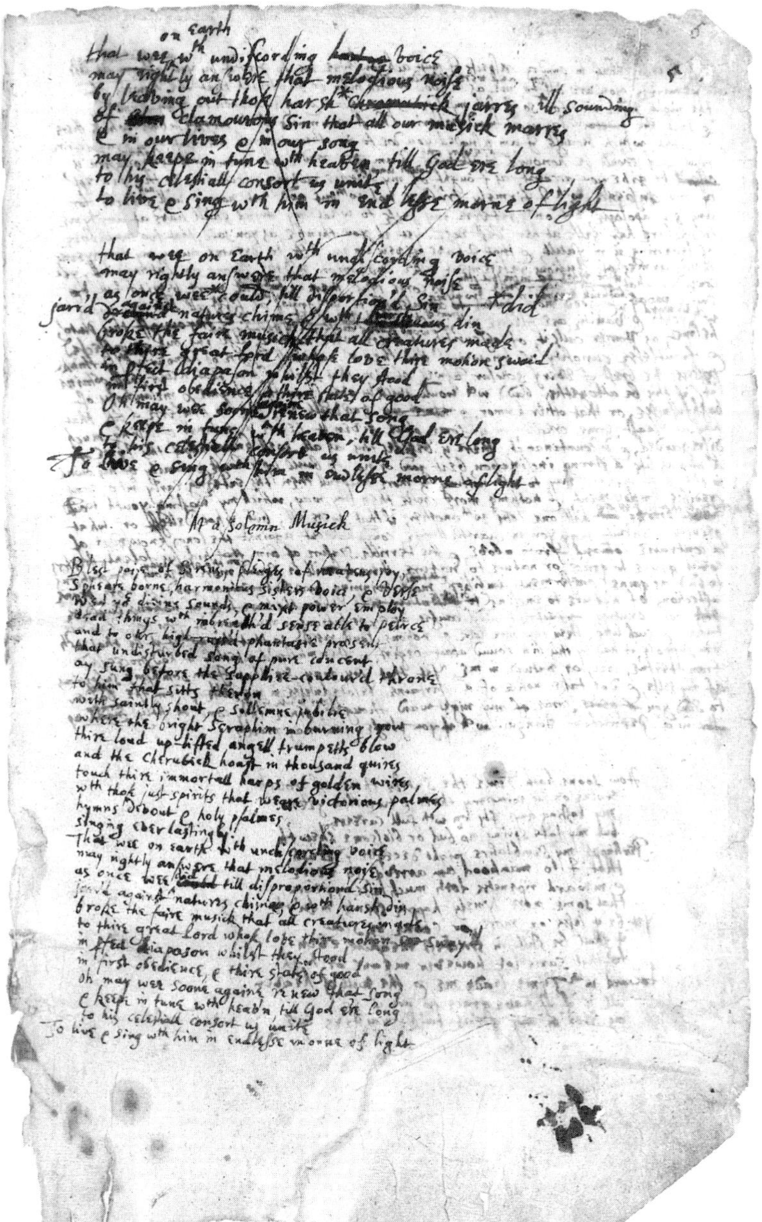

PLATE 4 *Milton's autograph second, third and fourth drafts of 'At a Solemn Musick' in the Trinity Manuscript: Cambridge, Trinity College Library,* MS *R. 3.4., p.5. (Original page size 302 × 188mm). Reproduced by permission of Trinity College Library, Cambridge.*

(*Fac.*, p.34; Young, XX^{v}).[35] The Cambridge transcriber also recorded a deceptively neat list of the topics found under the heading 'British Troy' by omitting a number of Milton's marginal references and additions (*Fac.*, pp.35–36; Young, XXI^{v}–XXII^{v}). Most noticeably, Young untangled the texts of 'Baptistes' and 'Sodom' – the former of which overran the latter due to Milton's additions – by giving each a separate page, and silently interpolating two of Milton's expansions that ran onto pages facing the main body of the text (*Fac.*, pp.36–39; Young, XXIII^{r-v}).

Young did not limit his rearrangement of portions of the Trinity Manuscript to the prose sections. In the text of 'Comus', for example, Young followed Milton's marginal instructions regarding the so-called 'pasted leaf': 'that wch follows heere is in the pasted leafe begins *poore Ladie* and first behold this &c.' (*Fac.*, p.21). Young not only copied Milton's directions (less the deleted '*poore Ladie*'), but inserted the 35 lines from the leaf between lines 671 and 707 (*Fac.*, p.20; Young, XI^{v}–XII^{r}; 'Comus', ll.672–706). Young did reproduce the arrangement of the lines as they appear on the original leaf, with lines 678–86 written as a cramped addition in the right margin. Earlier in 'Comus', Young had silently entered the sixteen lines (349–64) written on the now-missing fragment known as 'the paper over against' (from Milton's marginal note 'read the paper over against'; *Fac.*, p.15; Young, VIII^{r}).

Although certainly offenses against pure transcription, Young's rearrangement of the multiple drafts of the concluding song from 'Comus' and portions of 'Lycidas' suggest that he took a serious interest in the Trinity Manuscript as evidence of Milton's habits of composition. In the Trinity version of 'Comus', the first 34-line draft of the Spirit's epilogue – the whole of which has been crossed out – and the final expanded version appear on facing pages ('Comus', ll.976–1023; *Fac.*, pp.26–27). Young, however, brought the two versions together on a single page divided into two columns, with the preliminary draft on the left, and the final on the right, and thus allowed a close comparison, or even collation, of the two (Young, XIV^{v}).

Likewise with 'Lycidas', Young created what is essentially a parallel-text edition of the poem. In Milton's original, the first page devoted to the pastoral elegy contains four drafts of three different passages (ll.1–14, 142–151 [two drafts], and 58–63; *Fac.*, p.28). Two of these drafts are preliminary only (ll.1–14, and the first of ll.142–151) and two are final and thus keyed by Milton for insertion in the text of the whole poem that follows (*Fac.*, pp.29–32). Young did not copy these four passages as they appear on one single page, nor did he (as elsewhere) silently insert them at their appropriate places in the continuous text. Instead, he copied the continuous draft of 'Lycidas' only on *recto* pages, and left the *versos* blank for the entry of the draft passages opposite their final versions (in the cases of the preliminary ll.1–14, 142–151) and the inserted portions opposite (but not in) the positions indicated for them by Milton (Young, XVIII^{v}–XIX^{v}).

Young's 'edition' of these two portions of the Trinity Manuscript shows that he shared Dr Johnson's interest in the evidence of Milton's compositional process. Some thirty years before Young, Johnson too had viewed the Trinity Manuscript and judged it 'pleasant to see great works in their seminal state pregnant with latent possibilities of excellence', adding that there could not be 'any more delightful entertainment than to trace their gradual growth and expansion, and to observe how they are sometimes suddenly advanced by accidental hints, and sometimes slowly improved by steady meditation'.[36] Young evidently agreed.

The significance of Arthur Young, Jr's transcript of the Trinity Manuscript can be summarized under two heads: textual, and more generally, literary historical. Readings not extant in the Trinity Manuscript today but preserved by Young are confined to the following locations: 'Arcades', ll.33–45, 84–95 (*Fac.*, pp.1–2; Young, Ia^{v}–b^{r}); 'Comus', ll.349–65, the 'paper over against' (*Fac.*, p.15; Young, VIII^{r}); the lower-left margin and bottom of the page containing outlines for Biblical tragedies (*Fac.*, p.34; Young XX^{v}–XXI^{r}); and the lower-left margin of the page containing outlines for British tragedies (*Fac.*, p.36; Young, XXII^{v}). Young's transcript of the first 45 lines of 'Arcades' proves that the first leaf of the Trinity Manuscript (*Fac.*, pp.1–2), now severely mutilated in its lower half, was whole at least as late as 1792. Both the decay of the first leaf and of the leaf containing the outlines for tragedies probably attest to the amount of 'tourist traffic' that these leaves in particular had to bear – what Wright described as 'the carelessness with which it was treated when it was too freely shown to visitors.'[37] The first leaf of any work usually is, of course, the first stop for both the casual and the serious observer, and more hands have probably turned this single leaf than any other in the thin volume. The marginal fraying of the tragedy outlines on *Fac.* 34 can no doubt be explained by the fact that on the *recto* of that leaf lies what has certainly always been the greatest attraction of the whole manuscript, the first two sketches of the nascent epic, *Paradise Lost*.

But the greatest textual significance in the Young transcript is undoubtedly the copy of the lines of 'Comus' contained on the now-missing 'paper over against'. Young's copy does not restore lines otherwise lost from the Milton canon, since the passage appears in the 1637 printed edition, and since Henry Todd also transcribed the 'paper', still *in situ*, in 1799 for his 1801 edition of Milton's complete works. Todd, however, who prints the lines in his textual appendix to 'Comus', does not preserve Milton's orthography. Young's copy, then, supersedes Todd's, and provides a helpful confirmation of S. E. Sprott's reconstruction of the passage in his parallel edition of the early texts of the masque.[38]

Young's transcript is also important as much for the readings it proves were *not* extant in 1792 as for those that were. If we can assume that most of the damage caused by casual observers occurred in the nineteenth century – an assumption corroborated by Young's and Todd's late eighteenth-century readings – it might be suggested that the significant *lacunæ* noted by Young in 1792 were present when Charles Mason gathered the loose leaves for binding in 1736. In addition, Young's transcription indicates that the process of repairing the tattered leaves with 'crude patchings' – which the editors of the 1970 Scolar Press facsimile claim were 'effected in the nineteenth century'[39] – had actually begun in the eighteenth century. First, Young drew into his own transcription with a dotted line the largest *lacuna* found in the entire Trinity Manuscript – the finger-shaped gouge that curves downward from the top left corner of the leaf containing the first two drafts of 'At A Solemn Musick' (*see* PLATES 3–4). This significant loss, at least, cannot be blamed on the Victorians.

Proof of patching in the Georgian period is found in the text of 'Arcades' on the *verso* of the damaged first leaf (*Fac.*, p.2; Young, I[b^{r}]). The 1969–70 restoration of the Trinity Manuscript discovered that Milton's marginal addition of two lines had been covered by one of the 'crude patches'. The patch is clearly visible in the 1899 Wright facsimile (p.2), where it obscures the bracketed addition of two lines beginning '*though* [ ]/*yet we* [ ]'. The complete lines uncovered in 1969 read '*though [Syr]inx yor Pans mistresse were / yet we[ll m]ight Syrinx wait on her*' ('Arcades', ll.106–7; *Fac.*, p.II and 2). Young, however, only saw the following: '*though Spring yor* [ ]/*yet well might* [ ]'. Although not as extensive as the one removed in 1969, a patch did cover half of the two lines when Young copied them in 1792.

Finally, it has been nearly twenty-five years since William Riley Parker pointed to modern scholars' surprising neglect of Milton's eighteenth-century bibliography. To date, that gap in scholarship has not been filled.[40] In addition to providing textual scholars of Milton with a valuable new text to be collated and compared with existing ones, Young's 1792 transcript of the Trinity Manuscript holds great importance for literary historians of the eighteenth century as yet another piece of evidence of the Georgian fascination with Milton. That fascination played itself out in the century not only in terms of poetic influence, but also in efforts to identify and analyze Milton's palaeography, to establish reliable copy-texts, and to produce complete, definitive editions of his works. Young's transcript provides further proof of the vigour of Georgian Milton studies.

APPENDIX I

A summary of the contents of Arthur Young, Jr's Transcript of the Trinity Manuscript, Princeton University Library Coll. No. C0140 (Gen. MSS, Misc.), Box 'MERS – MIT', showing verse line numbers keyed to the Columbia edition of Milton's works, page numbers for the corresponding pages of the 1970 Scolar Press *Facsimile* of the original Trinity Manuscript, and noting Arthur Young's marginalia and variations on the ordering of texts as found in the Trinity Manuscript.

[Ai^{r}]	Arthur Young's title page: POEMATA|MILTONI|MANV=SCRIPTA|Copied from the|Originals by|Arthur Young|of|Trinity College|Cambridge|1792
[Ai^{v}]	Latin inscription from TM title page (*Fac.*, p.I); Young's signature and date, '(Transcrib'd October.5.1792) by Arthur Young. of Trinity Coll–'.
I[a^{r}]	'Arcades', ll.1–34. (*Fac.* p.1)
I[a^{v}]	'Arcades', ll.35–83. (*Fac.* pp.1–2)
I[b^{r}]	'Arcades', ll.84–109. (*Fac.* pp.2–3)
I[b^{v}]	'At a Solemn Musick', draft one, ll.1–28; draft two, ll.1–16. (*Fac.* p.4)
II[a^{r}]	'At a Solemn Musick', draft two, ll.17–28; draft three, ll.17–28; draft four, ll.1–28. (*Fac.* p.5)
II[a^{v}]	Letter to an Unknown Friend, draft two (*Fac.*, p.7), with Sonnet 7. Young omits draft one of the Letter (*Fac.*, p.6), except that he supplies the text of Sonnet 7 from draft one which Milton did not recopy for draft two.
II[b^{r}]	Letter to an Unknown Friend, draft two, cont., omitting one sentence ('and though this were enough ... *to omit out ward cases*'); 'On Time'; 'Upon the Circumcision', ll.1–14. (*Fac.*, pp.7–8)
II[b^{v}]	'Upon the Circumcision', ll.15–28; Sonnet 8, with note 'this not Miltons writing'; Sonnet 9. (*Fac.*, pp.8–9)
III^{r}	Sonnet 10. (*Fac.*, p.9)
III^{v}	*blank* (Trinity MS has 3 blank pages; *cf. Fac.* between pp.9–10)
IV^{r}	'Comus', ll.1–25. (*Fac.*, p.10)
IV^{v}	'Comus', ll.26–71. (*Fac.*, pp.10–11)

V^{r}	'Comus', ll.72–114. (*Fac.*, pp.11–12)
V^{v}	'Comus', ll.115–159. (*Fac.*, p.12)
VI^{r}	'Comus', ll.160–205. (*Fac.*, pp.12–13)
VI^{v}	'Comus', ll.206–244. (*Fac.*, pp.13–14)
VII^{r}	'Comus', ll.245–290. (*Fac.*, p.14)
VII^{v}	'Comus', ll.291–334. (*Fac.*, pp.14–15)
VIII^{r}	'Comus', ll.335–374 (*Fac.*, pp.15–16; ll.350–365 are supplied from the now-missing 'paper over against').
VIII^{v}	'Comus', ll.375–412. (*Fac.*, p.16)
IX^{r}	'Comus', ll.413–457. (*Fac.*, pp.16–17)
IX^{v}	'Comus', ll.458–497. (*Fac.*, pp.17–18)
X^{r}	'Comus', ll.498–546. (*Fac.*, p.18)
X^{v}	'Comus', ll.547–593. (*Fac.*, pp.18–19)
XI^{r}	'Comus', ll.594–643. (*Fac.*, pp.19, 21)
XI^{v}	'Comus', ll.644–698. (*Fac.*, pp.21, 20)
XII^{r}	'Comus', ll.699–750 (*Fac.*, p.21; *NB*: ll.671–703 are transcribed from the so-called 'pastéd leaf', *i.e. Fac.*, p.20).
XII^{v}	'Comus', ll.751–778 (Young does not transcribe the heavily-struck 25 lines deciphered by Wright, *Fac.*, p.22), 805–820. (*Fac.*, pp.22–23)
XIII^{r}	'Comus', ll.821–857. (*Fac.*, p.23)
XIII^{v}	'Comus', ll.858–915. (*Fac.*, pp.23–24)
XIV^{r}	'Comus', ll.916–958. (*Fac.*, pp.24–25)
XIV^{v}	'Comus', ll.959–974 (*Fac.*, p.25); then, in parallel columns, the draft and final version of the Spirit's epilogue-song. In left column, draft one (34 lines) is faced on the right by the first 34 lines of the second draft (ll.975–1009). In TM these two versions stand on facing pages (*Fac.*, pp.26–27).
XV^{r}	'Comus', ll.1010–1022. (*Fac.*, p.27)
XV^{v}	Lycidas', ll.1–14 (draft one, *Fac.*, p.28), positioned opposite same lines on facing page.
XVI^{r}	'Lycidas', ll.1–48. (*Fac.*, p.29)
XVI^{v}	'Lycidas', ll.58–63 (draft one, *Fac.*, p.28), positioned opposite same lines in draft on facing page.
XVII^{r}	'Lycidas', ll.49–93. (*Fac.*, pp.29–30)
XVII^{v}	*blank*
XVIII^{r}	'Lycidas', ll.94–138. (*Fac.*, pp.30–31)
XVIII^{v}	'Lycidas', ll.142–151 (draft one), 142–151 (draft two). In TM, these two drafts stood on the same page (*Fac.*, p.28) with draft one of ll.1–14 (*Fac.*, p.28; Young XV^{v}). Young has moved the drafts of ll.142–151 to stand facing the final version on his XIX^{r} (*Fac.*, p.31), where appears Milton's marginal note for the passage's insertion ('Bring the rathe &c.').
XIX^{r}	'Lycidas', ll.139–141, 151–186. (*Fac.*, pp.31–32)
XIX^{v}	'Lycidas', ll.187–193. (*Fac.*, p.32)
XX^{r}	Three character outlines for 'Paradise Lost'. (*Fac.*, p.33)
XX^{v}	Third outline for 'Paradise Lost', concl. (*Fac.*, p.33). Outlines for

tragedies on Old Testament themes (in two columns, as in TM, *Fac.*, p.34, from 'The Deluge' through 'Moabitides'.)

XXI^{r} Outlines for tragedies on Old Testament themes, cont. in two columns, from 'Achan' through 'Ahab' (*Fac.*, p.34).

XXI^{v} Outlines for tragedies from British history, numbers 1–16 (*Fac.*, p.35).

XXII^{r} Outlines for tragedies from British history, numbers 17–26 (*Fac.*, pp.35–36).

XXII^{v} Outlines for tragedies from British history, numbers 27–33 (*Fac.*, p.36). Young silently omits the prose fragment found at the bottom right of the final page of British subjects, and adds it instead to the text of 'Sodom' (Young XXIII^{v}).

XXIII^{r} Prose outlines for 'Abram from Morea' and 'Baptistes' (*Fac.*, p.37).

XXIII^{v} Prose outline for 'Sodom' (*Fac.*, pp.37–38).

XXIV[a] New Testament subjects, prose outline for 'Adam unparadiz'd' (*Fac.*, p.38).

XXIV[b] Prose outlines for 'Scotch stories', 'Moabitides of Phineas', and 'Christus patiens' (*Fac.*, p.39). In TM (*Fac.*, p.39) two passages are continued from the facing page (*Fac.*, p.38). Young silently removes these passages to their indicated places at the conclusion of 'Sodom' (Young XXIII^{v}) and the foot of 'Adam unparadiz'd' (Young XXIV^{r}).

XXIV[c] Sonnet 13 (two drafts); Sonnet 11, ll.1–6 (*Fac.*, p.40).

XXIV[d] Sonnet 11, ll.7–14; Sonnet 14 (two drafts) (*Fac.*, pp.40–41).

XXV^{r} Sonnet 12, with note 'The alterations in the two following, are ^not^ written in Miltons hand *and* they corrected [*sic*] in another. AY.'; Sonnet 15; Sonnet 16, ll.1–6, with the note 'This not *in* Miltons hand writing. AY.' (*Fac.*, p.44). *NB:* Young silently omits the four sonnets (nos. 11, 12, 13, 14) copied in the hand of the so-called 'scribe Y' on page 2 of TM's apparently misbound quarto gathering (*Fac.*, pp.43, 42).

XXV^{v} Sonnet 16, ll. 7–14; Sonnet 17, with the note 'To appearance the same hand as preceding.' (*Fac.*, pp.44–45).

[XXVI]^{r} 'On the forcers of Conscience' (Young does not transcribe the overstruck direction '*to come in as is directed in the leafe before*'); Sonnet 21, ll.5–14, with note 'diff. hand. fro preced. to app.'; Sonnet 22, ll.1–4 (*Fac.*, pp.45–46).

[XXVI]^{v} Sonnet 22, ll.5–14; Sonnet 23 (*Fac.*, pp.46–47); and the title 'On the new forcers of Conscience und[er] ye long Parlament' which is not used here or elsewhere in TM (*cf. Fac.*, p.45; Young, [XXVI]^{r}).

APPENDIX II

Arthur Young, Jr's transcript of 'Comus', lines 350–365, from the so-called 'paper over against' (Young, VIII[r]).

> *-------------------------of innumerous bowes
> but o that haplesse virgin our lost sister
> where may she wander now, whether betake her
> from the chill dew amoungst rude burrs & thistles?
> phapps some cold banke is her boulster now
> or gainst the rugged bark of some broad elme
> Leans her unpillow'd head fraught wth sad fears.
> what if in wild amazment & affright
> or while wee speake within the direfull graspe
> of savage hunger, or of savage heat?
> 1 Brother. peace brother, be not over exquisite
> to cast the fashion of uncertaine evills
> for grant they be so; while they rest unknowne
> what need a man forestall *the* his date of greife
> and ran to meet what he would most avoid.
> or if they be but false alarms of feare
> how bitter is *this* such selfe delusion
> I doe not thinke my sister &c

NOTES

This essay owes its existence – but none of its weaknesses – to the collegial charity of Professor Emeritus Maurice Kelley and Professor Thomas P. Roche, Jr.

1 For a full discussion of the manuscript's history, *see* the introduction to W. Aldis Wright's *Facsimile of the Manuscript of Milton's Minor Poems, Preserved in the Library of Trinity College, Cambridge* (Cambridge, 1899). A helpful summary of the MS's contents, keyed to the standard Columbia edition of Milton's works, is found in John T. Shawcross's *Milton: A Bibliography for the Years 1624–1700* (Binghamton, N.Y., 1984), pp.7–9.

2 Samuel Leigh Sotheby's *Ramblings in the Elucidation of the Autograph of Milton* (London, 1861) contains the first photo-facsimiles of pages from the Trinity Manuscript. Wright's facsimile has been superseded by that of the Scolar Press (1970), which retains Wright's transcription but provides new photographs of the manuscript taken after its careful restoration in 1969–70. Unless otherwise noted, all subsequent references to the Trinity Manuscript will be to the Scolar Press facsimile, abbreviated *Fac.* Note that page numbers refer to those of the transcript, not the manuscript.

3 Princeton University Library Coll. No. C0140 (Gen. MSS, Misc.), Box 'MERS – MIT', hereafter 'Young'. Dr Beal has drawn my attention to the use of the Trinity Manuscript by the eighteenth-century antiquarian Francis Peck. Peck, in his own annotated manuscript collection of Milton's verse now in the British Library (Additional MS 28637), frequently cites variant readings from the Trinity MS,

especially in his notes on the sonnets, but, like the eighteenth-century editors of Milton, makes no attempt at facsimile transcription from the Trinity text.

4 All biographical information, unless otherwise noted, is taken from the *Dictionary of National Biography*.

5 John G. Gazley, *The Life of Arthur Young, 1741–1820* (Philadelphia, 1973), p.vii.

6 Gazley, *Life*, p.147.

7 BL Add. MS 35126, f.199; quoted in Gazley, *Life*, p.147. In the same letter, Valpy laments 'the unaccountable loss of your manuscript poems.' Early biographers also attribute four novels from the 1760s and 1770s to Young, Sr. The *DNB* lists them as *The Fair American, Sir Charles Beaufort, Lucy Watson,* and *Julia Benson, or the Innocent Sufferer.* For their attribution to Young, *see* Gazley, *Life*, pp.10–11.

8 Valpy to Young, Sr, March, 1785, in Arthur Young, *The Autobiography of Arthur Young*, ed. M. Betham-Edwards (London, 1898), p.133.

9 For Frances Burney's lively account of her weekend at Bradfield Hall, where she also met and received the compliments of the *emigré* Duc de la Rochefoucauld-Liancourt, *see The Journals and Letters of Fanny Burney*, ed. Joyce Hemlow, vol. I (Oxford, 1972), pp.231–48.

10 *The Eton College Register, 1753–1790*, ed. Richard Arthur Austen-Leigh (Eton, 1921), p.582.

11 Thomas Harwood, *Alumni Etonenses . . . to the Year 1797* (Birmingham, 1797), pp.96–97.

12 Young, *Autobiography*, pp.142–43.

13 W. W. Rouse Ball and J. A. Venn, *Admissions to Trinity College Cambridge, Vol. III, 1702–1800* (London, 1911), p.315.

14 Gazley, *Life*, p.244.

15 BL Add. MS 35126, ff.468–69. Quoted in Gazley, *Life*, p.244.

16 BL Add. MS 35126, ff.478–79. Quoted in Gazley, *Life*, p.245.

17 John G. Gazley, 'The Reverend Arthur Young, 1769–1827: Traveller in Russia and Farmer in the Crimea', *Bulletin of the John Rylands Library*, 38 (pp.360–405), p.361. D. J. McKitterick has suggested to me that Young probably won the Hooper declamation cup, which still exists as a college prize.

18 Capel Lofft, a radical Whig, differed – often in public and in print – with Arthur Young, Sr, on almost every political issue of the day. The two men, however, maintained an amicable social relationship, with Lofft contributing to Young's *Annals*, and even opening his home, Troston Hall, to Young's daughter during her last illness. *See* Gazley, *Life*, pp.148–50, 158, 371–72.

19 Capel Lofft, ed., *Paradise Lost* (Bury St Edmund's, 1792), p.i. For his edition, Lofft collated those of 1667 and 1672.

20 Capel's edition of Shakespeare, like his nephew's of Milton, was based on a careful collation of early editions, and appeared in ten volumes in 1768, with the three-volume *Notes and Various Readings* following posthumously in 1783.

21 Lofft, ed., p.xxvii.

22 For a description of the manuscript transcript *see* W. W. Greg, *Catalogue of the Books Presented by Edward Capell to the Library of Trinity College* (Cambridge, 1903), p.165. Not insignificantly, Capel dedicated his projected edition to Dr Zachary Pearce, Bishop of Rochester (1690–1774), another Trinity alumnus and Fellow, who wrote a sustained critique of Bentley's infamous 1732 edition of Milton, which he published in 1733 as *A Review of the Text of the Twelve Books of Milton's* Paradise Lost *in which the Chief of Dr. Bentley's Emendations are Considered.*'

23 Gazley, 'Reverend Arthur Young', pp.362–4.

24 ibid., pp.373, 402.

25 Each sheet bears the same watermark: on the right half a Britannia, similar to Heawood's nos.201–221, faced on the left by the monogram 'E & P': *see* Edward Heawood, *Watermarks Mainly of the Seventeenth and Eighteenth Centuries* (Hilversum, Holland, 1940).

26 Any foliation supplied by me is contained in square brackets [ ].

27 The lines reproduced on the card are: the inscription, first line, and initials ('I.M.') from the first draft of Sonnet XIII (*Fac.*, p.43); 'Comus', l.507 (*Fac.*, p.18); 'Arcades', ll.17, 14 (*Fac.*, p.1); the title, date and first line and a half from the second draft of 'Lycidas' (*Fac.*, p.29); followed by the same line and a half from the first draft (*Fac.*, p.28); the title of Sonnet 14 (*Fac.*, p.41), 'Comus', l.14 (*Fac.*, p.10); and Sonnet XV, ll.7–8 (*Fac.*, p.44).

28 Young's most outstanding gaffes occur in his copy of the (admittedly tangled) outlines for tragedies, where, for example, Milton's 'Gideon Idoloclastes' (*Fac.*, p.34) becomes 'Gideon Holoclastes' (Young, XXI^r), and the 'counselers 2.' in the sketch for 'Dinah' (*Fac.*, p.34) appear as the garbled 'tounsdaz 2.' (Young, XX^v).

29 Sotheby's sale catalogue, 19 July 1990, lot 11.

30 'Comus', l.332; *Fac.*, p.15, Young, VII^v. I follow Wright's practice of italicizing deleted readings.

31 'Comus', l.254 (*Fac.*, p.14).

32 Young, VII^r.

33 *Fac.*, p.22; Young XII^v. The struck lines appear elsewhere as ll.672–77, 662–664, and much altered as ll.692–702, plus four lines not used elsewhere. *See* the note on these lines in the Columbia *Works*, vol.1, pt.2, pp.553–54.

34 John Steadman, 'Milton's Outlines for Tragedies', in *Complete Prose Works of John Milton*, 8 vols. (New Haven, 1982), vol. VIII (ed. Maurice Kelley), p.541.

35 It should be noted, however, that Young does not move the expanded outline for 'Moabitides or Phineas' (*Fac.*, p.39) to stand after its first mention (*Fac.*, p.34), but leaves it in its original position after the 'Scotch stories' (Young, XXIV^v).

36 Samuel Johnson, *Lives of the English Poets*, 3 vols., ed. George Birkbeck Hill (Oxford, 1905), vol.I., p.124.

37 Wright, p.2.

38 S. E. Sprott, ed., *A Maske: The Earlier Versions* (Toronto, 1973), p.94. Professor Sprott bases his reconstructed text on the edition of 1637 'according to Milton's probable spelling and punctuation in 1637' (p.11).

39 *Fac.*, pp.I–II. The introduction is unsigned.

40 William Riley Parker, *Milton, A Biography*, 2 vols. (Oxford, 1968), vol.2, p.1199. John Shawcross's bibliographic work is a major exception. His bibliography of early Milton texts, *op. cit.*, brings us to the threshold of the century. His *Milton 1732–1801, The Critical Heritage* (London and Boston, 1972) provides an invaluable anthology of primary texts in eighteenth-century Milton criticism and, in its introduction (pp.1–39), the only systematic survey of Milton's critical fortunes in the period. For a non-bibliographic study of Milton's poetic influence in the Augustan Age, *see* Dustin Griffin, *Regaining Paradise: Milton and the Eighteenth Century* (Cambridge, 1986).

Marvell, R. F. and the Authorship of 'Blake's Victory'

ELSIE DUNCAN-JONES

I

In 1990 Margarita Stocker and Timothy Raylor reported the discovery of 'a new Marvell manuscript' among the papers of Samuel Hartlib, now at the University of Sheffield.[1] The manuscript, which they reproduce, is a version, though with many minor differences and thirty-six lines omitted, of the poem printed in Marvell's *Miscellaneous Poems* (1681) under the title '*On the Victory obtained by* Blake *over the* Spaniards, *in the Bay of Sanctacruze, in the Island of* Teneriff. 1657'.[2] The title in the Hartlib manuscript is 'To his HIGHNESSE. In his late Victory in the Bay of Santa Cruz, in the Island of Tenarif'.

The purpose of the present article is to report the existence of another manuscript of this poem with much the same title as the Hartlib (which from now on I call *H*), namely, 'To his Hignesse On his late Victory in the Bay of Sancta Cruze in the Island of Tenariff 57'.[3] (The '7' seems to have been corrected from '8'). This version of the poem is close to, though not identical with *H* and shorter by two lines. A feature which prevents me from calling it another new Marvell manuscript is that it is signed at the end with the initials 'R. F.' after the date 'July 9 57'. The R. F. manuscript (which I shall refer to as *P*) is to be found at Petworth among papers once belonging to Roger Boyle, Baron Broghill and first Earl of Orrery (1621–76): it is now the property of Lord Leconfield who has kindly given me permission to describe and reproduce it. I am also much indebted to Dr Alison McCann of the West Sussex Record Office at Chichester, curator of the Petworth archive. Above all I acknowledge my debt to the expertise of my friend Hilton Kelliher of the British Library who inspected the manuscript and gave me his findings.

I was led to R. F.'s manuscript by a more or less casual reading of the biography of *Roger Boyle, First Earl of Orrery* by Kathleen M. Lynch.[4] On page 90 Miss Lynch mentions that in 1657 Orrery (then Lord Broghill) wrote 'Verses to his Highness on his late Victory in the Bay of Sancta Cruze in the island of Teneriff'. In these verses, says Miss Lynch, he praised 'undaunted Blake' and Cromwell's 'resistless genius'. Recognising these phrases as occurring in the poem attributed to Marvell and investigating further I found that the poem ascribed by Miss Lynch to Broghill-Orrery is indeed in substance that printed in Marvell's *Miscellaneous Poems*, 1681, but in a version shorter by thirty-eight lines and with a title near to that of the manuscript found in 1990 at Sheffield. Miss Lynch must of course have seen the manuscript at Petworth but overlooked the fact that it is signed, not as she perhaps took it, R. B., for Roger Boyle, but R. F. The F. is unmistakable. She also somehow missed the connection with Marvell. I have Hilton Kelliher's authority for saying that the handwriting of this version is certainly not Orrery's.[5] Nor, in my judgment, dissenting from Miss Lynch, is the style in the least like his.

The text of this version occupies the first five pages of four unfoliated and unpaginated leaves, measuring approximately 288 × 198mm, that were formed when one bifolium was set inside another. The rest of the manuscript is blank, except for a much later endorsement on the verso of the final leaf, reading 'Verses to His Highness on Victory, Sancta Cruz Island of Teneriffe'. The paper carries a watermark consisting of three circles arranged in a column and surmounted by a crown, the middle circle incorporating the letters 'A O' and the top one a cross. In height the mark measures 80mm and the crown is 20mm at its widest point.[6] The chain-lines are spaced at some 37mm. Pin-holes are visible toward the centre folds, where the leaves had at one time been secured. Numerous folds and some discolouration in the document show that it has been carried as a packet.

The hand is a sprawling and ill-controlled one with a rather variable tendency to slope to the right. The only catchwords ('A choyce which': *P*, line 105) occur on the penultimate page, but there are none at all to link the two bifolia. This has less to do with the fact that the copying runs to the very foot of the page than that the transcriber realised at this point that four pages would be insufficient to complete the text, and so was obliged to add the inner bifolium. After this he was able to reduce the hitherto rather excessive number of lines per page. The text itself, which is written in a light brown ink, shows clear signs of having been reviewed after the initial copying. In particular, the punctuation at the ends of the lines on the first page seems to have been added later. Apparently the same darker shade

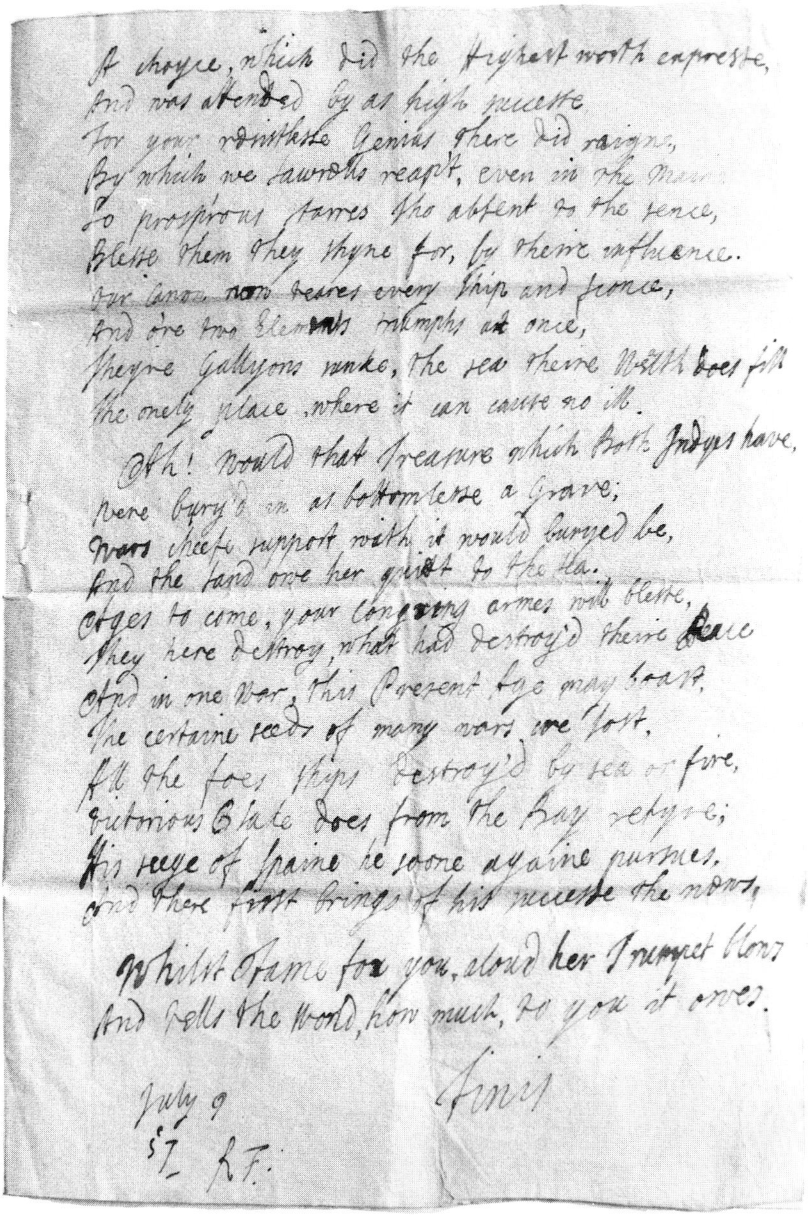
A choyce, which did the highest worth expresse,
And was attended by as high successe
For your resistlesse Genius there did raygne,
By which we laurells reap't, even in the Maine
So prosperous starres tho absent to the sence,
Blesse them they shyne for, by theire influence.
Our Canon now teares every Ship and Sconce,
And ore two Elements triumphs at once,
Theyre Gallyons sinke, the sea theire Wealth does fill
The onely place, where it can cause no ill.

Ah! would that Treasure which both Indyes have,
were bury'd in as bottomlesse a Grave;
Wars cheefe support with it would buryed be,
And the Land owe her quiet to the Sea.
Ages to come, your Conquering armes will blesse,
They here destroy, what had destroy'd theire Peace
And in one War, this Present Age may boast,
The certaine seeds of many wars are lost.
All the foes Ships destroy'd by sea or fire,
Victorious Blake does from the Bay retyre;
His seege of Spaine he soone againe pursues,
And there first brings of his successe the news,

Whilst Fame for you, aloud her Trumpet blows
And tells the World, how much, to you it owes.

Finis

July 9
57 R.F.

PLATE 1 *The last page of 'Blake's Victory': Petworth House Archives, Orrery Papers 13187. (Original page size 288 × 198mm). Reproduced by permission of Lord Leconfield.*

of ink used here also occurs in two over-inked phrases occurring in the middle of the final page, and in the final lines of the poem. The implication seems to be that this is a scribal fair-copy, though if so the scribe was not a very professional one, being content at the paragraph beginning 'The Peeks proud height' (*P*, line 41), towards the foot of the second page, with no fewer than two false starts, each given a separate line and each crudely deleted.

It may be wondered why *P* had lain so long unnoticed. It has of course been duly catalogued by the Historical Manuscripts Commission which gives the first and last lines of the poem.[7] The reason why it was not long ago linked with the poem in Marvell's *Miscellaneous Poems* must be that H.M.C. prints the signature 'R. F.', and that the first line quoted is not the first line of *1681*, 'Now does *Spains* Fleet her spatious wings unfold'. *P* has the same first line as *H*, 'The Spaniards fleet from the Havanna now', not known before the appearance of the important Stocker-Raylor article.

There are subsidiary points of some interest that I shall deal with later, but the great interest of the manuscript at Petworth is that it is signed with initials other than 'A. M.'. This may, I hope, turn the scales against the notion that this often crude and markedly unskilful poem must be ascribed to Marvell. In the centuries during which the poem has been before the public I cannot find that any editor or biographer of Marvell has expressed admiration of it, except the adoring and often uncritical Grosart who calls it 'a great celebration'.[8] Augustine Birrell in his book on Marvell in the English Men of Letters series found the lines 'not worthy of so glorious an occasion'.[9] Pierre Legouis in his *André Marvell* objected to the trifling conceits, the gross flattery of Cromwell, the unrelenting denigration of Spain.[10] Much later, in his revision (1971) of Margoliouth's edition Legouis remarked that if 'Blake's Victory' were banished from the canon it would be no loss to Marvell's reputation, 'literary or moral'.[11] But he did not feel that there was enough evidence against it to disregard the authority of the Folio of 1681. Legouis would certainly have welcomed the appearance of R. F.

Even when the attribution to R. F. was unknown there was one piece of external evidence against the poem's being Marvell's. It has been removed bodily from the copy of *Miscellaneous Poems* acquired in 1946 by the Bodleian Library, believed to have belonged to Marvell's relatives, the Popples; and this even though its removal meant that five stanzas of 'Upon Appleton House' had to be replaced by a handwritten copy.[12] Critics differ about the authority of the corrections and alterations in this volume. Legouis was sceptical, as were Hugh MacDonald and Margoliouth.[13] Doubts are also expressed by Thomas Clayton and Warren Chernaik.[14] It often strikes one that while some undoubted errors have been corrected others of equal or greater importance are left unchanged. For instance, in line 23 of 'The Garden', 'Fair Trees! Where s'eer you barkes I wound', 'where s'eer' is heavily corrected to 'where s'ere'; but 'you' for 'your' remains uncorrected.[15] I cannot agree with Professor Lord that the volume has been 'painstakingly prepared'.[16] Some poems seem to have been tinkered with capriciously, or merely to bring them into line with later usages. Indeed, some alterations seem to have been made without full understanding. I would instance the alterations made to '*Hortus*', the substitution of 'seeming' for 'Teeming' in line 35 of 'Eyes and Tears' and, most striking because it is an alteration in a poem published in Marvell's life-time and presumably seen by him through the press, the changing of 'and' to 'that' in line 25 of Marvell's commendatory poem to the second edition (1674) of *Paradise Lost*.[17] As the line stands in *1674* it provides an answer to two problems stated earlier in the poem. First, Marvell had doubts whether the materials for *Paradise Lost* could be dealt with satisfactorily; second, he had feared that somebody else (of course Dryden is here intended) might meddle with Milton's poem and make a play of it. The answer to the first is 'But I am now convinc'd'; to the second, 'and none will dare / Within thy Labours to pretend a Share'. The alteration of 'and' to 'that' makes the line an answer to one problem only – a change that could surely not be authorial.

Whatever their reason for doing so, in removing 'Blake's Victory' from the volume of Marvell's poems the owner or owners of the Popple volume were certainly right. G. de F. Lord in his 1968 edition prints 'Blake's Victory' among poems of doubtful authenticity because of its absence from the Bodleian volume.[18] Annabel Patterson in *Marvell and the Civic Crown* boldly calls the poem 'a piece of unquestioning and uninteresting propaganda' and remarks that if Marvell really wrote this poem he must have changed his mind regarding the question of Cromwell's accepting the crown 'and on the nature of political commentary'.[19] I would add that the unlikeness that she discerns between 'Blake's Victory' and Marvell's genuine work is particularly striking if 'Blake's Victory' is compared with the poem Marvell published two years earlier, *The First Anniversary of the Government under his Highness the Lord Protector*.[20] There is a particular crudity in R. F.'s choosing to address his poem directly to the Protector himself so that his flatteries are uttered as it were to the Protector's face. Marvell in *The First Anniversary* is so conscious of the offensiveness of exaggerated praise that at one point he employs the device of imagining that Cromwell is dead, that he had really perished in the carriage accident of 1654:

> So with more Modesty we may be True,
> And speak as of the Dead the Praises due:
> (lines 187–188)

Again, while R. F. in the Folio version seems to wish that Cromwell should accept the title of King:

> The best of Lands should have the best of Kings.
> (line 40)

Marvell two years earlier had made Cromwell's accepting the title of King something that his enemies would rejoice in:

> O could I once him with our Title see,
> So should I hope yet he might Dye as wee.
> (*The First Anniversary*, lines 391–392)

These are particular points. When the shelter of Marvell's name is removed it is easy to see that the quality of mind is most certainly not Marvell's and the quality of the versification is often not even that of a practised poet. Could the author of *The First Anniversary* have been guilty of such lines as

> The Air was soon after the fight begun,
> Far more enflam'd by it, then by the Sun.
> (*F*, lines 121–22)

or

> That Bay they enter, which unto them owes,
> The noblest wreaths, that Victory bestows.
> (*F*, lines 115–16)

or

> But this stupendious Prospect did not neer,
> Make them admire, so much as they did fear.
> (*F*, lines 79–80)

Most strikingly, would Marvell have been capable of calling the news of Blake's victory 'The saddest news that ere to *Spain* was brought' (line 165)? To say this is to forget the news of the defeat of the Armada, less than seventy years earlier. Blake's victory was certainly an extraordinary one. Clarendon in his *History of the Rebellion* does full justice to this feat of Cromwell's navy: 'The whole action was so miraculous that all men who knew the place concluded that no sober men, with what courage soever endued, would ever undertake it; and they could hardly persuade themselves to believe what they had done'.[21] But in terms of the damage to Spain, although the loss of six great galleons, ten smaller ships and very many lives, so close to a heavily fortified shore, must have been a bitter blow, it could hardly compare with the news of the defeat of the Armada, in the memorable year of 'Eighty-eight'. What was R. F. thinking of, or failing to think of, when he wrote this line? To do him justice he removed it from both the shorter versions.

Stocker and Raylor assume that the Hartlib text is earlier than *1681*. I am sorry to dissent. I am convinced that *1681* is the earliest of the three texts of the poem we now have. (I leave out of consideration the first published text of the poem, that in Bulteel's collection of 1674, which has been collated with *1681* by Margoliouth and which allowing for its removing all references to Cromwell seems to be relying on the same text as *1681*.[22]) And I believe that the latest text of the three is R. F.'s, dated 9 July 1657.

The most striking difference between *1681* and the other two is that both of these omit the twenty-four lines in praise of the Canary Islands (*P*, lines 25–52). This lengthy description might well have been cut as disproportionate in a poem about a naval action. But it also contains various doubtful political propositions of which R. F. might well have repented, most famously the suggestion that Cromwell should annex the Canary Islands on the perhaps not very logically impressive grounds that 'The best of lands should have the best of Kings' (line 40). The lines on the beauties of the Canaries (lines 25–38) are not the worst in the poem, though it is hardly idiomatic to make Heaven 'pour . . . Trust' (not even 'pour down trust') on them. In any case it seems very unlikely that the passage should have been added after 9 July 1657, the date on *F*. Blake died early in August and any addition made then must surely have contained a reference to his death.

Unlike most of the changes I shall concern myself with, the alteration to the first line is not obviously an improvement. 'Now does *Spains* Fleet her spatious wings unfold' has a more confident air than 'The Spaniards fleet from the Havanna now' (*H*, *P*). But the later version has a little more substance, telling us where the fleet sailed from. I would suggest that the change was made partly on the grounds that the original line too much resembles the opening line of the poem the celebrated Waller had written on a naval action of Cromwell's fleet in 1656[23]:

> Now, for some ages, had the pride of Spain
> Made the sun shine on half the world in vain;

These lines were so much admired that Etherege's Dorimant, a connoisseur of poetry, is found quoting them fifteen years later, at the very beginning of *The Man of Mode*.[24] R. F. was not to know that this was to be so, but he was perhaps sufficiently indebted to Waller not to wish to risk the comparison. For instance R. F.'s phrase 'Capatious Gallions' (line 7) is borrowed from Waller. What in my judgment is R. F.'s best couplet, one of the few that would not disgrace Marvell, develops a conceit of Waller's in a poem to Henrietta Maria:[25]

> So prosperous Stars, though absent to the sence,
> Bless those they shine for, by their Influence.
> (*F*, lines 147, 148)

Waller long before had written of

> . . . . . the rich spangles that adorn the sky
> Which, though they shine for ever fixed there,
> With light and influence relieve us here.
> ('Of the Queen', lines 36–38)

Before coming to the many instances in which R. F. is, in my judgment, clearly making efforts to improve his composition I must deal with what appears to be a considerable change for the worse. In *1681* the news of the presence of Blake's fleet is said to be

> A grief, above the cure of Grapes best juice.
> (line 82)

H and *P* both alter 'Grapes' to 'Wines', clearly ridiculous. But, as can be seen from the reproduction of the Petworth MS (PLATE 1) *P* has a cross (X) marked above the first letter of 'Wines'. I believe that what R. F. intended to write was 'Vines best juice', good sense, and a variation from the 'rich Grape' of line 53. R. F.'s revisions often seem to show a wish to vary his vocabulary.

It would be tedious to compare minutely the differences between the versions of a not very good poem no longer to be accepted as Marvell's. I content myself with samples. First, as to matter of fact. As I have already said, *H* and *P* both remove the couplet most open to criticism on factual grounds

> The saddest news that ere to *Spain* was brought,
> Their rich Fleet sunk, and ours with Lawrel fraught.
> (*F*, lines 165, 166)

It is not only that R. F. here forgets about the news of the defeat of the Armada: the fleet sunk by Blake was no longer 'rich'. It was known at the time that 'all the bullion had been landed and most of the goods' by the Spaniards.[26] Another factual point: although as Clarendon says 'the slaughter on board the [Spanish] ships and on the shore was incredible' no account that I have seen suggests that there were no survivors; and it is indeed most unlikely with so much help available on a shore so near to the ships.[27] *1681* however commits itself to the statement that all the Spaniards perished:

> Never so many with one joyful cry,
> That place saluted, where they all must dye.
> (lines 69–70)

H and *P* are not so rashly specific, changing the second line to

> That place did greete where they are doom'd to dy;
> (*F*, line 38)

Again: *1681* surely exaggerates the power of seventeenth-century cannon fire when it states that

> Torn Limbs some leagues into the Island fly
> (line 133)

One of my reasons for thinking *P* later than *H* is that although *H* leaves this unchanged, *P* alters 'leagues' to 'miles', a mile being a third of a league.

It is not always possible to distinguish between the effects of a desire for stylistic improvement and a laudable desire to tone down the exaggerated emphasis that *1681* lays on the cowardice of the Spaniards. Either or both might have prompted the omission from *H* and *P* of what is perhaps *1681*'s clumsiest couplet, that in which R. F. compares the degree of the Spaniards' wonder at the height of the Peak of Teneriffe with the degree of their fear of the English fleet:

> But this stupendious Prospect did not neer,
> Make them admire, so much as they did fear.
> (lines 79–80)

In line 83 the change of 'Terrour' to 'Wonder' is a welcome indication of a desire to play down Spanish timidity. Perhaps R. F. had reflected that too much emphasis on this somewhat lessened the English achievement.

The omission of lines 59–60 is of some interest as showing, I believe, that R. F. was trying to improve his versification. The rhymes in this couplet are 'Oar' / 'more'. The rhymes in the succeeding couplet are 'War' / 'far'. 'More' in the first couplet rhymes with 'War' in the succeeding couplet; so the 'Oar' / 'more' couplet is removed.

It would be otiose to list all the small changes in vocabulary made in an effort to avoid repetition. *H*'s version of line 21 is

> So that such darkness would suppress their fear

P replaces 'suppress' by 'dispell', surely an improvement, apart from the fact that 'suppress' is used elsewhere in the poem. Again, while *1681* describes the sea as 'large, and deep' (line 154) both *H* and *P* have the more adequate 'bottomlesse'.

It is perhaps worthwhile to consider the changes R. F. makes to the final couplet, though in no version is it very impressive. *1681* has

> Whilst Fame in every place, her Trumpet blowes,
> And tells the World, how much to you it owes.
> (lines 167, 168)

H makes no change. *P* alters 'in every place' to 'for you, aloud'. My conjecture is that the author had observed that he had already used the expression 'in every place' in *H*, line 70, 'Those Forts w*hi*ch doe in every place appear', replacing the rather childish-sounding 'so high and strong' in *1681*. He might also have reflected that 'in every place' repeats the point made by 'tells the World'. However, 'for you, aloud' is no less feeble than 'in every place', perhaps feebler. Here as often in his poem R. F. lacks matter to fill up his line. In contrast it may be remembered that when Marvell alludes to the hackneyed image of Fame's trumpet he enlivens it by introducing the grotesque effect that blowing a trumpet has on a trumpeter's features:

> . . . the breathing Trees;
> Which in their modest Whispers name
> Those Acts that swell'd the Cheek of Fame.
> ('*Upon the Hill and Grove at* Bill-borow',
> (lines 62–64)

It would be strange indeed if Marvell who had dealt so delicately with the praise of Fairfax should several years later have dealt so crudely with Cromwell's.

Who was R. F.? The most famous poet of these initials writing in 1657 was of course Richard Fanshawe, whose authorship is, however, out of the question both as a devoted royalist and as an accomplished writer. The English Roman Catholic priest whom Marvell had met and satirized in Rome in 1645 has the right initials. Marvell's satire shows us Flecknoe as appallingly eager to share what Marvell considered his 'hideous verse' – he begins to recite the moment that Marvell has mounted the stairs.[28] Flecknoe himself says that in every place he cultivated the best company that was to be found.[29] In 1657 he seems to have been in England, trying to ingratiate himself with Cromwell. In 1654 he had dedicated his play *Love's Dominion* to Cromwell's favourite daughter the Lady Elizabeth Claypole. To judge from Marvell's poem, Marvell in Rome, however much he detested Flecknoe's poetry, had behaved with flawless politeness, entertaining at his table both Flecknoe and a noble but very quarrelsome young companion who had turned up by chance. Flecknoe in London in 1657 might well have sought out Marvell, both as an old friend and as one usefully close to the seats of power – an ideal recipient for Flecknoe's latest poetical endeavour. And Marvell might have preserved the manuscript as a rather dire memento of another trying occasion. It would indeed have been a striking example of what Marvell calls 'Chance's better Wit' if a longish specimen of Flecknoe's verse had been included in Marvell's *Miscellaneous Poems* and passed for centuries unchallenged.[30]

Tempting as the idea may be, I cannot believe that Flecknoe is our man. In the first place, the handwriting of *P* is certainly not Flecknoe's.[31] Flecknoe has the reputation of a bad poet and R. F. in my view is not a good one. But the feebleness of Flecknoe is quite unlike the feebleness of R. F. 'Blake's Victory' for all its flaws is too coherent, sustained and factual to have been within Flecknoe's range. Flecknoe's longest poems are still relatively short, and he is not interested in fact, even in a biography. The extraordinary little book, described by himself as 'a short-breath'd Pamphlet', that he published in 1658 called, significantly, *The Idea of his Highness Oliver later Lord Protector* is almost without factual substance. It is perhaps worth noting also that so far from thinking, as the author of 'Blake's Victory' does, that Cromwell's 'resistless genious' (*F*, line 145) could operate at long distance Flecknoe here is of the opinion that the comparative failure of Cromwell's war with Spain was due to Cromwell's absence.[32] Again, Flecknoe, who calls himself a man of peace, is most unlikely to have set about describing a naval action. Flecknoe has his own voice, though sometimes a feeble one: it is always straining after epigram and effect.

Hilton Kelliher has kindly brought to my notice several other R. F.s writing verse in the 1650s – one a translator of Martial and another the author of a pair of poems published in February 1650/1, called *Mercurius Heliconicus*, nos. 1 and 2. This second R. F.'s style is crabbed and learned. The first poem adopts a position rather like that of Marchamont Needham in his pamphlet *The Case of the Commonwealth of England* . . . (London, 1659).[33] R. F.'s thesis here is that Change is inevitable and since God

. . . modeliz'd a new
Our ancient moderation, tis but due
And requisite in us, obsequiously
To blesse the Ordinance of the most high.

The second poem, addressed to the ruler rather than the subject, advances the proposition that 'Each several he is his own Machiavel': the ruler is advised to 'sheare [his] Subject close, and bare'.[34] There are allusions to Tiberius and Galba. The couplets are very unlike those of 'Blake's Victory': this R. F. constantly makes the sense overflow from one couplet to the beginning of the next, in a manner then becoming old-fashioned. My impression is that he was an older man than the R. F. of 'Blake's Victory'; and certainly a much cleverer one. These two poems, though not very poetical, are haunting and remarkable and might figure in a discussion of Marvell's 'Horatian Ode', though hardly of 'Blake's Victory'.

One might have hoped for a clue to R. F.'s identity from the publication of 'Blake's Victory' in 1674 in the volume published by the younger John Bulteel called *A New Collection of Poems and Songs. Written by several Persons. Never Printed before*. The reissue of 1678 adds that the collection was *written by several of the great wits of our present age, as I.D. T.F. S.W. C.O. I.B. &c.* Presumably Bulteel felt that the great scoop among this very disparate lot was an unpublished poem of Dryden's to Lady Castlemaine. All one learns to our purpose from this collection is that Bulteel thought R. F.'s poem worth printing, even though he had in 1674 to take some trouble to disguise its numerous flattering references to Cromwell. On the other hand Bulteel gave the poem no very honourable place, tucking it into the end of his volume, third from the last, followed immediately by a rather improper poem translated from the French. Had R. F.'s been a distinguished name his initials might conceivably have appeared with those of, among others, John Dryden: not so. At least one of Bulteel's contributors, C. O. (Corbett Owen), was long dead when the volume appeared and R. F. may not have survived till 1674.

A subsequently famous R. F. who was probably in England from about 1655, and was extruded from the living of Godmersham in 1662, is Robert Ferguson, the plotter.[35] (Possibly Ferguson is the 'learned Scotch gentleman' mentioned in Marvell's letter to Sir Edward Harley of 3 May 1673.[36]) A poem from his hand would indeed have been a curiosity and worth preserving: but 'Blake's Victory' is not marked by either the Scotticisms or the learning that characterise Ferguson's known writings. Also it is unlikely that so devious a character would have employed the rather simple-minded plan of trying to ingratiate himself with Cromwell by giving him almost all the credit for the achievement of his seamen. The more sophisticated Waller in his naval poem of 1656 had justly observed that there was no need to give Cromwell the credit for the victories of others, he had enough of his own:

> Let the brave generals divide that bough,
> Our great Protector hath such wreaths enow;
> His conquering head has no more room for bays;
> (lines 103–5)

After considerable searches I have to confess that I have no R. F. to offer. My impression is that he was a young man. One cannot build safely on his forgetting the Armada; such slips are often unaccountable. Still it seems likely that he was young, and no very practised writer. He thought well enough of his own abilities to enter a field that at the time must have been felt to belong to the admired Waller, who had produced two poems on naval events. (This seems to have been a genre not previously practised. Apart from Deloney's ballads there seems, for instance, to be no poem of note even on the Armada earlier than Macaulay's.[37]) At the same time R. F. was modest enough to try to remove what he, or someone he consulted, perceived as faults of fact and style.

It has to be remembered that we do not know when or how Marvell acquired his copy of 'Blake's Victory'. It might have found a place among his papers at any time between 1657 and 1678. Otherwise one might build on the suitability of the three recipients of R. F.'s poem to construct a scenario of an R. F. who knows his way about the literary and political world of 1657. All three recipients, Hartlib, Broghill and Marvell, were well placed to show the poem to Cromwell if they were so minded. Marvell was at that time the least distinguished of the three; but since 1653 when he was chosen to act as tutor to the young William Dutton he had had an undoubted channel of communication with Cromwell. His letter to Cromwell of that year makes it clear that it is Cromwell who has given him his post, Cromwell who has placed him and Dutton with Oxenbridge, and it is to Cromwell that Marvell will report on 'any little particularityes' of Dutton's progress.[38] In France in the autumn of 1656 it was known that there was some talk of Dutton's marrying into Cromwell's family, for James Scudamore in the well-known letter I discovered in which he calls Marvell an Italo-Machiavellian mentions that the French call the boy *le genre du Protecteur* (the Protector's son-in-law).[39] There is no doubt that Marvell had ample access to Cromwell. I am obliged to dissent from the suggestion in Stocker's and Raylor's article that Marvell in 1657 would have needed the patronage of Hartlib. The fact that in 1654 Marvell had published his *First Anniversary of the Government under O. C.* with the government printer Thomas Newcomb is one indication that he was already well-known to the authorities. More strikingly, a comparison of Marvell's poem with the speech Cromwell made dissolving Parliament on 22 January 1654/5 suggests that Marvell had read Cromwell's speech before it was delivered or, more likely, that Cromwell had read Marvell's poem.[40]

It would have been fitting that R. F. should present Broghill with the most carefully revised copy of his poem. Son of the great Earl of Cork, brother of the famous Robert Boyle and of Milton's friend Lady Ranelagh, Broghill was himself already celebrated both as a soldier and as the author of the much admired romance *Parthenissa*. His fame as author of verse tragedies is post-Restoration, but in 1657 he was already a poet and a friend of the poets Davenant and Cowley. (Davenant in a poem addressed to Broghill in the year of Blake's victory indeed compared 'the rising prospect of your wit' to that same Peak of Teneriff so unmemorably celebrated by R. F.[41]

> The *Teneriff*, ascending to the Sky
> Lifts not so sharp a spire, nor mounts to high;

Broghill in 1657 was also one of Cromwell's intimate friends. Miss Lynch mentions that in the same month of July 1657 in which R. F. dates his poem to Broghill he stayed for some days with the Protector at Hampton Court.[42] It is hard to imagine him bothering Cromwell with 'Blake's Victory', unless R. F. had more to recommend him than his powers as a poet. Our best hope of discovering the identity of R. F. – really of interest only as it might concern Marvell – is that someone may come across another specimen of the (alas, not very distinctive) hand.

II

TO THE READER.

> These are to Certifie every Ingenious Reader,
> that all these Poems, as also the other things
> in this Book contained, are Printed according
> to exact Copies of my late dear Husband,
> under his own Hand-Writing, being found since
> his Death among his other Papers, Witness my
> Hand this 15*th* day of *October*, 1680.
> *Mary Marvell.*

The remainder of this article can be little more than a definition of ignorance. We do not know when or how 'Blake's Victory' came to be among Marvell's papers. We do not know how the compiler of the Folio came to print 'Blake's Victory' as Marvell's. We do not know with certainty who the compiler was. Mary Marvell in the short letter which, strangely, is the only piece of prefatory matter, does not say she is the compiler, though it is a natural assumption in the absence of any other name.[43] What is clear is that the presence in the volume of a poem not Marvell's invalidates the only claim she does make, namely that to her knowledge everything that it contains has been printed from copies in Marvell's handwriting. It is all but impossible to imagine circumstances that might have caused Marvell to copy out in his own hand an unrevised poem of little merit and some length.

It may be said that the prefatory letter makes another claim implicitly, viz. that its author is Marvell's widow. This claim, contrary to most recent scholars, I incline to allow. Grosart and C. H. Firth both accepted it, on the grounds that in March 1679 the Prerogative Court of Canterbury had granted her (together with a creditor, one John Green) the administration of Marvell's effects.[44] Grosart's remark 'I do not see that it was possible for "Mary Marvell" to have obtained this "administration" without satisfying the authorities that she was the widow' seems to me just. Then among the details unearthed by Professor Tupper is the telling one that in 1682, in a court of law, Mary named a date and place for the marriage, 13 May 1667, Holy Trinity, Little Minories.[45] A fact unknown to Tupper, and one perhaps therefore not given due weight, is that the church in question, being a royal peculiar, was one where valid marriages could be and were, in considerable numbers, performed clandestinely, that is without banns or licence. Since all she claimed was a clandestine marriage the objection that Marvell's friends and relations did not know of it becomes unimportant. The registers that would prove the case are at present missing: there is no reason to think that they were missing three hundred years ago. It is known that in the seventeenth century the registers, as one might expect, were carefully kept and guarded.[46]

It might be argued that the question of Mary's marital status is irrelevant to the present discussion. A housekeeper of long standing is likely to have been as well acquainted with Marvell's handwriting as any lawful wife. Yet fraud in one thing makes it easier to suspect fraud in another, though it is hard to see what purpose could have been served by deliberately printing 'Blake's Victory' as Marvell's. If, as is overwhelmingly probable, what we have here is a genuine mistake, how did it come about? Some similarity in the handwriting to that of Marvell himself? R. F.'s handwriting is not in the least like Marvell's. Or some similarity to that of a scribe employed by Marvell? There is no indication, perhaps little likelihood, that Marvell did employ one.

Was the compiler of the volume at this moment in great haste? She, he, or they must have paused for some time over the title. The original was presumably: *To his Highness the Lord Protector. . .* This has been changed so as to exclude the reference to Cromwell and to give due prominence to Blake: *On the Victory obtained by Blake. . .* (To 'obtain' a victory, which today sounds like a genteelism, is traditional English.)[47] Nothing has been done to make the poem itself more acceptable to the authorities in 1681. This is in keeping with the compiler's general treatment of the Cromwellian poems; but in this instance the reader, deprived of the knowledge that the whole poem is a direct address to the Protector, is left with a number of unexplained 'your's. Bulteel in 1674 had been at pains to suggest that the 'you' is England.[48]

Although as Annabel Patterson shrewdly shows, the poem itself is not Marvellian in matter or manner, a hurried glance might have left the compiler (particularly perhaps if he or she were no connoisseur of poetry) believing it was genuine. Marvell's authentic verse does sometimes touch on naval matters, Marvell did glory in Cromwell's naval achievements, he had indeed once mentioned Blake by name. Again the eye might pick up here and there an occasional distinctive-seeming phrase that had occurred in Marvell's verse; for instance the 'all-seeing Sun ('Blake's Victory', line 13) appears in the fifth stanza of 'Eyes and Tears'.[49] (This expression, first used by Giles Fletcher, is in fact relatively common.)[50] Then in lines 27–28 of the Bilborough poem Marvell had mentioned that same Peak of Teneriff about which R. F. hovered so infelicitously.[51]

Why such haste? It might be significant that 'Blake's Victory' is followed immediately by 'Thyrsis and Dorinda', far and away the most faulty text in the Folio.[52] Here the compositor seems to have lost his wits. (But if 'Blake's Victory' was inserted in a hurry the hurry is to be felt in the acceptance of the text as genuine rather than in the text itself which has relatively few errors.) Is it possible that these two poems were substituted hastily for something that had to be removed?

One of the few things that we know about the compiling of the Folio is that after the 'Horatian Ode', *The First Anniversary* and most of the 'Poem upon the Death of O. C.' had been set up they were removed from all except two known copies.[53] We do not know whose nerve had failed: most likely the publisher's. The only name to appear except his was to be Mary Marvell's and the authorities would have been unlikely to pursue an obscure widow. When it is recalled that Milton's sonnets to Fairfax and to Cromwell were both withheld from publication till 1694 the boldness of the plan to publish Marvell's three cancelled poems in 1681 seems astonishing.[54] Is it perhaps more likely to have been Mary Marvell's than that of any of the bankrupt bankers whom Marvell had sheltered? Theirs are the only other names that have ever been suggested. They were surely men of the world who knew the temper of the times. Although there have been attempts to find highly sophisticated reasons for the arrangement of the poems in the Folio it is possible to see it as not beyond the reach of commonsense. First a number of poems that would have been congenial to the pious Dissenters who were Marvell's greatest admirers: last the poems that were most dangerously Cromwellian: in the middle a more or less random collection. Such an arrangement would not have been beyond the powers of any one literate and reasonably intelligent, as Mary must have been.

Returning to the business of the mistaken inclusion of 'Blake's Victory': supposing that this poem and the one immediately following, 'Thyrsis and Dorinda', hurriedly replaced more dangerous material, can we conjecture what that might have been? In *The First Anniversary* (lines 117–124) Marvell does make a public (though unsigned) proclamation of his intention to write a poem encouraging princes (unnamed) to root out Roman Catholicism, to 'massacre the Whore':

> Unhappy Princes, ignorantly bred,
> By Malice some, by Errour more misled;
> If gracious Heaven to my Life give length,
> Leisure to Time, and to my Weakness Strength,
> Then shall I once with graver Accents shake
> Your Regal sloth, and your long Slumbers wake:
> Like the shrill Huntsman that prevents the East,
> Winding his Horn to Kings that chase the Beast.
> (lines 117–124)

Marvell's intentions sound undiplomatically fierce and such a poem, if he ever wrote it, would certainly have been obnoxious to the authorities in 1681. But the phrase 'with graver Accents', occurring in a context already impassioned, suggests to me that the poem was to be in the Latin tongue, as is to be expected of one meant at that time for foreign eyes. And I guess that Latin poems, even in 1681, would have been regarded as relatively safe. The puzzle remains.

Marvell's two eighteenth-century editors, Cooke and Thompson, agree that Mary Marvell was not Marvell's wife, that she compiled the volume of 1681, and, astonishingly, that in publishing some of the poems she did Marvell a disservice. Cooke says that they were 'not all to the Honour of the deceased'.[55] Thompson accuses her of sacrificing Marvell's fame to the desire of making money.[56] Whatever they were objecting to, it was not 'Blake's Victory': both give that what might be considered a place of honour, next to the poem on Milton's *Paradise Lost*. Cooke makes a particular point of having 'castrated' his volume of such poems as he was sure were not Marvell's.[57] In fact he omits only Marvell's translation from Brebeuf and the Latin couplets '*Inscribenda Luparae*'. Why he omitted the former I have no notion. '*Inscribenda Luparae*' was no doubt omitted because he could not believe that Marvell would ever have written in praise of Louis XIV. Evidently he knew nothing of the competition (with a prize of a thousand pistoles) promoted by Colbert that had set so many English pens at work in 1671.[58] As Professor Bradbrook conjectured long ago the poems Cooke wished away are likely to have been such love poems as 'Daphnis and Chloe' and 'Ametas and Thestylis'.[59] These would have been felt unsuitable to the figure of the austerely virtuous patriot that the eighteenth century had made of Marvell. Miss Bradbrook also suggests that in printing the love poems Mary Marvell was stupidly injuring her own claim to be an 'inconsolable' widow. How a genuine widow would actually have behaved in this respect in 1681 is difficult to establish. But it does appear that the compiler of the volume makes no attempt to present Marvell in a consistent light, political or personal. 'Tom May's Death' with its insulting references to the great Parliamentary generals is there as well as the poems in praise of Cromwell; 'Ametas and Thestylis' as well as 'Upon a Drop of Dew'. Better to have erred by including, by whatever mistake, the poem on 'Blake's Victory' than by excluding deliberately 'To his Coy Mistress'. A century later Captain Thompson, a poet himself and one who should have known Marvell's handwriting extremely well, having edited his letters from the originals, printed as Marvell's, from a manuscript of poems 'some written by his own hand, and the rest copied by his order', pieces composed long after Marvell's death by Addison and Malet.[60]

NOTES

1 'A new Marvell Manuscript: Cromwellian Patronage and Politics', *English Literary Renaissance*, 20 (1990), 106–162.

2 *Miscellaneous Poems*, London, 1681, pp.104–108: *see Poems and Letters of Andrew Marvell*, ed. H. M. Margoliouth, 3rd edn. rev. by Pierre Legouis, with the collaboration of E. E. Duncan-Jones (Oxford, 1971), vol. I, pp.119–124.

3 Petworth House Archives: Orrery Papers 13187 (a folder containing three manuscript poems).

4 University of Tennessee Press, 1965.

5 Orrery's hand of the period is found in a letter to John Thurloe of 1657 in British Library, Birch MS 4158, f.66.

6 The general type is recorded by Edward Heawood, *Watermarks mainly of the 17th and 18th Centuries*, Hilversum, 1950, nos.249–264. The earliest of these (no.251) is dated to 1656.

7 Sixth Report, 1877, Appendix, p.318, col. b.

8 *Complete Works, in verse and prose, of Andrew Marvell, M.P.* (London, 1872), vol. I, p.9.

9 *Andrew Marvell* (London, 1905), pp.70–71.

10 *André Marvell* (Paris, 1928), p.108.

11 *Andrew Marvell*, 2nd edn. (1968), p.108.

12 Bodleian MS Eng. poet. e. 49, p.103.

13 Pierre Legouis, *André Marvell*, 2nd edn. (New York, 1965), p.198; Hugh MacDonald, *The Poems of Andrew Marvell* (London, 1956), pp.xix, xx; and *Poems and Letters of Andrew Marvell*, ed. H. M. Margoliouth, 2nd edn., vol. I, p.235.

14 Thomas Clayton, '"Morning Glew" and other Sweat Leaves in the Folio text of Andrew Marvell's major pre-Restoration poems', *English Literary Renaissance*, 2 (Autumn 1972), pp.356–375; and Warren Chernaik, *The Poet's Time* (Cambridge, 1983), pp.206–7.

15 Bodleian MS Eng. poet. d. 49, p.49 (reproduced in facsimile in *Miscellaneous Poems*, 1681, Menston: Scolar Press, 1973).

16 Andrew Marvell, *Complete Poetry* (New York, 1968), p.xxxi (repr. London, 1984, p.xxv).

17 *Poems and Letters of Andrew Marvell, ed. cit.*, vol. I, pp.53–55, 15–17 and 137–139.

18 Lord, *ed. cit.*, (1968), p.xxxii and 266–70 (and *see* repr., 1984, p.xxvii, 266–70).

19 *Marvell and the Civic Crown* (Princeton, N.J., 1978), pp.70–71.

20 *Poems and Letters of Andrew Marvell, ed. cit.*, vol. I, pp.108–119.

21 *History of the Rebellion and Civil Wars in England*, Book XV, No.56 (ed. by W. Dunn Macray, Oxford, 1888, vol. VI, p.36).

22 *A New Collection of Poems and Songs. Written by several Persons . . .* (London, 1674), pp.109–116.

23 *The Poems of Edmund Waller*, ed. G. Thorn Drury (1893), p.151, 'Of a War with Spain, and Fight at Sea', lines 1–2.

24 *Man of Mode*, Act I, sc.1, lines 1–2: *see* edn. by John Barnard, New Mermaid Plays (London, 1979), p.7.

25 *Ed. cit.*, p.78, 'Of the Queen'.

26 Public Record Office, *Calendar of State Papers: Venetian, 1657–1659*, p.64.

27 Clarendon, *ed. cit.*, vol. VI, p.37.

28 *Poems and Letters, ed. cit.*, vol. I, p.87, line 20.

29 *A Relation of ten Years Travells in Europe, Asia, Afrique, and America* (London, [?1654]), 'To the Reader', sig. [A3]: '. . . all that know me, knowing I never willingly converse but with the noblest in every place, finding them still in every respect the best.'.

30 'Upon Appleton House', line 585 (*ed. cit.*, vol. I, p.75).

31 Flecknoe's hand is found in British Library Additional MS 21508, f.4: reproduced in W. W. Greg, *English Literary Autographs* (Oxford, 1928), Pt. II, No. LVI (d–f).

32 *The Idea of His Highness Oliver, late Lord Protector, &c. with certain brief reflexions on his Life* (London, 1659), p.41.

33 *Mercurius Heliconicus, No.1 Or, the Result of a safe Conscience. Whether it be necessary to subscribe to the Government now in being* (London, 1651) [dated in the Thomason copy to 3 Feb. 1650/1].

34 *Mercurius Heliconicus, No.2. Or, a short Reflexion of Moderne Policy* (London, 1651) [dated in the Thomason copy to 12 Feb. 1650/1].

35 *Dictionary of National Biography*, ed. Sir Leslie Stephen (London, 1889), vol. XVIII, pp.350–53.

36 *Poems and Letters of Andrew Marvell, ed. cit.*, vol. II, p.328.

37 *Works of Thomas Deloney*, ed. F. O. Mann (Oxford, 1912), pp.479–482; and Macaulay's *Lays of Ancient Rome* (London, [1907]), pp.249–56.

38 Ibid., pp.304–305 (with facsimile).

39 E. E. Duncan-Jones, 'Marvell in 1656', *Times Literary Supplement*, 2 December 1949, p.791.

40 Wing C7171.

41 'To the Earl of Orrery', lines 100–2, in *The Shorter Poems and Songs from the Plays and Masques*, ed. A. M. Gibbs (Oxford, 1972), p.109.

42 Lynch, *op. cit.*, p.90.

43 *Miscellaneous Poems* (1681), half title: *see Poems and Letters of Andrew Marvell, ed. cit.*, vol. I, p.8.

44 Grosart, *ed. cit.*, vol. I, p.lii; and C. H. Firth, 'Marvell, Andrew', *Dictionary of National Biography*, vol. XXXIII, p.329.

45 Fred S. Tupper, 'Mary Palmer, alias Mrs. Andrew Marvell', *Publications of the Modern Language Association*, 53 (June 1938), pp.367–92.

46 E. M. Tomlinson, *A History of the Minories* (London, 1907), pp.205, 206, and 389 *et seq.*

47 O.E.D., 2nd edn. (Oxford, 1989), sub 'Obtain', *v. trans.* 2a; and *see v. intrans.* 4.

48 Bulteel's title reads simply 'On The Victory over the *Spaniards* in the *Bay* of *Sancta Crux*, in the Island of *Teneriffe*'.

49 *Poems and Letters of Andrew Marvell, ed. cit.*, vol. I, p.16.

50 Giles Fletcher, *Christ's Victorie* (Cambridge, 1610), xxxiv, 'heauen's all-seeing eye'.

51 '*Upon the Hill and Grove at* Bill-borow *To the Lord* Fairfax', in *Poems and Letters of Andrew Marvell, ed. cit.*, vol. I, p.60.

52 *Poems and Letters of Andrew Marvell, ed. cit.*, vol. I, pp.19–21.

53 British Library C.59.i.8, which includes the cancelled signatures R2–T1 and U2–X2 (13 leaves) and a copy in the Huntington Library, which retains the cancelled sigs. R2–T2 (8 leaves) only.

54 *The Poems of John Milton*, ed. John Carey and Alastair Fowler (London, 1968), pp.321–322 and 325–326.

55 *The Works of Andrew Marvell*, ed. Thomas Cooke (London, 1726), vol. I, p.x.

56 *The Works of Andrew Marvell*, ed. Capt. Edward Thompson (London, 1776), vol. III, p.489.

57 *Ed. cit.*, vol. I, p.36.

58 E. E. Duncan-Jones, 'Marvell's "Inscribenda Luparae"', *Times Literary Supplement*, 26 April 1957, p.257.

59 M. C. Bradbrook and M. G. Lloyd-Thomas, *Andrew Marvell* (Cambridge, 1961), p.148.

60 *Ed. cit.*, vol. I, pp.vi, xiv–xxiv.

'More Copies of it abroad than I could have imagin'd': Further Manuscript Texts of Katherine Philips, 'the Matchless Orinda'

ELIZABETH H. HAGEMAN AND ANDREA SUNUNU

At the close of an article we wrote for volume 4 of *EMS*, we quoted Katherine Philips's comment to Sir Charles Cotterell on the success of her translation of Corneille's *Pompey*: 'There are . . . more Copies of it abroad than I could have imagin'd'.[1] That assertion is applicable to the results of our recent research on Philips's writing and her contemporary reputation. Initially, we thought of her as a poet whose writing circulated among a limited, though perhaps ever-widening, circle of friends and acquaintances, but we have revised that view in the light of manuscript items we have discovered. When we examined them beside early copies of Philips's work listed in Patrick Thomas's edition of her poems and also those located by Peter Beal and recorded in his recent *Index of English Literary Manuscripts*,[2] we came to realize how significant a role Philips played in what Arthur Marotti calls the 'ongoing social discourse' of seventeenth-century manuscript culture.[3] In fact, we now see that Philips provides a near-perfect case study of a mid-seventeenth-century coterie poet whose work suited, or was made to suit, a wide range of literary tastes. Crafted as verse to be read (or sung) in specific literary and historical circumstances, her poems circulated in single sheets, in manuscript compilations, and also in printed books. As they were recopied, her poems were often reordered, placed in new contexts, or rewritten to suit other people's purposes. At least one of her readers linked her with seventeenth-century French poets; some of her readers sought consolation in her poems about death; and others highlighted her image as a loyal friend and chaste lover. Some poets commented directly on Philips's accomplishments, and others wrote verses to or about Orinda and other figures named in her poems and letters. As her century wore on, both male and female readers were inspired to transcribe, extract, answer, adapt, supplement, and imitate the writing of the poet named on the title page of the 1667 folio edition of her works, 'the most deservedly Admired Mrs. Katherine Philips, The matchless Orinda'.[4]

I. POETRY OF EXCHANGE

Like other poets of her century, Philips often uses what Margaret Ezell has characterized as 'interactive genres, literary forms which invite the reader's response'[5] (or, we would add, which allow the reader to imagine that he or she is overhearing a private conversation). Among Philips's poems are verse letters, ventriloquist poems, pairs of poems such as 'For Regina' and 'To J.J. esq: upon his melancholly for Regina', dialogues in which Orinda converses with her friends or in which they exchange ideas with one another, poems that pointedly recast the language of other poets, and poems that answer – sometimes agreeing with, sometimes debating – verses by other authors.

We have located the poem by the Welsh clergyman Vavasor Powell (1617–70) that incited Philips's 'Upon the double murther of K. Charles, in answer to a libellous rime made by V.P.' Reproduced here as PLATE 1, it is preserved in Aberystwyth, National Library of Wales (Powis Castle, [1959 deposit], Herbert of Cherbury MSS and papers, parcel 14/7a[ii]). Philip Wyn Davies, who kindly examined the manuscript for us, writes in a letter of 5 July 1993 that 7a(i) and 7a(ii) 'contain a journal kept by Captain Henry Herbert (later fourth baron Herbert of Chirbury, died 1691) when serving in Colonel Sir Henry Jones's regiment with the French army in 1671–3. . . . The journal is followed by two blank folios which are in their turn followed by the stubs of [a number of] excised pages. The poem by Vavasor Powell is on the verso of the next folio after the stubs. The hand appears to be that of the journal, the hand of Captain Henry Herbert'. Henry Herbert, the younger son of Richard Herbert (1600?–55) and Mary Herbert (née Egerton), was the nephew of Alice, Countess of Carbery, whom Philips celebrated in one of her poems. The poem is headed 'Of *the* late K. Charles of Blessed Memory', the phrase 'of Blessed Memory' perhaps suggesting that the heading was supplied by a royalist; if the phrase is Powell's, it is an ironic statement of the 'Comend[ation]' of Charles that the poet says he recently 'heard *and* saw' (line 1).

Taken together, Powell's and Philips's verses illustrate the seventeenth-century controversy over the Two Tables of the Ten Commandments in which 'Puritans' argued for the primacy of the First Table (Commandments I–IV, which treat one's duties to God)

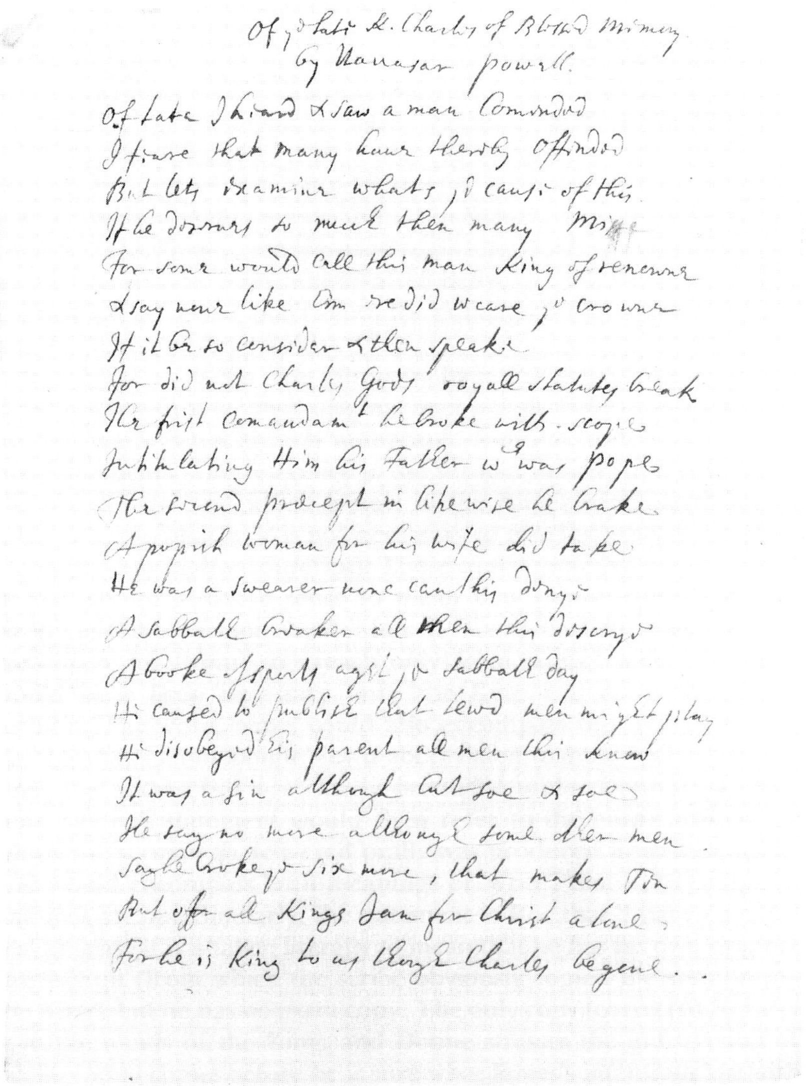

Of ye late K. Charles of Blessed Memory
by Vavasor powell.

Of late I heard & saw a man Commended
I feare that many have thereby Offended
But lets examine whats ye cause of this
If he deserves so much then many misse
For some would call this man King of renowne
& say none like him ere did weare ye crowne
If it be so consider & then speake
For did not Charles Gods royall statutes break
The first Comandamt he broke with scope
Intitulating Him his Father wch was pope
The second precept in likewise he brake
A popish woman for his wife did take
He was a swearer none can this denye
A sabbath breaker all then this descrye
A booke of sports agst ye sabbath day
He caused to publish that lewd men might play
He disobeyed his parent all men this knew
It was a sin although but soe & soe
He say no more although some deem men
Saythe broke ye six more, that makes Ten
But of all Kings I am for Christ alone
For he is King to us though Charles be gone.

PLATE 1 *'Of the Late K. Charles of Blessed Memory by Vavasor Powell': Aberystwyth, National Library of Wales, Powis Castle (1959 deposit), Herbert of Cherbury* MSS *and papers, parcel 14/7a(ii), fol. 7b. (Original size 220 × 173mm). Reproduced by permission of the National Library of Wales.*

and 'Anglicans' maintained the significance of the Second Table (Commandments V–X, which deal with one's responsibilities to one's neighbours). High-church Protestants argued – in the words of Thomas Pierce in 1659 – that 'The most material part of godliness is moral honesty. . . . The Second Table is the touchstone to our obedience to the First'. As J. Sears McGee explains, they 'regarded the First Table requirements as entirely fulfilled by honest participation in the prescribed rituals [of the English Church] and [believed] that puritan attacks upon those rituals were unjustified; second, that the mark of a good Christian was avoidance of theological controversy and concentration upon Second Table duties; and finally, that an acceptable measure of perfection in those duties was attainable by using Christ as an exemplar'. Conversely, low-church Protestants 'define[d] all sin in terms of idolatry', following William Perkins's argument that 'the ground of the nine later commandments is the first[,] "Thou shalt have no other gods before me"'. They focused on what they saw as 'remainders of popery' in the English Church, and they considered *The Book of Sports*, which allowed activities such as archery and dancing after divine services on Sundays, 'a direct breach of the Fourth Commandment', which enjoins observance of the sabbath.[6] For Fifth Monarchists such as Powell, then, Charles I seemed an idolatrous usurper of Christ's kingdom.[7]

Powell's thesis is that Charles broke 'Gods royall statutes' (line 8): 'The first comandam*en*t [Thou shalt have no other gods before me] he broke with scope/Intitulating Him his Father w*hi*ch was pope' (lines 9–10), the word 'Father' perhaps alluding to the Lord's Prayer and the word 'Intitulating' (entitling) connoting a 'crowning' of the pope as God. The second commandment (that one not create false idols), he broke when he 'A popish woman [Henrietta Maria] for his wife did take' (line 12). He broke the third commandment – against swearing – 'none can this denye' (line 13); and he broke the fourth – 'all men this descrye' – with 'A booke of sports ag*ain*st *th*e Sabbath day' (lines 14–5). The fifth commandment Powell treats ambiguously, perhaps because he thought that disobeying an evil parent is not important ('although but soe *and* soe', line 18) or perhaps because of the theory that breaking the final six commandments is only the logical outcome of violating the First Table of the Law. Glossing over '*th*e six more' (line 20), Powell closes with an epigrammatic assertion of his doctrine of kingship: 'of all Kings I am for Christ alone:/For he is King to us though Charles be gone' (lines 21–2).

That Philips does not mention Powell's odd count of the commandments – his listing five and then referring to 'six more, that makes Ten' (line 20) – could suggest that the Herbert copy of Powell's verses is a variant text of the one she knew, her copy perhaps reading 'five more'. By declining to respond to the charge that 'Charles . . . broke God's lawes' ('Upon the double murther', line 11), she sidesteps the first and longest part of Powell's agument and emphasizes instead the slanderous speech and treasonable actions of the king's countrymen (line 23). She then undercuts Powell by acknowledging that 'Christ *will* be King' (line 29; emphasis ours) and reminding Powell that Christ commands a peaceable kingdom.

Powell also presents his verses as an answer to others' opinions, but his tone differs markedly from Philips's. He writes as though with calm concern, inviting his readers, 'lets examine whats *th*e cause' (line 3) of the praise of Charles as 'King of renowne' (line 5). Rather than entering easily into a public conversation, Philips claims that she does not even think of political matters. As a woman, she resembles Croesus's 'sonne whose father's danger nigh/Did force his native dumbnesse, and untye/The fettred organs' (lines 3–5; *see* Herododus, I. 85).[8] Her 'passion' (line 7) rises as the poem progresses. Alluding to Parliamentarians' recent sequestering of Royalists' lands, she commands Powell not to 'sequester our common sense' (line 26) or to ignore Christ's law of forgiveness. This poem, like others of Philips's, is about speaking truly. And, like many of her poems, it takes much of its power from the speaker's identity as a woman, a person from whom her culture expected silence.

As Philips responded to other writers, so too did her contemporaries answer her verses – Henry Hall, for example, in lines we quoted in our previous article, and an anonymous author who criticized her poem 'The Soule'. Although Patrick Thomas prints the latter response to Philips (*Poems*, pp.371–2) from a text in an eighteenth-century manuscript book of English poems and translations from Welsh into English (National Library of Wales, MS I Brogyntyn 28, fol. 34), he says only that the last two lines of Philips's poem – 'And those who yield to what their souls convince,/Shall never need another Law' – 'are paraphrased in [that] anonymous poem'. What we would note is that the anonymous poet first rewrites Philips's conclusion, changing 'And those who yield to what' to 'who yeild to all *tha*t', and then mocks the statement as a misguided expression by a member of 'The charming sex':

> Mrs Kath: Phillips her Verses on
> the Soul. the 2 last lines thus
> Paraphras'd. *th*e lines are these

> – who yeild to all *tha*t does their Souls convince
> shall never need another Law.

— — — — — — — — — — — —

When e're wrong notions take *the* place of Truth
well may *the* soul be-wilder'd goe astray
instead of Love *the* safest guide of youth
affected Modesty perverts *the* way.

Varnish'd dissembling gives an awkward dress
To warmth *and* beauty for *our* comforts made
and striving to adorne it makes it less
when *the* false colours strike too deep a shade

The charming sex will need no other Law
Let them but follow Love *and* natures choice
Nor be by crooked maximes kept in awe
Since their owne souls can give them best advice.[9]

Altogether different in tone are the verse 'conversations' which can be found in Oxford, Balliol College MS 336, a notebook in which Nicholas Crouch (*fl.* 1640–90), a fellow of Balliol, transcribed Latin and English poems. The Latin verses include Thomas Master's description of the game of shuffleboard; the English poems, Sir Charles Sedley's verses on Mary Napp beginning 'As in those Nations, where they yet Adore'. In his catalogue of the collection, Sir Roger Mynors notes on fol. 6v a list of some of the coterie names in Philips's circle and on fols 10r through 11r transcripts of two of her poems from the early 1650s, their titles here 'To Alicia Count*ess* of Carbery Coming into Wales' and 'In Nobilem Palæmonem'. The latter is Philips's poem beginning 'This is confest *pre*sum'tion; for had I' addressed elsewhere to Francis Finch, who in 1653 signed with the sobriquet 'Palæmon' an essay entitled *Friendship* and addressed to 'D. Noble *Lucasia-Orinda*'. Noting that Finch was a gentleman commoner at Balliol before entering the Inner Temple, Patrick Thomas suggests, plausibly, that Crouch may have received the poems from him (p.46). Neither Thomas nor Mynors noticed, however, that on fols 7r through 9v are another poem by Philips and two more that are almost certainly hers.[10]

On fols 7v–8v is the poem known as 'Lucasia', beginning in all other known copies, 'Not to obleige Lucasia by my voice', but here copied without a heading and with the name 'Syndænia' in each of the five lines where one would expect to see the coterie name for Anne Owen. The poem preceding this one (fol. 7r; PLATE 2), headed 'Syndænia', begins 'Soe to be good, that all men shall confesse'; the third (fols 9r-v; PLATES 3–4), transcribed without a heading and beginning 'Mad*am*: I doe not these few Lines indite', is addressed to an unnamed woman. Both are written in a style and with the fervour

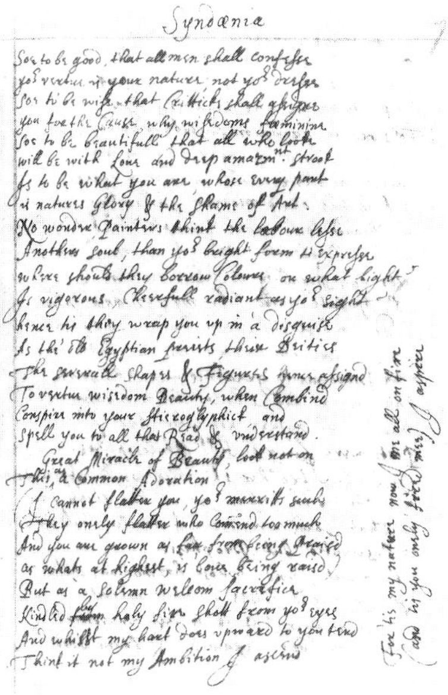

Syndænia

For to be good, that all men shall confesse
yor vertue is your nature, not yor dresse
For to be wise, that Critticks shall assigne
you for the Cause why wisdoms feminine
For to be beautifull that all who looke
will be with Love and deep amazm[nt]. strooke
Is to be what you are, whose every part
is natures Glory & the shame of Art.
No wonder Painters think the labour lesse
Another soul, than yo[r] bright form to expresse
where should they borrow Colours, or what light
Is vigorous, Cheerefull radiant as yo[r] sight
hence tis they wrap you up in a disguise
As the old Egyptian preists theire Deities
The severall shapes & Figures once assignd
To vertue wisdom Beauty, when Combind
Conspire into your Hieroglyphick and
Spell you to all that Read & understand.
Great Miracle of Beauty, look not on
This, as a Common Adoration
I cannot flatter you, yo[r] merrits such
They only flatter who Commend too much
And you are grown as far from being Praised
as whats at highest, is from being raisd
But as a Solemn welcom sacrefice
Kindled by holy fire shott from yor eyes
And whilst my hart does upward to you tend
Think it not my Ambition to ascend

For tis my nature now I am all on fire
and tis you only (fire) [illegible] aspire

PLATE 2 *'Syndænia': Oxford, Balliol College Library* MS *336, fol. 7r. (Original size 185 × 135mm). Reproduced by permission of the Master and Fellows of Balliol College, Oxford.*

that could identify them as friendship poems by Philips. Topoi familiar to readers of her poems appear throughout both encomia: the lady's 'vertue is [her] nature, not [her] dresse'; the poet is one of many people awestruck by 'Majestique beauties' which are 'such as will teach a Religion/to sencles things, who worship *and* admire/when you with yo*ur* bright form doe them inspire'. The speaker contrasts her own inadequacies with her subject's grandeur, and she uses images of reading and writing to express Syndænia's effect on her and on the world at large. The metrical patterns, too, are Philips's – the iambic couplets, often with a verb at the end of the first line, often with a medial caesura in the second; and the rhyme words resemble those she uses in her panegyrics. The sobriquet 'Syndænia' would seem appropriate in Philips's circle of friends, for it could derive from the Greek verb 'syndænumi' whose English translation would be 'to feast together' or 'to entertain together'. Although no related Greek noun exists, an English seventeenth-century poet might have used a feminine 'ia' ending – as in 'aletheia' (truth) or 'eleutheria' (freedom) – to create an abstract noun to be understood as 'the person with whom I feast', an English equivalent of the word 'friend' or, better

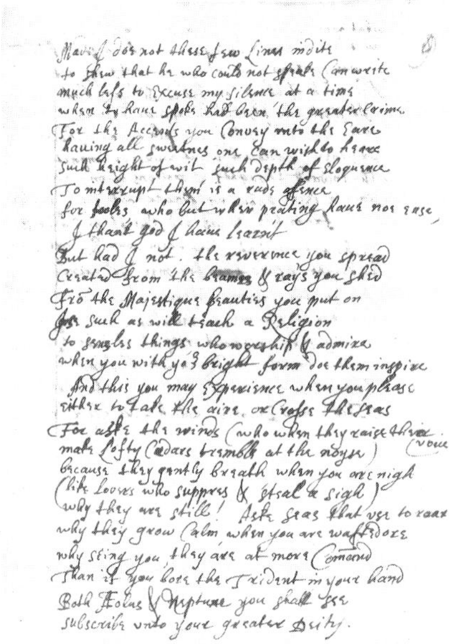
Madam
I doe not these few Lines indite
to shew that he who could not speake Can write
much less to Excuse my silence at a time
when to haue spoke had been the greater Crime.
For the Accords you Conuey into the Eare
hauing all sweetness one Can wish to heare
Such height of wit such depth of Eloquence
To interrupt them is a rude offence
for fools who but when prating haue noe ease
I thank god I haue learnt
But had I not. the reverence you spread
Created from the beames & rays you shed
Fro the Majestique beauties you put on
Is such as will teach a Religion
to senseless things who worship & admire
when you with yor bright form doe them inspire
And this you may Experience when you please
either to take the aire, or Crosse the seas
For aske the winds (who when they raise their voice
make Lofty Cedars tremble at the noyse)
because they gently breath when you are nigh
(like Lovers who suppress & steal a sigh)
why they are still! Aske seas that use to roar
why they grow Calm, when you are wafted ore
why sting you they are at more Command
Than if you bore the Trident in your hand
Both Æolus & Neptune you shall see
subscribe unto your greater Deity.

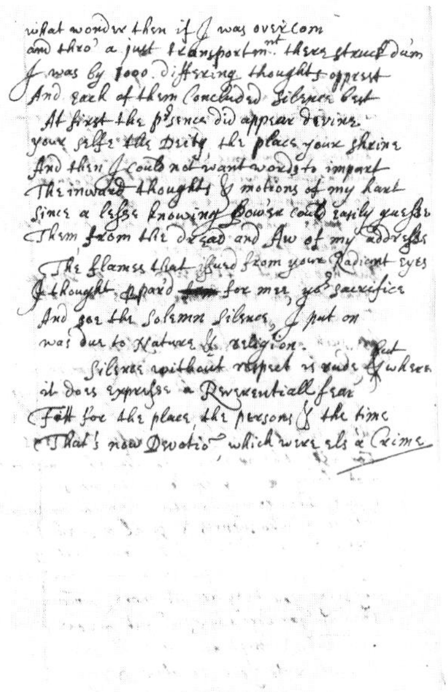
what wonder then if I was overcom
and thro' a just transport^mt there struck dum
I was by 1000 differing thoughts oppresst
And each of them Concluded Silence best
At first the p^rsence did appear devine
your selfe the Deity the place your shrine
And then I could not want words to impart
The inward thoughts & motions of my hart
Since a lesse knowing Bowser could easily guesse
Them from the dread and Aw of my addresse
The flames that issued from your Radiant eyes
I thought prepared for mee yor sacrifice
And for the Solemn silence I put on
was due to Nature & religion.
But Silence without respect is rude & where
it does expresse a Reverentiall fear
Felt for the place, the persons & the time
That's now Devotion which were els a Crime

PLATES 3–4 *'Madam: I doe not these few Lines indite': Oxford, Balliol College Library* MS *336, fol. 9r–v. (Original size 185 × 135mm). Reproduced by permission of the Master and Fellows of Balliol College, Oxford.*

still, 'companion', itself a word deriving from the notion of someone with whom bread is shared.

Against the assumption of Philips's use of the sobriquet 'Syndænia' is the possibility that either Nicholas Crouch or Francis Finch, who was himself a poet, inserted the name 'Syndænia' in poems Philips wrote for Lucasia. Moreover, one detail might suggest that someone other than Philips composed one or both of the two 'new' poems in Orinda's voice. Although Philips herself could have used the pronoun 'he' in line 2 of the verse letter beginning 'I doe not these few Lines indite/to shew that he who could not speake Can write' (*see* PLATE 3) as an indefinite pronoun meaning 'anyone', a male scribe might consciously have altered the word to make the poem apply to himself or, if he did not realize that the poem's author was female, to correct what he saw as an error, or else he might unconsciously have inserted a variant. Yet 'he' might signal a male poet accepting a challenge offered in the final line of the Lucasia/Syndænia poem: 'But they admire best, who dare Imitate'. Nevertheless, given their stylistic and circumstantial similarities with Philips's own verse, the likelihood is that the two previously unrecorded poems are indeed by her and that they, along with the Lucasia/Syndænia poem, were written under a temporary variant sobriquet used for Anne Owen between the composition of 'To the truly noble, and obleiging Mrs: Anne Owen (on my first approaches)' and 29 December 1651, the date of 'To the excellent Mrs A. O. upon her receiving the name of Lucasia, and adoption into our society'.

A more complicated instance of Philips's participation in a literary exchange emerges in a comparison of her early poem beginning 'A marryd state affords but little ease:/The best of husbands are so hard to please' and a longer anti-marriage poem that incorporates most of Philips's sixteen lines, the latter quoted by Margaret J. M. Ezell in her comments on the 'wry sophistication and detachment' with which some seventeenth-century women poets treated marriage.[11] Professor Ezell has kindly pointed out to us that the poem she quotes in *The Patriarch's Wife*, 'Advice to Virgins. By a Lady' (beginning 'I cannot but congratulate,/The happy Omen of your last Nights Fate') in Oxford, Bodleian MS Firth c. 15, fols 335–7, is also extant in slightly different versions in Bodleian MS Eng. misc. c. 292, fol. 110, and Nottingham, University Library, Portland Papers PwV 40, fol. 242r-v, and PwV 41, pp. 149–50. These longer anti-marriage poems suggest a variety of possibilities: that Philips's poem was expanded by a later seventeenth-century woman, whose verses were then copied and modified by others, for instance, or that the manuscript in Philips's hand is a copy of a (perhaps truncated) version of an earlier poem by someone else that resurfaced elsewhere later in her century. Another alternative – most interesting, perhaps, in view of its implications for a history of women's participation in England's manuscript culture – is that Philips's 'A marryd state' is one in a series of women's poems in which proverbial lines such as 'The best of husbands are so hard to please' and 'A virgin state is crown'd with much content' lead toward a triumphant contradiction of the image of a virgin leading apes in hell commonly used in Renaissance England to discourage spinsterhood (here quoted from Bodleian MS Firth c.15, fol. 337):

And therefore Madam, be advis'd by me,
Turn, Turn Apostate to Loves Deity
Suppress wild Nature, if she dare rebell
There's no Such Thing as leading Apes in Hell.
(lines 59–62)

A somewhat similar puzzle is to be found in London, British Library, Additional MS 29921, a seventeenth-century duodecimo miscellany. On fol. 67v the couplet 'Tho every thing may love, yet tis a Rule/He cannot be a friend that is a fool' is annotated, 'Mr Venninge things

Worth thinking on 3d centurye 81', with the further information, ''Tis also in a large Poem of Mrs. Cath. Philipp's Entitled [The Friend] in her Works in folio. p.94. These 2 lines are in her 9th Stanza p.96: It is her 64th Poem in her folio printed AD. 1678'. Mr Venninge is Ralph Venning (1621?–74), a non-conformist preacher who, after the Act of Uniformity of 1662, was pastor of an independent congregation in London's Fenchurch Street – in the same street as St Gabriel Fenchurch, where the 1648 marriage allegation linking Katherine Fowler and James Philips declared they would be married. Fenchurch Street is near Bucklersbury, where Katherine Fowler was born and her half-brother Joshua Fowler still lived in the 1660s. Venning's *Things Worth thinking on; or, Helps to Piety,* entered in the Stationers' Register on 13 February 1664/5, was printed in editions dated 1664 and 1665. Venning uses the couplet on friendship in the 81st entry in his fourth (not third) century of meditations. Although it is possible that Venning and Philips took the couplet from a common source, Venning could have read Philips's 'A Friend' in manuscript (the poem's presence in National Library of Wales MS 775B indicates it was probably written before 1658) or in the edition of her poems printed in January 1663/4, more than a year before *Things Worth thinking on.*

That the person who transcribed Additional MS 29921 was well-acquainted with Philips's poetry is clear from his identification of Venning's quotation from her work and also from his entering, on fols 115v and 116r, three passages in which Philips treats the desirability of controlling one's passions: lines 97–100 of 'L'Accord du Bien', lines 39–40 of 'Invitation to the Country', and lines 77–80 of 'The Soul' – each passage attributed to 'Orinda' and numbered with the folio page from which it is taken. Earlier, on fols 82r–83r, in a section described in the Table of Contents as a group of poems by one J. Baynes, is a poem imitating her 'A retir'd friendship, to Ardelia', the same poem that the Duke of Monmouth recast to create a song we noted in our previous article – the poem from which Anne Finch, Countess of Winchilsea (1661–1702) probably chose her own sobriquet.[12] This imitation is transcribed as is the rest of the manuscript – in a neat hand combining secretary and italic forms.

Its attribution is in heavy Chancery script: after consulting several paleographers, we can say that the ascription appears to be to one 'J B de [or a] K [or R] W'. Here again we find motifs that echo throughout Philips's verse: phrases such as 'the dull World', 'tyranny of Fate', and 'secure from strife and noise', and the idea that friendship is a virtuous union of souls. Awkward metrical patterns in the last four stanzas, however, and rhyme words such as 'about us'/

'without us' show that this poet has not fully succeeded in adopting Philips's cadences:

On Friendship.

Come my Fidelia, Let us smile
At the dull World, and in this Arbour
Wee'l innocently sitt a while
Free from the Cares which Great ones harbour.

Nought ill dares here disturb our Joyes,
Whilst others aim at Crowns *and* sway
We rest secure from strife and noise,
Happier (since so we think) then they.

No envyous tongues our rest controul
But in our Friendships innocence
We find a powrefull Calm of soul
Thats worth our precious times expence.

Nothing can touch our happy state
Founded on vertues changeless nature
Which feare no tyranny of Fate
Nor any sublunary Creature.

What tho the Heavens their wheel do roll
Let them roll on, wee'l constant stand
Their influence reaches not the Soul
Vertue can Nature countermand.

What though the stars twinkle *and* gaze
And dance their fairy-round about us
We fear no mischief from their raids
Nor any thing that moves without us.

In this whole World a friend thats just
Is all the true Content we have,
Such sympathize even in their dust,
And love tho parted in the Grave.

Nor Age nor death shall alter me
Nor absence which at last will make
The greatest Friends seek liberty –
And new ones to their bosomes take.

Dearest Fidelia thou and I
Will seal with Life the bond of Friend
Our Loves tho sever'd ne'r shall die
But shall be constant to the End.

Also relevant here is a poem recently located by Rashelle F. Trefousse in the July 1694 issue of the *Gentleman's Journal.*[13] 'Friendship. An Elegy, by Lucasia' could indeed be by Anne Owen herself, but we suggest that it could also be a ventriloquist poem written by another member of their circle – or by a later reader who perceived a conflict between Orinda's female friendships and love for her husband. The elegy, in fact, could be written in response to 'To my dearest Antenor on His parting', for it begins with an account of Orinda's sorrow at Antenor's departure:

> As cooing Turtles do in the loss bemoan
> Of their kind mates, and murmer all alone;
> So for *Antenor* does *Orinda* mourn,
> Nor can rejoyce till the dear man return.
> (lines 1–4)

The poem's speaker is jealous of that love ('In vain I plead for sacred Friendship's tyes') and asserts the supremacy of lost friendship: 'Her Days had Pleasure, and her Nights had Rest;/Strong was the Passion, yet serene her mind' (lines 11 and 20–21). Realizing that Orinda will be happy only if she knows that Antenor will return safely, 'Lucasia' closes, 'Thus in his absence I might Reign a while/And rival Love and Friendship recocoucile [*sic*]' (lines 47–8).

Our final example of poetry of exchange may be found in an exemplar of the 1664 edition of Philips's poems now in Northampton, Massachusetts, William Allen Neilson Library, Smith College. In each of three places in the 1664 printed text, one omitted line is indicated by asterisks. In the Smith College copy, two of these three lacunae have been supplied by an apparently contemporary reader writing in a neat print hand, not at first sight easily distinguished from the book's typeface. In 'To the noble Palæmon on his incomparable discourse of Friendship' he or she has inserted 'Thy Chains would be but like embracing Arms', and in 'To my dear Sister, Mrs. C. P. on her Nuptial', 'Delude the Soul, and are but worthless Joyes', in neither instance duplicating lines which do appear in other extant printed or manuscript sources.[14] As this contemporary reader attempts to guess the missing words, we see him or her engaging in – if not to answer, then to complete by a process of personal invention – the texts of two of Katherine Philips's poems.

II. MANUSCRIPT COLLECTIONS RELATING TO WOMEN

Given the number of poems Philips wrote about female friends, relatives, and members of the royal family, it is not surprising that among Philips manuscripts listed in Beal's *Index* are several manuscript books which have interesting connections with women. For example, the text proper of Washington, D.C., Folger Shakespeare Library MS V. b. 231, a scribal copy of the 1669 printed edition of Philips's works, is preceded by a 20-line poem headed 'Cassandra preferr'd to Orinda', Cassandra perhaps being the owner of the manuscript. Beginning 'Let Cowley and the Rest theire fancy trye/ That ne're Orinda's name should dye' (lines 1–2), the poem concludes with the assertion that if 'pindars greatest fame' (*i.e.*, Cowley) had seen Cassandra's 'face', 'vertue', and 'witt', he would have had to admit 'We have a greater then Orinda now/Then if, Cassandra once I but Rehearse/In fancy he's baffled and In verse' (lines 18–20).[15] The binding of New Haven, Yale University MS Osborn b 118 suggests a connection with Philips's Lucasia, for it is stamped with the crest of the family of Marcus Trevor, Viscount Dungannon, whom Anne Owen married in 1662. Stamped initials 'I D' on either side of the crest, we note, may conceivably mark the volume as having belonged to Lucasia's son John (1668–87).[16] In the manuscript compiled by Elizabeth Lyttelton, daughter of the Norfolk antiquary Sir Thomas Browne (Cambridge University, Additional MS 8460), is an unattributed transcript of Philips's 'The Virgin'. And the Chetwode manuscript in the library of St Paul's Cathedral, known for its copies of Donne's sermons, is inscribed 'Katherine Butler. Given me by Father May 1693'; it has, at the other end from the sermons, an unpaginated poetical miscellany in the same hand as the inscription and introduced with the phrase 'A Common Place Book 1696'. With extracts from such poets as Juvenal, Ariosto, Dryden, and Orrery are six from one of the folio editions of Philips – three of them (lines 39–40 of 'Invitation to the Countrey', nine stanzas of 'Friendship', and stanza six from 'Friendship in Emblem, or the Seale, to my dearest Lucasia') listed in Beal's *Index* and three more besides: 'Against Pleasure', here headed 'How slight, *and* trifling *the* Pleasures of *the* World'; lines 5–12 from 'Rosania's private marriage', headed 'That *the* Greatest Things are done w*i*thout a noise or bustle'; and lines 1–22 of 'The World', headed 'The Miserable State of Human Life'.

But perhaps the most interesting example of Philips's poems being collected by or for a woman is found within British Library, Harley MS 6900, a collection of French poems including Philips's elegy on the Queen of Bohemia (fol. 68r–v) and her poem to the Duchess of York 'Who commanded Mrs. Philips to send her what *ver*ses she had written' (fol. 69r-v).[17] This volume is, indeed erroneously, described in the Harley catalogue as possibly having belonged to Philips. Clues to the actual owner of the manuscript emerge in the phrase 'Pour

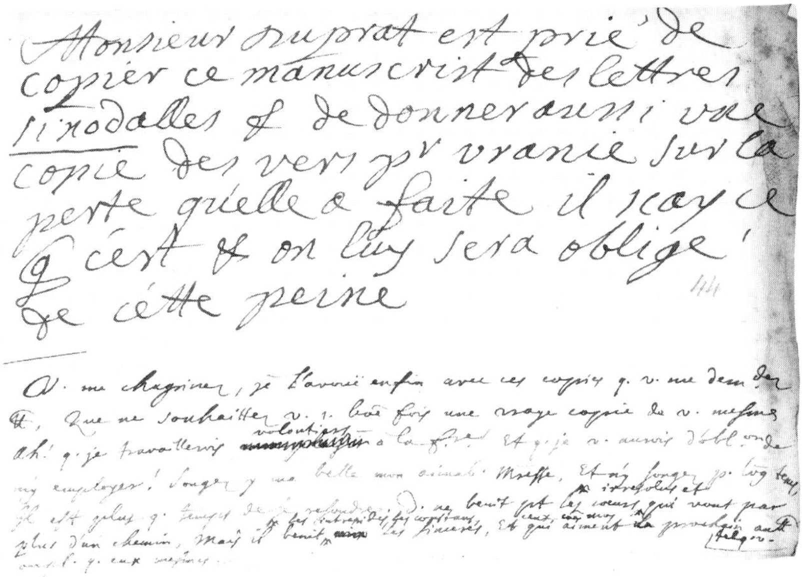
Monsieur duprat est prié de copier ce manuscrist des lettres sinodalles & de donner aussi une copie des vers pr vranie sur la perte quelle a faite il scay ce q cést & on luy sera oblige de cétte peine

PLATE 5 *Note to Monsieur Duprat and the beginning of his reply: London, British Library, Harley* MS *6900, fol. 44r. (Original size 120 × 170mm).*

Mademoiselle Hardy', which appears, with the name 'Hardy' crossed out, upside down on a sheet of paper bound in with the manuscript as folio 44. The inserted slip (PLATE 5) comprises a scribbled note in French to a Monsieur Duprat and a subscribed reply, dated 'Avr. 15. 83', to the request: 'Monsieur Duprat est prié de copier ce manuscrist des lettres si nodalles *et* de donner aussi une copie des vers p*our* uranie sur la perte qu'elle a faite il scay ce q*ue* c'est *et* on luy sera obligé de cette peine' [Monsieur Duprat is asked to copy this manuscript of letters so knotty and also to give a copy of the verses to Urania for the loss she has suffered he knows what it is and we shall be grateful to him for his trouble'] (fol. 44r).

Addressing first 'U' (fol. 44r) and then 'Iris' – 'Vous q*ue* mon esprit craint et vous q*ue* mon coeur aime' [You whom my spirit fears and you whom my heart loves] (fol. 44v), and calling himself 'Tyrsis', Monsieur Duprat responds that complying with the request is no burden, but an honour. Monsieur Duprat remains unidentified, though, conceivably, he may be the same Monsieur Duprat whose library, listed in a 78-page catalogue now owned by the Bodleian Library (8°F 128 [7] Linc.), contained many French books and was sold at auction on Tuesday, 2 May 1699.[18] The date '1662/Jan. 9th' on fol. 3r of Harley MS 6900 offers a *terminus a quo* for the poem beginning on that folio, for Harley MS 6900 itself, or for a collection upon which Harley MS 6900 is based. Monsieur Duprat's hand is almost certainly that of the manuscript itself, for the cursive note and the more formal scribe's hand share a number of similar letter-forms: *Q, L, d,* and *p,* for example. Yet which of the two requested copies Harley MS 6900 may be we cannot determine – or even whether Monsieur Duprat is being asked, in 1683, to make additional copies of his own Harley MS 6900. The relationship between 'Mademoiselle Hardy', 'Urania', and 'Iris' compounds the ambiguity, for 'Uranie' may or may not be another sobriquet for the 'Iris' to whom Monsieur Duprat writes, just as 'Mademoiselle Hardy' may be either 'Uranie' or 'Iris' or neither, and the name 'Hardy' either French or English.[19] The watermark, which consists of the letters 'I', 'D', and 'C' centered above a bunch of grapes and punctuated with two inverted hearts, may well signal that the paper is French, for as Joe Nickell, who kindly examined the watermark of Harley MS 6900 for us, notes, 'grapes-watermarked paper typically came from France'.[20] Although French paper was of course used in England in the late 1600s, it is possible that this manuscript was actually transcribed in France and that 'Mademoiselle Hardy' is the 'Mademoiselle Hardy' listed in Carolyn C. Lougee's Appendix Two, '*Précieuses* of Uncertain Identity'.[21]

The references to 'Uranie', 'Iris', and 'Tyrsis' fit in with the pastoral names that appear in the works of seventeenth-century French *précieuses* and *précieux* poets whom scholars have always seen as major influences on Philips's poetic style, poets well represented among the thirty-four French poems transcribed in Harley MS 6900.[22] Interestingly, Philips mentions both of her own poems in a letter to Cotterell on 3 May 1662: aware that the Duchess of York has praised her work – 'I have been told', she writes, 'that when her Highness saw my Elegy on the Queen of BOHEMIA, she graciously said, it surpriz'd her' (pp.32–3), Philips asks Cotterell to revise her poem to the Duchess: 'it shall not be seen at Court, till you have first put it in a better Dress, which I know you will do, if it be capable of Improvement; if it be not, commit [it] to the Flames . . . . If it passes your Judgment in any degree, let me have your Remarks upon it, and I will correct it by them, and send the Dutchess another Copy, in obedience to the Commands she was pleas'd to lay upon me, that I should let her see all my Trifles of this nature' (p.32). The Harley copy of the poem to the Duchess of York (PLATE 6) differs in a number of details from the other extant versions of the poem, the Harley variants just possibly witnessing to an attempt by Cotterell to fulfill Philips's request that he put the poem 'in a better Dress'; alternately, this version could

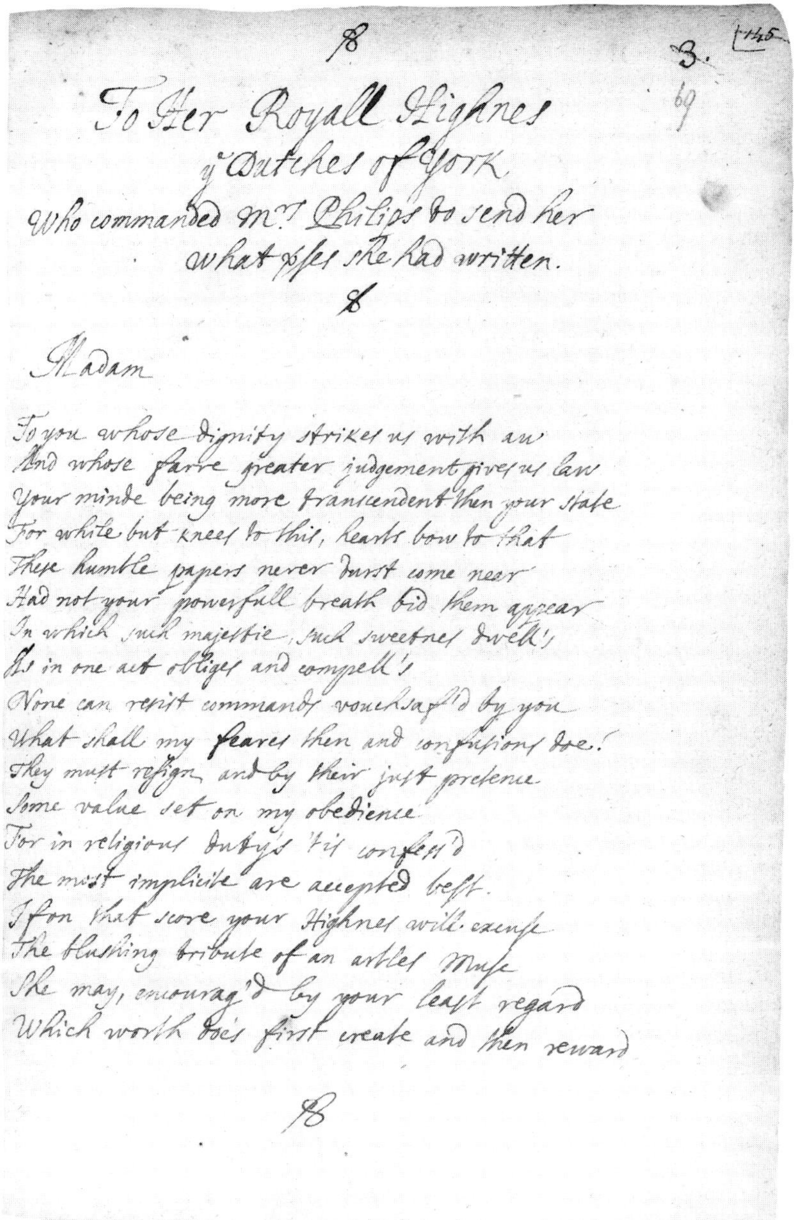

To Her Royall Highnes
ye Dutches of York
Who commanded Mrs Philips to send her
what Verses she had written.

Madam

To you whose dignity strikes us with aw
And whose farre greater judgement gives us law
Your minde being more transcendent then your state
For while but knees to this, hearts bow to that
These humble papers never durst come neer
Had not your powerfull breath bid them appear
In which such majestie, such sweetnes dwell's,
As in one act obliges and compell's
None can resist commands vouchsaf'd by you
What shall my feares then and confusions doe!
They must resign, and by their just pretence
Some value set on my obedience
For in religious duty's 'tis confess'd
The most implicite are accepted best.
If on that score your Highnes will excuse
The blushing tribute of an artles Muse
She may, encourag'd by your least regard
Which worth doe's first create and then reward

PLATE 6 *Katherine Philips, 'To Her Royall Highnes* the *Dutches of York': London, British Library, Harley* MS *6900, fol. 69r. (Original size 297 × 184mm).*

predate the one used as the source of the other known copies of Philips's poem.

That Philips's two late royalist poems, as well as one other (anonymous) English poem in the volume, are written in the same hand as the rest of the manuscript indicates that its owner and/or its scribe believed them to belong, in some way, with the French poems: at the least, the same person who valued the French poems admired Philips's works as well; at the most, its owner thought of Philips as an English colleague of French seventeenth-century *précieux* and *précieuses* poets. For the majority of the French poems in Harley MS 6900 that we have succeeded in identifying are written by members of the circle centered upon the French novelist Madeleine de Scudéry (1607?–1701), known as 'Sapho' and the 'Reine du Tendre'[23] and believed by her contemporaries to have written *Almahide*, from which Philips translated the poem headed in the Rosania manuscript and the printed editions 'A Pastoral of Mons. de Scudery's in the first volume of Almahide. Englished'.[24] Preciosity began around 1610 at the *salons* of Catherine de Vivonne, Marquise de Rambouillet (1588–1665) whose *chambre bleue* became an 'alternative court, a new center of power' that fostered conversation as 'a fine art' recognized by foreign visitors as the essence of French culture.[25] It was in the *chambre bleue* that Corneille read his *Polyeucte, martyr* and that Madeleine de Scudéry first gained a following for her prose romances. The Marquise de Sévigné's comment, 'the Hôtel de Rambouillet was the Louvre',[26] testifies to the movement's importance, for despite Molière's famous satire against it, *préciosité* 'began as a feminist movement, inspired by early 17th-century projects for women's education'.[27] Though Madame de Rambouillet continued to hold court until her death, the end of the civil war known as the *Fronde* (May 1648-February 1653) ushered in a new era of bourgeois *salons*, the most famous of which was Madeleine de Scudéry's. When she returned to Paris with her brother after he lost the governorship Madame de Rambouillet had obtained for him, Mademoiselle de Scudéry set up her own Saturday gatherings at her home in the Marais.

Evidence of Philips's own interest in contemporary French poetry takes various forms, including her explicit admiration of 'the Countess of SUZA's Elegy' (Letter of 18 March 1661/2, p.21) and her request that Cotterell send her 'a Copy of [his] Translation of *Le Temple de la Mort*' (Letter of 20 August 1662, p.48);[28] but she was also indirectly connected with French literary activity: Cotterell translated a prose romance by Gautier de Costes, Seigneur de La Calprenède (1610?–63), husband of a known *précieuse*, and John Davies dedicated to Philips his translation of the ninth part of *Hymen's Praeludia: or, Love's Masterpiece*, another work by La Calprenède.[29]

The contents of Harley MS 6900 are listed in full below as an appendix, from which it can be seen that at least two of the poems ('Elegie sur une Jalousie' [fols 46v–48v] and 'Elegie' beginning 'Je vien, cruelle Iris, les yeus baignés de larmes' [fols 52v–56r]) are by Henriette de Coligny, Comtesse de la Suze (1618–73), for whose poetry Philips expressed admiration in the letter mentioned above. At least four others are by Paul Pellisson-Fontanier (1624–93), devoted friend of Madeleine de Scudéry and often linked in print with Madame de la Suze. One more, 'Sur un Saphir retrouvé' (fol. 34v), may be by Madame de la Suze or by Pellisson.

Harley MS 6900 provides further evidence of Philips's affinity with the coterie poetry of her French contemporaries, even as it arranges its poems so that many of them respond to each other. For example, the poem of compliment that heads Harley MS 6900 – 'Pourquoi cacher une aimable personne' [Why hide a lovable person] – prefigures the compliments paid by Pellisson's four poems about 'Sapho'. In his 'Caprice contre L'Estime, A Sapho' Pellisson admits that he can no longer hope to get to 'Tendre' – that he will never be loved, only esteemed – but his tone lightens in his three later poems in the manuscript: in 'La Fauvette. Dialogue' Pellisson uses his pseudonym 'Acante' ('Achante'/'Acanthe' in Harley MS 6900), pitting himself against 'La Fauvette' ('the warbler'), who, in Sapho's absence, will serve as audience. Later, after a series of eight enigmas, the Countess returns to lament in the 'Elegie' beginning 'Je vien, cruelle Iris, les yeus baignés de larmes/Me jetter à vos pieds et vous rendre les armes'. [I go, cruel Iris, with eyes bathed in tears/To throw myself at your feet and to give up my arms to you] (fol. 52v), and then Pierre Perrin's 'Sur une absence, Virelais' follows, facetiously explaining that love has never withstood the test of absence.

Though separated by twelve blank pages from the French poetry, the sequence of three English poems (fols 68r–70v) also includes the French pattern of both praise and riddle: for Philips's two explicit encomia of Queen and Duchess are followed by a riddling coda in 'Song', which begins 'That beauteous Creature for whom I am a Lover/I must not, I will not, I cannot discover' and leads into a guessing game: the person who 'both kills my heart, *and* makes it live,/ Is either call'd Mary, or Betty, or Nan,/ Now, guesse if you can,/Now guesse if you can' (fol. 70r). Thus we see Philips's poetry coming full circle: written in the *précieux* mode and for coterie circulation, her poems are here placed in the company of poems by the very French poets whose work inspired her admiration.

III. MEMORIAL VERSIONS AND ADAPTATIONS

Best known today for her friendship poems, Katherine Philips was also the writer of elegies and epitaphs commemorating the death of relatives, acquaintances, and members of the royal family. As Joan Applegate's discovery (reported in volume 4 of *EMS*) of the musical score verifies, one – 'On the death of my first and dearest childe, Hector Philipps' – was set to music by Henry Lawes. Four others (the epitaph for her son beginning 'What on Earth deserves our Trust?' and epitaphs for John Collier, Regina Collier, and John Lloyd) were engraved on church monuments; the last, the ventriloquist poem Philips wrote for her sister-in-law Cicily to use on Lloyd's monument in Cilgerron Church, survives until the present day. Were it not for the existence of her autograph manuscript, National Library of Wales, MS 775B, however, we would not know the poem on the monument to be Philips's, for the heading, 'IN MEMORY OF HER DEARE *AND* HONOURED HUSBAND JOHN LOYD OF KILRHIWE ESQ WHO DYED *THE* 11TH OF JULY 1657 IN THE 36TH YEARE OF HIS AGE, *AND* LYES BURIED UNDERNEATH', says nothing of the authorship Philips asserted when, in copying out the poem in NLW MS 775B, she noted that it is 'inscrib'd on his Monument in Kilgarron (in *th*e person of his wife').

As Catherine Cole Mambretti notes in her dissertation on Philips (p.45), some thirty-five years after Philips wrote 'In memory of F.P. who dyed at Acton 24 May. 1660 – 13th of her age', that poem on the death of her stepdaughter Frances was adapted to create an epitaph on an infant named Mary Morris. That Mary Morris's epitaph was actually inscribed on a monument is suggested by its appearance in a collection of contemporary epitaphs, New Haven, Yale University, Osborn MS fb 143 (p.24). We have also found the epitaph to Mary Morris in a similar manuscript, Folger Library MS W. b. 455 (p.41), this a collection ascribed to one 'R S', *c.*1705, entitled *Delectus epitaphiorum Anglo-Latinorum tam veter7m quam recentium.* Transcribed here from the Folger copy, Mary Morris's epitaph is made up of lines 1–2 and 7–10 of Philips's 90-line elegy:

On Mary Morris 1695 aged 3 Quart*ers* and 9 days.

> If I could ever Write a lasting Verse
> It should be laid, dear Saint, upon thy Herse.
> Ah! beauteous Blossom, too untimely dead:
> Whither, oh Whither is thy Sweetness fled?
> Where are the Charms that always did arise
> From the prevailing Language of thy Eys.

Parish records for Acton, Middlesex, where Philips's mother lived in

May 1660 with her fourth husband Philip Skippon, do not include the year 1660, and no monument bearing Frances Philips's name survives in St Mary's Church in Acton. We are left, then, with the supposition that Mary Morris's friends or family found the material for her epitaph in a printed text of Philips's poem, though the possibility perhaps remains that the 90-line elegy is an expanded version of an epitaph inscribed in Acton and then used to commemorate an even younger girl a third of a century later.[30]

Philips's epitaph on her son appears in another Yale University manuscript, Osborn MS c189, a seventeenth- or very early eighteenth-century volume indexed as 'Commonplace book: anonymous manuscript poetry of the 17th and 18th century, by various authors. [ca 1705]' in which are fourteen extracts from Philips, three of them from the epitaph on little Hector Philips. Of the other eleven, four appear to derive from seventeenth-century printed music books: on page 27 are eight of the sixteen lines of 'A Countrey life' (here headed 'In Praise of *the* Country') that are printed with a musical score in the fifth book of Henry Playford's *The Banquet of Musick* (1691), and 'A Farewell to Rosania', which appears with music by George Hart in the third book of *The Banquet of Musick* (1689); on page 29 are both of the Philips poems set to music in William King's *Poems by Mr Cowley and Others* (1688): 'Upon the engraving. K: P: on a Tree in the short walke at Barn-Elms' (here headed 'Upon graving a Name on a Tree' – in King's book it is headed 'Upon the graveing a Name on a Tree'), and 'Tendres desirs' (called here 'A Lover' – in the music volume it is headed 'Loves Cure'). The manuscript also contains seven extracts from Philips's *Pompey*, six of the seven, however, attributed or addressed to the wrong character. On page 24, for instance, one of Cornelia's couplets – 'But should all my endeavours prosper ill;/What I can't do, sure Cleopatra will' – is assigned to Caesar; and one of Caesar's couplets – 'But vainly we resist the Gods, who will/Their just decrees on Guilty men fulfill' – is given to Pompey, the titular character who never appears on stage. Although giving speeches to different characters would seem to be deliberate, the purpose of such adaptations remains puzzling.

On pages 21 and 22 of the volume are the three poems created from Philips's 'EPITAPH. ON HECTOR PHILLIPS', two in the voice of a parent who has lost a child: the first lamenting the early death of one of three children; the second, the death of a 'stripling' (Philips's son died as an infant). The third poem is generalized to comment on the vanity of all earthly things. Line numbers beside the following transcripts refer to lines copied or recast from Philips's epitaph; line 2 in the first poem, for example, is a revision of her line

6, 'A son, a Son is born at last':

A Parent, on *th*e death of a Child.

Seven years childles, marriage past, 5
Three Children then we had at last. 6
One a long life promised. 9
Yet in less than six weeks dead. 10

An Epitaph for A Youth.
Here lie's.

The Carkess of a happy spirit,
Bless*ed* by God's mercy *and* own merit.
Too promising, too great a mind, 11
In so small room to be confin'd; 12
Therefore, b'ing fit in Heaven to dwell, 13
He quickly broke the Prison shell. 14
So the subtle Alchymist 15
Can't with Herme's seal resist 16
The powerfull Spirit's subtler flight 17
But 'twill bid long good night. 18
And if the sun it so arise 19
Half so glorious as his eyes, 20
Like this stripling, take's a shroud 21
Buried in a morning Cloud. 22

The Vanity of Earthly things.

What on Earth deserves our trust; 1
Youth and Comfort both are Dust. 2
Long we gathering are with Pain 3
What one moment calls again. 4

Shortly after Philips's own early death (of smallpox, at the age of 32), her life and work were commemorated in a manuscript volume long known to Philips scholars. Created for Philips's 'Rosania', Mary Montagu (née Aubrey), National Library of Wales MS 776B is important as a witness to the textual history of Philips's poems and plays. This manuscript is also, we now see, important to literary historians because it is an exemplary seventeenth-century memorial volume in which Philips's own work is posthumously edited to create a collection whose whole concept hinges on the theme of triumph over death. As Julian Thomas of the National Library of Wales pointed out to us, its binding of blind-stamped black leather (PLATE 7) is an English 'sombre' binding such as one finds on Mourning Bibles and Prayer Books of the period.[31] Its dedicatory letter 'To the Excellent Rosania' (PLATE 8) is subscribed from her 'Most humble, *and* most devoted Servant Polex*ande*r'. To Claudia Limbert's suggestion that Philips

PLATE 7 *Binding of Rosania manuscript: Aberystwyth, National Library of Wales, MS 776B. (Original size of full opening 190×305mm; each cover 190 × 140mm). Reproduced by permission of the National Library of Wales.*

gave Sir William Temple the sobriquet 'Polexander', naming him from the eponymous hero of the romance by Marin le Roy, Sieur du Parc et de Gomberville (1600–74),[32] we can add that the name 'Polexandre' and several others familiar to Philips scholars – among them, 'Artaban' and 'Silvandre' – appear in a list in the prose *Recueil Sercy* in which we found the source of Philips's translation of 'Tendres desirs' that we reported in volume 4 of *EMS*. In that list Artaban's name is associated with 'Visite' (p.273) and 'Jalousie' (p.291); Silvandre's, with 'Complaisance' (p.276); and Polexandre's, with 'Declaration' (p.277).[33]

Polexander's letter to Rosania combines the compliment one might expect to accompany a gift with the consolation appropriate to a memorial volume: 'Orinda, though withdrawn, is not from you; In lines so full of Spirit, sure she lives; And to be with you, is that only spell, can share her with *th*e bright Abodes; your Eyes, her heaven on Earth; your Noble Heart her Center'. As part of his praise of Orinda, Polexander remembers her modesty: 'To appear in Print, how un-inclined she was?'. Ignoring the 1664 edition of 75 of Philips's poems and perhaps referring to his own manuscript as an edition,

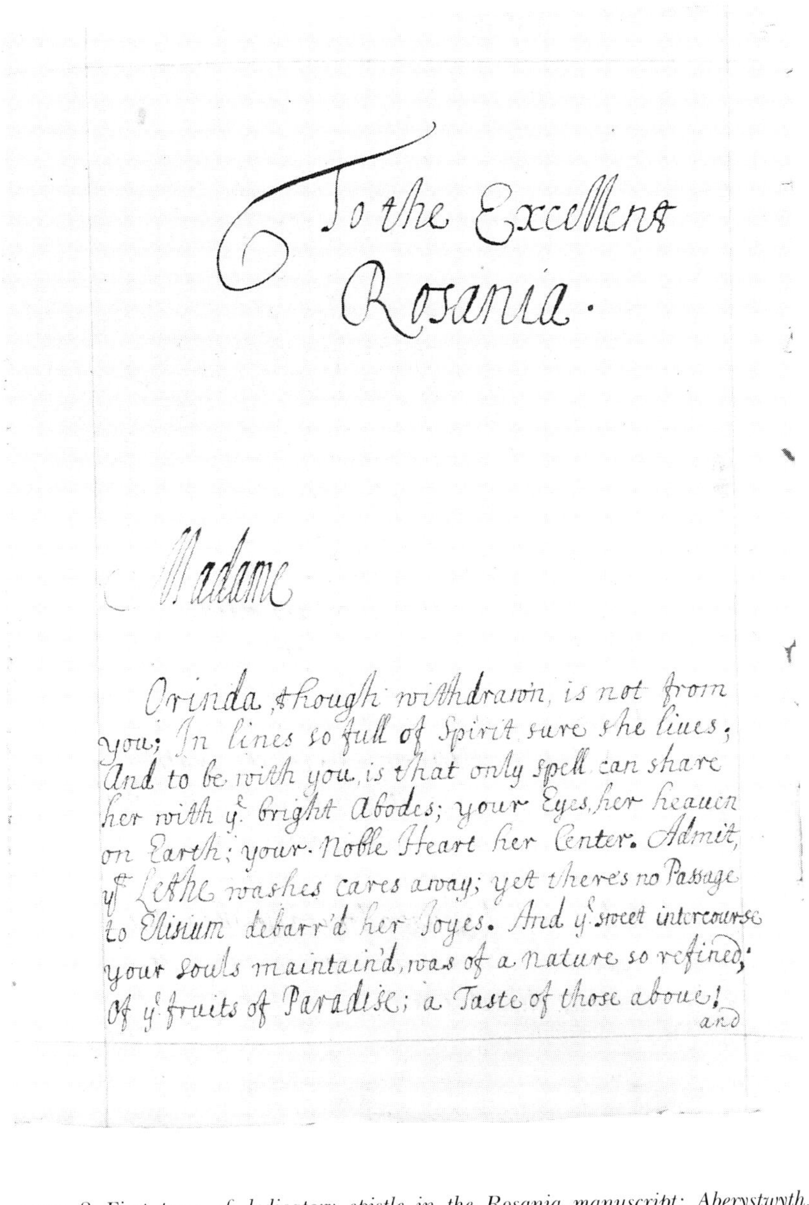

To the Excellent
Rosania.

Madame

Orinda, though withdrawn, is not from you; In lines so full of Spirit sure she liues; And to be with you, is that only spell can share her with ye bright Abodes; your Eyes, her heauen on Earth; your Noble Heart her Center. Admit, yt Lethe washes cares away; yet there's no Passage to Elisium debarr'd her Joyes. And ye sweet intercourse your Souls maintain'd, was of a nature so refined; Of ye fruits of Paradise; a Taste of those aboue; and

PLATE 8 *First page of dedicatory epistle in the Rosania manuscript: Aberystwyth, National Library of Wales,* MS *776B. (Original size 190 × 140mm). Reproduced by permission of the National Library of Wales.*

Polexander continues, '(I confess, an Edition, now, would gratify her admirers, and 'twere but a just remeriting that value, which (in hers, *and* their own Right) was *th*e Universall consent.)' After praising Rosania for 'expos[ing] your admirable Beauty to that spitefull Disease, (whence all our grief,)', the letter returns to consolation – 'Enjoy these dear Remains, no more as a sad Monument; nor to remind her past, but present State. Thus, will her Raptures be to your harmonious soul, a Jacobs-staff, to levell at her Gloryes' – before a final compliment for Rosania: 'Nor can these charming Poems, so absolute over our affections be themselves utterly insensible, how Soveraign a bliss its to be yours'.

Reflecting the seventeenth-century priority of drama over lyric poetry and also Philips's reputation in the mid-sixties as a successful dramatist, the volume begins with *Pompey* and Philips's incomplete translation of Corneille's *Horace*. Some blank pages precede Philips's five briefer translations and 91 of her original poems. Arranged in an order different from that of any other known collection and incorporating texts copied and/or adapted from a variety of different sources, they end with nine poems that offer religious consolation: 'To Mrs Wogan, my Honoured Friend, on *th*e Death of her Husband', 'In memory of *th*e most justly honour*e*d Mrs Owen of Orielton', 'In Memory of Mrs. E. H.', 'On Controversies In Religion', eighteen lines out of Henry More followed by Philips's verses beginning 'Eternall Reason', 'L'Accord du Bien', 'The Soul', 'Happiness', and 'Death' – the latter concluding with a quiet statement of Philips's acceptance of death:

> If I be sure my soul is safe,
> And that my Actions will provide
> My tomb a nobler Epitaph,
> Then that I onely liv'd *and* dy'd,
>
> So that in various accidents
> I Conscience may *and* Honour keep;
> I with that ease *and* innocence
> Shall dy, as Infants goe to sleep.
> (lines 21–28)

These stanzas seem to vindicate Polexander's opening statement that 'Orinda, though withdrawn, is not from you' and his assertion in the middle of the letter that 'Angels, thus, are still ascending, *and* descending. It was this, Orinda's matchless Pen aspired; And having bequeath'd you these clear Streams, you see how soon she thither took her flight, whence *th*e rich veine derived'.

IV. POEMS TO AND ABOUT ORINDA

In his *Index* Peter Beal calls attention to a collection of 73 of Philips's poems in 'a single, neat, non-professional hand' on pages 1–88 of Oxford, Worcester College MS 6.13, once owned by George Clarke (1661–1736), whose father, Sir William Clarke (1623?–66), gave evidence at James Philips's trial in 1661 (*see* British Library, Egerton MS 2979, fol. 116v). A note in the Clarke manuscript indicates that Louise I. Guiney identified the poems as Philips's in 1907, three years after her Appreciatory Note introduced J. R. Tutin's selected edition of Philips, but no subsequent Philips scholar has hitherto worked with the manuscript. The Philips poems are introduced by Abraham Cowley's 'Ode. On Orinda's Poems', headed here – as in the 1664 printed edition of 75 of her poems – 'To the most Exelently [sic] Accomplist Mrs Katharine Phillips upon her Poems', in which he asserts that Orinda 'Does man behind her in proud triumph draw/ And cancell greate Apolloes sallicke Law' (lines 5–6). At the end of the selection (p.88) is a quatrain in which one 'Mr J ff' (or perhaps 'Mr J H') also praises Philips by claiming that she surpasses male writers:

Written upon this last Copy
by Mr J ff

Madam *the* praises of yo*u*r friend shall live
By you who merit more then you canne give
While Women *tha*t would write like men pursue
What men shall overtake that write like you.

Although the friend in this poem may be Lady Elizabeth Carre, to whom the last Philips poem in the manuscript is addressed, the word 'Copy' in the heading could refer to the whole collection of poems. In this case 'friend' might be an error for 'friends'. Mr J ff/H could conceivably be John Finch (1626–82) or else James Howell (1594–1666), both of whom contributed poems, as did Philips, to the posthumous edition of William Cartwright's works (1651). But of course he could also be any number of other seventeenth-century men with those initials – James Harrington (1611–77), whose sister Elizabeth, Lady Ashton, was a neighbour of Cotterell's, is just one example – or he could be the person who copied out the manuscript.

A series of verses in which another poet – perhaps here a woman – expresses humble admiration for Orinda appears in British Library, Additional MS 28101, in which Catherine Cole Mambretti (p.48) located a transcript of Song 3 ('From lasting *and* unclouded Day') from *Pompey* (fols. 114r and 115r). As the catalogue indicates, this

'Family Miscellany' was compiled a good while after Philips's death, by 'Ashley Cowper, Clerk of the Parliaments, nephew of the first earl Cowper and uncle of William Cowper, the poet, consisting partly of extracts from authors of the second quarter of the 18th century, and partly of compositions by the collector himself and members of his family'. Elsewhere in that manuscript we have located three poems addressed to Orinda: 'To Orinda – advising to trust Fortune for a future Meeting' (fol. 26r), 'Business – to Orinda' (fol. 28r), and 'To Orinda. In Answer to a Letter chiding the Author for not Writing' (fol. 29r). These three poems are ascribed to one 'S C', just possibly Ashley Cowper's relative Dame Sarah Cowper of Panshanger, Hertfordshire (1643–1720), whose diary we quote in our Conclusion below. All three present Orinda as a virtuous source of inspiration, whether through the compliment, 'No more to Fortune will I humbly sue,/Since I have found a greater Goddess – You' (fol. 26r, lines 10–11); the question, 'How can I gain who have *Orinda* lost' (fol. 28r, line 8); or the acknowledgement, 'True my *Orinda* there was once a time,/ When too much writing was *your* Lovers Crime;/My Pen enjoy'd its Freedom to Excess,/I scribbled more but yet I lov'd you less' (fol. 29r, lines 1–4).

This epideictic pattern continues in yet another eighteenth-century compilation. Among manuscripts bequeathed to the British Museum by the historian and biographer Thomas Birch (1705–66) are Additional MSS 4223 and 4244, each of which contains brief biographical notes on Philips, and also Additional MSS 4456 and 4457 which include poems addressed to Orinda. On fol. 162r of Additional MS 4456 is a 15-line poem 'On Friendship. To Orinda' beginning 'Orinda! you the languid Song inspire', which, according to the library catalogue, is 'apparently in Birch's early hand'. A longer version of the same song, there beginning without reference to Orinda, ''Tis thou the languid song inspires' is on fols 165v–6r of Additional MS 4457, just after a 35-line poem beginning, 'Orinda! Sappho! Sister! Friend!/This doggrel Rhyme awake I send' (fols 163r–4r). The latter is a mildly amusing piece begging for 'Another Bard; another Friend' to be 'A Friend, more gay, and more polite,/Your gen'rous Friendship to requite' (lines 19 and 24–5). If not outstanding poetry, these verses do provide evidence of a continuing admiration of Philips and a sure sense that her coterie name was for many decades associated with songs about virtuous love and friendship – even in poems that show no evidence of their authors' having any personal knowledge of Philips or her immediate circle.

The legendary Orinda's name also appears in National Library of Wales MS 5308E (Herbert 14), a seventeenth- or eighteenth-century manuscript of poems by Donne, Beaumont, and others, including an ode to 'the worthy *and* generous Patriot Henry Herbert Esq*uire* uppon his happy *and* victorious Return to England' (this the same Henry Herbert in whose hand the Vavasor Powell poem discussed above appears to be written). In the first of four stanzas about a male poet's response to four ladies, the writer acknowledges his ineptitude before Orinda, whose virtue he describes in terms (except for the discordant word 'Adorable') reminiscent of Philips's descriptions of friends such as Lucasia:

> In Vain he Aims who has no force to hit,
> Who can describe divine Orinda's Wit?
> All outward Charm with that Perfection joyn'd
> Is but the bright Resemblance of her Mind,
> Adorable, Sublime, Correct, Immense
> Whose Ev'ry Grace is her Own Eloquence.
> (lines 1–6)

The second stanza treats a flirtatious and cruel 'Celia her friend with soft Obliging Air' whose 'Eyes,/Invite, and Guard the Tree of Paradise' (lines 7 and 11–12). The third treats 'Yong Sylvia', a person of 'Beauty, regardles Mien, and Innocence,/A sp'ritly Air, and Growing Excellence' (lines 13–15).[34] Altogether different from Orinda or Celia or Sylvia is Pulcheria, the lady this otherwise unsuccessful poet *can* 'sing' (line 20). His 'Trembling Muse' can celebrate her inviting 'full-ripe Modesty in blooming Youth/ . . . /Happy's the Man who May her favours Gain,/And knows to Value, what he dares Obtain' (lines 19 and 24–8).

Two pairs of poems we have located in an early eighteenth-century poetical anthology at the University of California at Los Angeles include a figure named Orinda who is the object of a poet's love. UCLA MS 170/68, a miscellany written mostly in the hand of a single scribe, has ruled pages, running titles, and, on fol. 108r–v, an incomplete index of the poems in the manuscript. In pencil on fol. 110v are written 'Miss Whard/Welchman/Worcester' and '1831'. Beginning with Rochester's 'Of Nothing' ('Nothing thou elder brother ev'n to Shade'), UCLA MS 170/68 includes poems by such writers as Wotton, Flatman, and Spratt. Walter Pope's 'Wish' is there, as are Buckingham's 'A Familiar Epistle to Mr Julian Secretary to *the* Muses' ('Thou com*m*on shore of this poetiq*ue* Town'), here attributed to Lord Buckhurst, and Montrose's 'An Epitaph on K[ing] C[harles] I'. Arranged according to the same interactive principles that inform Harley MS 6900, discussed above, this coterie manuscript includes a number of linked poems: Waller's 'The Storm on *th*e Death of O.

Cromwell' and Godolphin's 'The Answer to *th*e Storm', for example; Rochester's 'A Satyr on Man' and Lessey's 'Satyr in answer to that against Man'; 'Ephelia to Bajazet' and 'Bajazet to Ephelia'. The poem beginning 'After 2 sittings now our lady state', elsewhere entitled 'The Last Instructions to a Painter' and attributed to Marvell, is here headed 'Advice to a Painter. 3d part' and glossed 'A Scandalous poem'; following it are the first 170 lines of the poem beginning 'Nay paynter if thou dar'st design *tha*t fight', elsewhere entitled 'The Second Advice to a Painter', here headed 'The 2d *and* 3d advice to a Painter for drawing *th*e history of our Navall Actions *th*e 2 last year 1665 *and* 1666, In answer to Mr Waller'.

On fol. 49r–v of UCLA 170/68 is 'To Orinda', written in the person of Antenor – depicted not as Orinda's husband, but as an impatient lover – followed by a quatrain headed 'Antenor's Dream'. In 'To Orinda' Antenor asserts, 'willingly I was a Prisoner ta'en;/nay, I in secret even hugg'd my chain' (lines 7–8), but he says that now 'All *th*e town rings of young Antenor's flame' (line 18), and he wants to be free of Orinda. Despairing of the attempt, he closes,

> my last reserve shall be to drink *and* swear,
> grow frantick, mad, build Castles in *th*e air,
> whither on whimsyes mounted will I fly
> *and* all yo*ur* darts *and* batteryes defy.
> (lines 31–4)

'Antenor's Dream' (which we transcribe here in its entirety) then portrays Antenor after he has escaped from Orinda:

> Deep as *th*e grave all things a silence kept
> *and* free fro*m* cares *th*e young Antenor slept:
> w*he*n in a vision fair Parthenia came,
> Parthenia th'object of his tender flame.

Why Antenor dreams of Parthenia is unclear, for no Philips poems on Parthenia are currently known – although Beal records in his *Index* that a poem 'Orinda to Parthenia. Signed "Ka. Ph"' was reported to be in an unlocated manuscript, formerly Phillipps MS 4001, sold by Sotheby's in 1946.

The second pair of poems about falling in love with Orinda (on fols. 57r–59r of UCLA MS 170/68) would perhaps also be clarified by 'Orinda to Parthenia'. 'To Lysander' begins with the triplet, 'Well *the*n, Lysander, since you would be great, / May all thy wishes find a prosperous fate, / Mayst thou have Honour, titles, wealth *and* state'. Couplets in which the poet expresses a preference for a quiet, sensible life – his most fervent wish being, '*And* to compleat *th*e happyness of

Life, / may my Orinda be at last my Wife' (lines 30–1) – lead to a final tercet: 'This, my Lysander, if I once obtain, / I promise thee nor is my promise vain, / No other joys I'll look for but in Heav'n again' (lines 36–8). Then 'Love discover'd' chronicles the speaker's transformation into a lover/poet: 'Fro*m* Cowly *and* his brethren chips I fetch'd' (line 9); 'I spoke, I wrote, nay, I e'en thought in Rhyme' (line 14). At line 21 he names his lady: 'Orinda's form still in my fancy plaid / . . . / Or prose, or verse w*ha*tever I design'd / Only Orinda could employ my mind' (lines 21–4). He struggled to escape from Cupid, who was joined by Parthenia; and the poet finally freed himself – 'Till in a muses shape *th*e Urchin drest / . . . I entertain'd w*i*thin my breast' (lines 81–2).

On fol. 10v, between two poems on the death of Rochester and Spratt's ode 'On the death of O. Cromwell' (the latter glossed, 'A poem too too [*sic*] good for *th*e Subject') is an unattributed poem addressing neither Orinda nor her creator Katherine Philips, but female readers of her printed poems. 'To the Ladyes On Mrs Philip's Poems' (PLATE 9) is replete with topoi often seen in writing about Renaissance women: it comments, for instance, on women's preaching, on their wielding pens rather than needles, on their writing 'manly' verse. With an erotic wit, this poet offers a double-edged compliment:

> We of the gown, o*ur* former cares deplore
> Wee'll throw by books *and* study women more:
> Or Ladyes since you'r in the press, wee'll read
> Your volumes over *and* with greater heed.
> (lines 19–22)

Whereas 'J C', the broadside poet who in 'An Elegie, Upon the Death of the most Incomparable, Mrs. Katharine Philips, The Glory of Her Sex' published in 1664 (Wing C53) wrote that 'She, who in Tragique buskins drest the Stage, / Taught Honour, Love, and Friendship to this Age', this poet (also referring, as did Cowley, to Orinda's cancelling the Salick law) claims that women's writing turns the world upside down:

> Thus You grow masculine apace, in troth
> You wear the Breeches *and* the Buskin both.
> Verses of old were us'd in Charms, but You
> Charm with your faces *and* your Verses too;
> And, maugre what the Saliq*ue* law denies,
> Yet still in numbers you will tyranize.
> (lines 29–34)

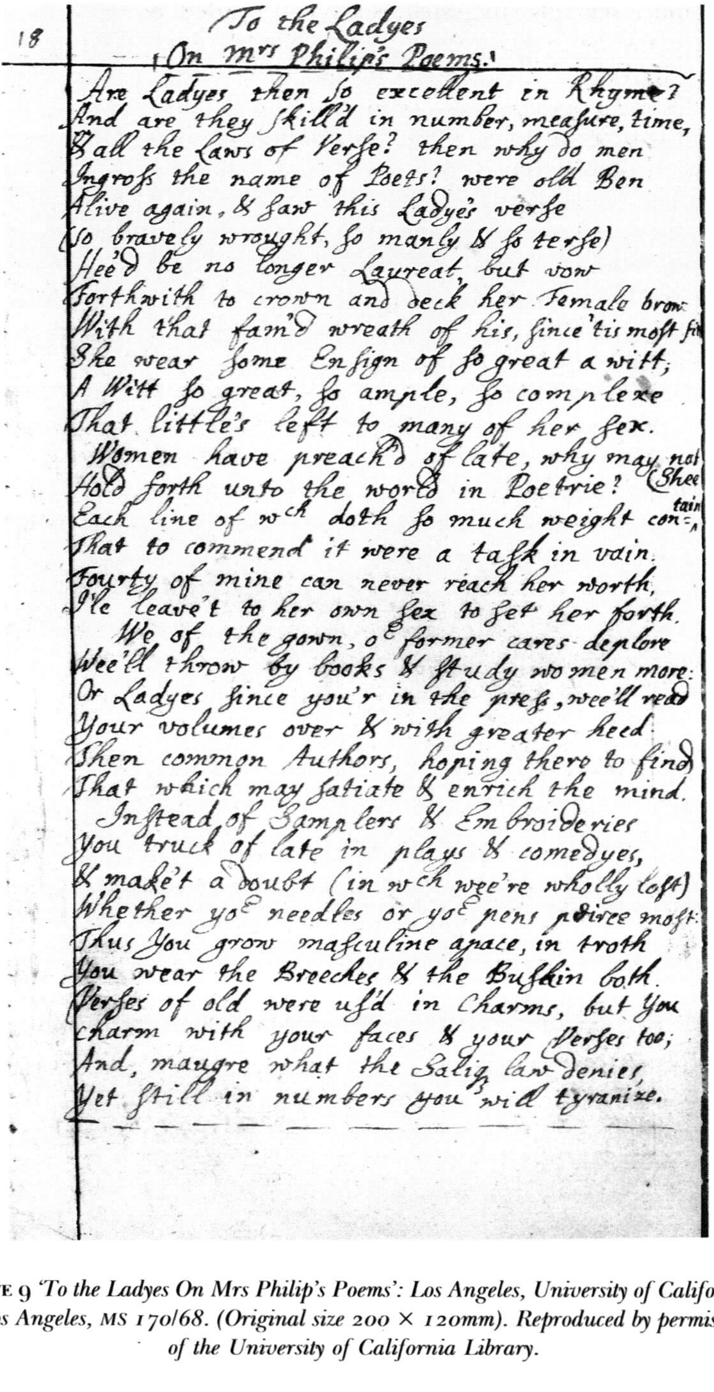

18

To the Ladyes
On Mrs Philip's Poems.

Are Ladyes then so excellent in Rhyme?
And are they skill'd in number, measure, time,
& all the Laws of Verse? then why do men
Ingross the name of Poets? were old Ben
Alive again, & saw this Ladye's verse
(So bravely wrought, so manly & so terse)
Hee'd be no longer Laureat, but vow
Forthwith to crown and deck her Female brow
With that fam'd wreath of his, since 'tis most fit
She wear some Ensign of so great a witt;
A Witt so great, so ample, so complexe
That little's left to many of her sex.
Women have preach'd of late, why may not (Shee
Hold forth unto the world in Poetrie?
Each line of wch doth so much weight contain
That to commend it were a task in vain.
Fourty of mine can never reach her worth,
Ile leave't to her own sex to set her forth.
We of the gown, our former cares deplore
Wee'll throw by books & study women more:
Or Ladyes since you'r in the press, wee'll read
Your volumes over & with greater heed
Then common Authors, hoping there to find
That which may satiate & enrich the mind.
Instead of Samplers & Embroideries
You truck of late in plays & comedyes,
& make't a doubt (in wch wee're wholly lost)
Whether your needles or your pens [illegible] most:
Thus You grow masculine apace, in troth
You wear the Breeches & the Buskin both.
Verses of old were us'd in Charms, but You
Charm with your faces & your Verses too;
And, maugre what the Saliq law denies,
Yet still in numbers you will tyranize.

PLATE 9 *'To the Ladyes On Mrs Philip's Poems': Los Angeles, University of California at Los Angeles, MS 170/68. (Original size 200 × 120mm). Reproduced by permission of the University of California Library.*

Even more sexually suggestive is a poem headed 'Song' in Bodleian Library, MS Rawlinson poet. 94, a miscellany compiled *c.*1680–90 by John Chatwin of Emmanuel College, Cambridge. The manuscript includes imitations of Anacreon and translations from Petronius; several pastoral dialogues; poems with titles such as 'A Satyr against the Gout' and 'Camilla display'd Naked in Bed'; and two poems about other late seventeenth-century women poets, 'To Astrea on her Poems', beginning 'Too long, (alas!) have these unhappy Times / Groan'd under Nonsense and poor jingling Rhymes', and 'In Pious Memory of Mrs Ann Killigrew. a Pindarique', beginning 'How! Poetry and Painting both in One, / Two mighty Arts So closely joyn'd'. The Orinda poem parodies Philips's friendship poems, its ideal audience being readers who remember lines such as the opening quatrain of 'Friendship's Mysteries': 'Come, my Lucasia, since we see / That miracles men's faith do move / By wonder and by Prodigy, / To the dull, angry world let's prove / There's a religion in our Love'. The author of this anapestic song, however, creates a tone altogether different from Philips's:

Song.

1.

Come, come my Orinda and now let us prove
The Secret enjoyments of innocent Love,
In excesses of Rapture enfolded wee'll lye,
And in melting Embraces together wee'll dye;
  Whilst the Gods that Sit crown'd with the fullness of bliss,
  Shall envy and wish for a pleasure like this.

2.

Then let the Dull Lobor complain of his Miss,
And Say that She's rude to deny Him a Kiss;
Let Him Sigh too and whine, and trouble his Mind,
For his nauseous Jilt that is grown So unkind;
  I value not Jove nor his Goddesses charms,
  So long as I'me blest in Orinda's Soft Arms.

The 'comedy' of this verse arises, of course, from a play on the idea that Orinda's name is synonymous with chaste love – this poet boldly imagining that he might enjoy with her erotic experiences denied other would-be lovers.[35]

On 8 April 1663, Philips wrote to Sir Charles Cotterell, 'I have had many Letters and Copies of Verses sent me, some from Acquaintance, and some from Strangers, to compliment me upon POMPEY . . . they are so full of Flattery, that I have not the Confidence to send them to you' (*Letters*, p.78). Our PLATE 10 reproduces what may be one of those poems, 'On the famous Orinda and her Pompey', now in the

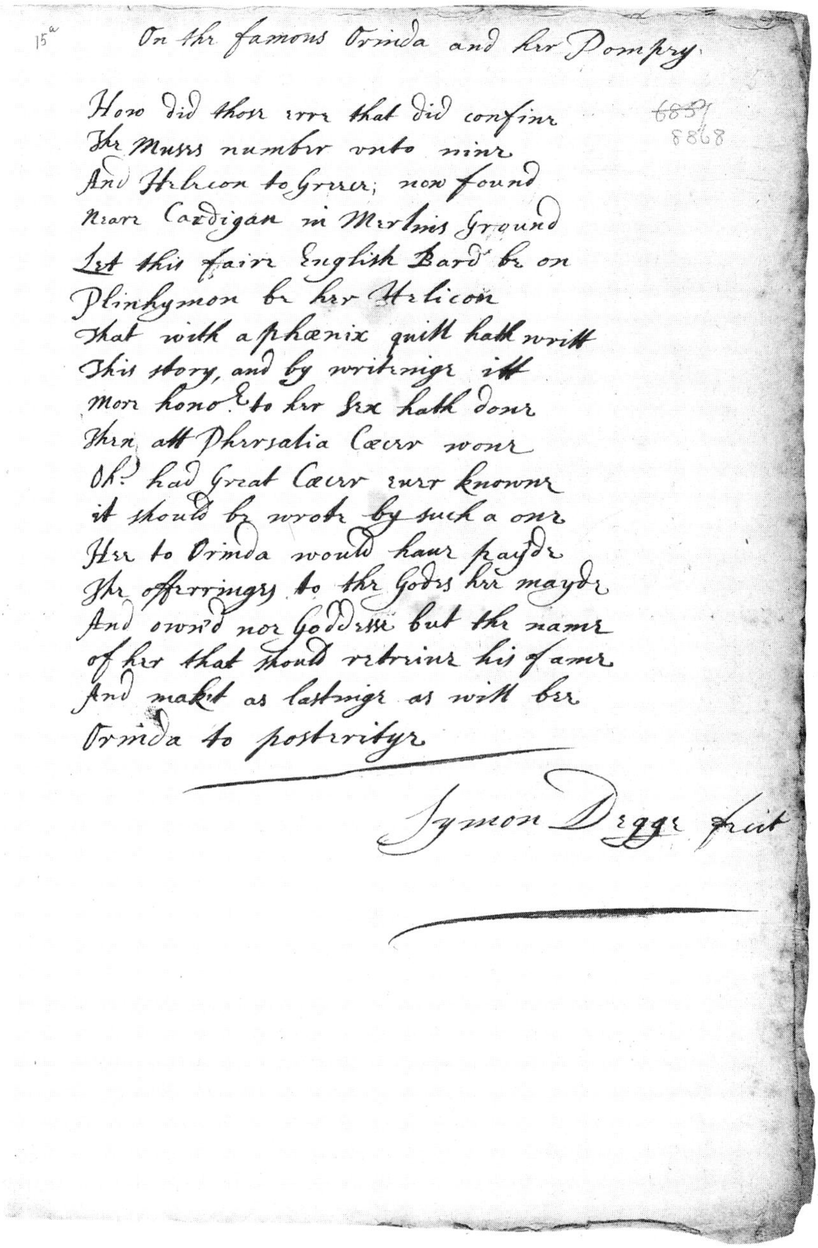

15a

On the famous Orinda and her Pompey

6859
8868

How did those erre that did confine
The Muses number unto nine
And Helicon to Greece; now found
Neare Cardigan in Merlins Ground
Let this faire English Bard be on
Plinhymon be her Helicon
That with a phœnix quill hath writt
This story, and by writinge itt
More hono.r to her sex hath done
Then att Phersalia Cæsar wone
Oh! had Great Cæsar ever knowne
it should be wrote by such a one
Hee to Orinda would have payde
The offerringes to the Gods hee mayde
And own'd noe Goddesse but the name
of her that should retreive his fame
And make it as lastinge as will bee
Orinda to posteritye

Symon Degge fecit

PLATE 10 *'On the famous Orinda and her Pompey' ascribed to Symon Degge: San Marino, California, Huntington Library, EL 8868. (Original size 300 × 203–206mm). Reproduced by permission of the Henry E. Huntington Library.*

Huntington Library among the papers of John Egerton, third Earl of Bridgewater (1646–1701), nephew of the Countess of Carbery. Symon Degge (1612–1704), to whom it is ascribed, was a reader at the Inner Temple. A royalist and judge of West Wales (1660), recorder of Derby (1661), steward of the manor court of Peverel (1662), and justice of the Welsh marches (1662), Degge is a contemporary of Philips, a person thinking of Orinda not as a disembodied name or emblem of love and friendship but as a Welsh writer. He emphasizes the Welsh connection as he celebrates a tenth muse 'now found / Neare Cardigan in Merlins Ground' (lines 3–4), and he closes with the assertion that had Caesar known Philips would translate *Pompey* (in which he is a character), he would have 'own'd noe Goddesse but the name / of her that should retreive his fame / And mak't as lastinge as will bee / Orinda to posteritye' (lines 15–18).

CONCLUSION

When Philips died on 22 June 1664, Sir Edward Dering (1625–84) echoed the title page of the 1664 edition of *Poems. By the Incomparable Mrs. K.P.* when he wrote in a household book recently catalogued as British Library, Additional MS 70887, 'my very deare friend Mrs Katharine Phillips a woman of excelling worth *and* vertues *and* of a prodigious wit, fruitfull in many incomparable poems, departed this life, to the universall losse of this nation, at London of the small pox' (fol. 10v).[36] Heralded three years later on the title-page of the folio edition of her works as the 'matchless Orinda', Philips served as a model for a number of women writers of the next decades – Anne Killigrew; Mary, Lady Chudleigh; Mary Astell; Anne Finch, Countess of Winchilsea; Jane Barker; Elizabeth Rowe; Mary Barber; and Mary Masters are all authors whom Marilyn L. Williamson lists as 'self-acknowledged followers' of Philips.[37] Writing as Philoclea to her Philander, John Locke, Damaris Masham (née Cudworth) also models herself on Philips when she says, 'But this brings me . . . to the Subject of Poetry, and to makeing my excuse for not Writeing in Verse, Since that Rhimeing Humour not onely went soon off But I have Almost forsworne ever Leting it come on Againe, Since what was intended onely for my Owne Diversion I find has Unawares (to Use Mrs Phillips's words) expos'd me to the Severitie of the Wise and the Railerie of the Witts, Altho not in any Printed Volume'.[38]

'Mrs Phillips's words' in Masham's letter are paraphrased from a letter Philips wrote in January 1663/4 to Cotterell to circulate among their friends as a defense against the publication of the 1664 edition of her *Poems;* a text of that letter was subsequently printed in the Preface to the 1667 folio (*Letters*, pp.147–52). With those words, Philips claimed for herself and, by extension, for her poems the kind of feminine decorum that allowed the approval of a polite society that generally regarded the writing of literature to be beyond woman's ken.[39] Philips's well-documented success in claiming the adjective 'virtuous' allowed poems by Philips to join verses by such writers as Cowley, Waller, and Flatman to 'Counterballance and refute sufficiently any ill use that may be made' (fol. 4v) of poems by Lucretius, Ovid, Catullus, and Rochester transcribed in *The Muses Magazine*, a two-part poetical miscellany dated 1705 and now catalogued as Bodleian Library, MS Rawlinson poet. 173. It also led John Evelyn to write in his diary of 'the virtuous *Mrs. Philips*' in contrast to 'that – – – Castlemaine' when the king's mistress acted in a court performance of Philips's *Horace* in 1668.[40]

Katherine Philips's reputation was so unlike that of her contemporary the 'eccentric' Margaret Cavendish, Duchess of Newcastle (1624?–74), that Evelyn's wife Mary would contrast her with Cavendish, whose 'discource' she describes as 'empty whimsicall and rambling, as her Books, ayming at science difficulties and high thoughts, terminating commonly in nonsence Oathes and folly'. '[W]hat contrary miracles dos this Age produce', Mary Evelyn continues, 'This Lady and Mrs Philips, the one transporded [*sic*] with the shadow of reason the other possessed of the substance and insensible of her treasure, and yet men who passe for learned and wise not only put them both in equall balance but make the greatnesse of the one wheigh downe the certaine and reall worth of the other'.[41] Philips's reputation for virtue seems also to lie behind Sarah Cowper's judgment on women writers written in a diary entry of 31 July 1701: 'I have mett with none to excel unless *th*e Admirable Mrs Philips, and wou'd sooner wish my self able to ha' compos'd the prayer we find in her poems than to be mistress of all the Gems, I ever yet saw belong to any Woman. The Dutch*ess* of Newcastle hath made a pudder with philosophy and verse'.[42] How twentieth-century readers might best read Philips's use of the humility topos in her letters and poems is another matter altogether, a matter, indeed, that has evoked a variety of responses from recent critics. Our own feeling is that Philips's use of this topos in poems such as the answer to Vavasor Powell which we discussed in Part I of this essay is wittily and wonderfully ironic. For the conclusion of the story of Croesus's mute son crying out 'in his fear and his grief'. says Herodotus, was that thereafter 'for all the days of his life he had power of speech'.

APPENDIX

THE CONTENTS OF BRITISH LIBRARY HARLEY MS 6900

1 Untitled poem beginning 'Pourquoi cacher une aimable personne' (fol. 1r).

2 Untitled Latin poem beginning 'Arcum Nola dedit' and its English translation beginning 'Nola did give a bowe' (fol. 1r).

3 'Sur la Carte de Tendre: Ballade', beginning 'Estimés vous cette carte nouvelle' (fol. 1v). By Jean Regnault de Segrais (1624–1701). Headed 'Sur la carte du Tendre' in *La Guirlande de Julie Pour Mademoiselle de Rambouillet Julie Lucine d'Angennes* (Bibliothèque Nationale, MS FR 19142, fol. 208v, col. 1), a manuscript of 62 madrigals composed by various hands, including Corneille's. Charles de Sainte-Maure, Marquis and later Duc de Montausier (1610–90), began this collection in homage to his future wife Julie d'Angennes (1607–71), daughter of Madame de Rambouillet, and presented it to her on her thirty-fourth birthday in 1641. Also in *Nouveau recueil de diverses poésies, composées par plusieurs autheurs* (Paris, 1656) – (hereafter *Recueil Sercy*), III – *see* Frédéric LaChèvre, *Bibliographie des Recueils Collectifs de Poésies publiés de 1597 à 1700*, tome deuxième (*1636–1661*) (Paris, 1903), p.477.

4 'Madrigal', beginning 'Si malgré mes soucis malgré votre rigueur' (fol. 2r). Ascribed to Molière (Jean-Baptiste Poquelin, 1622–73) by P. LaCroix, *Poésies diverses attribuées à Molière ou pouvant lui être attribuées* (Paris, 1869). In *Recueil Sercy*, III (1656) – *see* LaChèvre, pp.380 and 630. Although Molière may at first seem out of place among the *précieux* poets, it is worth noting that Pellisson wrote the Prologue to Molière's play *Les Fâcheux* and that Molière himself, in the Preface to his *Les Précieux ridicules*, emphasized his mockery of the incompetent apes of excellence.

5 'Autre' [Another madrigal], beginning 'Va, ne te gesne point, cours aimable infidelle' (fol. 2r). Headed 'Madrigal' in *La Guirlande de Julie, Pour Mademoiselle de Rambouillet Julie Lucine d'Angennes* (Bibliothèque Nationale MS FR 19142, fol. 208v, col. 2). Also in *Recueil Sercy*, III (1656) – *see* LaChèvre, p.642.

6 'Les Quatre saisons de l'année', beginning 'Du fantasque Orion les funestes orages' (fols. 3r–34r).

7 'Sur un Saphir retrouvé', beginning 'Je suis plus content qu'un Roi' (fol. 34v). Headed 'Sur le recouvrement d'un saphir' in *Recueil de Pieces Galantes En Prose* et *en Vers, De Madame la Comtesse de La Suze, D'une autre Dame*, et *de Monsieur Pellisson. Augmenté de plusieurs Elegies*, tome premier (Paris, 1678), p.197.

8 'Caprice contre L'Estime, A Sapho', beginning 'Donc je ne doi plus pretendre' (fols 35r–36v). By Paul Pellisson-Fontanier (1624–1693) (known as Pellisson). In *Recueil de pièces galantes, en prose et en vers* (Paris, 1684), pp.154–60. Headed 'Caprice contre l'estime (à M*ademoise*lle de Scudéry)' in *Petit recueil de poésies choisies* (1660) – *see* LaChèvre, p.408. Also in *Recueil de Pièces Galantes en prose* et *en vers, de Madame la Comtesse de La*

Suze et *de Monsieur Pellisson. Augmenté de plusieurs piéces nouvelles de divers Auteurs* (Trévoux, 1725), tome 1, pp.200–7.

9 'A L'Orfelin, fameus graveur Pour l'obliger de faire la medaille du Duc de Mantoue', beginning 'Savant maistre de l'art, ton admirable main' (fol. 37r).

10 'L'Or, Idylle', beginning 'On dit que Jupiter étalant sa puissance' (fol. 38v).

11 'La Fauvette. Dialogue', beginning 'Puis que Sapho n'est point ici' (fols 39r–42v). By Pellisson. Headed 'Dialogue entre Acante et La Fauvette' in *Recueil de pièces galantes, en prose et en vers* (Paris, 1684), pp.135–46, and (Trévoux, 1725), pp.176–90. Also in *Bibliothèque Poëtique, ou nouveau choix des plus belles pieces de vers en tout genre, depuis Marot jusqu'aux Poëtes de nos jours. Avec leurs vies et des remarques sur leurs ouvrages* (Paris, 1745), tome 4, p.471.

12 Five stanzas – from what appears to be the end of a poem begun on missing pages – are crossed out line by line. The first of these stanzas begins, 'Si quelque fois mes yeus vous disent un mot d'elle' (fol. 43r).

13 'L'Oranger à Sappho', beginning 'Qu'on en parle, qu'on en gronde' (fols 43v, 45r). By Pellisson. Headed 'L'Oranger (à Sapho: M*ademoise*lle de Scudéry)' in *Le Nouveau Cabinet des Muses* (Paris, 1658) – *see* LaChèvre, p.409; 'L'Oranger: A Mademoiselle de Scudéry' in *Bibliothèque Poëtique* (Paris, 1745), tome 4, p.487, and 'L'Oranger À Sapho' in *Recueil de pièces galantes, en prose et en vers* (Paris, 1684), pp.161–4.

14 'Dialogue entre Acante et quelques pommes d'Api', beginning 'D'où venés vous, Belles Pommes?' (fols 45v–46r). By Pellisson. Headed 'Le Dialogue des pommes d'Api' in Alain Niderst's list of poems cited by Madeleine de Scudéry in her *Célanire* (1669) – *see* Niderst, *Madeleine de Scudéry, Paul Pellisson et leur Monde* (Paris, 1976), p.483.

15 'Elegie sur une Jalousie', beginning 'Pensers ou lon se plaist esperances flatteuses' (fols 46v–48v). By the Comtesse de la Suze (1618–73). Headed 'Elegie IV' in *Poésies de Madame la Comtesse de la Suze* (Paris, 1666); 'Sur une jalousie' in *Recueil de pièces galantes, en prose et en vers* (Paris, 1684), pp.10–11; 'III. Elegie sur une Jalousie' in *Recueil de Pièces Galantes* (1725), tome 1, pp.14–19; and 'Elegie' in *Le Nouveau Cabinet des Muses* (Paris, 1658) and *Recueil Sercy*, II (1653) – *see* LaChèvre, p.604.

16 'Ode', beginning 'Digne sang de tant de Heros' (fols 49r–50r). Headed 'A Mme La C. de S. Ode' in *Le Nouveau Cabinet des Muses* (Paris, 1658) – *see* LaChèvre, p.544.

17–24 (fols 50v–52r) and 27–30 (fol.58r–v). Enigmas.

We have identified nine of the twelve enigmas in Nos. 17–24 and 27–30 as the work of Charles Cotin (1604–82), an abbot known as the father of the French enigma and as the model for Molière's Trissotin in *Les Femmes Savantes* (R. Jouanny, ed., *Molière: Oeuvres Complètes* [Paris, 1962], tome 1, p.894, n.288, and tome 2, p.681). Each of the identified enigmas appears in at least one of the following editions: *Recueil des énigmes de ce Temps. Première Partie* (Paris, 1655); *Oeuvres Mesle'es de* Monsieur *Cotin, de l'académie françoise. Contenant énigmes, odes, sonnets, et épigrammes* (Paris, 1659); and

Recueil des Enigmes de ce Temps. Première Partie (Paris, 1661). Cotin's No. XI, p.12; XIX, p.20; XXXV, p.36; XL, p.41, XLI, p.42, XLIII, p.44, XLVII, p.48 [pagination incorrectly inverted as '84' in 1661 ed.], XLVIII, p.49, and LVI, p.57.

17 'Enigme', beginning 'Je puis comme les dieus découvrir les pensées' (fol. 50v).

18 'Autre', beginning 'Dans le Palais des Rois où le luxe commande' (fol. 50v). No. XI, p.12 (1655, 1659, and 1661).

19 'Autre', beginning 'Issus d'un Pere malhureus' (fol. 51r). No. XXXV, p.36 (1659 and 1661).

20 'Autre', beginning 'Lon voit en l'air une maison' (fol. 51r). No. XL, p.41 (1659).

21 'Autre', beginning 'Mon corps, quoi que petit a ses nerfs et ses veines' (fol. 51v). No. XIX, p.20 (1655, 1659, and 1661).

22 'Autre', beginning 'Mon corps est sans couleurs comme est celui des eaux' (fol. 51v). No. XLVII, p.48 (1655, 1659, and 1661).

23 'Autre', beginning 'D'un pere paresseus le destin me fit naître' (fol. 52r). No. XLI, p.42 (1659 and 1661).

24 'Autre', beginning 'Qui pourroit en beauté contre moi disputer' (fol. 52r). No. XLIII, p.44 (1655, 1659, and 1661).

25 'Elegie', beginning 'Je vien, cruelle Iris, les yeus baignés de larmes' (fols 52v–56r). By the Comtesse de la Suze. Headed 'V. Elegie' in *Recueil de pièces galantes, en prose et en vers* (Paris, 1684), pp.16–21, and in *Recueil de Pièces Galantes* (1725), pp.24–32.

26 'Sur une absence, Virelais', beginning 'A Lepreuve de l'absence'. (fols 56v–57v). By Pierre Perrin (1620–1675). Headed 'Sur une absence. Virelay' in *Le Nouveau Cabinet des Muses* (1658) and in Pierre Perrin, *Oeuvres* (1661) – *see* LaChèvre, p.512.

27 'Enigme', beginning 'Je fais suivre ici bas mes inconstantes lois' (fol. 58r). Cotin, No. XLVIII, p.49 (1659 and 1661).

28 'Autre', beginning 'Je suis fils de la Terre, et Vulcan me fassonne' (fol. 58r).

29 'Enigme', beginning 'Cibelle a fait mon corps que Vulcan a formé' (fol. 58v).

30 'Autre', beginning 'Celui dont la rigueur fatale a l'Univers' (fol. 58v). Cotin, No. LVI, p.57 (1659).

31 'Pour Mad*ame* d'Olonne malade du pied', beginning 'Comme si lon ouvroit desja votre cercueil' (fols 59r–60r).

32 'Pourtrait, adressé à Tirsis', beginning 'Entre les plus charmans objês' (fols 60v–61v).

33 'Epigramme De Madem*oise*lle Colletet', beginning 'Ou ma raison me trompe, ou je vois en effet' (fol. 62r). By Gilles Boileau (1631–69). Headed 'Epigramme de Mademoiselle**. Sur Scarron' in *Bibliothèque Poëtique, ou nouveau choix des plus belles pieces de vers en tout genre, depuis Marot jusqu'aux Poëtes de nos jours. Avec leurs vies et des remarques sur leurs ouvrages* (Paris, 1745), tome 1, p.396.

34 'Les Visions. À Mons*ieur* le Mar*écha*l de Grammont', beginning 'Je ne vous

écris point, Non faute de memoire' (fol. 62v). Marginal notation: 'Scudery'. Headed 'Les Visions. Au Mar*échal* de Gramont', but otherwise unidentified, in *Recueil Sercy*, III (1656) – *see* LaChèvre, p.570.
Note: Although we have not yet identified the poem entitled 'Pour Mad*ame* d'Olonne, malade du pied', Jean-Regnault Segrais mentions Madame d'Olonne in his *La Galerie des Portraits de Mademoiselle Montpensier: Recueil des Portraits et Eloges en vers et en prose des seigneurs et dames les plus illustres de France, la plupart composés par eux-mêmes. Dédiés à son altesse royale Mademoiselle* (Paris, rpt. 1860), p.172. 'Madame Dollonne' is also listed as No. 133 in Lougee's 'Index of Identifiable *Précieuses*', p.220. So too, le Maréchal de Grammont, named in the heading 'Les Visions à Mons*ieur* le Mar*éch*al de Grammont' (fol. 62v), is a member of the group about whom Segrais writes in *La Galerie des Portraits de Mademoiselle Montpensier*.

35 'Tableau de la vie humaine', beginning 'C'est une Loy connue en toute la Nature' (fols 63r–66r).

36 'Virelay', beginning 'C'est à bon droit q*ue* lon conda*mn*e à Rome' (fols 66v–67r).

37 'On the death of the Queene of Bohemia', beginning 'Although *the* most doe with officious heat' (fol. 68r–v). By Katherine Philips.

38 'To Her Royall Highnes *the* Dutches of York Who commanded Mrs. Philips to send her what *ver*ses she had written', beginning 'Madam/To you whose dignity strikes us with aw' (fol. 69r–v). By Katherine Philips.

39 'Song', beginning 'That beauteous Creature for whom I am a Lover' (fol. 70r–v).

NOTES

1 *The Collected Works of Katherine Philips, The Matchless Orinda*, Vol. II: *The Letters*, ed. Patrick Thomas (Stump Cross, Essex, 1990), p.60. Subsequent quotations from Philips's letters will be from this edition.

2 *The Collected Works of Katherine Philips, The Matchless Orinda*, Vol. I: *The Poems*, ed. Patrick Thomas (Stump Cross, Essex, 1990). Except in instances where the context makes clear that we are citing manuscript texts, our quotations from Philips's poems are from Thomas's edition. Where possible, Thomas uses manuscripts as copytexts, but he imposes upon them punctuation from printed editions. Peter Beal, *Index of English Literary Manuscripts*, Vol. II: *1625–1700*, Part 2: *Lee-Wycherley* (London and New York, 1993), includes most of our manuscript discoveries. We in turn are indebted to Dr Beal for sharing with us his knowledge of Philips's texts and for his enthusiastic support and participation in our project. It was he who called our attention to the Chetwood manuscript in St Paul's Cathedral Library, the Mary Evelyn letter, and the Clarke manuscript at Worcester College; he anticipated us in locating the Elizabeth Lyttleton manuscript at Cambridge.

3 'Malleable and Fixed Texts: Manuscript and Printed Miscellanies and the Transmission of Lyric Poetry in the English Renaissance', in *New Ways of Looking at Old Texts: Papers of the Renaissance English Text Society, 1985–1991*, ed. W. Speed Hill (Binghamton, New York, 1993), p.167.

4 In addition to Peter Beal and to people named elsewhere in the text or notes of this essay, we owe thanks for help with various parts of our research to P. A. Bullock, Anne Caiger, Sara S. Hodson, Carl Huffman, Daniel Huws, Yvonne McDaniel, Keith Nightenhelser, Joanna Parker, Martha Rainbolt, Mary Robertson, Marc Schwarz, Sara Jayne Steen, Marthe Tendjoukian, Joseph Wisdom, Hayley Wood, and Laetitia Yeandle. For financial support of the project, we thank the American Philosophical Society, the Folger Shakespeare Library, and the Center for the Humanities of the University of New Hampshire. For permission to reproduce photographs and/or transcripts of manuscript items now in their possession, we also thank Balliol, Christ Church, and Worcester Colleges and the Bodleian Library, Oxford; the Evelyn Trustees; the Folger Shakespeare Library; the Henry E. Huntington Library; the Osborn Collection, Yale University; the Library of the University of California at Los Angeles; the Ruth Mortimer Rare Book Room, Smith College Library; and the National Library of Wales.

When we have quoted directly from seventeenth-century texts, we have maintained their spelling and punctuation, though we have regularized *i, j, u, v,* and *w* to conform to modern usage, and we have expanded contractions such as 'y^e^' = '*the*' and '&' = '*and*' or '*et*'.

5 'The *Gentleman's Journal* and the Commercialization of Restoration Coterie Literary Practices', *Modern Philology,* 89 (1992), 328.

6 Our history of the controversy over the Two Tables is indebted to J. Sears McGee, *The Godly Man in Stuart England: Anglicans, Puritans, and the Two Tables, 1620–1670* (New Haven and London, 1976), especially pp.68–113. We follow him in using 'Puritan' to refer to 'those whose highest priority was the dissemination of "godly preaching" throughout England' and 'Anglican' to denote 'those more or less content with the episcopal organization and liturgy of the Church of England' (pp.9–10). For controversy incited by *The Book of Sports, see,* for example, Leah S. Marcus, *The Politics of Mirth: Jonson, Herrick, Milton, Marvell, and the Defense of Old Holiday Pastimes* (Chicago and London, 1986), or Kenneth L. Parker, *The English Sabbath: A Study of Doctrine and Discipline from the Reformation to the Civil War* (Cambridge, 1988).

7 B. S. Capp, *The Fifth Monarchy Men: A Study in Seventeenth-century English Millenarianism* (Totowa, New Jersey, 1972), pp.50–2. It was in Capp's quotations from Powell's poem that we first recognized the antecedent of Philips's 'Upon the double murther'.

8 Elizabeth Warren, *The old and good way vindicated* (London, 1646), sig. A3v, also compares herself to the dumb son of Croesus. Cited by Patricia Crawford, 'Women's published writings 1600–1700', in *Women in English Society, 1500–1800,* ed. Mary Prior (London and New York, 1985), p.226.

9 Our transcript of this poem replicates the format in which it is transcribed in Aberystwyth, National Library of Wales, MS I Brogyntyn 28, fol. 34.

10 Several weeks after we located these poems, we learned that we had been anticipated by James Brown and Patricia Sant. Their article announcing the poems is, we understand, forthcoming in *English Literary Renaissance*; we have accordingly refrained from printing a full transcription and from commenting in detail on the likelihood of the poem's being Philips's.

11 *The Patriarch's Wife: Literary Evidence and the History of the Family* (Chapel Hill and London, 1987), pp.106–8.

12 *See* Carol Barash, 'The Political Origins of Anne Finch's Poetry', *Huntington Library Quarterly,* 54 (1991), 346. Barash notes that 'Ardelia . . . is the female form of "ardelio," Latin for a meddler or busy-body. If Finch's speaker burns ardently with

transgressive political desires, those desires are on the verge of being ironized as the individual woman's private emotional concerns'.

13 'The Reputation of Katherine Philips', unpublished Ph.D. dissertation, City University of New York (1990), p.78. Trefousse apparently assumes the elegy is by Anne Owen.

14 The three lacunae in the 1664 edition (and also in the Clarke MS at Worcester College) are line 12 of 'On the Fair Weather just at Coronation'; line 6 of 'To my deare Sister Mrs. C. P. on her Nuptial'; and line 25 of 'To the noble Palaemon on his incomparable discourse of Friendship' – the 1664 text printing what is line 26 in all other known copies of the poem ('Drawn by the softer, and yet stronger Charms') as line 25 and following it with a line of asterisks. Other versions of the line missing from the Palaemon poem are 'Nations and people would let fall their armes' (NLW MS 775B, NLW MS 776B, and the Dering MS in Texas) and 'Nations and Armies would lay down their Arms' (1667 folio). Other versions of line 6 in the poem on Cicily Philips's marriage are 'Do but disturb and not adorn our Joys' (NLW MS 775B and Dering MS) and 'Are but a troublesome, and empty noise' (1667 folio); the line is also missing in NLW 776B.

We should like to thank Karen V. Kukil, Assistant Curator of Rare Books, for providing information and photocopies of the relevant pages of the Smith College volume.

15 That this Cassandra is not Philips's sister-in-law Cicily Lloyd (née Philips) is demonstrated by our discovery in the National Library of Wales of the inventory of the recently-deceased Cicily Lloyd's 'good scattels and Chattels' taken on 9 March 1660/1 (St David's Probate/1660/187).

16 Although Thomas observes the Trevor coat-of-arms on this binding (*Poems*, p.49), he does not call attention to John Dungannon as a possible owner.

17 While we were working on this essay, we discovered that Catherine Cole Mambretti, 'A Critical Edition of the Poetry of Katherine Philips', unpublished Ph.D. dissertation, University of Chicago (1979), and Rebecca Lynn Tate, 'Katherine Philips: A Critical Edition of the Poetry', unpublished Ph.D. dissertation, Texas Tech University (1991), collate the Philips poems from this manuscript. Neither of them, however, examines the contents of the manuscript as we do here.

18 *The Library of Mr DuPrat, Being A Collection of Philological, Historical and Theological Books, in the* Greek, Latin, Italian, Spanish, French *and* English *Tongues in all Volumes, will be sold by Auction at Toms Coffee-House adjoyning to Ludgate on* Tuesday *2d of* May *next 1699. By John Bullord.*

19 For examples of the popularity of the sobriquet 'Uranie' in seventeenth-century French poetry, *see* Sonnet 18 by Vincent Voiture (1597–1648), which became part of the posthumous controversy that pitted his 'Uranie' against the 'Job' of Isaac de Benserade (1613–91), and the poem 'A Madame de Pelissari, sur la perte d'un grand procès' by Etienne Pavillon (1628–1705). For the texts of Voiture's Sonnet 18 – 'Il faut finir mes jours en l'amour d'Uranie' – and the corresponding poem about 'Job' by Benserade, which became part of a famous controversy in the *précieux* salons, *see La poésie française du premier 17e siècle: textes et contextes*, ed. David Lee Rubin (Tübingen, 1986), p.302. For Pavillon's poem addressed to 'Uranie', *see Bibliothèque poëtique, ou nouveau choix des plus belles pieces de vers en tout genre: depuis Marot jusqu'aux Poëtes de nos jours. Avec leurs vies et des remarques sur leurs ouvrages* (Paris, 1745), tome 3, pp.193–5.

20 He also drew our attention to Heawood, No. 1026 (plate 147) and, especially, No. 3011 (plate 385), both of which include the letters *I*, *D*, and *C*. He observes of Heawood No. 3011 in which the three letters are punctuated with hearts as in the

Harley manuscript: 'It seems very likely to me that this represents a different size or grade of paper made by the same papermaker. The document is designated Paris, 1684, only one year after the most recent date ['Avr. 15. 83' on fol. 44] connected with the manuscript'.

21 *Le Paradis des Femmes*: *Women, Salons, and Social Stratification in Seventeenth-Century France* (Princeton, 1976), p.223.

22 For the French influence on Philips, *see* Philip Webster Souers, *The Matchless Orinda* (Cambridge, Mass., 1931), pp.143–5, and Patrick Thomas, *Katherine Philips ('Orinda')* ([Cardiff], 1988), *passim*, and the Introduction to his edition of *The Poems*, pp.7–11. Harley MS 6900 also includes one Latin poem and its translation into English on fol. 1r and five stanzas of an additional French poem, each line neatly crossed out, on fol. 43r. An older pagination of the manuscript indicates that two folios are now missing between fols 42 and 43.

23 The 'map of Tenderness' was a social game invented by Madeleine de Scudéry and played in the salons of the *précieuses*: this fanciful map, which marked numerous roads and by-ways in the rarefied country of tenderness, was printed in *Clélie* (1654). For a reproduction of 'La Carte du pays de Tendre', *see*, for example, Dorothy Anne Liot Backer, *Precious Women* (New York, 1974), p.195.

24 Although *Almahide, ou l'esclave reine* appeared with Madeleine's brother's name on the title page, the Scudérys' contemporaries believed most works nominally by him to have been his sister's. Modern scholars agree with this seventeenth-century attribution, except in the case of *Almahide*, which many critics ascribe to Georges de Scudéry (1601–67) because they consider it inferior to Madeleine de Scudéry's other works. *See* René Godenne, *Les Romans de Mademoiselle de Scudéry* (Genève, 1983), pp.307–14.

25 Joan DeJean, 1654: 'The Salons, "Preciosity," and the Sphere of Women's Influence,' *A New History of French Literature*, ed. Denis Hollier (Cambridge, Mass., and London, 1989), p.298.

26 Letter of 12 January 1680, in DeJean, p.298.

27 DeJean, p.302.

28 Thomas notes (*Letters*, p.48, n.10) that this poem, written in 1633 and published in 1646, by Philippe Habert (1605–37) was described by Paul Pellisson-Fontanier as 'une des plus belles pièces de notre poésie française'.

29 In Appendix One, 'Index of Identifiable *Précieuses*', Lougee lists La Calprenède's wife, née Madeleine de Lyée, as No. 89 (p.218). For references to the two English translations of La Calprenède, *see* Souers, pp.121 and 143–4.

30 Thomas, *Poems*, p.276, notes a twelve-line version of the poem on Frances Philips headed '(Upon a dear Friend dead:)' in Oxford, Bodleian Library, Rawlinson poet. MS 90, fol. 164v; it comprises Philips's lines 1–4 followed by four additional lines and then Philips's lines 85–90.

31 On sombre bindings, *see English Bindings, 1490–1940 in the Library of J. R. Abbey*, ed. G. D. Hobson (London, 1940), no. 64, and Howard M. Nixon, *English Restoration Bookbindings: Samuel Mearne and his Contemporaries* (London, 1974), pp.42–5.

32 'Katherine Philips: Another Step-Father and Another Sibling, "Mrs C: P.", and "Polex:r"', *Restoration*, 13 (1989), 4–5.

33 *Almanach d'Amour, Pour l'An de Grace 1663. Par le Grand Ovide Cypriot, Spéculateur des Ephémérides Amoureuses*, in *Recueil de pièces en prose, les plus agréables de ce temps. Composées par divers Autheurs*, Seconde partie (Paris, 1662), pp. 263–306. The *Almanach d'Amour* is mentioned in Pellisson's 'La Fauvette. Dialogue' in British Library, Harley MS 6900, fol. 40v, treated in Part II, above.

34 While 'Sylvia' is a common pastoral name, it is perhaps worth noting in the Centre for Kentish Studies a letter to Philips's friend Sir Edward Dering subscribed on 15 May 1669, 'Your indeared Silviae' (U350, C2/120).

35 A somewhat similar impulse may lie behind 'Orinda to Cloris' by Sir Charles Sedley, one of the 'Court Wits' whose collaborative translation of Corneille's *Pompey* rivalled Philips's. In Sedley's ventriloquist poem a rather worldly Orinda admonishes Cloris to 'Live, *Cloris*, then at the full Rate / Of thy great Beauty' (Lines 17–18); she should choose not a man known for wisdom or one successful in the realm of worldly honour, Orinda advises, but one of those who 'of Love their Business make, / In Love their whole Diversion take' (lines 29–30). *See The Poetical and Dramatic Works of Sir Charles Sedley*, ed. V. de Sola Pinto, Vol. I (London, 1928), pp.9–10.

36 We are indebted to Hilton Kelliher for calling our attention to this manuscript and for helping us with numerous other details as we wrote this essay.

37 *Raising Their Voices: British Women Writers, 1650–1750* (Detroit, 1990), p.21. Among copies of Philips's published poems owned by women is an exemplar of the 1664 edition now in the University Library, University of Illinois at Urbana-Champaign; its inscription, 'This book was given by Mrs Ann Pughe of Mathafarn to Lowry Nanney 1722', indicates a Welsh connection, for Matharvarn, in County Merioneth, is in northern Wales, 5½ miles north of Machynlleth. A copy of the 1667 edition in the Lilly Library, Indiana University, is inscribed, 'Hannah Deane Sept 17 1776'. In a private collection in America is a copy of the 1667 folio on which is written on the pastedown, 'Madam Anne Crewe Febr: 26: 6$\frac{8}{9}$, and on the third flyleaf – in a different hand – 'Madame anne [*sic*] Crewe her booke Oct: 2i [*sic*] 1672'. The catalogue of Sotheby's sale of George Thorn-Drury's collection on 16 June 1931 lists as Lot 1331 a copy of the 1669 edition in which 'on a flyleaf at the end are 24 blank lines of verse headed "The Teares of the Consort for Mr. Tighe Writt by My Lord Blessington 1679" and signed at the foot "Ann: Tighe. August 26th, 1680"'. A copy of the 1678 edition in the Furness Memorial Library, University of Pennsylvania, is inscribed 'Mary Parker / Her Book. 1743 / To Serena Norris'. Lower on the page is the name 'Debby Norris'; and above the women's names in smaller letters is written, 'Joseph Parker Nors is [presumably Norris] his Book 1772'. A copy of the same edition in the University Library, University of Illinois at Urbana-Champaign, is inscribed on its title page in what appears to be a seventeenth- or possibly eighteenth-century hand, 'Mary anne [*sic*] Herbert'.

The importance of Philips's poems, especially those on friendship, to the American writer Sarah Orne Jewett (1849–1909) and her circle is indicated by three volumes of Philips's poems once owned by Jewett and an essay by Jewett's friend Annie Fields. In the Houghton Library, Harvard University, is a copy of the 1664 edition inscribed with Jewett's signature and a presentation copy of J. R. Tutin's 1904 selection of poems for which Louise I Guiney wrote the introductory Appreciatory Note. The latter book is inscribed, 'To my dear Sarah Orne Jewett, Orinda's immemorial friend. L.I.G. Oxford, March 19, 1904'. In her dissertation, p.173, Rachelle F. Trefousse reports in Jewett's copy of the 1669 edition in the Berg Collection of the New York Public Library a note that Philips 'was the first to dignify the love and friendship of women for each other'. In *A Shelf of Old Books* (1895 – ascribed on the title page to 'Mrs. James T. Fields'), Annie Fields cites Keats's praise of 'To Mrs M. A. upon absence' and writes, 'Where else can we look in all literature for such an apotheosis of love between woman and woman – love on earth even as it is in heaven? She was a true lover indeed. Was there ever one quite like her?' After quoting several other poems from the 1678 edition, Fields closes with a commendation of Philips's 'true simple poetry' (pp.201 and 204).

It was evidently Alice Marsh Camron whose interest in Philips led in 1879 to the naming of a tract of land near Berkeley, California, 'Orinda Park'; in 1900, when it was incorporated, the work 'Park' disappeared, and the present town of Orinda, California, was established: *see The History of Orinda* (Orinda, 1970), pp.27–8.

38 *The Correspondence of John Locke*, Vol. II: *Letters nos. 462–848*, ed. E. S. de Beer (Oxford, 1976), p.793. De Beer opines that 'Lady Masham's verse resembles that of "To Rosania" and "L'Accord du Bien"' (p.793, n.2). Masham quotes two lines from Philips's 'L'amitié: To Mrs M. Awbry' in letter No. 830, p.735. We are grateful to Wayne Glausser for calling our attention to these letters.

39 Among many essays treating Philips's success in earning for herself a reputation for virtue in an age when women were expected to be 'chaste, silent, and obedient', *see* especially Paula Loscocco, 'Manly Sweetness': Katherine Philips among the Neoclassicals', *Huntington Library Quarterly*, 56 (1993), 259–79.

40 *The Diary of John Evelyn*, Vol. III: *Kalendarium, 1650–1672*, ed. E. S. de Beer (Oxford, 1955), p.505. J. H. K. Wing, Christ Church librarian, kindly confirmed for us that in Evelyn's manuscript diary there are three dashes before Castlemaine's name.

41 Oxford, Christ Church, Evelyn Papers (Mary Evelyn Box).

42 Quoted by Allan Pritchard, 'Editing from Manuscript: Cowley and the Cowper Papers', *Editing Poetry from Spenser to Dryden: Papers given at the sixteenth annual Conference on Editorial Problems*, ed. A. H. de Quehen (New York and London, 1981), p.66. It should, however, be noted that not all seventeenth-century readers found Margaret Cavendish to be hopelessly eccentric. Among, for example, George Etherege's early poems is 'To Her Excellence the Marchioness of Newcastle after the Reading of Her Incomparable Poems' beginning, 'With so much wonder we are struck'; it may be worth noting that a transcript of this poem is to be found on fol. 128r–v, immediately after Philips's 'To the Queen's Majesty in her Late Sicknesse' (fol. 127r–v), in British Library, Harley MS 3991. In the Houghton Library, Harvard University, is an autograph draft of a letter in which John Egerton, second Earl of Bridgewater (whose annotated copy of Philips's works is also in the Houghton Library) thanks the Duchess for a copy of her *Orations of divers sorts* and claims that 'having read so many Orations, upon so many severall persons, my admiration rises to so great a heighth, *that* I know not how to expresse it'.

The Badminton Manuscript: A New Miscellany of Restoration Verse

MICHAEL BRENNAN AND PAUL HAMMOND

At Badminton House, Avon, the seat of the Duke of Beaufort, is preserved a folio manuscript volume of 756 pages, bound in old calf (henceforth Badminton MS).[1] This volume, compiled throughout in the same hand, in probably the late seventeenth- or early eighteenth-century, contains four distinct collections of material, all of which were almost certainly copied from other manuscripts. The contents of the volume, described in more detail in APPENDIX I, is as follows:

1 'Anno Primo Regni Gul: et Mariae Regis et Reginae 1689 The Book of Establisment of their Majesties Houshold': the book of 'Household Establishments' (1689–97) of William and Mary (pp.1–71).
2 A collection of legal judgements and precedents (pp.75–212).
3 A verse miscellany of eighty-seven poems, including verses by John Wilmot, Earl of Rochester; Aphra Behn; Charles Sackville, Earl of Dorset; Sir George Etherege; Sir Carr Scroope; John Dryden; John Oldham; and John Sheffield, Earl of Mulgrave and Duke of Buckingham (pp.217–439).
4 'Observations concerning New fforest out of an old manuscript': copies of documents relating to the New Forest (pp.442–543).

The main purpose of this article is to focus attention upon the mode of compilation and literary significance of its large – and hitherto unexamined – collection of Restoration poetry. To this end, a detailed finding-list of all the poems included in Badminton MS, along with a first-line index, is provided as APPENDIX II. However, before examining the poems themselves, the other collections of material may prove to be of some assistance in considering the possible provenance and early ownership of this volume.

PROVENANCE

Only the relatively recent history of the Badminton MS can be established with any degree of certainty. According to notes made by Miss L. Redstone, archivist at Badminton between 1940 and 1942, the volume was brought to the Muniments Room in September 1941 from a kitchen-maid's room in the House, along with some other, unrelated items. It remained in the Muniments Room until 1978, when it was placed on deposit in the Gloucestershire Record Office; it was then returned to Badminton in 1989, where it was catalogued as FmE 3/12 by the present archivist, Mrs Margaret E. Richards.

If we assume for the moment that the Badminton MS has been in the possession of the Dukes of Beaufort since about the time of its composition, then either the first or second Dukes should first be considered as candidates for its ownership. However, it seems rather unlikely that Henry Somerset (1629–1699/1700), third Marquess of Worcester and first Duke of Beaufort, would have been much interested in its contents, since by the 1690s he was an old and ailing man. Furthermore, in 1688 he had been a firm opponent of the Prince of Orange and had refused the oath of allegiance when the Prince became King William III (although he finally took it in 1689). As a non-juror he was deprived of all his offices in 1690, except that of Keeper of the Forest of Dean (which he also lost in 1697), and he effectively retired from court to Badminton. In 1698 he suffered a further blow when his only son and heir, Charles Somerset (1660–98), Lord Herbert of Raglan and Marquess of Worcester, was killed in a coaching accident.[2]

Charles Somerset himself is perhaps another possible candidate for the original ownership of the Badminton MS, particularly since, unlike his father, he vigorously supported the Prince of Orange in 1688 and took an active interest in politics, serving as MP for Monmouthshire in 1679 and from 1689 until 1695. However, he held no court office after 1689, and would not necessarily have had ready access to the kinds of material contained in the Badminton MS.[3]

Moving down through the generations, Charles's son, Henry Somerset (1684–1714), second Duke of Beaufort and a notable Tory, appears at first sight to be a more feasible candidate for the ownership of this volume. However, the fact that its first item, the book of 'Household Establishments' of William and Mary (pp.1–71), ends abruptly in 1697, poses a significant problem in linking its origins directly with the second Duke of Beaufort, who was then only thirteen years old. In view of his youth, it seems rather unlikely that he was personally responsible for the actual compilation of the volume (unless it was copied out for him at a later stage in the early eighteenth-century), particularly since he pointedly absented himself from court until the accession of a Tory ministry in 1710. Nevertheless, the second Duke of Beaufort did serve as Warden of the New Forest from 1710 to 1714, and would certainly have been interested in the documents included in the volume which relate to that office (pp.442–543).

Although it seems necessary, therefore, to look beyond the immediate family of the Dukes of Beaufort to find the most likely candidate for the original owner of the Badminton MS, the key to this problem perhaps does lie in the material on the New Forest.[4] Charles Paulet (*c.*1630–1699), Marquess of Winchester, had been a keen supporter of William of Orange, with whom he had corresponded in Holland, and also assisted William after his landing in England. On 2 January 1689 Paulet was a member of the deputation of nonconformists who had presented their petition to William at St James's. In return for his support, he was created Duke of Bolton on 9 April 1689, the year in which the book of 'Household Establishments' of William and Mary begins. In the same year he also regained his place on the Privy Council. Most significantly for our purposes, he served as Lord Lieutenant of Hampshire and Warden of the New Forest from 1668 until 1676, and again from 1689 until 1699.[5]

The first Duke of Bolton's eldest surviving son, Charles Paulet (1661–1722), the second Duke, had been an equally ardent supporter of William, crossing over to Holland in order to escort him to England; and had carried the orb at William's coronation on 11 April 1689.[6] He was appointed as his father's successor as Warden of the New Forest in 1699, serving until 1710 when he was replaced by the second Duke of Beaufort.[7] It is possible, therefore, that the second Duke of Beaufort may have found the volume at Lyndhurst House, the Warden's residence, which after 1710 he refurbished at his own expense. He may then have decided to keep the volume as being both of general interest and of specific relevance to his Wardenship. Alternatively, it may simply have been included in error with his other personal effects, which were sent from Lyndhurst to Badminton after his death in 1714.[8]

Whatever the circumstances under which this folio volume first came to Badminton, it is certain that the second Duke of Beaufort, in addition to the material on the New Forest, would have been especially attracted by its miscellany of Restoration poetry. Both the first and second Dukes evinced a keen interest in political and satiric poetry, especially verses reflecting upon Restoration court life and members of the nobility. As is clear, for example, from unpublished correspondence at Badminton, the first Duke had been an early reader of Dryden's *Absalom and Achitophel*, soon after its publication in November 1681. Writing to his wife on 3 December 1681, the first Duke observed:

> I like Mr Dryden very well. I hope hee will goe on wth it [*Absalom and Achitophel*], tis somewhat abrupt as it is an[d] I am sure hee hath left out some of the Kings best friends; I wish his patron may make out the caracter hee gives of him.[9]

In the following year, both the first Duke of Beaufort, as Bezaliel, and his son, Charles Somerset (1660–98), were fulsomely commemorated in *The Second Part of Absalom and Achitophel* (1682), written by the poet and dramatist Nahum Tate with Dryden's assistance.[10]

Henry Somerset, the second Duke, was an intelligent and cultured man who maintained a wide correspondence, instigated various architectural schemes at Badminton and other properties, and was created DCL of St John's College, Oxford, in April 1706. The bulk of a large collection of panegyrical and satirical printed tracts, now in the British Library, was probably collected by him; and such items as a rare printed poem, *Thaliae Sacellum. A Congratulatory Poem on the Happy Marriage of . . . Henry Duke of Beaufort* (1702), commemorating his marriage on 7 July 1702 to Mary (1683–1705), daughter of Charles Sackville, Earl of Dorset, still remain in the Muniments Room at Badminton.[11]

THE BADMINTON MANUSCRIPT VERSE MISCELLANY

Restoration scribal miscellanies[12] such as the Badminton MS (as distinct from personal commonplace books) were often assembled by transcribing several small collections of poems, or even items on individual sheets, rather than by the complete transcription of a single exemplar. The scribe therefore acted to some extent as an editor on behalf of the customer or bookseller who commissioned him. The fact that the manuscript miscellanies often include the same poems, but rarely in exactly the same order, indicates that while working to a particular brief (say, to produce a collection of political satires or erotic poems) the scribe would be constrained in his arrangement of the material by the availability of copy texts. The special significance of the Badminton MS in this respect is that it shares substantially identical groups of poems with four other manuscripts, all of which were transcribed in the late seventeenth century, probably in the early 1680s:

1 Stockholm, Royal Library of Sweden, MS Vu. 69, also known as the Gyldenstolpe MS (henceforth cited as Gyldenstolpe).
2 Nottingham, University Library, Portland MS PwV 40 (henceforth PwV 40).
3 London, British Library, Harley MS 6913 (henceforth Harley 6913).
4 Nottingham, University Library, Portland MS PwV 38 (henceforth PwV 38).

This overlapping of material clearly indicates that small anthologies of contemporary poems on particular themes were available to scribes. It should be emphasised at this point that while a considerable number of Restoration manuscripts have been examined to locate these four comparable examples, our searches have been by no means exhaustive. Nevertheless, we hope that the conclusions given below will serve to indicate to other scholars the potential importance of examining not only the contents but also the order of contents in manuscript miscellanies.

TABLE 1

A comparative listing of poems in Badminton MS FmE 3/12; Royal Library of Sweden MS Vu. 69 (the Gyldenstolpe MS); Nottingham University Library Portland MS PwV 40; British Library Harley MS 6913; and Nottingham University Library Portland MS PwV 38.

BADMINTON MS item		GYLDENSTOLPE MS item		PORTLAND MS PwV 40 item		HARLEY MS 6913 item		PORTLAND MS PwV 38 item	
1	p.217	**1**	p.1	–	–	**1**	p.1	**1**	p.1
2	p.218	**2**	p.5	**104**	fol. 232[a]	–	–	–	–
3	p.227	**3**	p.21	**103**	fol. 228[b]	–	–	–	–
4	p.235	**4**	p.35	**90**	fol. 213[b]	–	–	–	–
5	p.235	**5**	p.37	**94**	fol. 218[a]	–	–	–	–
6	p.241	**6**	p.47	**85**	p.211	–	–	–	–
7	p.243	**7**	p.51	**88**	p.212[b]	–	–	–	–
8	p.244	**8**	p.53	**83**	p.203	–	–	–	–
9	p.246	**9**	p.59	–	–	–	–	–	–
10	p.247	**10**	p.61	–	–	–	–	–	–
11	p.248	**11**	p.63	–	–	**24**	p.123	–	–
12	p.251	**12**	p.71	**2**	p.1	–	–	–	–
13	p.255	**13**	p.77	**3**	p.5	–	–	–	–
14	p.260	–	–	**4**	p.11	–	–	–	–
15	p.262	**14**	p.87	**5**	p.12	–	–	–	–
16	p.263	**51**	p.227	**6**	p.13	–	–	–	–
17	p.268	**15**	p.89	–	–	–	–	–	–
18	p.273	**16**	p.97	**7**	p.19	–	–	–	–

BADMINTON MS item		GYLDENSTOLPE MS item		PORTLAND MS PwV 40 item		HARLEY MS 6913 item		PORTLAND MS PwV 38 item	
19	p.275	**17**	p.102	**8**	p.22	–	–	–	–
20	p.277	**18**	p.107	**9**	p.25	–	–	–	–
21	p.281	**19**	p.113	**14**	p.29	–	–	–	–
22	p.284	**20**	p.119	**15**	p.32	–	–	–	–
23	p.286	**21**	p.123	**16**	p.34	–	–	–	–
24	p.288	**22**	p.127	**17**	p.36	–	–	–	–
25	p.289	**23**	p.129	**18**	p.37	–	–	–	–
26	p.290	**24**	p.131	**19**	p.38	–	–	–	–
27	p.291	**25**	p.132	**20**	p.39	–	–	–	–
28	p.292	**29**	p.145	**21**	p.40	–	–	–	–
29	p.296	**26**	p.133	**22**	p.45	–	–	–	–
30	p.300	**27**	p.141	**23**	p.48	–	–	–	–
31	p.301	**28**	p.144	**24**	p.49	–	–	–	–
32	p.302	**31**	p.157	**25**	p.50	–	–	–	–
33	p.303	**30**	p.153	**26**	p.51	–	–	–	–
34	p.305	**32**	p.159	**27**	p.53	–	–	–	–
35	p.307	**39**	p.174	**28**	p.56	–	–	–	–
36	p.308	**33**	p.163	**29**	p.56	–	–	–	–
37	p.309	**34**	p.165	**30**	p.57	–	–	–	–
38	p.310	**35**	p.167	**31**	p.59	–	–	–	–
39	p.310	**36**	p.168	**32**	p.59	–	–	–	–
40	p.311	**37**	p.169	**33**	p.60	–	–	–	–
41	p.313	**41**	p.176	**34**	p.62	–	–	–	–
42	p.314	**38**	p.173	**35**	p.63	–	–	–	–
43	p.314	**42**	p.177	**36**	p.64	–	–	–	–
44	p.315	**40**	p.175	**37**	p.64	–	–	–	–
45	p.315	**43**	p.178	**38**	p.65	–	–	–	–
46	p.316	**45**	p.182	**39**	p.66	–	–	–	–
47	p.317	**44**	p.179	**40**	p.66	–	–	–	–
48	p.318	**46**	p.183	**41**	p.68	–	–	–	–
49	p.319	**47**	p.185	**42**	p.69	**2**	p.5	**2**	p.3
50	p.321	–	–	–	–	–	–	–	–
51	p.322	–	–	–	–	–	–	–	–
52	p.323	–	–	–	–	–	–	–	–
53	p.325	**48**	p.189	**43**	p.71	**3**	p.9	**3**	p.9
54	p.332	**50**	p.211	**47**	p.87	–	–	–	–
55	p.343	**52**	p.237	**51**	p.105	**15**	p.79	**15**	p.75
56	p.348	**53**	p.245	**98**	fol. 222[a]	**4**	p.21	**4**	p.21
57	p.358	**54**	p.261	–	–	**5**	p.37	**5**	p.37
58	p.365	**49**	p.203	**44**	p.79	**6**	p.49	**6**	p.47
59	p.368	**57**	p.279	–	–	**7**	p.55	**7**	p.53
60	p.369	–	–	–	–	**8**	p.57	**8**	p.55
61	p.370	**56**	p.275	–	–	**9**	p.59	**9**	p.57
62	p.373	**55**	p.273	–	–	**10**	p.63	**10**	p.61
63	p.374	**65**	p.312	–	–	**11**	p.67	**11**	p.63
64	p.376	–	–	–	–	**12**	p.71	**12**	p.67
65	p.378	–	–	–	–	**14**	p.77	**14**	p.73
66	p.379	**59**	p.285	–	–	**16**	p.87	**16**	p.83

BADMINTON MS item		GYLDENSTOLPE MS item		PORTLAND MS PwV 40 item		HARLEY MS 6913 item		PORTLAND MS PwV 38 item	
67	p.386	**63**	p.299	–	–	**19**	p.105	**19**	p.101
68	p.388	–	–	–	–	**20**	p.109	**20**	p.105
69	p.389	–	–	–	–	**22**	p.115	**22**	p.111
70	p.391	**64**	p.310	–	–	**23**	p.119	**23**	p.115
71	p.392	–	–	–	–	**25**	p.129	**24**	p.119
72	p.397	–	–	–	–	**26**	p.137	**25**	p.127
73	p.401	–	–	–	–	**28**	p.151	**26**	p.133
74	p.406	–	–	–	–	**29**	p.159	**27**	p.139
75	p.409	–	–	–	–	**30**	p.165	**28**	p.143
76	p.413	–	–	–	–	**31**	p.171	**29**	p.151
77	p.414	–	–	–	–	**32**	p.173	**30**	p.153
78	p.416	–	–	–	–	**34**	p.180	**31**	p.157
79	p.416	–	–	–	–	**35**	p.181	**32**	p.158
80	p.416	–	–	–	–	**36**	p.183	**33**	p.159
81	p.418	–	–	–	–	**37**	p.187	**34**	p.163
82	p.421	–	–	–	–	**38**	p.193	**35**	p.167
83	p.423	–	–	–	–	**39**	p.197	**36**	p.171
84	p.428	–	–	–	–	**40**	p.205	**37**	p.179
85	p.429	–	–	–	–	**41**	p.209	**38**	p.183
86	p.433	–	–	–	–	**42**	p.215	**39**	p.187
87	p.433	–	–	–	–	**43**	p.215	–	–

As Table 1 indicates, the Badminton MS shares not merely the same poems, but substantially the same – and for much of the material exactly the same – running order with Gyldenstolpe and PwV 40 for the first two-thirds of the collection, while the last third matches exactly the order of contents in Harley 6913 and PwV 38. David Vieth has already noted the links between Gyldenstolpe and PwV 40,[13] and has suggested possible interpretations of the arrangement of the poems into thematic groups.[14] Some anomalies in the match between the manuscripts deserve particular comment. The fact that Badminton MS item 14 exists in the same position in PwV 40 suggests that its absence from Gyldenstolpe may be due to scribal or editorial censorship, since it is a particularly crude and obscene poem. (Pepys included it in the manuscript supplement which he had bound up with his copy of the 1680 edition of Rochester).[15] The mismatch of Badminton MS with Gyldenstolpe and PwV 40 around items 16 and 17 also suggests editorial intervention, but of a different kind. Badminton MS moves from Mulgrave's 'The Enjoyment' to Aphra Behn's 'The Imperfect Enjoyment'; Gyldenstolpe does not give Mulgrave's poem here, but includes it much later; PwV 40 has Mulgrave's poem but not Behn's. There was clearly doubt about whether or not to associate the two pieces, but at least one other compiler came to the same decision as the compiler of Badminton MS, for New Haven,

Yale University Library MS Osborn b 105 has Mulgrave's poem followed by Behn's.[16] It is not possible to determine who was responsible for the editorial decisions behind the compilation of the poetical section of Badminton MS: it could have been the scribe of the Badminton MS, or it could have been someone else who arranged the material which he was copying. The term 'compiler' is used to avoid implying that the scribe was necessarily responsible for editorial decisions.

Another mismatch occurs at the point at which Badminton MS introduces Rochester's literary satires. Items 28 to 31 form what Vieth has identified as a linked group: Rochester's 'An Allusion to Horace', Scrope's reply 'In Defence of Satire', Rochester's rejoinder, 'On the Supposed Author', and Scrope's final 'Answer'.[17] Badminton MS places these poems in what Vieth has established to be their chronological (and logical) order, whereas Gyldenstolpe places 'An Allusion to Horace' at the end of the group. Perhaps the compiler of Gyldenstolpe recognized the linked group, but not the most appropriate order for the poems; or perhaps Rochester's long satire (which we know from other manuscripts to have circulated separately) was not to hand at the right moment.

Items 34 to 48 are a group of songs and love poems chiefly by Rochester. Badminton MS and Gyldenstolpe agree on the items included, but there are small variations in the order, suggesting that while the compilers were deriving their material ultimately from the same bundle, the poems (presumably written originally on separate leaves) were slightly shuffled. It is worth noting that Badminton MS items 34–46 occur in the same order (with only one poem differently placed) in Leeds University Library, Brotherton Collection, MS Lt 54, so it would seem that this group of songs and love poems had a separate circulation.[18]

Items 50 to 52 are poems on Edward Howard, which Gyldenstolpe omits. These poems evidently formed a linked group, though they seem to have circulated singly for the most part; they do, however, appear together in Yale MS Osborn b 105.[19] The compiler of Badminton MS sensibly placed them here next to 'Mac Flecknoe', another satire on an inept dramatist.

Turning now to the links between Badminton MS and PwV 40, we find that from items 12 to 49 the two manuscripts present exactly the same order of material, with only two anomalies: (1) PwV 40 omits Badminton MS item 17, as already mentioned; (2) PwV 40 adds a group of poems between Badminton MS items 20 and 21 (this is a group of erotic poems which is inserted into PwV 40 and disrupts the original foliation). It also omits Badminton MS items 1 to 11, a substantial group of poems by or associated with Rochester which could easily have been transmitted together in a single fascicle that was not available to the copyist of PwV 40. Some of these poems, however, are included towards the end of PwV 40.

From items 56 to 87 Badminton MS is replicated by Harley 6913 and PwV 38, except that the other manuscripts occasionally add other poems; the order, however, is exactly the same. The reasons why Badminton MS omits the poems which are included in Harley 6913 and PwV 38 can only be conjectured, but one can imagine that item 13 in PwV 38, Thomas Flatman's 'Song Upon Ld Rochester's Death', might have been omitted because it appeared in print in Flatman's *Poems and Songs* (1682). Items 17 and 18 in PwV 38 are perhaps too outspoken in their criticism of the King: 'Tacit de vita Agric: An Allusion' (item 17) stresses the need for kings to govern according to the law, while 'The Looking Glass' (item 18) is a satire on the Duchess of Portsmouth and her relationship with Charles II. Item 21 in PwV 38, 'A Plurality Parson', might have been omitted by a compiler who objected to satirical treatment of ecclesiastical matters. After the end of the shared sequence, PwV 38 continues with further poems on figures in court circles. The poems which Badminton MS shares with PwV 38 and Harley 6913 are topical and political satires, and those which can readily be dated come from late 1680 (item 72) or 1681 (items 73, 74, 81, 83, 86). It is notable that Gyldenstolpe finishes at Badminton MS item 70, in 1680, which is the date which Vieth conjectures for the transcription of Gyldenstolpe. In effect, then, Badminton MS combines two distinct, though related, collections: the first a group of poems by Rochester and his circle from the 1670s, finishing at 1680 (approximately duplicated by Gyldenstolpe and PwV 40); and the second a collection of political satires from the very early 1680s (duplicated by Harley 6913 and PwV 38).

TEXTUAL LINKS BETWEEN BADMINTON MS AND OTHER MANUSCRIPTS

Since Badminton MS is apparently not a straight transcript of any other extant manuscript, but a copy of groups of poems which also survive in these other closely related copies, one would expect Badminton MS to have demonstrable – but not exclusive – textual links with Gyldenstolpe, PwV 40, Harley 6913 and PwV 38. We may expect the chain of transmission to vary from poem to poem, or from group to group, and in many cases the textual variants are not sufficient for the establishment of a precise stemma. Nevertheless, it

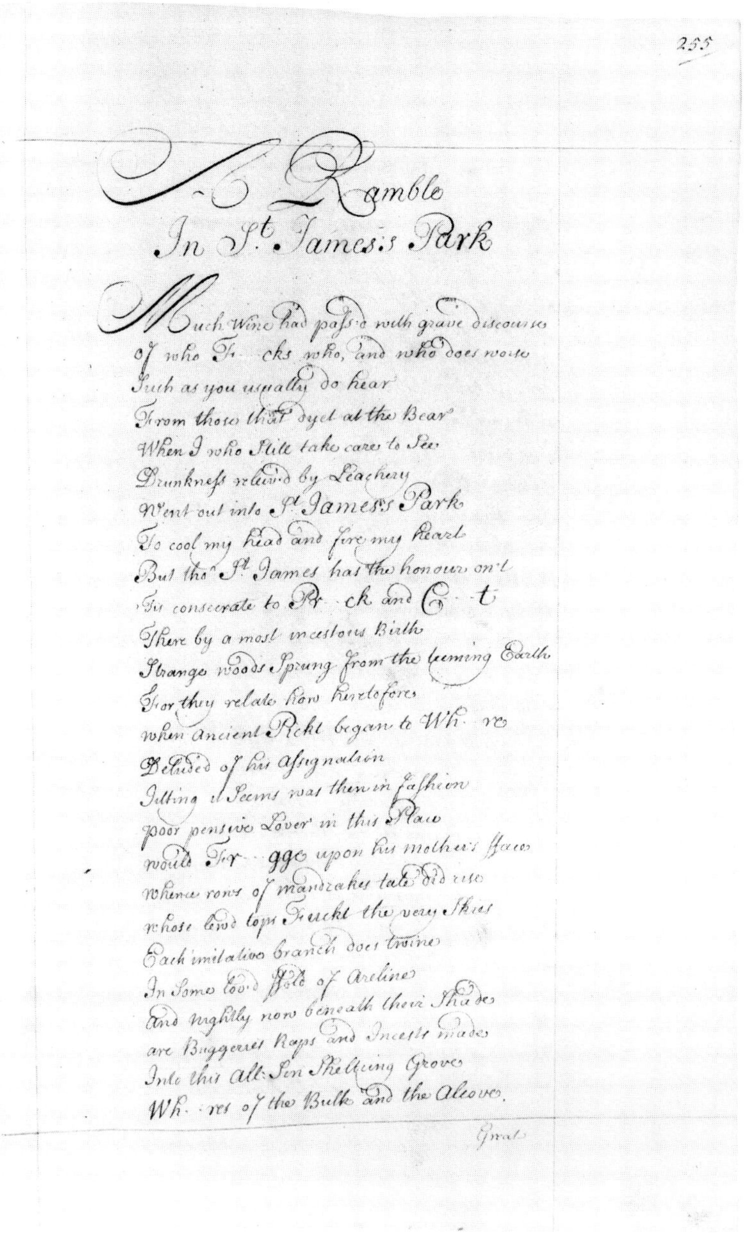
255

A Ramble
In St. James's Park

Much Wine had pass'd with grave discourse
Of who F--cks who, and who does worse
Such as you usually do hear
From those that dyet at the Bear
When I who still take care to see
Drunkness reliev'd by Leachery
Went out into St. James's Park
To cool my head and fire my heart
But tho' St. James has the honour on't
'Tis consecrate to Pr--ck and C--t
There by a most incestous Birth
Strange woods spring from the teeming Earth
For they relate how heretofore
when ancient Pickt began to Wh--re
Deluded of his Assignation
Jilting it seems was then in fashion
poor pensive Lover in this Place
would Fr--gge upon his mother's face
Whence rows of mandrakes tale did rise
whose lewd tops Fuckt the very Skies
Each imitative branch does twine
In some lov'd Fold of Aretine
And nightly now beneath their Shade
are Buggeries Rapes and Incests made
Into this All-Sin Sheltring Grove
Wh--res of the Bulk and the Alcove.

Grat

PLATE 1 *The beginning of Rochester's 'A Ramble in St. James's Park': Badminton* MS, *p.255. (Original page size 240 × 360mm). Reproduced by permission of His Grace the Duke of Beaufort.*

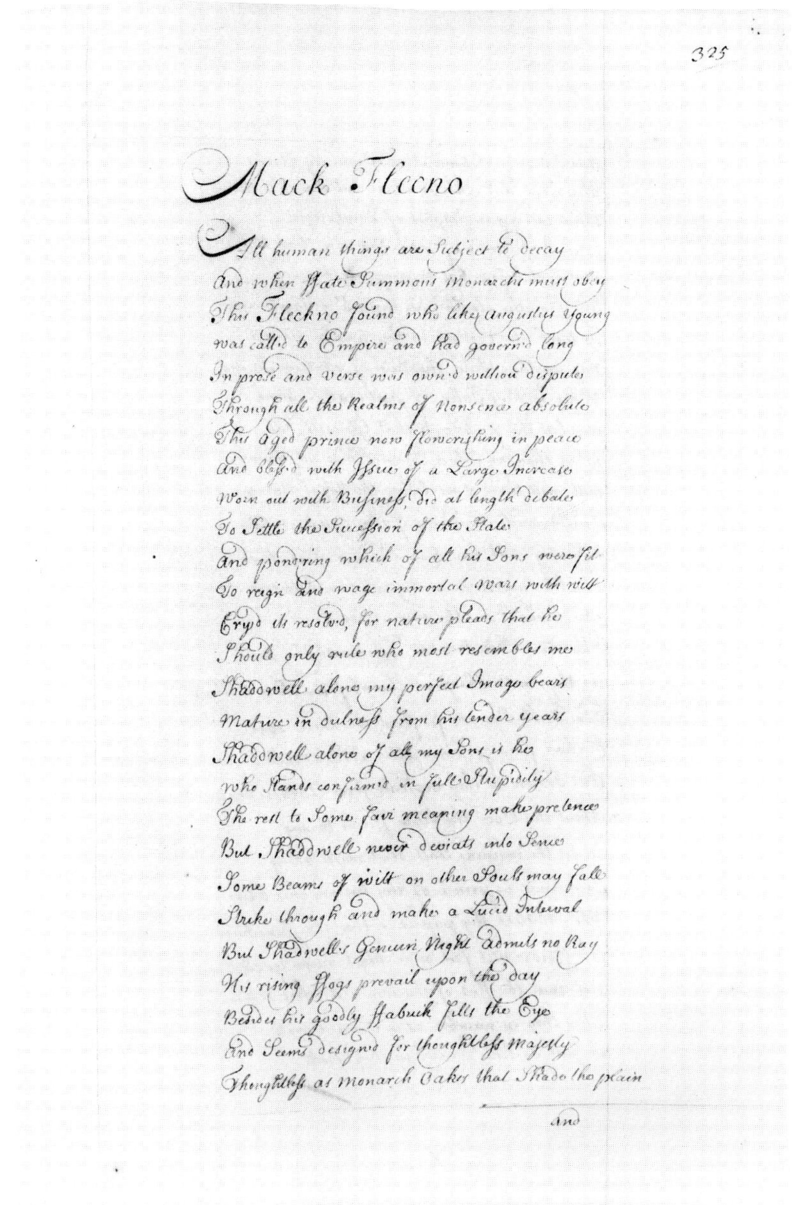

PLATE 2 *The beginning of Dryden's 'Mack Flecno': Badminton* MS, *p.325. (Original page size 240 × 360mm). Reproduced by permission of His Grace the Duke of Beaufort.*

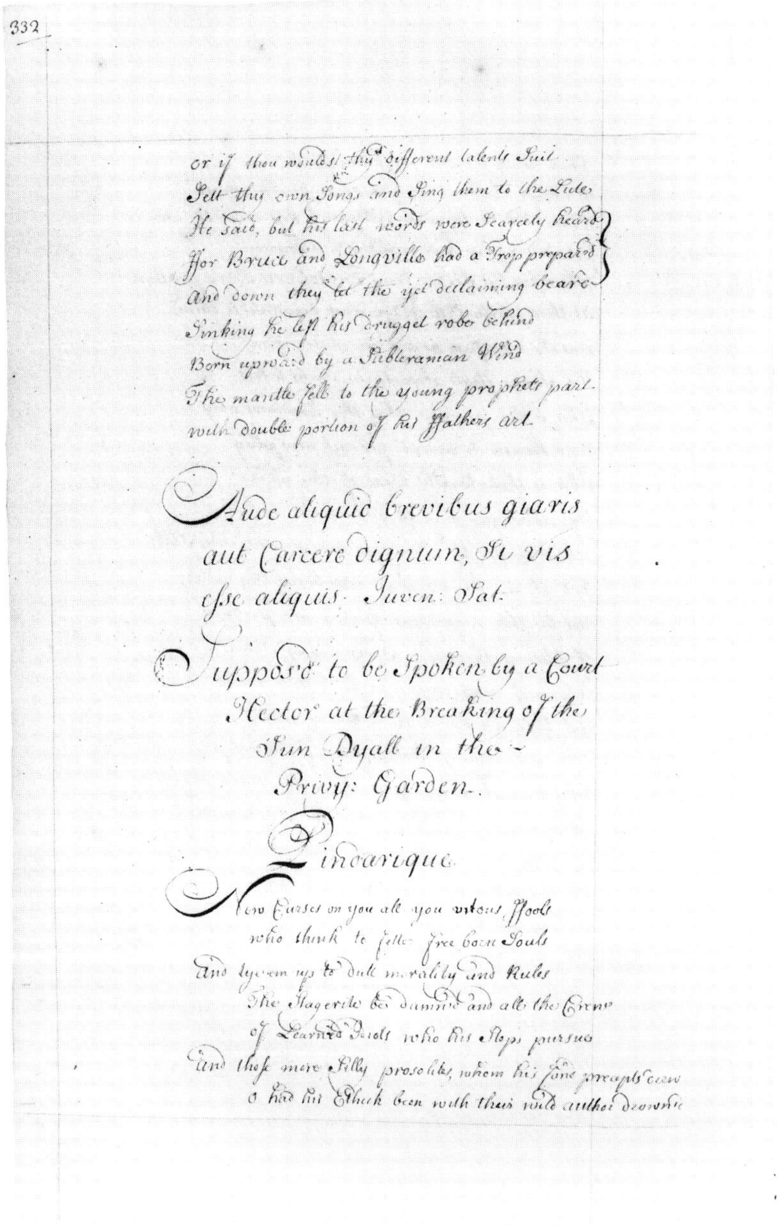
332

Or if thou wouldst thy different talents suit
Sett thy own Songs and Sing them to the Lute
He said, but his last words were scarcely heard
ffor Bruce and Longville had a Trap prepar'd
And down they let the yet declaiming beard
Sinking he left his drugget robe behind
Born upward by a Subterranean Wind
The mantle fell to the young prophets part
with double portion of his ffathers art

Aude aliquid brevibus giaris
aut Carcere dignum, si vis
esse aliquis. Juven: Sat.

Suppos'd to be Spoken by a Court
Hector at the Breaking of the
Sun Dyall in the
Privy: Garden.

Pindarique

New Curses on you all you virtous ffools
who think to fetter free born Souls
And tye em up to dull morality and Rules
The Stagerite be damn'd and all the Crew
of Learned Idiots who his Steps pursue
And those mere Silly proselites, whom his fond precepts drew
O had his Ethick been with their vile author drown'd

PLATE 3 *The end of Dryden's 'Mack Flecno' and beginning of Oldham's 'Pindarique': Badminton* MS, *p.332. (Original page size 240 × 360mm). Reproduced by permission of His Grace the Duke of Beaufort.*

is possible to demonstrate the textual affiliations of Badminton MS with these and other Restoration manuscripts in the case of a small sample of poems where the textual variants are sufficiently substantial.

(i) *Dryden's 'Mac Flecknoe'*

The textual problems of 'Mac Flecknoe' have been set out by Vieth in his important article, 'Dryden's *Mac Flecknoe:* The Case Against Editorial Confusion'.[20] Vieth's discussion is supplemented by Paul Hammond's account of the text of 'Mac Flecknoe' in Leeds MS Lt 54.[21] The stemma which Vieth establishes is given in Table 2 (with Leeds MS Lt 54 added as M15).

TABLE 2

THE STEMMA OF DRYDEN'S 'MAC FLECKNOE'

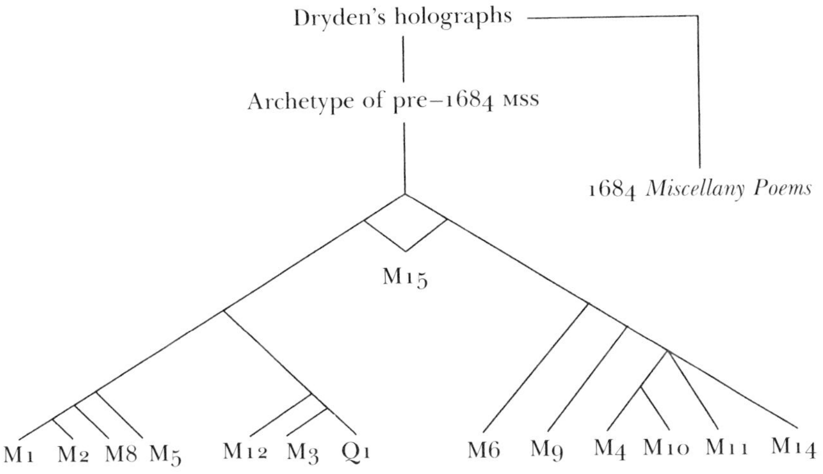

If we collate the Badminton MS against the authorized printed text published in *Miscellany Poems* (1684), the results are as follows (substantive variants only):

1684	MS
11	was] were
12	war] wars
13	'tis] its
108	sat] sate
111	arround] about
117	nor] or
126	Poppies] poppey

15*etc*	Sh———] Shadwell
29	of] to
33	clad] cloath'd
33	Norwich] Rustick
35	I] of
35	whilom] whilsom
39	tim'd] tun'd
41	And] When
41	Hymn] him
44	trembling] trembles
45	At] As
48	A——] Aston
50	Floats] wafts
53	André] Andrew
55	Though] Thou
58	bore] wore
59	he ne'er would] he'd never
60	for] with
63	anointed] appointed
64	to] by
74	its] his
75	form'd] nurs'd
76	Where] These
78	little] like
82	this] the
82	vanisht] varnish'd
84	war] wars
88	Pile] pale
92	it] he
96	Fame] pomp
97	Bun-Hill] Bumhill
98	Carpets] Carpet
107	Throne] Seat
107	of] on
126	were] was
128	that] the
128	time] times
139	Heavens] Heaven
140	farr] fair
142	his] his own
146	Ignorance] arrogance
149	Writ] write
150	toyl] Soile
157	'em] them
157	thy] thine
159	future] after
160	Issue] issues
161	too . . . 164 wit] *omitted*
165	thou] tho
168	Formal's] Formall
177	on] or
179	Nicander's] Alcander's
181	Whip-stitch] Whipstick
181	my] mine
183	When] Where
183	Muse] Scenes
183	Fletcher] Fletcher's
184	transfuse] translate
185	transfus'd] transfuse
195	writ] write
196	But sure thou'rt] Yet thou art
197	gentle] gentler
208	Ten] a
210	thy^{2}] the
213	sent] let
213	Bard] beard
215	upwards] upward

The relation between Badminton MS and the other manuscripts can be established fairly easily. First, Badminton MS occupies a terminal position on the stemma, as it has a number of unique readings, none of much interest except for the variant at line 97 where the scribe has responded too readily to the poem's scatalogical imagery by writing 'Bumhill' for 'Bunhill'. Next, we can see that Badminton MS belongs on the right hand side of Vieth's clearly divided stemma, for at line 179 it reads 'Alcander's' instead of 'Nicander's': this marks it out as belonging with M4, M6, M9, M10, M11 and M14; other readings which associate it with the same branch of the stemma are 'Yet' (196), 'wafts' (50) and 'varnish'd' (82). We can be more precise about the position of Badminton MS on the stemma by identifying points where it agrees with other single manuscripts or small groups:

Single MSS
M5: 13, 165
M10: 63, 76 (M10 has 'There'), 126b

Groups of Two MSS
M4, M10: 41a, 45, 183 (twice), 213
M4, M14: 59
M6, M10: 146
M10, M14: 168
M6, M11: 181
M9, M10: 184

Groups of Three MSS
Q1, M4, M10: 58
M2, M5, M6: 39
Q1, M1, M9: 111
M1, M11, M13: 128a
M4, M5, M10: 208
M1, M2, M11: 117

In this textual tradition there are many minor agreements which result either from cross-contamination or from scribes independently arriving at the same minor variant (as in the case of the trivial coincidences of Badminton MS with M5), but when allowance is made for these, it is clear that the most consistent agreements are between Badminton MS and M4 and M10, particularly the latter. It is probable that Badminton MS belongs on the stemma (as M16) in approximately this position:

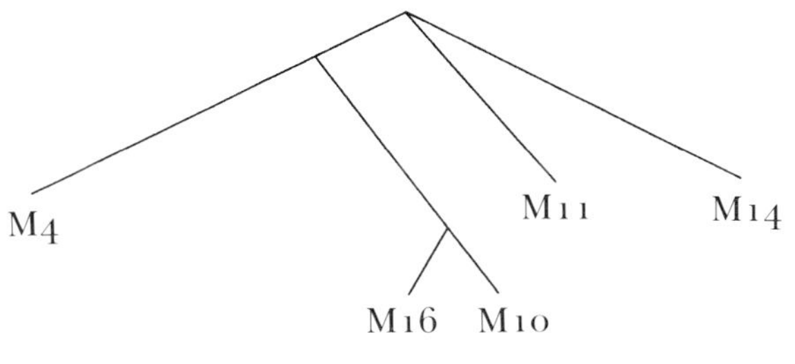

If we now translate these symbols back into the manuscripts for which they stand, we find:

M4: British Library Harley MS 6913
M10: Portland MS PwV 38
M11: Portland MS PwV 40
M14: Gyldenstolpe MS

It seems, then, that the Badminton MS text of 'Mac Flecknoe' is most closely related to the text as found in exactly those manuscripts with which it has already been shown to be connected on the basis of the order of items.

(ii) *Rochester's 'Satire Against Reason and Mankind'*

This poem is found in Badminton MS, Gyldenstolpe and PwV 40, although the latter includes it in a group of poems towards the end of the manuscript, out of the shared sequence. This suggests that the compiler of PwV 40 was at this point working from different material from the compilers of Badminton MS and Gyldenstolpe, and this supposition is confirmed by an examination of the textual evidence.

Keith Walker, in his 1984 edition of Rochester's poems, lists PwV 40 amongst the manuscripts which he has examined, but overlooks its text of this poem.[22] Nor does he print a stemma for it, or offer any analysis of the relationship between the manuscripts. Since the textual tradition has not been mapped, this investigation will necessarily be more limited than in the case of 'Mac Flecknoe'. We will consider first the links between Badminton MS and Gyldenstolpe, and return to PwV 40 later. If we take from Walker's collation those readings which he records as being unique to Gyldenstolpe, or which Gyldenstolpe shares with only a small number of other witnesses, we have the basis for a comparison with Badminton MS. Badminton MS agrees with Gyldenstolpe in its apparently unique readings at the following points:

Text printed by Walker] Gyldenstolpe
61 has freely] freely has
70 find out] out
91 Before the spacious *World*, his *Tub*] A Tubb, before the spatious world
152 mean] vain
175 the proud] this proud
188 Since] For
206 with] even with

Badminton MS also belongs to small groups of manuscripts which share variant readings with Gyldenstolpe MS at lines 18, 55, 64, 85, 122, 131, 201. However, it disagrees with Gyldenstolpe at line 51 (where Gyldenstolpe and two other manuscripts read 'that' for 'this'), and line 65 (where Gyldenstolpe and Harvard fMS Eng 623 read 'a Beast' for 'Beast'). However, these minor divergences are much less significant than the many substantive agreements. But while Badminton MS and Gyldenstolpe are closely linked in the textual transmission

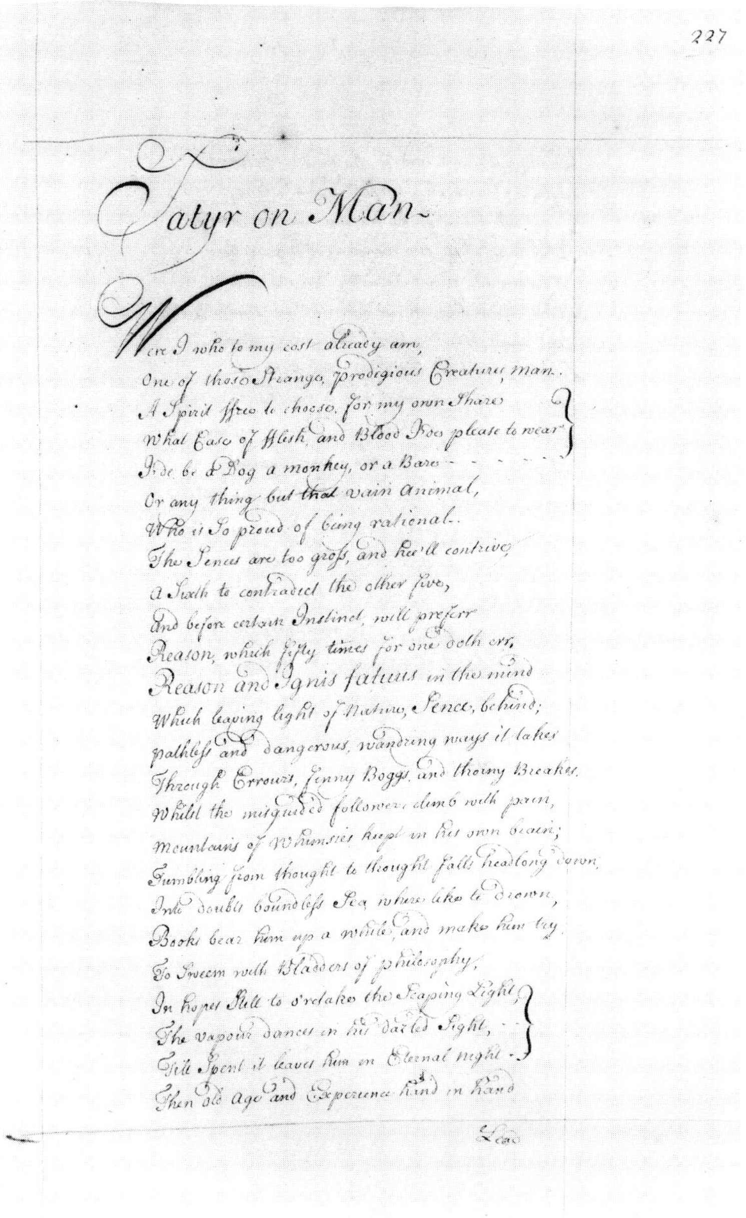

227

Satyr on Man-

Were I who to my cost already am,
One of those Strange, prodigious Creatures, man.
A Spirit ffree to choose, for my own Share
What Case of fflesh, and Blood I'd please to wear
I'de be a Dog a monkey, or a Bare - - - -
Or any thing but that vain animal,
Who is So proud of being rational.
The Sences are too gross, and hee'll contrive
a Sixth to contradict the other five,
And before certain Instinct, will preferr
Reason, which fifty times for one doth err,
Reason and Ignis fatuus in the mind
Which leaving light of Nature, Sence, behind;
pathless and dangerous, wandring ways it takes
Through Errours, ffenny Boggs, and thorny Breakes.
Whilst the misguided follower climb with pain,
mountains of Whimsies heapt in his own brain;
Tumbling from thought to thought falls headlong down,
Into doubts boundless Sea where like to drown,
Books bear him up a while, and make him try,
To Swim with Bladders of philosophy,
In hopes Still to o'retake the Scaping Light,
The vapour dances in his dazled Sight,
Till Spent it leaves him in Eternal night -
Then old Age and Experience hand in hand

Lead

PLATE 4 *The beginning of Rochester's 'Satyr on Man': Badminton* MS, *p.227. (Original page size 240 × 360mm). Reproduced by permission of His Grace the Duke of Beaufort.*

of this poem, PwV 40 is not associated with them: none of the variants listed above as being shared by Gyldenstolpe and Badminton MS is found in PwV 40. Evidently, then, the group of Rochester's poems included at the end of PwV 40 come from a significantly different source from that used by Badminton MS and Gyldenstolpe.

(iii) *Rochester's 'The Disabled Debauchee' (entitled 'The Maim'd Drunkard' in Badminton MS)*

This poem has a sufficiently large number of variants in its textual tradition to make comparison potentially fruitful, although once again no stemma has been published by editors of Rochester. Of Badminton MS's fifteen substantive variants from the text printed by Walker (which he based on the 1680 edition), three are apparently unique: line 25, 'with' for 'worth'; line 29, 'pale' for 'cold'; and line 39, omission of 'And'. One variant is shared uniquely with Gyldenstolpe: line 20, 'does' for 'shall'. Three are shared with Gyldenstolpe and Leeds Brotherton Collection MS Lt 54: at lines 8, 37, 38. Eight are shared with groups of manuscripts which include Gyldenstolpe: at lines 1, 11, 12, 17, 18, 19, 21, 30. Badminton MS, therefore, is closer to Gyldenstolpe in this poem than to any other manuscript. PwV 40 (again not consulted by Walker for this poem) agrees with his text against Badminton MS and Gyldenstolpe in all cases except at line 21. This confirms the conclusions about the different textual origins of the Rochester material in the later part of PwV 40.

(iv) *Rochester's 'Upon Nothing'*

The textual history of this poem is unusually complex, as has been shown by Harold Love.[23] It comes within the shared sequence in Badminton MS, Gyldenstolpe and PwV 40. Badminton MS agrees with PwV 40 (apparently uniquely) in reading 'unto' in line 1, but elsewhere it does not agree with PwV 40: for example, at line 33 it reads 'design' for 'designs', and at line 43 'disguises' for 'disguise' – both minor variants. In two cases, however, it agrees with PwV 40, Gyldenstolpe and one other witness: at line 42, in reading 'Where' for 'And' (along with Yale MS Osborn fb 142); and at line 47, in reading 'fidelity' for 'civility' (along with the 1715 printed edition). Though this evidence is limited, it does tie the three manuscripts together textually. Love had already assigned Gyldenstolpe and PwV 40 to the small group of manuscripts which he has designated the '"at first" group' (the others are Edinburgh University Library MS Dc.1.3; Yale MS Osborn fb 142; and Harvard fMS Eng. 623), and he commented that all the manuscripts in this group are, or derive from, commercially produced miscellanies, and therefore use a text available in one scriptorium.[24]

(v) *Dorset's 'Colin'*

This poem exists in Badminton MS, Gyldenstolpe, Harley 6913 and PwV 38; some of the extant manuscripts have been collated in the second volume of *Poems on Affairs of State*, which takes Harley 6913 as its copy-text.[25] The only significant variant which all four manuscripts share is at line 15, where they have 'as a' for 'was a' in the other witnesses. Otherwise Badminton MS, Gyldenstolpe and PwV 38 agree against Harley 6913 at line 5 (Harley 6913 has 'him on' for 'on him'); at line 30 (Harley 6913 has 'was' for 'were'); and in keeping lines 50–1 (which Harley 6913 omits). Badminton MS does, however, agree with Harley 6913 and PwV 38 at line 87, in reading 'nigh' against 'near' in Gyldenstolpe. The agreements are worth noting; the variants in Harley 6913 which the others do not share are explicable as errors by the copyist of Harley 6913.

(vi) *Mulgrave's 'An Essay upon Satire'*

This poem provides further evidence of strong textual links between the four manuscripts: at the following points Badminton MS, Gyldenstolpe, Harley 6913 and PwV 38 agree together, and with Yale MS Osborn Phillipps 7440 (now b 113), against the other witnesses collated in the first volume of *Poems on Affairs of State*:[26]

Text printed in *POAS*] Text of Badminton MS

20	aim] hit
25	grossest] greatest
44	fool] fop
50	dancing] gaudy
133	I'll not pay only, I'll admire him too] I'll pay him justly and admire him too
158	For sense sits silent and condemns for weaker] For some sit silent and condemn the weaker ['other' in PwV 38]
192	his brisker] he in former
226–9	*omitted*

Moreover, Badminton MS, Gyldenstolpe, Harley 6913 and PwV 38 agree against all the other witnesses in reading 'greater' for 'other' at line 40, and in omitting line 118. At line 42, where the other witnesses read 'correction', Harley 6913, PwV 38 and Badminton MS have 'connection', while Yale MS Osborn Phillipps 7440 and Gyldenstolpe have 'conviction'. At line 157 Badminton MS, PwV 38 and Gyldenstolpe read 'has' for 'have' in the other witnesses. The text in PwV 40 does not appear in the sequence shared with Badminton MS and Gyldenstolpe, and generally does not agree with their readings; however, PwV 40 does read 'hit' at line 20 and 'gaudy' at line 50, so there are some minor links. The most interesting textual point here is that Badminton MS, Gyldenstolpe, Harley 6913 and PwV 38 have clear textual links, since 'An Essay upon Satire' occurs towards the end of the sequence shared by Badminton MS with Gyldenstolpe, and towards the beginning of the sequence shared by Badminton MS with Harley 6913 and PwV 38: the textual links, therefore, point towards a common scriptorium origin for all four manuscripts.

(vii) *Conclusion*

The exact nature of the textual links between these five manuscripts could only be established by an exhaustive collation, not only of these five but of all other manuscripts containing the poems which these include. But the present sample investigations have at least suggested some basic conclusions.

1 The unusual links between these manuscripts in terms of their order of contents are matched by significant correspondences between the textual variants which they share.
2 The textual links are strong in poems which have quite different textual histories – 'Satire Against Reason and Mankind', 'Mac Flecknoe' and 'An Essay on Satire' – suggesting that the copyists shared a common copy-text (or copy-texts which themselves shared a recent common original) even for poems which did not usually circulate together.
3 Nevertheless, the textual links between the manuscripts vary from poem to poem, sometimes even within what we might suppose to have been a linked group (such as some of the poems of Rochester), suggesting that even within such groups the copyists were sometimes working from different exemplars.
4 The five manuscripts *may* all have derived from the same scriptorium, although in the case of Badminton MS this would have been (at least) at one remove, since it is plainly not itself a scriptorium manuscript.

APPENDIX I: Badminton Muniments Room FmE 3/12

Description of Contents

page	*contents*
	[2 blank leaves]
p.1	'Anno Primo Regni Gul: et Mariae Regis et Reginae 1689 The Book of Establisment of their Majesties Houshold An Establisment of the yearly Charge of their Majesties Dyet and Incidents for House Keeping . . . to commence the 1st April 1689:'
pp.2–5	[Diets of the King (p.2), the waiters and maids of honour (p.3), the chaplain (p.4) and 'Additions to the several Dyets' (p.5)]
pp.6–10	[Provisions and household goods]
p.10*	[p.11 misnumbered p.10]
p.11	[Provisions for the chapel]
p.12	'Incidents to be allowed in such proportions as the Officers of the Green Cloth shall find necessary for our Service . . .'
pp.13–14	[Incidents]
pp.15–20	'Wages and Board Wages to our Household Officers and Servants that are continued in their Several Offices and places to attend our present Service'
p.21	'Allowances to such old Houshold Servants that Served King Charles the First and King Charles the Second both of Blessed Memory in Forreign Parts'
p.22	'Stipends allowed to such old Houshold Servants of his Late Majesty King Charles wch are not now Employ'd in their Majesties Service, But are admitted to Supernumeraries to their present Maj:'
p.23	[Stipends]
p.24	'Allowances in Money by way of pension granted by King Charles the 2d of Blessed Memory, and continued by the Late King James the 2d to Serts Widows and others hereafter nam'd to continue during our pleasure'
p.25	[Pensions]
pp.26–8	'Wages and Board Wages to our Officers and Servants of the Chamber' [including the Lord Chamberlain, private secretaries, cupbearers, carvers, servers, gentlemen ushers, daily waiters, esquires of the body, servers of the chamber, pages of the presence and bedchamber, master of the Jewel House, barbers, clerks of the Signet and Privy Seal, surgeons, apothecary, groom porter, gentlemen of the guns, surveyor of the chamber, grooms of the stool, gentlemen ushers of the privy chamber and laundress of the Queen's body]
p.29	[Eleemozin]
p.30	'The Establishment of the Officers and Servants belonging to our Chappel Royal Closet and Vestry' [including references to

	'M^{r} of the Musick Doctor Blow for teaching and keeping ten Children of the Chappel' (at £24 per annum each); and 'Organ Keeper Henry purcell, for keeping the organs in Repair' (£56 per annum)]
p.31	'Chappel at St James's'
p.32	'An Establishment containing the Number of all such Horses as we think fit to allow for our own Service'
pp.33–7	'The Stables'
p.38	[blank]
pp.39–40	'The Stables'
pp.41–2	'The Number of Carriages to be allowed at our [and the Queen's] Removes'
p.43	'To be allowed unto our Houshold Officers and Servants for riding wages . . . during the time of our Residence at Windsor or Hampton Court'
pp.44–5	'An Extract of the whole Charge contained in this Book of Establism^{t}'
pp.46–9	'Ordinances to be observed for the Regulating Acco^{ts} and the well governing our House'
p.50	'Sum Total of the Book of Establishment' [includes a payment of £30 in April 1689 to 'Thomas Shadwell Esqr poet Laureat']
pp.51–2	[blank]
p.53	'Abstract of the Acco^{ts} of the publick Revenues Taxes and D[ebits ?]'
pp.54–66	'Money borrowed from Mich^{s} 1692 to Mich^{s} 1693 Viz^{t}.'
p.67	[blank]
p.68	'A List of the Remains at Mich^{s}. 1693 on the heads underwritten'
p.69	'Acco^{t}. Shewing how much hath been borrowed upon the Revenue. Taxes and Exq^{r} in the same year '
pp.70–1	[Accounts]
pp.72–4	[blank]
p.75	'Judicature in Parliament The Execution of all our Laws hath been long since distributed by parliament unto the Inferior Courts in Such as the Subject is directed where to complain and the Justices how to redress wrongs and punish Offences'
pp.75–212	[Legal judgements and precedents]
pp.213–16	[blank]
pp.217–439	[Verse Miscellany]
pp.440–1	[blank]
pp.442–89	'Observations concerning New fforest / out of an old manuscript'
pp.490–2	[blank]
pp.493–543	[New Forest account, continued]

pp.544–748	[blank and unnumbered]
pp.749–50	'Index of what papers are contain'd in this Book – relating to N: Forest'
pp.751–4	[blank]

APPENDIX II: A FINDING LIST OF POEMS IN BADMINTON MS FME 3/12

Abbreviations

ARP	D. M. Vieth, *Attribution in Restoration Poetry* (New Haven and London, 1963).
Badminton MS	Volume of memoranda and verses owned by the Duke of Beaufort, Badminton House, Avon, Muniments Room FmE 3/12.
CPR	*Complete Poems of John Wilmot, Earl of Rochester*, ed. D. M. Vieth (New Haven and London, 1968).
Crum	*First-Line Index of English Poetry 1500–1800 in Manuscripts of the Bodleian Library, Oxford*, ed. M. Crum, 2 vols (Oxford, 1969).
Gyldenstolpe	*The Gyldenstolpe Manuscript Miscellany of Poems by John Wilmot Earl of Rochester, and other Restoration Authors*, ed. B. Danielsson and D. M. Vieth, Stockholm Studies in English, 17 (Stockholm, 1967).
Harley 6913	Verse miscellany in British Library, Harley MS 6913.
Harris	*The Poems of Charles Sackville, Sixth Earl of Dorset*, ed. B. Harris (New York and London, 1979).
POAS1	*Poems on Affairs of State: Augustan Satirical Verse 1660–1714*, Volume I: 1660–1678, ed. G. de F. Lord (New Haven and London, 1963).
POAS2	*Poems on Affairs of State: Augustan Satirical Verse 1660–1714*, Volume II: 1678–1681, ed. E. F. Mengel, Jr., (New Haven and London, 1965).
PwV 38	Verse miscellany in the Portland collection, deposited in 1949 by the Duke of Portland in the library of the University of Nottingham. Portland MS PwV 38 is paginated from pp.1 to 257 and [258] to [263].
PwV 40	Verse miscellany in the Portland collection, deposited in 1949 by the Duke of Portland in the library of the University of Nottingham. Portland MS PwV 40 is paginated from pp.1 to 211, and then marked only with folio numbers from fols 212^{a} to 247^{a}, with fol. 232 mistakenly used twice (and thus described below as fols 232^{a-d}).
Thorpe	*The Poems of Sir George Etherege*, ed. J. Thorpe (Princeton, 1963).
Walker	*The Poems of John Wilmot, Earl of Rochester*, ed. K. Walker (Oxford, 1984).

Wilson *Court Satires of the Restoration*, ed. J. H. Wilson (Columbus, Ohio, 1976).

NOTE: The attributions provided here are those which have been proposed by modern editors. There are no attributions in the manuscript.

1 (pp.217–18)
Prologue
Gentle Reproofs have long been try'd in vain,
Edmund Ashton
Gyldenstolpe, p.1 (no 1)
Harley 6913, p.1 (no 1)
PwV 38, p.1 (no 1)
CPR, 226; *ARP*, 266–8; *Gyldenstolpe*, 321

2 (pp.218–26)
A Letter from Artemiza
Chloe in verse, by your Command I write,
Rochester
Gyldenstolpe, p.5 (no 2)
PwV 40, fol. 232[a] (no 104)
CPR, 203; *ARP*, 378–81; *Gyldenstolpe*, 321–2; Crum, C198

3 (pp.227–34)
Satyr on Man
Were I who to my cost already am,
Rochester
Gyldenstolpe, p.21 (no 3)
PwV 40, fol. 228[b] (no 103)
CPR, 200–2; *ARP*, 370–5; *Gyldenstolpe*, 322–3; Crum, W317

4 (p.235)
Regime de Viver
I rise at Eleven, and I dine about Two,
(possibly) **Charles Sackville, Earl of Dorset**
Gyldenstolpe, p.35 (no 4)
PwV 40, fol. 213[a] (no 90)
CPR, 228; *ARP*, 86–7, 168–72, 411–12; *Gyldenstolpe*, 323; Crum, I417; Harris, 186–7

5 (pp.235–41)
Satyr
What Timon does old age begin to approach
Rochester
Gyldenstolpe, p.37 (no 5)
PwV 40, fol. 218[a] (no 94)
CPR, 193–4; *ARP*, 453–4; *Gyldenstolpe*, 323

6 (pp.241–3)
The maim'd Drunkard
As some old Admiral in former war
Rochester
Gyldenstolpe, p.47 (no 6) 'The Maim'd Drunkard'
PwV 40, p.211 (no 85) 'The Disabled Debauch')
CPR, 205; *ARP*, 384–5; *Gyldenstolpe*, 324; Crum, A1663
Usually known as 'The Maimed Debauchee' or 'The Disabled Debauchee'

7 (p.243)
Seneca Troas
After Death nothing is and nothing Death
Rochester
Gyldenstolpe, p.51 (no 7)
PwV 40, p.212[b] (no 88)
CPR, 215–16; *ARP*, 397–9; *Gyldenstolpe*, 324; Crum, A718

8 (pp.244–6)
The Disappointment

Naked she clasp'd me in her longing arms,
Rochester
Gyldenstolpe, p.53 (no 8) 'The Dissapointment' (Naked she lay clasp'd in my longing Armes)
PwV 40, p.203 (no 83) 'The Imperfect Enjoym[t].' – according to Vieth, copied from the Pforzheimer edition of Rochester's poems (A–1680PF)
CPR, 187; *ARP*, 381–2; *Gyldenstolpe*, 325; Crum, N3
Usually known as 'The Imperfect Enjoyment'

9 (p.246)
On Marriage
The Clogg of all pleasure the Luggage of Life
Unknown
Gyldenstolpe, p.59 (no 9)
CPR, 233; *Gyldenstolpe*, 325; Crum, T408

10 (p.247)
Upon leaving his Mistress
'Tis not that I am weary grown
Rochester
Gyldenstolpe, p.61 (no 10)
CPR, 195–6; *ARP*, 403–4; *Gyldenstolpe*, 325–6

11 (pp.248–51)
A Dewil Between two Monsiers upon My Lady Be. . .t's C. .t with their change of Government from monarchicall to Democratical.
In Milford Lane near to S[t]. Clements Steeple
(possibly) either **Charles Sackville, Earl of Dorset** (Gyldenstolpe, 326) or **Henry Savile** (Gyldenstolpe, 326; Crum, I1404), or both (Harris, 118)
Gyldenstolpe, p.63 (no 11)
Harley 6913, p.123 (no 24)
Crum, I1404; *Gyldenstolpe*, 326–7; Harris, 118–23

12 (pp.251–4)
From E. R. to E. M.
Dear Freind
I hear this town does so abound
Rochester
Gyldenstolpe, p.71 (no 12)
PwV 40, p.1 (no 2)
CPR, 213–14; *ARP*, 369–70; *Gyldenstolpe*, 327; Crum, D82[b]; *POAS1*, 348
Usually known as 'An Epistolary Essay from M. G. to O. B. upon their Mutual Poems'

13 (pp.255–60)
A Ramble In S[t]. James's Park
Much Wine had pass'd with grave discourse
Rochester
Gyldenstolpe, p.77 (no 13)
PwV 40, p.5 (no 3)
CPR, 187; *ARP*, 375–7; *Gyldenstolpe*, 328; Crum, M541

14 (pp.260–1)
Advice To a C. . . .t Monger
F. .cksters you that will be happy
Unknown
PwV 40, p.11 (no 4)
CPR, 226; *ARP*, 489

15 (p.262)
Nestor
Vulcan contrive me such a Cupp:
Rochester
Gyldenstolpe, p.87 (no 14)
PwV 40, p.12 (no 5)
CPR, 191; *ARP*, 405–7; *Gyldenstolpe*, 328–9; Crum, V72
Usually known as 'Upon His Drinking a Bowl'

16 (pp.263–7)
The Enjoyment
Since now my Silvia is as kind as ffair,
John Sheffield, Earl of Mulgrave
Gyldenstolpe, p.227 (no 51) 'The Appointment'
PwV 40, p.13 (no 6) 'The Enjoymt.')
CPR, 232; *ARP*, 481–3; *Gyldenstolpe*, 348; Crum, S578

17 (pp.268–72)
The Imperfect Enjoyment
One day the amorous Lysander
Aphra Behn
Gyldenstolpe, p.89 (no 15)
CPR, 231; *ARP*, 448–50; *Gyldenstolpe*, 329; Crum, O1162

18 (pp.273–5)
Familiar Letters.
Dreaming last night of Mistress Farley
Charles Sackville, Earl of Dorset
Gyldenstolpe, p.97 (no 16)
PwV 40, p.19 (no 7)
CPR, 226; *ARP*, 438–9; *Gyldenstolpe*, 329–30; Harris, 105–8

19 (pp.275–7)
Answer
As Crafty Harlots use to shrink
George Etherege
Gyldenstolpe, p.102 (no 17)
PwV 40, p.22 (no 8)
CPR, 223; *ARP*, 439–40; *Gyldenstolpe*, 329–30; Thorpe, 38–9

20 (pp.277–80)
Second Letter
If I can guess the Devil Choack me
Charles Sackville, Earl of Dorset
Gyldenstolpe, p.107 (no 18)
PwV 40, p.25 (no 9)
CPR, 228; *ARP*, 440–41; *Gyldenstolpe*, 329–30; Harris, 112–14; Thorpe, 40–2

21 (pp.281–3)
Answer To the Second Letter
So Soft and Amorously you write
George Etherege
Gyldenstolpe, p.113 (no 19)
PwV 40, p.29 (no 14)
CPR, 233; *ARP*, 441; *Gyldenstolpe*, 329–30; Thorpe, 43–5

22 (pp.284–5)
Ephelia
How far are they deceiv'd who hope in vain
(probably) **George Etherege**
Gyldenstolpe, p.119 (no 20)
PwV 40, p.32 (no 15)
CPR, 227; *ARP*, 465–7; *Gyldenstolpe*, 330–1; Crum, H1381; *POAS1*, 342; Thorpe, 9–10

23 (pp.286–7)
A very Heroicall Epistle In answer to Ephelia
Madam
If you're deceiv'd 'tis not by my heart
Rochester
Gyldenstolpe, p.123 (no 21)
PwV 40, p.34 (no 16)
CPR, 227; *ARP*, 468–70; *Gyldenstolpe*, 331; Crum, I1089; *POAS1*, 345

24 (pp.288–9)
Poet Ninny
Curst by that Just Contempt his ffollies bring
Rochester
Gyldenstolpe, p.127 (no 22)
PwV 40, p.36 (no 17)
CPR, 212; *ARP*, 470–1; *Gyldenstolpe*, 331

25 (pp.289–90)
My Lord all Pride
Bursting with pride the loath'd Imposthume Swells
Rochester
Gyldenstolpe, p.129 (no 23)
PwV 40, p.37 (no 18)
CPR, 213; *ARP*, 471–2; *Gyldenstolpe*, 331; *POAS1*, 414

26 (p.290)
A Letter
Madam
I cannot change as others do
(probably) **Sir Carr Scroope**
Gyldenstolpe, p.131 (no 24)
PwV 40, p.38 (no 19)
CPR, 227; *ARP*, 434–6; *Gyldenstolpe*, 331–2

27 (p.291)
Answer
I F. . .ck no more than others do
Rochester
Gyldenstolpe, p.132 (no 25)
PwV 40, p.39 (no 20)
CPR, 210–11; *ARP*, 436–7; *Gyldenstolpe*, 331–2

28 (pp.292–6)
An allusion to Horace The Tenth Satyr of the first Book Nempe incomposito dixi pede
Well Sir 'tis granted I Said Dryden's Rhimes
Rochester
Gyldenstolpe, p.145 (no 29)
PwV 40, p.40 (no 21)
CPR, 207; *ARP*, 386–9; *Gyldenstolpe*, 332–3; Crum, W289; *POAS1*, 358

29 (pp.296–300)
In Defence of Satyr
When Shakespear, Johnson Fletcher rul'd the Stage
Sir Carr Scroope
Gyldenstolpe, p.133 (no 26)
PwV 40, p.45 (no 22)
CPR, 235; *ARP*, 390–4; *Gyldenstolpe*, 332–3; Crum, W1441; *POAS1*, 364

30 (pp.300–1)
On the Suppos'd Author of a late Poem in defence of Satyr
To task and torture thy unmeaning Braine
Rochester
Gyldenstolpe, p.141 (no 27)
PwV 40, p.48 (no 23)
CPR, 208; *ARP*, 394–6; *Gyldenstolpe*, 332–3; Crum, T3193; *POAS1*, 371

31 (p.301)
Answer By way of Epigramme
Rail on, poor feeble Scribler, Speak of me
Sir Carr Scroope
Gyldenstolpe, p.144 (no 28)
PwV 40, p.49 (no 24)
CPR, 232; *ARP*, 396–7; *Gyldenstolpe*, 332–3; *POAS1*, 373

32 (p.302)
On M[rs]. W. .llis
Against the Charmes our Ballox have
Rochester
Gyldenstolpe, p.157 (no 31)
PwV 40, p.50 (no 25)
CPR, 211; *ARP*, 433–4; *Gyldenstolpe*, 334

33 (pp.303–4)
NOTHING
Nothing thou Elder Brother unto Shade
Rochester
Gyldenstolpe, p.153 (no 30)
PwV 40, p.51 (no 26)
CPR, 206; *ARP*, 399–403; *Gyldenstolpe*, 333–4; Crum, N430

34 (pp.305–7)
Ovid
O nunquam pro me satis indignate Cupido
To Love
Oh Love hou cold art thou to take my part
Rochester
Gyldenstolpe, p.159 (no 32)
PwV 40, p.53 (no 27)
CPR, 186; *ARP*, 382–4; *Gyldenstolpe*, 334–5; Crum, O665

35 (p.307)
To Corinna
What cruel pains Corrinna takes
Rochester
Gyldenstolpe, p.174 (no 39)
PwV 40, p.56 (no 28)
CPR, 183; *ARP*, 420–1; *Gyldenstolpe*, 337; Crum, W424

36 (p.308)
Woman's Honour
Love bid me hope and I obey'd
Rochester
Gyldenstolpe, p.163 (no 33)
PwV 40, p.56 (no 29)
CPR, 175; *ARP*, 421–2; *Gyldenstolpe*, 335

37 (p.309)
The Submission
To this moment a Rebell I throw down my arms
Rochester
Gyldenstolpe, p.165 (no 34)
PwV 40, p.57 (no 30)
CPR, 175; *ARP*, 423–4; *Gyldenstolpe*, 335–6

38 (p.310)
Thirsis
Give me leave to raill at you
Rochester
Gyldenstolpe, p.167 (no 35)
PwV 40, p.59 (no 31)
CPR, 172; *ARP*, 414–16; *Gyldenstolpe*, 336

39 (pp.310–11)
[no title]
Nothing adds to your fond fire
(probably) **Rochester's wife**
Gyldenstolpe, p.168 (no 36)
PwV 40, p.59 (no 32)
CPR, 230; *ARP*, 417–18; *Gyldenstolpe*, 336, where Vieth comments: 'The first of this pair of lyrics is probably by Rochester. The second, an answer to the first, is probably by his wife. In Gyldenstolpe the copyist evidently did not know he was transcribing two separate poems: the second song carries no heading, and the heading of the first song is inappropriate, since the second stanza is plainly addressed by a man to a woman. A similar situation is presented by the texts in Portland MS PwV 40, p.59, which are closely related to those in the Gyldenstolpe MS: the first poem is also headed "To Thirsis", and the second poem follows on the same page as if it were part of the first. The Portland texts are independent of printed sources and carry no ascriptions'.

40 (pp.311–12)
Song
Fair Cloris In a piggstay lay
Rochester
Gyldenstolpe, p.169 (no 37)
PwV 40, p.60 (no 33)
CPR, 183; *ARP*, 413–14; *Gyldenstolpe*, 336

41 (p.313)
To Phillis
Phillis be gentler I advise

Rochester
Gyldenstolpe, p.176 (no 41)
PwV 40, p.62 (no 34)
CPR, 183; *ARP*, 418–20; *Gyldenstolpe*, 336; Crum, P165

42 (p.314)
Love and Life
All my past Life is mine no more
Rochester
Gyldenstolpe, p.173 (no 38)
PwV 40, p.63 (no 35)
CPR, 199–200; *ARP*, 425–8; *Gyldenstolpe*, 337

43 (pp.314–15)
Song
While on those Lovely Looks I Gaze
Rochester
Gyldenstolpe, p.177 (no 42)
PwV 40, p.64 (no 36)
CPR, 173–4; *ARP*, 429–31; *Gyldenstolpe*, 337

44 (p.315)
The Fall
How blest was the Created State
Rochester
Gyldenstolpe, p.175 (no 40)
PwV 40, p.64 (no 37)
CPR, 198; *ARP*, 428–9; *Gyldenstolpe*, 338

45 (pp.315–16)
Song
Amintor lov'd and liv'd in pain
Unknown
Gyldenstolpe, p.178 (no 43)
PwV 40, p.65 (no 38)
(not in *CPR*, *ARP*, or Crum).

46 (p.316)
Love to a Woman
Love a Woman th'art an Ass
Rochester
Gyldenstolpe, p.182 (no 45)
PwV 40, p.66 (no 39)
CPR, 190; *ARP*, 412–13; *Gyldenstolpe*, 339–40

47 (pp.317–18)
Song
In the ffeilds of Lincoln's Inne
(probably) **Sir Charles Sedley**
Gyldenstolpe, p.179 (no 44)
PwV 40, p.66 (no 40)
CPR, 228; *ARP*, 404–5; *Gyldenstolpe*, 339; Crum, I1524

48 (p.318)
Song
As trembling prisoners Stand at Bar
Alexander Ratcliffe
Gyldenstolpe, p.183 (no 46)
PwV 40, p.68 (no 41)
Gyldenstolpe, 340 (not in *CPR* or Crum).

49 (pp.319–21)
Julian
In verse to ease thy wants I write
(probably) **Anthony Carey, fifth Viscount Falkland**
Gyldenstolpe, p.185 (no 47)
PwV 40, p.69 (no 42)
Harley 6913, p.5 (no 2)
PwV 38, p.3 (no 2)
CPR, 229; *Gyldenstolpe*, 340–3

50 (pp.321–2)
To E. H. upon his Late poem
As when a Bulley draws his Sword
Edmund Ashton
CPR, 223; *ARP*, 445–6; Crum, A1721; *POAS1*, 339

51 (pp.322–3)
To E. H. upon his late poem
Come on ye Critticks find one fault who dares
Charles Sackville, Earl of Dorset
CPR, 225; *ARP*, 442–5; Crum, C569; *POAS1*, 338; Harris, 7–9

52 (pp.323–4)
To E. H. upon his late poem
Thou damn'd Antipodes to common Sence
Unknown (possibly Buckhurst, Wycherley or Henry Savile)
CPR, 234; *ARP*, 446–8; Crum, T2155; *POAS1*, 340

53 (pp.325–32)
Mack Flecno
All human things are Subject to decay
John Dryden
Gyldenstolpe, p.189 (no 48)
PwV 40, p.71 (no 43)
Harley 6913, p.9 (no 3)
PwV 38, p.9 (no 3)
ARP, 485–6; *Gyldenstolpe*, 343–7; Crum, A958; *POAS1*, 378

54 (pp.332–42)
Aude aliquid brevibus giaris [*sic*] aut Carcere dignum, si vis esse aliquis Juven: Sat.
Suppos'd to be Spoken by a Court Hector at the Breaking of the Sun Dyall in the Privy: Garden
Pindarique
Now Curses on you all you vitous ffools
John Oldham
Gyldenstolpe, p.211 (no 50)
PwV 40, p.87: 'Suppos'd to be spoken . . .' [etc.] (no 47)
CPR, 230; *ARP*, 458–61; *Gyldenstolpe*, 348; Crum, W463; *The Poems of John Oldham*, ed. H. F. Brooks with R. Selden (Oxford, 1987), 57–67, 400–404

55 (pp.343–7)
Colon
As Colon drove his Sheep along
(probably) **Charles Sackville, Earl of Dorset**
Gyldenstolpe, p.237 (no 52)
PwV 40, p.105 (no 51)
Harley 6913, p.79 (no 15)
PwV 38, p.75 (no 15)
CPR, 223; *ARP*, 488; *Gyldenstolpe*, 348–50; *POAS2*, 168; Harris, 124–35

56 (pp.348–57)
Essay on Satyr.
How dull and how insencible abeast
John Sheffield, Earl of Mulgrave
Gyldenstolpe, p.245 (no 53)
PwV 40, fol. 222[a] (no 98)
Harley 6913, p.21 (no 4)
PwV 38, p.21 (no 4)
Gyldenstolpe, 350–1; Crum, H1370; *POAS1*, 401

57 (pp.358–64)
Barbara Priamidum Sileat Miracula Memphis
Of all the wonders Since the world began
Unknown
Gyldenstolpe, p.261 (no 54)
Harley 6913, p.37 (no 5)
PwV 38, p.37 (no 5)
CPR, 230; *Gyldenstolpe*, 352–3

58 (pp.365–8)
A Familiar Epistle to M[r]. Julian Secretary the Muses
Thou common Shore of this poetick Town
(possibly) **George Villiers, Duke of Buckingham**

Gyldenstolpe, p.203 (no 49)
PwV 40, p.79 (no 44)
Harley 6913, p.49 (no 6)
PwV 38, p.47 (no 6)
Gyldenstolpe, 347; Crum, T2152; *POAS1*, 388; *Buckingham: Public and Private Man*, ed. C. Phipps (New York and London, 1985), 155–7, 255–7

59 (pp.368–9)
A Letter from the D: of M: to the King
Disgrac'd, undone, forlorn, mad ffortun's Sport
Unknown
Gyldenstolpe, p.279 (no 57)
Harley 6913, p.55 (no 7)
PwV 38, p.53 (no 7)
CPR, 226; *Gyldenstolpe*, 357–9; Crum, D332; *POAS2*, 254

60 (pp.369–70)
Ross's Ghost
Shame of my Life disturber of my Tomb
(possibly) **Wentworth Dillon, Earl of Roscommon**
Harley 6913, p.57 (no 8)
PwV 38, p.55 (no 8)
CPR, 232; Crum, S356; *POAS2*, 251

61 (pp.370–2)
A Ballad To the tune of an old man With a Bed:full of Bones
In famous Street near Whetstons park
Unknown
Gyldenstolpe, p.275 (no 56)
Harley 6913, p.59 (no 9)
PwV 38, p.57 (no 9)
CPR, 228; *Gyldenstolpe*, 355–7

62 (pp.373–4)
A Letter
Worthy S^r.
Though wean'd from all those Scandelous delights
Unknown
Gyldenstolpe, p.273 (no 55)
Harley 6913, p.63 (no 10)
PwV 38, p.61 (no 10)
CPR, 234; *Gyldenstolpe*, 353–4

63 (pp.374–6)
The Chronicle Out of M^r. Cowly
'Tis thought tall Richard first possest
Unknown
Gyldenstolpe, p.312 (no 65)
Harley 6913, p.67 (no 11)
PwV 38, p.63 (no 11)
CPR, 234; *Gyldenstolpe*, 373

64 (pp.376–7)
Pindarick
Let Ancients boast no more
Unknown
Harley 6913, p.71 (no 12)
PwV 38, p.67 (no 12)
CPR, 229

65 (p.378)
A Ballad
Of all Quality Whores modest Betty for me
Unknown
Harley 6913, p.77 (no 14)
PwV 38, p.73 (no 14)
CPR, 230; Wilson, 47

66 (pp.379–86)
Rochester's Farewell
Fill'd with the noysom folly of the Age
(possibly) **Charles Sackville, Earl of Dorset**
Gyldenstolpe, p.285 (no 59)
Harley 6913, p.87 (no 16)
PwV 38, p.83 (no 16)
CPR, 234; *Gyldenstolpe*, 361–5; Crum, T2722; Harris, 190–2

67 (pp.386–88)
The Angler
Me thinks I See the mighty Monarch Stand
Unknown
Gyldenstolpe, p.299 (no 63)
Harley 6913, p.105 (no 19)
PwV 38, p.101 (no 19)
CPR, 229; *Gyldenstolpe*, 366–7; Crum, M341; *POAS2*, 190

68 (p.388)
Upon Six holy Sisters that mett at a Conventicle to alter the popish word of preaching
Six of the ffemale Sex and purest Sect
Sir John Harington
Harley 6913, p.109 (no 20)
PwV 38, p.105 (no 20)
CPR, 232–3; Crum, S779

69 (pp.389–90)
A Ballad
To honourable Court there latly came
Unknown
Harley 6913, p.115 (no 22)
PwV 38, p.111 (no 22)
CPR, 235

70 (pp.391–2)
Satyr
Must I with patience ever Silent Sitt
Unknown
Gyldenstolpe, p.310 (no 64)
Harley 6913, p.119 (no 23)
PwV 38, p.115 (no 23)
CPR, 229; *Gyldenstolpe*, 371–2; *POAS2*, 205

71 (pp.392–6)
The parting Between Sireno and Diana
Close by a Stream whose flowry bank might give
Sir Carr Scroope
Harley 6913, p.129 (no 25)
PwV 38, p.119 (no 24)
Crum, C328

72 (pp.397–400)
Satyr
Curse on those Criticks Ignorant and vain
Unknown
Harley 6913, p.137 (no 26)
PwV 38, p.127 (no 25)
Crum, C821; Wilson, 36

73 (pp.401–5)
Utile Dulce
Muse let us change our Stile and live in peace
Unknown
Harley 6913, p.151 (no 28)
PwV 38, p.133 (no 26)
Crum, M548; Wilson, 49

74 (pp.406–8)
An Essay of Scandal
Of all the plagues with which this world abounds
Unknown
Harley 6913, p.159 (no 29)
PwV 38, p.139 (no 27)
CPR, 230; Crum, O54; Wilson, 63

75 (pp.409–13)
The Ladies March
Stamford's Countess led the Van
Unknown
Harley 6913, p.165 (no 30)
PwV 38, p.143 (no 28)
CPR, 233; Crum, S1111

76 (p.413)
The Sham prophecy
In sixteen hundred Seventy Eight
Unknown
Harley 6913, p.171 (no 31)

PwV 38, p.151 (no 29)
CPR, 228; Crum, I1480

77 (pp.414–15)
A Ballad
Have you heard of a Lord of Noble Descent
Unknown
Harley 6913, p.173 (no 32)
PwV 38, p.153 (no 30)
CPR, 226–7; Crum, H327

78 (p.416)
Riddle me Riddle me What is this
A Load of Gutts wrapt in a Sallow Skin
Unknown
Harley 6913, p.180 (no 34)
PwV 38, p.157 (no 31)
CPR, 223

79 (p.416)
A pert imitation of all the Flatteries of Fate
All the world can't afford
Unknown
Harley 6913, p.181 (no 35)
PwV 38, p.158 (no 32)
CPR, 223; Crum, A1031

80 (pp.416–18)
To the Tune of If Dr. P —— take Exceptions
Stamford is her Sexes Glory
Unknown
Harley 6913, p.183 (no 36)
PwV 38, p.159 (no 33)
CPR, 233

81 (pp.418–21)
A Panegyrick
Of a great Heroine I mean to tell – –
Unknown
Harley 6913, p.187 (no 37)
PwV 38, p.163 (no 34)
CPR, 230; *POAS2*, 242

82 (pp.421–3)
Some Nonsence To the Tune of the Magpyes
Old weinscott was i'th'right – with a hey, with a hey
Unknown
Harley 6913, p.193 (no 38)
PwV 38, p.167 (no 35)
Crum, O1041

83 (pp.423–8)
An Heroick poem
Of Villains, Rebells Cuckolds, pimps and Spies,
Unknown
Harley 6913, p.197 (no 39)
PwV 38, p.171 (no 36)
CPR, 230–1; *POAS2*, 228

84 (pp.428–9)
Scots Song
Yee London ladds be Sorrey
Unknown
Harley 6913, p.205 (no 40)
PwV 38, p.179 (no 37)
Crum, O167

85 (pp.429–32)
Scandal Satyr'd
Of all the ffools these fertile times produce
Unknown
Harley 6913, p.209 (no 41)
PwV 38, p.183 (no 38)
CPR, 230; Crum, O39

86 (p.433)
Canto
Nan and Franck two quondam ffriends
Unknown
Harley 6913, p.215 (no 42)
PwV 38, p.187 (no 39)
CPR, 230; Crum, N6

87 (pp.433–9)	**Unknown**
Canto	Harley 6913, p.215 (no 43)
Of Civil Dudgeon many a Bard	*CPR*, 230; *POAS2*, 235

FIRST LINE INDEX POEM NO.

NOTES

See above pp.193–4 for a list of abbreviations used in these notes.

1 Badminton Muniments Room, FmE 3/12 (formerly 600.1.20). The binding, which has been extensively damaged by damp, measures 245 × 375mm; and the pages, which remain in good condition, measure 240 × 360mm. We are grateful to His Grace the Duke of Beaufort for giving permission for this article to be published; and to Mrs Richards for information on the provenance of FmE 3/12.

2 Biographical works consulted include the *Dictionary of National Biography*; *The Dictionary of Welsh Biography Down to 1940* (1949), pp.916–19; G. E. Cokayne *et al.*, *The Complete Peerage*, 13 vols (1959), Vol. XII, Pt. ii, pp.846–63; P. R. Newman, *Royalist Officers in England and Wales, 1642–1660* (New York and London, 1981), p.351. Various papers of the first Duke of Beaufort relating to his titles and honours, public offices, political and parliamentary involvements, and private correspondence are preserved in Badminton Muniments Room (catalogue reference FmE).

3 Some of Charles Somerset's papers are preserved in Badminton Muniments Room (catalogue reference FmG).

4 This suggestion was first made by Mrs Richards.

5 The first Duke of Bolton was, by some accounts, a highly eccentric character. For example, *The Complete Peerage*, Vol. II, p.211, cites Bishop Burnet's impressions of him: 'he was a man of a strange mixture. He had the spleen to a high degree and affected an extravagant behaviour; for many weeks he would not open his mouth till such an hour of the day when he thought the air was pure. He changed the day into night, and often hunted by torch-light . . . He was a man of most profuse expense, and of a most ravenous avarice to support that; and tho' he was much hated, yet he carried matters before him with such authority and success, that he was in all respects the great riddle of the age'.

6 Descriptions of the second Duke of Bolton's character are even less flattering than those of his father. *The Complete Peerage*, Vol. II, p.212, recounts: 'Bishop Burnet's character of him, with Dean Swift's remarks thereon *in italics*, is as follows: "Does not make any figure at Court. *Nor anywhere else. A great Booby*". Tom Hearne's account is, "A most lewd, vicious man, a great dissembler and a very hard drinker". Lady Cowper in her *Diary* writes that he is generally to be seen with his tongue lolling out of his mouth'. From July 1715 until April 1717 the second Duke of Bolton served as Lord Chamberlain, with responsibility for the London theatres.

7 After the second Duke of Beaufort's death in 1714, the second Duke of Bolton was reappointed as Warden until his own death in 1722, and was himself then succeeded in the post by his son, Charles Paulet (1685–1754), third Duke of Bolton.

8 This unofficial process of taking possession of documents formerly owned by one's predecessor in a public office was not uncommon. The first Duke of Beaufort, for example, who served as both Warden of the Forest of Dean (1660–97) and President of Wales (1672–89), in each case brought back to Badminton relevant papers, which had once been owned by his predecessors in these offices. *See* Badminton Muniments Room, FmE 2/3/1–3 (Forest of Dean) and FmE 2/7/2–8 (Council of Wales).

9 Badminton Muniments Room, FmE 1/14.

10 *The Works of John Dryden*, General editor H. T. Swedenberg, Jr.; *Volume II Poems 1681–1684*, edited by H. T. Swedenberg, Jr., and V. A. Dearing (Berkeley, Los Angeles and London, 1972), pp.89–90 (lines 941–966).

11 The Badminton copy of this work (FmH 4/3) bears hand-painted, ornamental page-borders and the bookplate of the second Duke. The only other known copy of this poem – not listed in D. F. Foxon's *English Verse 1701–1750*, 2 vols (Cambridge, 1975) – is found in two volumes (as yet uncatalogued) of printed tracts, acquired by the British Library in 1982. Much of this collection, almost certainly once housed at Badminton, may have been drawn together by the second Duke of Beaufort, since sixty-six of its seventy-three items were printed between 1700 and 1714, including popular satires by Sir Richard Blackmore, Nicholas Brown, Thomas Parnell, William Pittis, Nahum Tate, John Tutchin, and Edward ('Ned') Ward; panegyrical poems to members of the royal family and aristocracy by Beckwith Spencer and Thomas Yalden; and various miscellaneous items, such as Joseph Trapp's *Ædes Badmintonianae* (1701), a 'country house' poem in praise of the Beaufort seat; two 1702 elegies on the death of William III; a poem by 'S. P. Gent', entitled *Britannia Triumphans* (1703), on James Butler (1665–1745), Duke of Ormonde, who married the first Duke of Beaufort's eldest daughter, Mary (d.1733), in 1685; John Phillips's, *Blenheim, a Poem* (1705) and Joseph Addison's *The Campaign* (1705), both commemorating the Duke of Marlborough's triumph at the battle of Blenheim in 1704; and various poems on the impeachment and trial of Henry Sacheverell in January 1710. Michael Brennan is grateful to Dr M. Jannetta of the British Library for his assistance in consulting these two volumes.

12 Besides *ARP* and *Gyldenstolpe* the principal previous studies of Restoration scribal miscellanies are W. J. Cameron, 'A Late Seventeenth-Century Scriptorium', *Renaissance and Modern Studies*, 7 (1963), 25–52; P. Hammond, 'The Robinson Manuscript Miscellany of Restoration Verse in the Brotherton Collection, Leeds', *Proceedings of the Leeds Philosophical and Literary Society: Literary and Historical Section*, 18 (1982), 275–324; H. Love, 'Scribal Publication in Seventeenth-Century England', *Transactions of the Cambridge Bibliographical Society*, 9 (1987), 130–54; H. Love, 'Scribal Texts and Literary Communities: the Rochester Circle and Osborn b. 105', *Studies in Bibliography*, 42 (1984), 219–35.

13 *Gyldenstolpe*, pp.xxvi–xxvii.

14 *Gyldenstolpe*, pp.xvii–xix, xxv.

15 Cambridge, Magdalene College, Pepys Library, item no. 810^2, pp.8–10.

16 *ARP*, pp.448, 481. Harvard fMS Eng 636 has the same arrangement.

17 *See ARP*, pp.137–63; *Gyldenstolpe*, pp.332–3.

18 *See* Hammond, pp.305–7.

19 *ARP*, p.97.

20 *Harvard Library Bulletin*, 24 (1976), 204–45.

21 *See* Hammond, *op. cit.*

22 Walker, pp.147, 195–6.

23 *The Text of Rochester's 'Upon Nothing'*, Centre for Bibliographical and Textual Studies, Monash University, Occasional Papers, 1 (1985).

24 Ibid, p.33.

25 *POAS2*, pp.523–4.

26 *POAS1*, pp.477–8.

The illuminator of Gloucester

MICHAEL GULLICK

The rise of urban based professional illuminators who worked where they lived rather than lived where they worked dates from the end of the twelfth century. A survey of the documentary evidence concerning named illuminators in England reveals that much of the evidence comes from only two places, London and Oxford, an accident of survival and publication rather than a truthful reflection of the centres of manuscript production.[1] One centre unrepresented in the survey is Gloucester and this absence can now be rectified. One *Thome illuminatori* was granted, with his heirs, land before the castle gate at Gloucester by Thomas Hamlin, abbot of Gloucester from 1179 to 1205, for an annual rent of 6d. The abbey half of the original chirograph has survived (*see* PLATE 1) which shows that the transaction was purely a civil one with no suggestion that Thomas the illuminator was an abbey servant. Presumably he was a lay professional who lived and worked in Gloucester at about the turn of the twelfth and thirteenth centuries.[2]

Thomas is important not only as an early English illuminator who can be connected to a particular place but also as one of only two or three twelfth-century lay artists described as illuminators from anywhere in Europe. Roger *illuminator* occurs in an Oxford deed of about 1190 and John *Luminarius* in a London grant of about 1200.[3] The earliest continental illuminator known to me is *Robertus illuminatori* who leased a shop in the Rue Neuve Notre Dame in Paris in 1224.[4]

The earliest certain use of the words illuminator or illumination in connection with book decoration appears to be the description of himself in a famous self portrait by the late-eleventh-century Norman monk Hugo *pictor* as *pictoris et illuminatoris*.[5] After this is the late-eleventh-century Tuscan manuscript with a note stating that its scribe wrote and *coloratus et illuminatus* the book.[6] The Stavelot Bible, completed in 1097, was *scriptura, illuminatione, ligatura* by Goderan

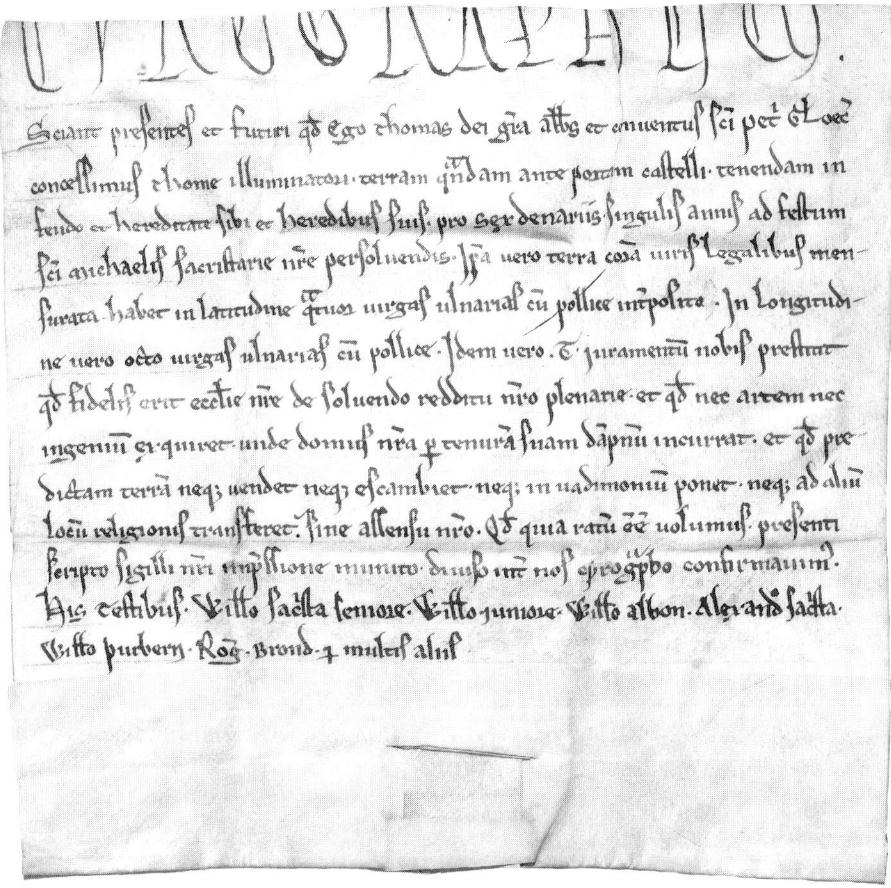

PLATE 1 *Gloucester, Cathedral Library, Dean & Chapter Archives, Charter V.3a (detail, slightly reduced, omitting seal). Reproduced by permission of the Dean & Chapter of Gloucester Cathedral.*

and others, and the Spainish Silos Beatus manuscript of 1109 was *compleuit . . . ab integro illuminabit.*[7] Orderic Vitalis, writing in the early-twelfth-century, described William, a late-eleventh-century monk of St Evroul in Normandy, as *scriptor et librorum illuminator.*[8] In Alsace in 1154 a note concerning the production of the Guta-Sintram Codex includes the words *miniatum uero siue illuminatum.*[9] These are the only examples of the use of the words illuminator or illumination known to me before about 1200.

Earlier than 1200 manuscripts were *ornavit*, *decoravit*, or *pinxit*, sometimes even *fecit*, and *scripsit* (or words similar to these). Those who made them were sometimes described as *pictor* but more commonly *scriptor* or nothing at all.[10] The earliest *pictor* of whom I am aware who can be certainly connected to book decoration is *Magius archipictor* who began the Tábara Beatus, completed after his death in 970.[11] Next in date is the unknown English monk and *pictor* who left a self portrait in the eleventh century Bury Psalter,[12] followed by the Spaniard *Fructosus pictor* who signed a manuscript of 1055.[13]

Later in the eleventh century come Hugo *pictor* and Robert Benjamin *pictor*, both Normans,[14] and there are several more in the twelfth century. Hildebert, a German who probably came from the area of Cologne and worked in Bohemia,[15] Engilbert *pictor et scriptor*, who made the Springiersbach Homiliary,[16] Oliver, who worked at Anchin,[17] and Werner, who worked at Zwiefalten.[18] The four twelfth century artists were probably all laymen.[19] What is most striking about the majority of these occurences of the word *pictor* is the association of the word with self portraits.

In the cases where a *pictor* can be firmly associated with the decoration of manuscripts the term is not always as particular as it might suggest. Hugo *pictor* was almost certainly a scribe as well as an artist,[20] and the same is probably true of Hildebert.[21] Equally the term *scriptor* may have a specific meaning, but before 1200 it was not always used to describe those who only wrote manuscripts. A mid-eleventh century manuscript made at St Germain-des-Près is signed *Ingelhardus decorauit. scriptor honestus*,[22] and a note in an Italian manuscript probably made in Pisa in 1168 refers to Adalbert as *scriptori de licteris maioris de auro et de colore*.[23] An earlier Italian manuscript, made at the turn of the tenth and eleventh centuries, was signed in drawn letters touched with colour within a decorated page *scriptor Ubertus in felix*,[24] and an eleventh century manuscript from St Vaast has an elaborately decorated full page panel with the words *Albertus scripsit* woven within the decoration.[25] Ubert and Albert were both virtually certain to have been artists and scribes.

These examples of verbal and visual ambiguity in pre-1200 manuscripts are a salutory warning concerning the fluidity of medieval vocabulary. However it does appear that an increase in the use of the word illuminator to describe those who decorated manuscripts coincides with the rise of urban-based professionals. An intriguing question is the extent to which the words *pictor* and *illuminator* were synonomous during the latter part of the twelfth and into the thirteenth centuries. Might Anselm *pictor* who had a house in Fleet Street close to St Bride's church 1186 × 1188, when he is mentioned in a charter with a parchmenter and others, have been an illuminator? Only a few years later this part of London is known to have associations with members of the booktrade.[26]

Documentary evidence can be deceptive and difficult to interpret but as more of it is found, published and collected, it will be easier to use in conjunction with the evidence of manuscripts themselves. Thomas the illuminator of Gloucester adds to our stock of knowledge not only because of the fact of his existence but also his existence prompts questions about how those who decorated medieval books perceived themselves and how they were called.

NOTES

1 M. A. Michael 'English Illuminators *c.*1190–1450; A Survey from Documentary Sources', *English Manuscript Studies 1100–1700*, 4 (1993), 62–113. To the list of illuminators can be added John Fowler who was paid in 1398–99 for work executed for Westminster Abbey, *see* J. A. Robinson and M. R. James *The Manuscripts of Westminster Abbey* (Cambridge, 1909) p.9.

2 Gloucester Cathedral, Archives of the Dean and Chapter ch.V.3a. Professor R. B. Patterson is preparing an edition of the abbey charters for the Bristol and Gloucester Archeological Society.

3 Michael, 'English Illuminators', p.79, with references.

4 L. Brièle and E. Coyecque, *Archives de l'Hotel-Dieu de Paris 1157–1300* (Paris, 1894), p.86.

5 O. Pächt, 'Hugo Pictor', *Bodleian Library Record*, 3 (1950–51), 97 and pl.5c, J. J. G. Alexander, *Medieval Illuminators and their Methods of Work* (New Haven and London, 1992), fig. 13.

6 K. Berg, *Studies in Twelfth Century Tuscan Illumination* (Oslo, 1968), pp.29 and 206–7.

7 A. G. Watson, *Catalogue of Dated and Datable Manuscripts c.700–1600 in the Department of Manuscripts, the British Library* (London, 1979), nos. 321 and 61 respectively.

8 M. Chibnall (ed.), *The Ecclesiastical History of Orderic Vitalis*, 2 (Oxford, 1968), p.86. For the tentative identification of some surviving manuscripts with the artist and scribe *see* F. Avril, 'La Décoration des Manuscrits dans les Abbayes Bénédictines de Normandie aux xie et xiie siècles', *Ecole nationale des chartes positions des thèses* (Paris, 1963), p.28.

9 J. Walter, 'Les miniatures du codex Guta-Sintram de Marbach-Schwarzenthann 1154', *Archives alsaciennes d'histoire de l'art*, 4 (1925), 18–19. For their portraits *see* Alexander, *Medieval Illuminators*, fig. 28.

10 The variety in terminology and vocabulary in inscriptions and colophons in pre-1200 manuscripts is considerable. The most accessible printed source for the majority of them is *Colophons de manuscrits occidentaux des origines au xvie siècle*, 6 vols (Fribourg, 1965–82) compiled by the Benedictines of Le Bouvret.
For the problems in interpreting and understanding this material *see* H. Hoffmann, *Buchkunst und Königtum im ottonischen und frühsalischen Reich*, Monumenta Germaniae Historia, Schriften 30–1 (Stuttgart, 1986), pp.42–79, Alexander, *Medieval Illuminators*, pp.5–10.

11 M. C. Díaz, *Codices Visigoticos en la Monarquia Leonesa* (Leon, 1983), p.319, n.54.

12 The damaged inscription around the portrait was first noticed by R. Kahsnitz, *Der Werdener Psalter in Berlin* (Dusseldorf, 1980), p.220; Alexander, *Medieval Illuminators* p.10 and fig. 12.

13 Díaz y Díaz, *Codices Visigoticos*, p.285.

14 For Hugo *see* n.5 above and for Robert Benjamin *see* T. Rud, *Codicum Manuscriptorum Ecclesiae Cathedralis Dunelmensis* (Durham, 1825), pp.110–11; Alexander, *Medieval Illuminators*, fig. 14.

15 Hildebert signed a full page miniature *H pictor* and left a self portrait underneath, Alexander, *Medieval Illuminators*, fig. 18. His name is known from another self portrait in which he is identified as *Hildebertus*, Alexander, fig. 19. For the two manuscripts *see* A. Legner (ed.), *Ornamenta Ecclesia. Kunst und Künstler der Romanik* 1 (Cologne, 1985), no.B.48.

16 A. Legner (ed.), *Rhein und Maas. Kunst und Kultur 800–1400*, 2 (Cologne, 1972), no.63; Alexander, *Medieval Illuminators*, fig. 21.

17 A. Boutemy, 'Enluminures d'Anchin au temps de l'Abbé Gossuin (1131/1133 à 1165)', *Scriptorium*, 11 (1957), 235–6 and 247; P. Černý, 'Die romanische Buchmalerei in der Abtei Saint-Sauveur in Anchin', *Nederlands Kunsthistorisch Jaarboek*, 36 (1985) 55–7; Alexander, *Medieval Illuminators*, fig. 23.

18 S. von Borries-Schulten, *Die Romanischen Handschriften der Württembergischen Landesbibliothek Stuttgart. I. Provenienz Zwiefalten* (Stuttgart, 1987), no.73; Alexander, *Medieval Illuminators*, fig. 20; R. Kuithan, '*Wernherus pictor* und *Reinhardus Mundrichingen*', in *Vinculum Societas. Joachim Wollasch zum 60. Geburstag*, eds. F. Neis, D. Poeck and M. Sandmann (Sigmaringendorf, 1991), pp.68–82.

19 Oliver *pictor* left a self portrait in one of the manuscripts he decorated showing himself as tonsured and wearing a white habit. It has been suggested that he was a Cistercian but from the wording of the colophon of the manuscript I am inclined to think he was more likely to have been a layman.

20 M. Gullick, 'The Scribe of the Carilef Bible: A New Look at Some Late-Eleventh-Century Durham Manuscripts', in *Medieval Book Production: Assessing the Evidence*, ed. L. L. Brownrigg (Los Altos Hills, 1990), pp.74–5 with references.

21 The inscriptions in the famous portraits of Hildebert and Everwin in a Prague manuscript, Alexander, *Medieval Illuminators*, fig. 19, appear to have been written by the scribe of the text above. The script can be associated with the part of Germany from where Hildebert came and not with Bohemia. It seems a reasonable deduction that Hildebert wrote and decorated the Prague manuscript.

22 C. Samaran and R. Marichal, *Catalogue des manuscrits en écriture latine portant des indications de date, de lieu ou de copiste*, 3 (Paris, 1974), p.255.

23 Berg, *Twelfth Century Tuscan Illuminatio*, p.206.

24 P. Pirri, 'La scuola miniaturistica de S. Eutizio in Val Castoriana presso Norcia nei secoli x–xii', *Scriptorium*, 3 (1949), 5–6 and pl.5.

25 S. Schulten, 'Die Buchmalerei des 11. Jahrhunderts im Kloster St Vaast in Arras', *Münchner Jahrbuch der Bildendenkunst*, 7 (1956), 72 and fig. 44.
There are hints in some pre-1200 texts of an equation of writing and painting which deserves investigation. It is touched upon by O. Guyotjeannin, 'Le Vocabulaire de la Diplomatique en Latin Medieval', in *Vocabulaire du livre et de l'écriture au Moyen Age*, ed. O. Weijers (Turnhout, 1989), p.126 and n.22 where mention is made of the use of *depingere* for *scribere*.

26 *Charters and Documents Illustrating the History of the Cathedral, City and Diocese of Salisbury*, Rolls Series 97 (London, 1891), no.54; Michael, 'English Illuminators', pp.68–69.

Thomas Hyngham, Monk of Bury and the Macro Plays Manuscript

JEREMY GRIFFITHS

The *Index of Middle English Verse* and its *Supplement* list 23 copies of the rendering of Boethius's *De Consolatione Philosophiae* in Middle English verse, attributed to John Walton of Oseney Abbey.[1]

Another copy of Walton's *Boethius* may be added to those recorded in the *Index*.[2] The manuscript consists of 104 vellum leaves, 260 × 170mm, in 13 gatherings of 8 leaves, copied in a single column of 34 lines. The manuscript is in a contemporary binding of tawed leather on wooden boards, lacking one gathering of 8 leaves before the present first leaf. The text begins with the second line of stanza 68, 'Bot for þei wer enfo*ur*med in my lore' (*see* PLATE 1).[3]

The manuscript was copied in an *anglicana formata* script by one scribe and may be dated on palaeographical grounds to the first quarter of the fifteenth century. The hand is characterised by a certain stiffness, especially in the formation of descenders in letters such as **y** and **h**, with some variability of size of individual letters, a number of broken strokes and a characteristic treatment of the letter **g**, written above the line, projecting above the x-height.

The scribe may be identified with the hand that copied Cambridge, Pembroke College, MS 307, Gower, *Confessio Amantis*; London, British Library, MS Arundel 119, Lydgate, *Siege of Thebes*; and the second hand of Tokyo, Takamiya Collection, MS 54, *South English Legendary*.[4]

The copy of Walton's Boethius was sold at Christie's, 25 April 1949, lot 16 from the library of the Free School at Kirkleatham, Yorkshire, founded in 1676 by Sir William Turner (d.1692), Wool Draper and Lord Mayor of London.[5]

The earlier provenance of the manuscript is attested by several ownership inscriptions, some only partly legible. The first of these, in

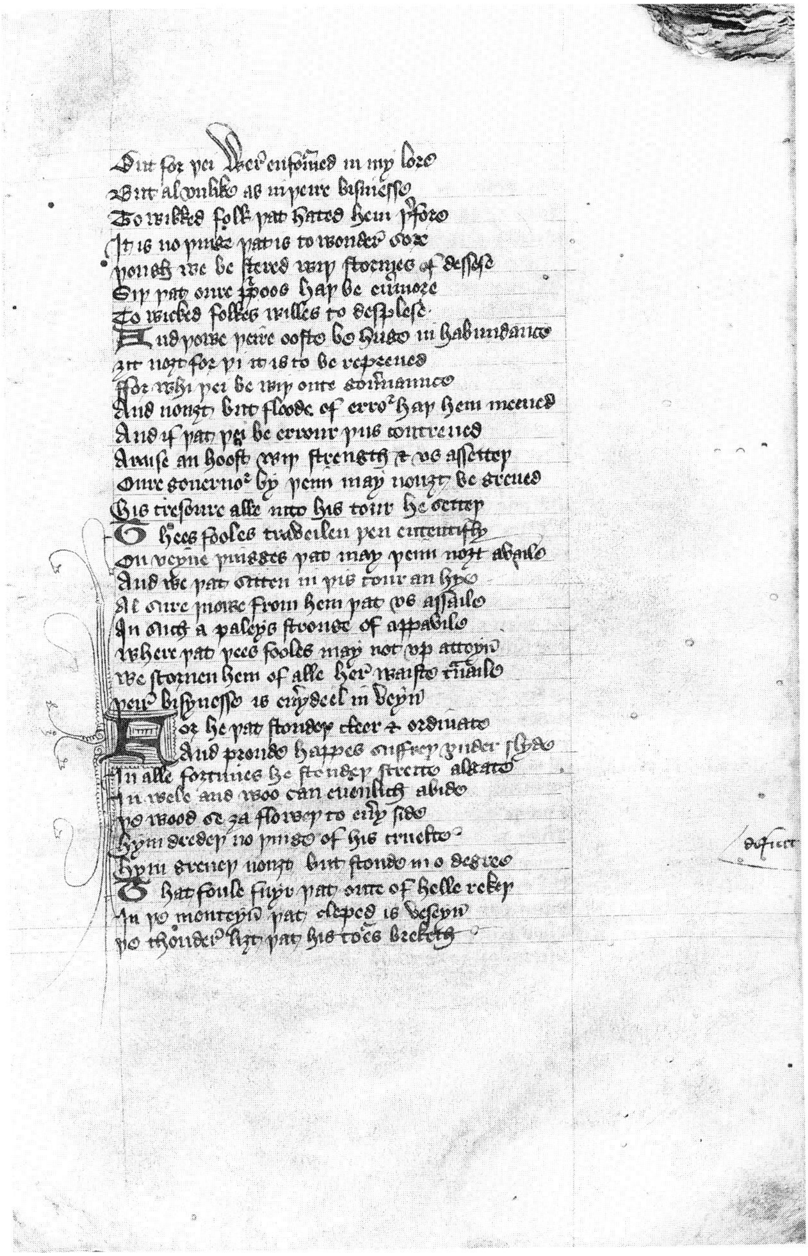

PLATE 1 *Oslo & London, The Schøyen Collection,* MS *615, Walton's translation of Boethius, fol. 1r (Original page size 260 × 170mm). Reproduced by permission.*

what appears to be an early fifteenth-century hand, is visible under ultra-violet light on a front flyleaf: 'Ego d*omi*na Elizabeth d*omi*na de Richo Mont⟨e?⟩ lego istu*m* librum/Roberto Godebowe armigero'. This form of words seemed to me to suggest that Elizabeth may have been prioress of a religious house at 'Richo Monte' or Richmond and there are incomplete early records of a house of Benedictine nuns at Richmond, Yorkshire.[6] Commenting upon a draft of this article, Dr A. I. Doyle has however told me in correspondence that the inscription refers, in his opinion, to a Lady Richmond and not to a nun, though he has been unable to suggest an immediate identification of this individual.[7]

The erased inscription states that Elizabeth left the manuscript to Sir Robert Godebowe. A second erased inscription on the same flyleaf in a contemporary hand, again read under ultra-violet light, suggests that the manuscript was disposed of by his executors: 'M*emorandum* q*uo*d Iohannis Tr⟨ ⟩ istum librum de execut⟨ ⟩/R*o*b*er*ti Godebowe'.

The 'Iohannis Tr⟨ ⟩' who appears from the erased inscription on the recto of the flyleaf to have acquired the manuscript from the executors of Sir Robert Godebowe stated his ownership in a partly erased inscription on the verso of the same leaf: 'Iste liber constat Ioh*anni* ⟨ ⟩' (*see* PLATE 2 (a)).

The first name in this inscription is overwritten in a hand that added a further inscription of ownership, in a more current fifteenth-century hand: 'Iste liber constat [Ioh*anni*] Thome Hyngham Mo*nach*o diui Ed*mundi*/de Bury'.

These inscriptions indicate that the manuscript passed soon after its completion from Elizabeth de Richmond to Sir Robert Godebowe, thence from his executors to one Johannes, and so to Thomas Hyngham, a monk of Bury St Edmunds.

The additions over erasure stating Thomas Hyngham's ownership of the manuscript on the verso of the flyleaf, which carries the offset of the original decoration from the lost first page, may be identified as the hand of the ownership inscriptions on fols 121r and 134r of the Macro Plays manuscript, now Washington, Folger Library, MS V.a.354, which read: 'O liber si quis cui constas forte queretur/ hyngham que monacho dices super omnia consto'.[8] The flyleaf inscription in the Walton manuscript is in a more current version of the hand than the ownership inscriptions in the Macro Plays manuscript, but the similarity of individual letter-forms (especially **h**, **y** and **g**) and the characteristic use and form of superscript **a**, written above the final minim of the last letter in the name Hyngham, confirm the identity of the hands.[9]

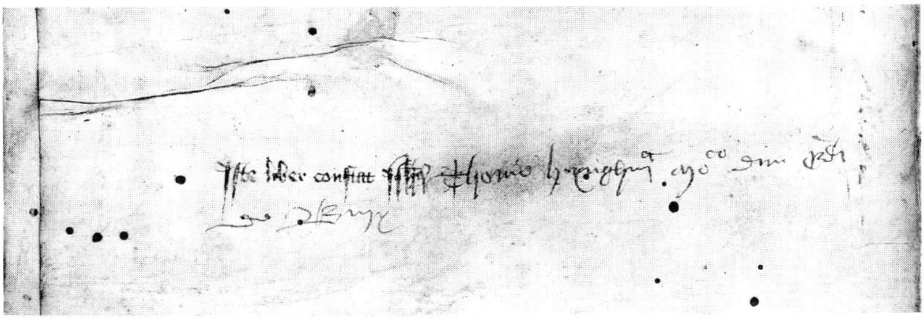

a

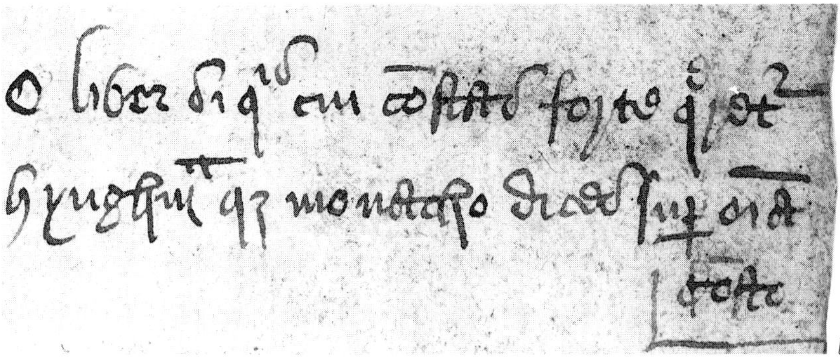

b

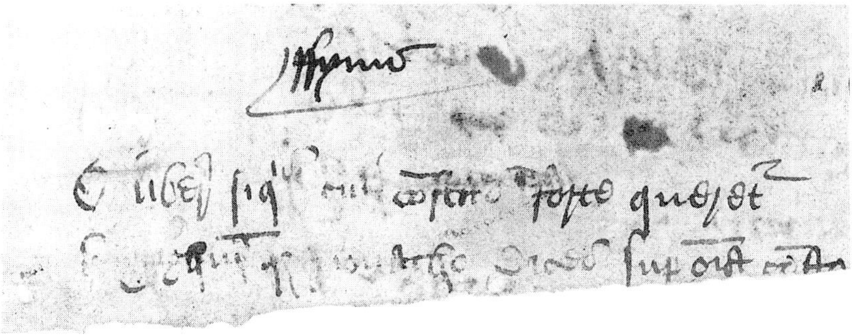

c

PLATE 2 *(a) Oslo & London, The Schøyen Collection,* MS *615, Walton's translation of Boethius, ownership inscription on front flyleaf (detail, reduced). Reproduced by permission.*
(b) Washington, Folger Library, MS *V.a.354, The Macro Plays, ownership inscription on fol. 121r (detail, actual size). Reproduced by permission of the Folger Shakespeare Library.*
(c) Washington, Folger Library, MS *V.a.354, The Macro Plays, ownership inscription on fol. 134r (detail, actual size). Reproduced by permission of the Folger Shakespeare Library.*

The Hyngham inscriptions in the Macro Plays manuscript appear on fol. 121r, at the end of the copy of the morality play *Wisdom*, and on fol. 134r, at the end of the copy of the play *Mankind* (*see* PLATE 2 (b) and (c)). Richard Beadle has argued convincingly that both *Wisdom* and most of *Mankind* were copied by the same hand. He has also suggested, through a detailed comparison of letter-forms, that the Hyngham inscriptions are in the same 'varied hand' that copied the stage-directions to the two plays and that this hand, in turn, is a variant of the hand of the main text, concluding that 'Hyngham himself, or someone who wrote very similarly, is likely to have been the W[isdom]-M[ankind] scribe'.[10]

As Dr Beadle makes clear, the identification of the hand of the Hyngham inscriptions with that of the stage-directions and of the text of *Wisdom* and most of *Mankind* names the scribe of this part of the Macro Plays manuscript as 'monk Hyngham', with a number of possible candidates amongst the monastic houses of East Anglia around 1475.[11] The further identification of this hand with the inscription in the copy of Walton's Boethius allows the scribe of *Wisdom* and most of *Mankind* to be identified as the Benedictine monk Thomas Hyngham and allows the probable place of copying of this part of the Macro Plays manuscript to be established as Bury St Edmunds.[12]

NOTES

1 Carleton Brown and Rossell Hope Robbins, *The Index of Middle English Verse* (New York, 1943), and Rossell Hope Robbins and John L. Cutler, *Supplement to The Index of Middle English Verse* (Lexington, 1965), no.1597. The Helmingham Hall copy listed by Brown and Robbins with a query, seems to be a ghost. 14 manuscripts were known to K. Schummer, *John Waltons metrische Ubersetzung der Consolatio Philosophiae: Untersuchung des Handschriftenverhaltnisses und Probe eines kritischen Textes*, Bonner Studien zur Englischen Philologie VI (Bonn, 1914).

2 The manuscript is now Oslo & London, The Schøyen Collection, MS 615. I am indebted to Mr Schøyen for the opportunity to study the manuscript and for permission to reproduce photographs of it.

3 *Boethius: De Consolatione Philosophiae translated by John Walton*, ed. Mark Science, EETS OS 170 (London, 1927). If the Schøyen manuscript originally contained both the Preface and the Prologue, it would lack 537 lines of text, which would occupy just over 15 pages, or 8 leaves, in the layout of the manuscript. The pattern of the surviving leaf signatures, which begin with **di** on the present fol. 17r, the first leaf of quire iii, appears to confirm the loss of just a single gathering before the present first leaf. On the first leaf the marginal note 'deficit' indicates the omission of a line in stanza 71, as in 7 other copies of the work (*see* Science, p.xli; Schummer, pp.lxiv–lxv). 68 lines (stanza 733, line 6 to stanza 743, line 3; Science, pp.257–260) are omitted between fols 77v and 78r, in the middle of quire x, with no apparent loss

of leaves, probably reflecting the turning over of two leaves at a time in the exemplar; none of the manuscripts collated by Science for the EETS edition appears to share this lacuna.

4 I am indebted to Professor T. Takamiya for providing me with information about this manuscript.

5 The manuscript was purchased by Maggs Bros. It appeared subsequently in Bernard Quaritch Limited, Catalogue 897 (1969), item 51 and passed into a private collection in the United Kingdom, whence it was purchased for the Schøyen Collection; *see Medieval Libraries of Great Britain: A list of Surviving Books*, ed. N. R. Ker, second edition (London, 1964), p.22 and *Supplement to the Second Edition*, ed. Andrew G. Watson (London, 1987), p.6.

6 D. Knowles and R. Neville Hadcock, *Medieval Religious Houses: England and Wales* (London, 1971), p.264.

7 I am indebted to Dr Doyle and to Dr M. B. Parkes of Keble College, Oxford for their comments upon a draft of this article. Dr Doyle has further pointed out to me that the will of a Robert Godebowe, Esq. of Folkygham, Lincs., dated 1430, is Public Record Office, Prerogative Court of Canterbury Wills, 15 Luffenham. I was unable to investigate this further before the article went to press.

8 *See The Macro Plays: A Facsimile Edition with Facing Transcriptions*, ed. David Bevington (New York and Washington, 1972) and Seymour De Ricci, *A Census of Medieval and Renaissance Manuscripts in the United States and Canada*, ii (New York, 1937), p.2272, no.5031.

9 I am indebted to Dr Richard Beadle of St John's College, Cambridge for confirming this identification following his own detailed comparison of the inscriptions in the two manuscripts, which he discussed in a paper given to the Manuscripts Conference at the University of York in July 1991.

10 Richard Beadle, 'The Scribal Problem in the Macro Manuscript', *English Language Notes*, 21 (1984), 1–13, especially pp.8–9. From a careful examination of the facsimile, I, myself, can see no reason to believe that the Hyngham inscriptions and the stage-directions are not in the same hand as the main text of the plays *Wisdom* and most of *Mankind*.

11 Beadle, pp.12–13.

12 In view of the probable location of the copying of *Wisdom* and *Mankind* in Bury St Edmunds, it is of interest to note existing evidence for dramatic activity in the town in the later Middle Ages, as summarised by Gail McMurray Gibson, 'Bury St Edmunds, Lydgate, and the N-Town Cycle', *Speculum*, 56 (1981), 56–90.

Manuscripts at Auction: January 1992 to December 1992

H. R. WOUDHUYSEN

This list is intended to provide a summary of manuscript items copied or owned in the British Isles between 1100 and 1700 that have appeared for sale at the major auction houses in London and New York and in other auction houses or booksellers' catalogues, where these have been available to the compiler. We would be pleased to receive notice of any auction or booksellers' catalogues containing relevant items for the period from January 1993.

The list cannot aim to be exhaustive but is offered as a guide to these materials. Where known, the names of purchasers and prices paid (including the buyer's premium) have been given, and also the present locations of the manuscripts or their subsequent appearance in booksellers' catalogues.

Items that can be dated approximately to before 1500 are indicated by an asterisk (*) before the lot or item number.

All medieval manuscripts written or illuminated in the British Isles have been included, as have manuscripts written or illuminated abroad but which can be shown to have been in the British Isles before 1700. Charters, grants of land and other items of mainly archival interest have generally been excluded.

For the later period, 1500–1700, manuscripts of chiefly literary, rather than historical, interest have been included. Royal letters and documents are generally omitted, as are single letters written by statesmen, ecclesiastics and other public figures, maps and surveys, heraldic manuscripts, manuscript cookery books and collections of recipes are also generally excluded.

Abbreviations

AL(s)s	Autograph letter(s) signed
attrib.	attributed to
D(s)s	Document(s) signed
ill.	illuminated

L(s)s Letter(s) signed
W(s)s Warrant(s) signed

LONDON

Bloomsbury Book Auctions

28 May 1992

201 ALLEN (THOMAS?): two sermons each subscribed 'By Mr Allen 1667'. Formerly Phillipps MS 22324. £132 to Edwards.

216 SIDNEY (ALGERNON): 10 ALss (3 signed, 3 with initials and 4 unsigned) to Benjamin Furly, Leicester House or London, 29 November [1677] – 8/18 April [1678]. £440 to Johnson.

224 SEVENTEENTH-CENTURY MSS: copies of Lss and Dss, including texts by Philip Stanhope, second Earl of Chesterfield, Ashley and Clifford, William Stanhope, and William Platt. £143 to Gulley.

234 DENBY (EARL OF): MS notebook, including accounts of his participation in the action against the Duke of Monmouth and in the wars of William of Orange in the Low Countries, 1685–1727. £220 to National Army Museum.

236 HOUSE OF LORDS: proceedings upon impeachments from 1666 to 1681, eighteenth century. Former owners include John Walker Heneage, Graham Bower and Grotius Society. £198 to Lawbook Exchange.

239 LEVETT (JOHN): Memorandum book, *c*.1688–1701. Former owners include the Marquess of Crewe. Unsold.

244 SCOTTISH CHURCH: sermons, *c*.1679. Texts include sermons by Andrew Gray, Samuel Rutherford and one preached at Kircudbright, 20 June 1634. £143 to Edwards.

25 June 1992

131 PEPYS (SAMUEL): ALs to his nephew, John Jackson, Lisbon, 4 March 1701. £2,090 to Maggs.

132 PEPYS (SAMUEL) and MENNES (SIR JOHN): retained copy of a letter to the Justices of the Peace of the county of Gloucester, Navy Office, 24 September 1663. Unsold.

141 GAMMON (HANNIBAL): *Oratio contra Gentes*, dedicated to Dudley, Lord North, partly authograph, *c*.1607–19. £605 to Gammon.

Christie's

24 June 1992

*77 MORE (SIR THOMAS): *A Treatise to receyve the Blessed Bodye of our*

Lorde, MS copy on paper in a single secretary hand, second half of the sixteenth century. Binding includes a bifolium from a Choir-book, MS on vellum in Latin, England, late thirteenth century. Former owners include John Burns and Manhattan College, New York. £4,180 to D. A Smith.

85 ALCHEMY: MS on paper, partly copied from a compilation of 1677, 1702. Texts include extracts from John Heydon and Hartman, *Chymicall secrets* and an epitaph on the Duke of Buckingham in English and Latin. £770.

358 BOYLE (ROBERT): Ls to Samuel Clarke, [London], 8 August 1668. £990.

21 October 1992 (John Sparrow Sale)

288 WALLER, (EDMUND): ten MS poems written in two hands in a copy of Edmund Waller, *Poems*, 1686, late seventeenth century. £2,860 to Quaritch. Now in the Brotherton Collection, University of Leeds.

25 November 1992

*18 SOUTH-ENGLISH LEGENDARY: fragment of a leaf from a MS on vellum in Middle English, possibly from Leicester Museum MS 18 D 59, Southern England, *c.*1310–20. £4,620 to Quaritch.

*20 BOOK OF HOURS, USE OF SARUM: ill. MS on vellum in Latin, Rouen, *c.*1445. Decoration includes seven large, defaced miniatures by the Talbot Master. £2,640.

Phillips

11 June 1992

26 LONDON, ST MARGARET'S, WESTMINSTER: Church Wardens' Accounts kept by Michael Arnold and Nicholas Bonham, 9 April–5 November 1666, audited by Emery Hill and Francis Dorington, 9 September 1667, 1666–7. £506.

46 HENRY VIII: Ls, the text in the hand of Peter Vannes, to Antonioto Adorno, Duke of Genoa, thanking him for his dealings with his two secretaries, Richard Pace and Bryan Tuke, and with Cardinal Wolsey, London, 14 July 1524. £5,500.

47 CHARLES I: Ls, the text in the hand of Georg Weckherlin, to Frederick William of Brandenburg introducing the King's legate, Joseph Avery, [Windsor], 23 January 1642. £572.

12 November 1992

129 PEPYS (SAMUEL) = Sotheby's 13 December 1990, lot 411. Unsold.

Sotheby's

28 April 1992

699 ELIOT (SIR JOHN): *The Monarchie of Man*, MS copy on paper, 'Ex[amine]d July 1774 by Jos: Cocks', *c.*1774. £33 to Browning.

715 HOLLOND (JOHN): *Brief Discourse of the Navy*, MS copy on paper, mid-seventeenth century. Former owners include the Earl of Dartmouth, Patshull House, Wolverhampton. £550 to Maggs.

28 May 1992

79 SEVENTEENTH-CENTURY COMMONPLACE BOOK: MS largely in French with a few pages in English, written in at least two Italic hands, early seventeenth century. Texts include quotations from Plutarch and Cornelius Agrippa. Unsold.

23 June 1992

*3 FRAGMENTS: collection of fifty fragments and leaves, MSS on vellum in Latin, mainly English, late twelfth to seventeenth centuries. Former owners include A. H. Philpot and Spurgeon's College. £2,860 to Maggs.

*86 BOOK OF HOURS, USE OF SARUM: ill. MS on vellum in Latin, Southern Netherlands, probably Bruges, third quarter of the fifteenth century. Made for export to England. Decoration includes five large initials (two cut out) with full ill. borders. Former owners include John Wythym, A. H. Philpot and Spurgeon's College (MS 2). £1,870 to Rouse.

*88 BOOK OF HOURS, USE OF SARUM: ill. MS on vellum in Latin, Southern Netherlands, almost certainly Bruges, *c.*1450–70. Made for export to England. Decoration includes seventeen very large ill. initials with full borders, twenty-two large historiated initials and four large half-page miniatures. Former owners include Alexander Murray, Sir Frank Brangwyn and Campion Hall, Oxford (MS 3). £12,100 to Newmann Walter.

*89 BOOK OF HOURS, USE OF ROME: ill. MS on vellum in Latin, Northern France, perhaps Paris, late fifteenth century. In a contemporary English binding. Decoration includes panel borders throughout, four small miniatures with three-quarter ill. borders and twelve large miniatures with full borders enclosing smaller miniatures. Former owners include Sir Frank Brangwyn and Campion Hall, Oxford, (MS 2). £9,900 to Fogg.

*92 BOOK OF HOURS, USE OF SARUM: ill. MS on vellum in Latin, England, perhaps London, late fifteenth century. Decoration includes nine very large initials with three-quarter ill. borders and three very large initials with full borders. Former owners include the Roberts and Strangman families, 'P. W.', W. Lyon Wood and Francis Edwards. £11,000 to Fogg.

30 June 1992

902 PARSONS (ROBERT): *The first Booke of the Christian exercise, appertaining to resolutio[n] corrected and newly imprinted Anno 1584*, MS copy on paper, 1654. £165 to Humber.

21 July 1992

9 BACON (SIR FRANCIS): copy of 'The World's a Bubble', written as a four-stanza version, with other poems transcribed by Thomas Everard on a single leaf, with the name Sarah Amler, *c.*1620s–30s. £550 to Quaritch.

12 EVELYN (JOHN): DS on vellum with seals, by John and Mary Evelyn, Charles and Amphilis Theyer of Coopers Hill, Brockworth, Gloucestershire, and John Jekyll, concerning land and premises at Deptford and land in Gloucestershire formerly owned by Sir Richard Browne, 2 October 1685. Unsold.

20 [SHAKESPEARE (WILLIAM)]: fragment of a MS of an unrecorded Elizabethan or Jacobean play containing a scene between a tapster and two thieves similar to one in *1 Henry IV*; extracted from a copy of Homer, *Odyssea*, ed. C. Gesner (Geneva, 1586), *c.*1590s–early 1600s. Unsold. Now in The Schøyen Collection MS 1627.

198 [OVERTON (ROBERT)]: DS by Charles II ordering Overton to be delivered by Sir Thomas Morgan, Governor of Jersey, to Captain Thomas Gardiner, counter-signed by Lord Arlington, Whitehall, 6 December 1671. £990 to Overton.

208 DERING (SIR EDWARD, SECOND BARONET): autograph journal for October 1675 to February 1679. £3,080 to Maggs.

209 DERING (SIR EDWARD, SECOND BARONET): autograph gardening journal December 1671 to March 1675. £3,300 to Maggs.

210 FAWKES (GUY): DS on vellum with seal, an indenture between Fawkes and Christopher Lomleye of York, tailor, concerning property and land in York and Clifton, witnessed by Dionis Baynebrigge, John Jackson and Christopher Hodgson, 14 October 1591. £4,620 to West.

213 HERALDRY: MS collection, including two drawings of a catafalque, a treatise on the right to bear arms, genealogical accounts with descriptions of the arms of various families, accounts of Cornish families, with a title-page of the 1690s by Thomas Penson, principally early seventeenth century. Unsold.

269 DUDLEY (SIR ROBERT, DUKE OF NORTHUMBERLAND AND EARL OF

WARWICK): MS, partly autograph and revised, of *Direttorio Marittimo*, including the preface written for its publication in *Dell'Arcano del Mare* and an autobiographical *Proemio*, *c.*1637–47. Unsold.

271 MAINWARING (SIR HENRY) = Sotheby's 23 June 1988 lot 209, with the scribe identified as Ralph Crane. £13,200 to Quaritch.

283 HERBERT (SIR HENRY, MASTER OF THE REVELS): LS, partly autograph, partly in the hand of Tom Browne, to Michael Mohan and the actors of the Cockpit Theatre in Drury Lane, concerning his right to censor all plays on the public stage and his demand for a lowering of the rates at the Cockpit, The Office of the Revels, 13 October 1660. Unsold.

306 MEADOWS (SARAH): MS of a religious treatise relating to the bringing-up of children, written before her death in 1688, late seventeenth–early eighteenth century. £550 to Marlborough.

307 WATTS (ISAAC): annotated copy of John Owen, *A Practical Exposition on the CXXX Psalm* (1669), dated 1693/4. £1,980 to Quaritch.

20 October 1992

65 SIDNEY (SIR ROBERT, VISCOUNT LISLE, FIRST EARL OF LEICESTER): DS by Sidney and his wife Lady Barbara for the leasing of land to Thomas Lewys *alias* Morrice, baker, 20 April 1616. £330 to Edwards.

7 December 1992

*2 (item 4) BREVIARY: leaf on vellum in Latin, mid-thirteenth century. Decoration includes three large initials. £800 to Weaver.

*6 PSALTER: two leaves from an ill. MS on vellum in Latin, Rhineland or perhaps Flanders or possibly England, second half (perhaps third quarter) of the thirteenth century. Decoration includes seven drawings of birds, animals and a fish, and five large historiated initials. £2,600 to Fogg.

*8 THE HUNGERFORD HOURS: five leaves from an ill. MS on vellum in Latin, East Anglia, perhaps, Ely, possibly Lincoln, *c.*1330. Former owners include Robert, Lord Hungerford, and his wife Margaret Botreaux. Decoration includes twelve large ill. initials, one enclosing a coat of arms resembling those of Sir John de Pateshull of Northamptonshire and Bedfordshire. £2,800 to Cooper.

*25 *NOVA STATUTA* = Sotheby's 6 December 1988, lot 10. £2,000 to Griffiths.

*37 ASTRONOMICAL TEXTS: four leaves from a MS on vellum in Latin, mid-thirteenth century. Texts include part of *De Quattuor Temporibus Anni*. Decoration includes large coloured diagrams. £4,800 to Quaritch.

*58 BOOK OF HOURS, USE OF SARUM: ill. MS on vellum in Latin, Southern Netherlands, probably Bruges, *c.*1400. Made for export to England. Former owners include Edward Hailstone and Major J. R. Abbey. Decoration includes seventeen very large initials with full borders and sixteen full-page miniatures. Unsold.

*59 BOOK OF HOURS, USE OF SARUM: ill. MS on vellum in Latin, perhaps London, *c.*1400. Former owners include Thomas Robard and the Rev. Nathaniel C. S. Poyntz. Decoration includes several catchwords with drawings and ill. initials throughout. £2,800 to Schuster.

*61 BOOK OF HOURS: forty-five leaves from an ill. MS on vellum in Latin, late fifteenth century. Former owners include William Bromley and J. A. Dortmond. Decoration includes three large ill. initials. Unsold.

14 December 1992

1 [BACON (SIR FRANCIS)]: MS draft of two Latin epigrams on Bacon, *c.*1620s. Former owners include Thomas Price of Llanyfyllin, Wales. £550 to Quaritch.

49 WOODDESON (JOHN), Rector of Radnage, Buckinghamshire: sermons, *c.*1681. With other later material. £1,375 to Fraser.

171 HOWARD (HENRY HOWARD, EARL OF NORTHAMPTON): five commonplace books, late sixteenth–early seventeenth century. Texts include a copy of a letter from Philip Howard, Earl of Arundel, to Sir Philip Sidney, 27 August [1583–5]. Former owners include Lord William Howard and John Maxwell. Sold with the Naworth Castle Library for £38,500 to Quaritch. Now in Durham University Library.

172 FIRE OF LONDON: Account of money paid to the Chamber of London for the relief of victims of the Fire, 1666. Unsold.

214 = Sotheby's 21 July 1992, lot 215. Unsold.

234 BARCLAY (ROBERT): notebook, predominantly autograph, partly in shorthand, *c.*1670s. Texts include religious writings probably relating to the *Catechism and Confession of Faith*, 1673, and an account of a vision on 20 June 1672. Unsold.

235 BARCLAY (ROBERT): MS copies of the 'Vindication of his Apology', late seventeenth–early eighteenth century, and of questions proposed by Charles Gordon to Barclay, his answers and Gordon's considerations of the answers, copied by Gordon's brother, Robert, late seventeenth century. £880 to Quaritch.

236 BARCLAY (ROBERT): two autograph pocket books, comprising a private journal from November 1678 to July 1690, with a continuation by his son to 1701, 1678–1701. Unsold.

237 BARCLAY (ROBERT): collection of Lss to Barclay with some to his son, February 1676–1752. Texts include scribal copy of a letter from George Fox, London, 31 June 1680; seven ALss from Elizabeth, Princess Palatine of the Rhine, and copies of two others by Barclay, February 1676–November 1677; ALs from James, Duke of York, Windsor, 27 June 1680; two ALss from the Earl of Perth and one from the Countess de Hornes, September 1676–November 1681; transcripts of nearly ninety letters to and from George Fox, William Penn, Sarah Fell and the Princess Palatine. £1,650 to Quaritch.

238 JAFFRAY (ALEXANDER): 'Journal or Diary' recounting his life in Scotland and religious experiences from 1614 to 1661, late seventeenth century. £3,850 to Quaritch. Now owned by Aberdeen Council.

239 BARCLAY (ROBERT): collection of sixteen Dss, relating to Barclay, 1683–90. Unsold.

240 BARCLAY (ROBERT, THE YOUNGER): MS copies of 'The Quaker's notion of the Divin light', 'Remarks upon Tho: Bonnets Confutation of Quakerisme', and other texts, *c.*1700s. £550 to Quaritch.

After lot 167, The Hulton Papers. Former owners include the third Earl of Essex, William Jessop and William Hulton.

1 LEICESTER (ROBERT DUDLEY, EARL OF LEICESTER): ALs to Queen Elizabeth I about the Spanish Armada, Tilbury, [20 or 27 July 1588]. Unsold.

2 LEICESTER (ROBERT DUDLEY, EARL OF LEICESTER): ALs to Queen Elizabeth I, mentioning Philip Sidney, Harden Castle, 1 June [1577]. £5,500 to Green.

3 ESSEX (ROBERT DEVEREUX, SECOND EARL OF ESSEX): forty-three ALss to Queen Elizabeth I, various places in France, Ireland, England and at sea, [7 October 1590–1601). Unsold.

4 ESSEX (ROBERT DEVEREUX, SECOND EARL OF ESSEX): autograph draft, extensively revised, of Essex's letter or 'Discourse', probably addressed to Sir Robert Cecil, recounting and justifying his Cadiz expedition, [1596]. Unsold.

5 ESSEX (ROBERT DEVEREUX, SECOND EARL OF ESSEX): scribal copy of a letter to Queen Elizabeth I, written before his Azores expedition, 'ffrom aboard the Dew repulce', 12 August [1597]. Unsold.

6 ESSEX (ROBERT DEVEREUX, SECOND EARL OF ESSEX): ALs to Lettice, Countess of Leicester, Leighs, Essex, 1 September [no year]. Unsold.

7 ESSEX (ROBERT DEVEREUX, SECOND EARL OF ESSEX): Ls, with autograph addition, to Roger Manners, Earl of Rutland, St Albans, 16 October [1596]. Unsold.

8 BACON (SIR FRANCIS): ALs to Robert Devereux, third Earl of Essex, York House, 7 November 1620. £13,200 to Quaritch. Now owned by Robert S. Pirie.

9 HOLLAND (SIR HENRY RICH, EARL OF HOLLAND): twenty ALss to Robert Devereux, third Earl of Essex, *c.*1630s. Unsold.

10 CHARLES LOUIS, *Elector Palatine*: ALs to Robert Devereux, third Earl of Essex, The Hague, 8/18 March 1639. Unsold.

BOOKSELLERS' CATALOGUES

Les Enluminures

Catalogue 1 (1992)

*40 Single miniature showing *Joseph's Coat Presented to Jacob*, attributed to the artist of Cambridge, Trinity College, MS B.11.7 (*see also* another miniature, Sotheby's, 19 June 1990, lot 53, probably from the same manuscript), London, *c.*1420. Ffr 300,000.

Simon Finch Rare Books

Catalogue Seventeen

43 CHAUCER Geoffrey: *Canterbury Tales*: transcription by William Pynwell of Manchester, John Rylands Library, MS Eng. 113, Horley, Oxfordshire, 1846–73. £700. Now in The Schøyen Collection, MS 1580.

Sam Fogg

Catalogue 15: Text Manuscripts of the Middle Ages and Renaissance

*4 BIBLE: ill. MS on vellum, in Latin, England, mid-thirteenth century, formerly owned by Sir Alfred Chester Beatty = Sotheby's, 24 June 1969, lot 48. £27,500.

*5 BIBLE: ill. MS on vellum, in Latin, England, 1260–1280. £32,500.

*19 BOOK OF HOURS: ill. MS on vellum, in Latin and Anglo-Norman, The Cornwallis Hours, London, mid-fifteenth century, obits of the Cornwallis family and of Margaret Haseley, nun of the Franciscan convent in London. Former owners include Andrew Gifford (1700–1784); Bristol Baptist College MS Z.d.38 = Sotheby's, 17 December 1991, lot 66. £22,000.

*24 JEAN DU VIGNAY: *De Ludo Scachorum*, MS in French, probably France, late fifteenth century, with early ownership inscription in Anglo-Norman. £7,500.

*26 CHRONICLE ROLL: ill. MS on vellum, in Latin, London, between 13 October 1453 and 15 March 1454, ends with Henry VI. Decoration includes 6 roundel miniatures, 9 ill. coats-of-arms by the scribe of Oxford, Bodleian Library, MS Lyell 33. £60,000.

*27 CHRONICLE ROLL: ill. MS on vellum, in Latin, London, between 1461 and 1464, lacks first membrane, ends with Edward IV, by the scribe of Oxford, Bodleian Library, MS Lyell 33. £10,000.

*37 BOOK OF HOURS: ill. MS on vellum, in Latin, Southern England, before 1483, made for the Roberts family of East Braxted, Essex = Sotheby's, 10 December 1969, lot 79. £16,500.

45 LEGAL FORMULARY AND COMMONPLACE BOOK: MS on vellum, in English, Latin and Anglo-Norman, England, East Anglia, possibly Colchester, *c.*1500–1509 with an addition in 1517. Former owners include George Thornhill. £15,000.

46 COMMONPLACE BOOK OF SIR WILLIAM STANFORD (1509–1558): MS on paper, in English, London, *c.*1500–1650, in blind-stamped wallet binding *c.*1500. £15,000.

47 ROYAL SUMMONSES AND LIST OF PROVISIONS FOR THE ENTHRONEMENT OF GEORGE NEVILLE, ARCHBISHOP OF YORK: MS on paper, in Latin, French and English, London, early sixteenth century. £4,500.

53 TESTA DE NEVILL: MS on paper, in Latin, in the hand of Robert Glover, Somerset Herald (1544–1588).

54 BURNHAM THORPE TERRIER: MS on paper, in Latin, 1574. £1,500.

55 HERALDIC COLLECTIONS: MS on paper, in English and Latin, England, 1560–1570. Former owners include Thomas, 17th Lord Dacre. £3,000.

57 ANTIQUITIES OF WINDSOR AND THE ORDER OF THE GARTER; FLOWER (WILLIAM) AND GLOVER (ROBERT): VISITATION OF NORTHUMBERLAND: MS on paper, in English and French, England, 1592 and 1575, in the hand of Robert Glover (1544–1588). £3,750.

58 HERALDIC COLLECTION: 'Catalogue of the Five Conquerors of this Island': ill. MS on vellum, in English, England, 1606. Former owners include 'Edm'd Waller'. £3,250.

61 BARONS OF ENGLAND: ill. MS on vellum, in English, England, 1625–1628. Dedicated to George Villiers, Duke of Buckingham. £1,750.

Maggs Brothers Ltd

Autograph Letters and Historical Documents, catalogue 1144

169 PEPYS (SAMUEL) = catalogue 1112, 1990, item 146.

Illuminated Manuscripts, Miniatures and Single Leaves, European Bulletin no. 17

*24 BIBLE: ill. leaf on vellum in Latin, probably Oxford, *c.*1230–40. Perhaps written by William de Brailes or in his workshop. Decoration includes a historiated initial of the prophet Malachi. £900.

*25 BIBLE: leaf on vellum in Latin, *c.*1220–40. Former owners include Otto Ege and perhaps Thomas Lever (1521–77). £125.

*39 BIBLE: ill. leaf on vellum in Latin, perhaps East Anglia, *c.*1350. Other parts of the Bible are in BL, Royal MS 1. E. IV and Bodleian, MS Bibl. lat. b. 4 and elsewhere. Decoration includes an initial 'U'. £700.

*46 THEOLOGY: bifolium from a work dealing with penance and absolution, *c.*1425. £100.

John Wilson

Catalogue 72

BOYLE (ROBERT) Ls, apparently to John Evelyn, 23 May 1657. £3,250.

ESSEX (ROBERT DEVEREUX, SECOND EARL OF ESSEX) Ls, to [Matthew Hutton], Archbishop of York, 18 March 1597/8. £3,250.

RALEIGH (SIR WALTER) Signature, detached. £450.

Michael Silverman

Catalogue 6

1 DYER (SIR EDWARD) Ds, a part-payment to Edward Stanhope of £10, 11 November 1596 £1,200.

Notes on Contributors

JULIA BOFFEY is Senior Lecturer in English at Queen Mary & Westfield College, University of London. She has published extensively on the audience and circulation of 15th- and 16th-century English verse.

MICHAEL BRENNAN is Senior Lecturer in English at the University of Leeds. His publications include a study of the patronage of the Herbert family, Earls of Pembroke (1988), and he is the editor of Lady Mary Wroth's pastoral drama *Love's Victory* (1988) and of the travel diary for 1611–1612 of Sir Charles Somerset (1993).

HUGH CRAIG is Associate Professor of English at the University of Newcastle, NSW. He is the author of *Sir John Harington* (1985) and editor of *Ben Jonson: The Critical Heritage* (1990). He is currently working on a study of dramatic styles in Jonson.

ELSIE DUNCAN-JONES, a former pupil of I. A. Richards at Cambridge, taught English at the University of Birmingham for forty years, retiring as Reader. Besides extensive periodical publications, her work has included collaboration with Pierre Legouis on the third edition (1970) of the Oxford English Texts *The Poems and Letters of Andrew Marvell*.

JEREMY GRIFFITHS is currently completing catalogues of the manuscripts at St John's College and Christ Church, Oxford, and has begun work on a catalogue of the manuscripts at Holkham Hall, Norfolk.

MICHAEL GULLICK runs The Red Gull Press. He has contributed an account of the medieval bindings at Hereford Cathedral to the recently-published catalogue of the cathedral's manuscripts and has published studies of medieval and modern scribal activity.

ELIZABETH H. HAGEMAN is Professor of English at the University of New Hampshire. With Andrea Sununu she is editing the works of Katherine Philips for the series 'Women Writers in English, 1350–1850' published by Oxford University Press.

RICHARD HAMER is Tutor in English at Christ Church, Oxford. His recent work has mainly been on early French and English translations of the *Legenda Aurea*.

PAUL HAMMOND is Senior Lecturer in English at the University of Leeds. He is the author of *John Dryden: A Literary Life* (1991) and editor of the Longman Edition of *The Poems of John Dryden: Volume 1: 1649–1681* (1994) and *Volume 2: 1682–1685* (1994).

LISA JEFFERSON is Research Assistant in the Faculty of Medieval & Modern Languages in the University of Oxford. She is currently engaged in a study of the surviving manuscripts of the Statutes of the Order of the Garter.

PETER McCULLOUGH, Junior Research Fellow at Trinity College, Oxford, received his Ph.D. in English from Princeton University. His first book, *The Sermon at the Courts of Elizabeth I and James I*, is forthcoming from the University of Massachusetts Press.

JEANNE SHAMI is Associate Professor of English at the University of Regina. She is currently completing a book on the politics of the late Jacobean pulpit. She has published various articles on John Donne, is one of the editors on the Donne *Variorum* project, and is publishing a parallel-text facsimile edition of the 1622 Sermon on the Gunpowder Plot with Duquesne University Press.

ANDREA SUNUNU is Associate Professor of English at DePauw University. With Elizabeth Hageman she is editing the works of Katherine Philips for the series 'Women Writers in English, 1350–1850' published by Oxford University Press.

H. R. WOODHUYSEN is Lecturer in English at University College, London. He has recently published a selection of Dr Johnson's writings on Shakespeare, and is currently completing a study of the texts of Sir Philip Sidney's works.

Notes for Contributors

1 Articles submitted should follow the journal's style-sheet, available on request. References in notes need cite only date and place of publication (not details of publisher).

2 Contributors are responsible for supplying their own illustrations together with the necessary permission to publish, the charges for which must be borne by the contributors themselves. Illustrations should be in the form of black and white glossy photographs (approximately 10 × 8 in./25.4 × 20.3 cm unless actual size). They should, ideally, be accompanied by the following information: (a) exact shelfmark or reference number in the collection or repository; (b) exact page or folio number (indicating recto or verso); (c) exact size of the original page; (d) exact wording of any descriptive caption required or specific acknowledgement for permission to reproduce; (e) any special instructions for the placing of the illustration in the article.

3 Two copies of each article should be submitted. The address for correspondence is: Jeremy Griffiths, St John's College, Oxford, OX1 3JP.

Index of Manuscripts

This index lists the present repositories of the manuscripts and individual printed books mentioned in the text (excluding the footnotes), listed alphabetically by location, together with the present locations of items in the section of Manuscripts at Auction on pp. 220–230, where these have been acquired by known private or public collections.

General Index

This index contains all the proper names appearing in the volume (with the few exceptions outlined below), including those in the list of Manuscripts at Auction on pp. 220–30, except for the names of buyers of individual items. The locations of items from the list of Manuscripts at Auction are given in the Index of Manuscripts, where items have been acquired by known private or public collections. The index excludes names appearing in the footnotes, titles of individual literary works by known authors (which are subsumed under the names of their authors) and place names mentioned only in passing.